VIRTUAL REALITY – HUMAN COMPUTER INTERACTION

Edited by **Xin-Xing Tang**

Virtual Reality – Human Computer Interaction

http://dx.doi.org/10.5772/3333
Edited by Xin-Xing Tang

Contributors

Giovanni Saggio, Manfredo Ferrari, Richard M. Levy, Stuart Gilson, Andrew Glennerster, Ying Jin, ShouKun Wang, Naifu Jiang, Yaping Dai, Umar Asif, J.P. Thalen, M.C. van der Voort, Alcínia Z. Sampaio, Joana Prata, Ana Rita Gomes, Daniel Rosário, Piovano Luca, Basso Valter, Rocci Lorenzo, Pasquinelli Mauro, Bar Christian, Marello Manuela, Vizzi Carlo, Lucenteforte Maurizio, Brunello Michela, Racca Filippo, Rabaioli Massimo, Menduni Eleonora, Cencetti Michele, Yusuf Arayici, Paul Coates, Zhuowei Hu, Lai Wei, Wilma Waterlander, Cliona Ni Mhurchu, Ingrid Steenhuis, Elham Andaroodi, Mohammad Reza Matini, Kinji Ono, Kazunori Miyata

Published by InTech

Janeza Trdine 9, 51000 Rijeka, Croatia

Publishing Process Manager Sandra Bakic
Typesetting InTech DTP Team
Cover InTech Design Team

Additional hard copies can be obtained from orders@intechopen.com

Virtual Reality – Human Computer Interaction, Edited by Xin-Xing Tang
p. cm.
ISBN 978-953-51-0721-7

For EU product safety concerns:
IN TECH d.o.o., Prolaz Marije Krucifikse Kozulić 3, 51000 Rijeka, Croatia,
info@intechopen.com or visit our website at intechopen.com.

Meet the editor

Xin-Xing Tang received the M.D. (2004) and Ph.D. (2007) degrees in mechatronic from Jilin University, Changchun, Jilin Province, China. From September 2008 to October 2010, he worked as a postdoctoral research fellow at Gifu University, Gifu, Japan. He currently works as an instructor at the School of Mechatronic Engineering, Changchun University of Technology, Changchun, Jilin Province, China. His research interests include virtual reality, tele-operation construction robot, machine vision, etc. At present, he is committed to the study of dexterous hand and vision bionics and tracking. He has published a lot of papers about virtual reality, image processing, tele-operation construction robot and vision bionics and tracking.

Contents

Preface

In recent years, virtual reality technology has become a very popular technology, which embodies the newest research achievements in the fields of computer technology, computer graphics, sensor technology, ergonomics, human-machine interaction theory. More and more people devote into this field and commit themselves to its research, development and application. Virtual reality technology has become one of the means for human to explore the world. What is brought to us by virtual reality? Firstly, it has changed our ideas. Now, the person, instead of computer, is the main body of information technology. Secondly, it has improved the human-machine interactive manner. Now, the natural interactive manner by hand and sound replaces the passive mode in the past. Thirdly, it has changed the manner of life and entertainment. In a word, virtual reality technology is an important technology to be paid attention, which will bring huge impact to our life and work.

The book aims to provide a broader perspective of virtual reality on development and application. In this book, we mainly introduce development trend and application of virtual reality. The book includes four parts, the first part is named as "virtual reality visualization and vision", which includes new developments in virtual reality visualization of 3D scenarios, virtual reality and vision, high fidelity immersive virtual reality included tracking, rendering and display subsystems. And the second part named as "virtual reality in robot technology" brings forth applications of virtual reality in remote rehabilitation robot-based rehabilitation evaluation method and multi-legged robot adaptive walking in unstructured terrains. And the third part named as "industrial and construction applications" is about the product design, space industry, building information modeling, construction and maintenance by virtual reality, and so on. And the last part, which is named as "culture and life of human", is about the culture life and multimedia technology.

At present, the virtual reality not only is used to improve the existing information system in human-computer interaction means, but also has impact on information organization and management, and even changes design principle of information systems, which will make it adapt to application requirements. However, our reviews regarding virtual reality is only limited to the robot, construction and industry, and culture life and multimedia technology. In fact, virtual reality only succeeds in penetrating total information systems by breaking through the limitation, which will get more healthy and rapid development. Although three-dimensional stereoscopic display device, head tracking device and rendering techniques based on image have been applied, many hardware and software problems need to be solved. Firstly, improve the hardware support by reducing the price of graphics accelerator and decreasing the dependence to three-dimensional stereoscopic display device. It is impossible for every information system to use the expensive graphics workstation and for everyone using the computer to wear the display device. Secondly, improve software development environment support. For example, whether it is possible that virtual reality display system can be generated only from the image directly, and no requiring manual rendering of three-dimensional geometric models, or the virtual reality environment can be rendered real time only by the software accelerator, that will be a problem. Therefore, it is necessary for us to summarize the available technology and application, and discuss the future development trend of virtual reality. Despite new advances in the field of virtual reality technology cannot be covered exhaustively in this volume, we hope this book will help readers to understand how to create and apply the virtual reality system.

Xin-Xing Tang Ph.D
School of Mechatronic Engineering,
Changchun University of Technology, Changchun, Jilin Province,
China

Section 1

Visualization of Virtual Reality and Vision Research

Chapter 1

New Trends in Virtual Reality Visualization of 3D Scenarios

Giovanni Saggio and Manfredo Ferrari

Additional information is available at the end of the chapter

http://dx.doi.org/10.5772/46407

1. Introduction

Virtual Reality (VR) is successfully employed for a real huge variety of applications because it can furnish major improvement and can be really effective in fields such as engineering, medicine, design, architecture and construction, education and training, arts, entertainment, business, communication, marketing, military, exploration, and so on. Therefore great efforts have been paid over time to the development of more and more realistic and sophisticated VR scenarios and representations.

Since VR is basically a three-dimensional representation of a not real environment, mainly due to computer-generated simulation, Computation and Visualization are the key technologies to pay attention to. But while the Computational Technology experienced an exponential growth during the last decades (the number of transistors on an integrated circuit doubles approximately every 18 months according to the Moore's law), the Technology devoted to Visualization did not catch up with its counterpart till now. This can represent a limit or, even, a problem, due to the fact that human beings largely rely on Visualization, and the human reactions can be more appropriate in front of spatial, three-dimensional images, rather than to the current mainly adopted two-dimensional Visualization of scenarios, text and sketches. The current adoption of flat panel monitors which represent only the "illusion" of the depth, does not completely satisfy the requirement of an "immersive" experience.

In VR, a Visualization in three dimensions becomes more and more mandatory, since it allows more easily the humans to see patterns, relationships, trends, .. otherwise difficult to gather.

This chapter describes the actual requirements for 3D Visualization in VR, the current state and the near future of the new trends. The final goal is to furnish to the reader a complete panorama of the state of the art and of the realizations under development in the research laboratories for the future possibilities.

To this aim we report the most significant commercial products and the most relevant improvements obtained with research prototypes for 3D Visualization in VR. In addition an interesting patented technology is described for which the screen is not made by a solid material as it usually occurs, so that the viewer can even *walk-through* the visualized scenario.

2. Requirements

The requirement for 3D Visualization in VR seems that can be now partially or, in some way, completely satisfied thanks to new possibilities offered by the latest technologies. We are not thinking to the "standard" 3D representation furnished by flat monitors, but real new 3D Visualization which can occur in a three-dimensional room environment, furnished by dedicated equipment, which allows to visualize any scenario from any perspective.

That's the way to realize the longed "real" immersive experience, even going beyond mere images visualized on a screen, toward ones that we can interact with and *walk-through* or *navigate-through* (the so called *Princess Leia effect* from the *Star Wars* movie) because no solid support for projection is necessary.

Today, the term VR is also used for applications that are not properly "immersive", since the boundaries of VR definition are within a certain blur degree. So, VR is named also for variations which include mouse-controlled navigation "through" a graphics monitor, maybe with a stereo viewing via active glasses. Apple's QuickTime VR, for example, uses photographs for the modelling of three-dimensional worlds and provides pseudo look-around and walk-trough capabilities on a graphic monitor. But this cannot be considered as a real VR experience.

So here we present and discuss new technologies and new trends in Virtual Reality Visualization of 3D Scenarios, also reporting our personal research and applications, especially devoted to new holographic systems of projection.

This chapter covers the aspects related to the Visualization tools for VR, talking of their requirements, history, evolution, and latest developments. In particular an novel authors' patented technology is presented.

We can expect from the future weaker and weaker boundaries between Real Environment (RE) and Virtual Environment (VE). Currently RE and VE are recognized to be the extremes of a continuum line where Augmented Reality (AR) and Augmented Virtuality (AV) lie too, according to the proposition of Milgram & Kishino (1994, see Figure 1). But we believe, in a near future, this line will become a circle, with the two extremes to be overlapped in a single point.

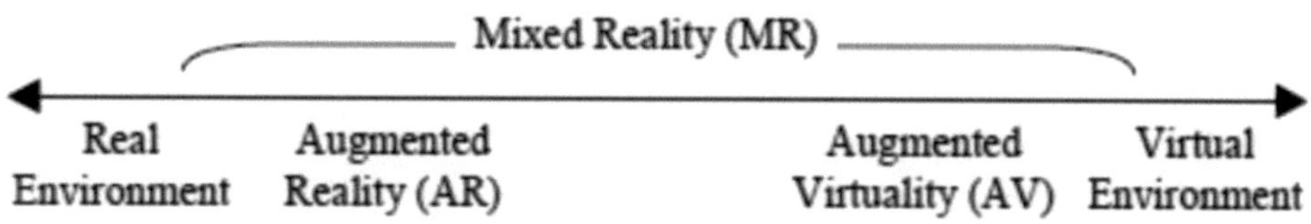

Figure 1. Virtuality-Reality Continuum

It means it will occur a difficulty or, even, impossibility for human senses to distinguish between Reality and Virtuality, and that's the real challenging goal. But, to this aim, the Visualization Technology needs to realize a burst of speed.

In the following we'll treat the new technology regarding Immersive Video, Nomatic Video, Head Mounted Displays, 3D AutoStereoscopy, Transparent Displays and HoloMachines. We will focus our attention in particular on 3D AutoStereoscopy and HoloMachines, since we have been spending efforts and gained experiences on these two technologies during latest years.

3. Actual state of new trends

Among all the commonly adopted methods to visualize a virtual or real scenario, there are some technologies worth to be mentioned as the more interesting ones, representing the actual state of new trends. So, in the following the Immersive Video, the Nomadic Video and the Head Mounted Displays are reported.

3.1. Immersive video

Immersive Video (IV) technology stands for 360° video applications, such as the Full-Views Full-Circle 360° camera. IV can be projected as multiple images on scalable large screens, such as an immersive dome, and can be streamed so that viewers can look around as if they were at a real scenario.

Different IV technologies have been developed. Their common denominator consists in the possibility to "navigate" within a video, exploring the scenario in all directions while the video is running. The scenario in generally available for a 360° view, but it is visible in a reduced portion at time, changeable according to the user's preference. Currently a few Company are devoted to IV technology, but their number is expected to growth exponentially. Let's consider here the major examples.

A first example comes from the Immersive Media® Company (www.immersivemedia.com) which is a provider of 360° spherical full motion interactive videos. The Company developed the Telemmersion® system, which is an integrated platform for capturing, storing, editing, managing spherical 3D or interactive video. A complete process of developing and building "spherical cameras", through the manipulation and storage of data to create the interactive imagery, to the delivery of the imagery and creating the immersive experience on a user's computer. Video shootings are realized by means of a spherical device in which different cameras are embedded in a way that images can be captured all around, with the only exception of the real base of the device. A limit comes from the not so performing Shockwave video format, but a "migration" to the Flash format can allow a partial improving of the performance.

The Global Vision Communication (www.globalvision.ch) furnishes technology regarding Immersive Video Pictures and Tours. In particular, their 360° interactive virtual tours can be easily integrated on existing website, or be a website themselves. Each individual panorama in a virtual tour is 360° HD-quality, clickable and draggable, linked to the others through hotspots for navigation and displayed on a customized map, featuring a directional radar. The virtual tour can be enhanced with sounds, pictures, texts, and hotpots.

The VirtualVisit Company (www.virtualvisit.tv) offers services related to 360° imagery too. Their services range from creation of 360° photography of facilities and programming high quality flash-, java- and iPhone/iPad compliant virtual visits.

The YellowBird® Company provides another example of end-to-end 360° video solutions (www.yellowbirdsdonthavewingsbuttheyflytomakeyouexperiencea3dreality.com). They shoot, edit, develop and distribute interactive 360° concepts with some of the most progressive agencies, broadcasters and brands around the world.

Another example we can mention is the Panoscope 360° (www.panoscope360.com), which consists of a single channel immersive display composed of a large inverted dome, a hemispheric lens and projector, a computer and a surround sound system. From within, visitors can navigate in real-time in a virtual 3D world using a handheld 3-axis pointer/selector. The Panoscope 360° is the basis of the Panoscope LAN consisting of networked immersive displays where visitors can play with each other in a shared environment. Catch&Run, the featured program, recreates a children's game where the fox can eat the chicken, the chicken can beat the snake and the snake can kill the fox. The terrain, an array of vertically moving rooftops, can be altered in real time, at random, or by a waiting audience trying to "help" players inside.

In the IV frame is concerned the European FP7 research project "3DPresence" (www.3dpresence.eu), which aims the realization of effective communication and collaboration with geographically dispersed co-workers, partners, and customers, who requires a natural, comfortable, and easy-to-use experience that utilizes the full bandwidth of non-verbal communication. The project intends to go beyond the current state of the art by emphasizing the transmission, efficient coding and accurate representation of physical presence cues such as multiple user (auto)stereopsis, multi-party eye contact and multi-party gesture-based interaction. With this goal in mind, the 3DPresence project intends to implement a multi-party, high-end 3D videoconferencing concept that will tackle the problem of transmitting the feeling of physical presence in real-time to multiple remote locations in a transparent and natural way.

Interesting immersive VR solutions come from CLARTE (www.clarte.asso.fr), which is a research centre located in Laval, France. In November 2010, CLARTE introduced the new

SAS 3+, a new Barco I-Space immersive virtual reality cube for its research projects. The I-Space is a multi-walled stereoscopic environment (made of three screens, each of 3x4 meters) that surrounds the user completely with virtual imagery. The SAS 3+ installation at CLARTE is powered with eight Barco Galaxy NW-12 full HD projectors and designed with three giant 4 by 3 meter glass screens.

The UC San Diego division of the California Institute for Telecommunications and Information Technology (Calit2, www.calit2.net), developed the StarCAVE system. It is a five-sided VR room where scientific models and animations are projected in stereo on 360-degree screens surrounding the viewer, and onto the floor as well. The room operates at a combined resolution of over 68 million pixels - 34 million per eye - distributed over 15 rear-projected walls and two floor screens. Each side of the pentagon-shaped room has three stacked screens, with the bottom and top screens titled inward by 15 degrees to increase the feeling of immersion. At less than $1 million, the StarCAVE immersive environment cost approximately the same as earlier VR systems, while offering higher resolution and contrast.

The IV technology is still quite "immature" and expensive but, despite all, it appears to be really promising, thus we can image the future with the current quality problems outmoded, and it will be possible to "navigate into" a movie in real effective ways, looking at the scene from a whatever point of view, even without pay attention to the leading actor but to a secondary scenario.

The IV technology experienced an improvement in performances thanks to new software plug-ins, the most interesting ones coming from Adobe and Apple.

In particular, the Flash® Immersive Video format, developed by Adobe, is especially adopted as a web solution to "navigate" in a street view, and keeping the mouse's cursor in the direction towards it is intended to go, the scene will change accordingly (see www.mykugi.com as an example).

Also Apple Inc. is interested in the IV technology, and developed the QuickTime Virtual Reality (QuickTime VR or QTVR) as a type of image file format. QTVR can be adopted for the creation and viewing of photographically-captured panoramas and the exploration of objects through images taken at multiple viewing angles. It functions as a plugin for the standalone QuickTime Player, as well as working as a plugin for the QuickTime Web browser plugin.

3.2. Nomadic video

A different way of visualization comes from the Nomadic Video (NV) approach realized by researchers of the Technische Universität Darmstadt (Huber et al., 2011). The display surface is not required to be dedicated and/or static, and the video content can change upon the surrounding context decided by the user. Everyday objects sojourning in a beam are turned into dedicated projection surfaces and tangible interaction devices. The approach is based on a pico-projector and on a Kinect sensor (by Microsoft Corporation). Pico-projectors and Kinect capabilities (motion tracking and depth sensing), might be able to turn any old surface into an interactive display (with varying results of course). Everyday objects, of the real scene surrounding the user, become a sort of "remote control", in a sense that the pico-projector plays different scenes according to their arrangement in the space. Makeshift display surfaces - a piece of paper or a book, for example - can be manipulated within a limited 3D space and the projected image will reorient itself, even rotating when the paper is rotated. The level of detail displayed by the projector can also be altered dynamically, with respect to the amount of display surface available. The NV system also allows everyday objects to function as a remote control since, for instance, a presentation can be controlled by manipulating an object within the camera's field of vision.

Another example of NV comes from the "R-Screen" 3D viewer, that was premiered at the Laval Virtual Exhibition, which is a VR 3-D devices and interactive technology conference that took place in Laval, France, on April 2009. The device is the result of collaboration between Renault's Information Technology Department and Clarté, the Laval Center for Virtual Reality Studies – which designed and built it. The 3D viewer enables users to walk around a virtual vehicle, as they would with a real vehicle. The "R-Screen" is a motorized screen pivoting 360° and measuring 2.50 m wide and 1.80 m high. It follows the movements of the user in such a way as to always be directly in front of the user. The system adopts several 3DVIA Virtools modules, including their VR pack. The concept was developed by Clarté and patented by Renault. A virtual, scale-one 3D image is displayed on screen. A computer updates the image according to the movements of R-Screen, enabling users to view the virtual vehicle from all angles.

3.3. Head Mounted Displays

The Head Mounted Display (HMD), also known as Helmet Mounted Display, is a visor that can be worn on the user's head, provided with one or two optical displays in correspondence of one or two eyes. The possibility to adopt one display for one eye, allows different images for the left and right eyes, so to obtain the perception of depth.

The HMD is considered to be the centerpiece for early visions of VR. In fact, the first VR system also highlighted the first HMD.

In 1968, computer science visionary Ivan Sutherland developed a HMD system that immersed the user in a virtual computer graphics world. The system was incredibly forward-thinking and involved binocular rendering, head-tracking (the scene being rendered was driven by changes in the users head position) and a vector rendering system. The entire system was so cumbersome that the HMD was mounted directly to the ceiling and hung over the user in a somewhat intimidating manner.

One of the first commercial HMD can be considered the Nintendo's Virtual Boy, a 3-D wearable gaming machine that went on sale in the 1990s, but bombed, partly because of the bulky headgear required as well as the image being all red.

A recent product was developed by technology giant Sony, that has unveiled a HMD named Personal 3D Viewer HMZ-T1, that takes the wearer into a 3D cinema of videos, music and games. The Sony's personal 3D viewer is being targeted at people who prefer solitary entertainment rather than sitting in front of a television with family or friends. Resembling a futuristic visor, the $800 device is worn like a pair of chunky goggles and earphones in one. It is equipped with two 0.7 inch high definition organic light emitting diode (OLED) panels and 5.1 channel dynamic audio headphone. The gadget enables the wearer to experience cinema-like viewing, equivalent to watching a 750 inch screen from 20 metres away.

But probably the more interesting HMD was developed by Sensics Inc. (www.sensics.com) with the SmartGoggles™ technology, based on which was realized the "Natalia", a highly-immersive 3D SmartGoggle available as a development platform to content and device partners, with the expectation that it will be available to consumers later in 2012. Natalia has got on-board: 1.2 GHz dual-core processor with graphics and 3D co-processor running Android 4.0; true 3D display 360 degree use; embedded head tracker for head angular position and linear acceleration; dual SXGA (1280×1024) OLED displays, supporting 720p, 64 degree field of view for excellent immersion; embedded stereo audio and microphone; WiFi and Bluetooth services.

Generally speaking, the HMDs have the advantages to be lightweight, compact, easy to program, 360° tracking, generally cheap (even if, for some particular cases, the cost can be as high as 40,000$), and let's experience a cinema-like viewing.

But, important drawbacks are a low resolution (the effective pixel size for the user can be quite large), low field of vision (Arthur, 2000), aliasing problems can become apparent, the high latency between the time a user repositions his/her head and the time it takes to render an update to the scene (Mine, 1993), effect of level-of-detail degradation in the periphery (Watson et al., 1997), the fact that the HMDs must be donned and adjusted, and that they are not recommended for people 15 years old and younger because some experts believe overly stimulating imagery is not good for teenagers whose brains are still developing.

Actually we can affirm that the HMDs did not take-off till now. In fact, outside of niche military training applications and some limited exposure in entertainment, the HMDs are very rarely seen. This is despite interesting commercial development from some very important players like Sony who developed the LCD-based Glasstron in 1997, and the HMZ-T1 during the current year.

4. Near future of new trends

4.1. AutoStereoscopy

Latest trend in visualization aims to furnish the "illusion of depth" in an image by presenting two offset images separately to the left and right eye of the viewer. The brain is then able to combine these two-dimensional images and a resulting perception of 3-D depth is realized. This technique is known as Stereoscopy or 3D imaging.

Three are the main techniques developed to present two offset images one for eye: the user wear eyeglasses to combine the two separate images from two offset sources; the user wear eyeglasses to filter for each eye the two offset images from a single source; the user's eyes receive a directionally splitted image from the same source. The latter technique is known as AutoStereoscopy (AS) and does not require any eyeglasses.

An improvement of the AS refers of AutoMultiscopic (AM) displays which can provide more than just two views of the same image. So, the AS realized by AM displays is undoubtedly one of the really new frontier that must be consider for the near future to realize the "illusion of depth", since leaves aside the uncomfortable eyeglasses and realizes a multi-point view of the same image. In such a way the user has not only the "illusion of depth" but the "illusion to turn around" the visualized object just moving his/her head position with respect to the source.

4.2. Alioscopy

The "feeling as sensation of present" in a VR scene is a fundamental requirement, and the AM displays go in that direction. So, we want here to present the "Alioscopy" display that is one realization of such technology, with which our research group is involved in.

The movements, the virtual interaction with the represented environment and the use of some interfaces are possible only if the user "feels the space" and understands where all the virtual objects are located. But the level of immersion in the AR highly depends on the display devices used. Strictly regarding the criteria of the representation, a correct approach for the visualization of a scenario helps to understand the dynamic behaviour of a system better as well as faster. But an interesting boost in the representation comes, in the latest years, from a 3D approach which offers help in communication and discussion of decisions with non-experts too. The creation of a 3D visual information or the representation of a "illusion" of depth in a real or virtual image is generally referred as Stereoscopy. A strategy to obtain this is through eyeglasses, worn by the viewer, utilized to combine separate images from two offset sources or to filter offset images from a single source separated to each eye. But the eyeglass based systems can suffer from uncomfortable eyewear, control wires, cross-talk levels up to 10% (Bos, 1993), image flickering and reduction in brightness. On the other end, AutoStereoscopy (AS) is the technique to display stereoscopic images without the use of special headgear or glasses on the part of the viewer. Viewing freedom can be enhanced: presenting a large number of views so that, as the observer moves, a different pair of the views is seen for each new position; tracking the position of the observer and update the display optics so that the observer is maintained in the AutoStereoscopic condition (Woodgate et al., 1998). Since AutoStereoscopic displays require no viewing aids seem to be a more natural long-term route to 3D display products, even if can present loss of image (typically caused by inadequate display bandwidth) and cross-talk between image channels (due to scattering and aberrations of the optical system). In any case we want here to focus on the AS for realizing what we believe to be, at the moment, one of the more interesting 3D representations for VR.

Current AutoStereoscopic systems are based on different technologies which include lenticular lens (array of magnifying lenses), parallax barrier (alternating points of view), volumetric (via the emission, scattering, or relaying of illumination from well-defined regions in space), electro-holographic (a holographic optical images are projected for the two eyes and reflected by a convex mirror on a screen), and light field displays (consisting of two layered parallax barriers). Figure 2 schematizes current AutoStereoscopic Techniques. See Pastoor and Wöpking (1997), Börner (1999) and Okoshi (1976) for more detailed descriptions.

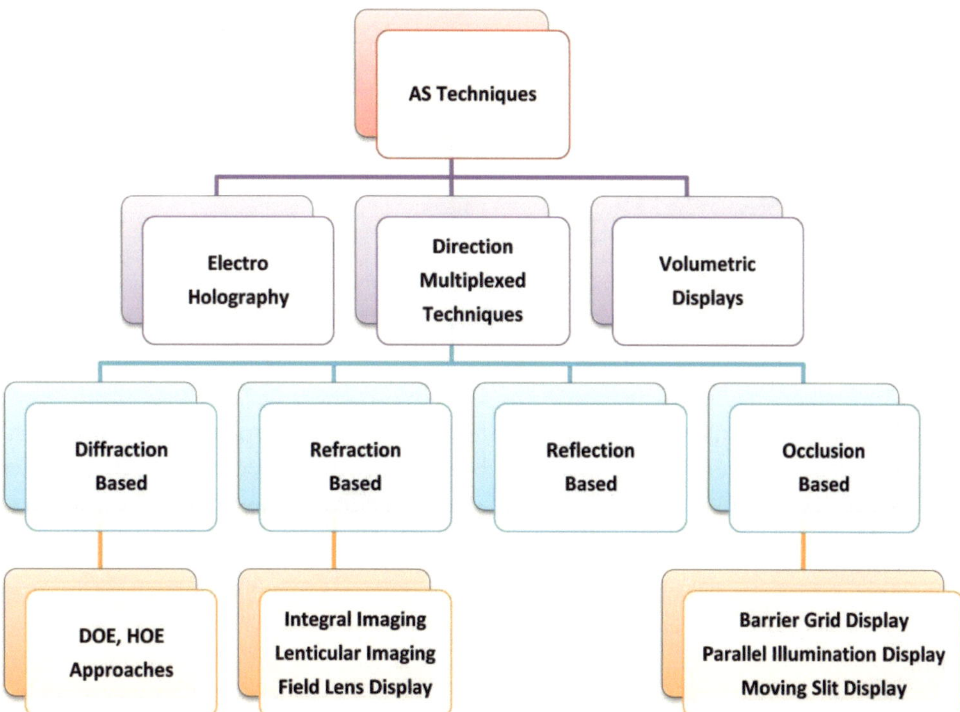

Figure 2. Schematization of current AutoStereoscopic techniques

Our efforts are currently devoted respect to four main aspects:

- user comfort,
- amount of data to process,
- image realism,
- deal with real objects as well with as graphical models.

In such a view, our collaboration involves the Alioscopy company (www.alioscopy.com) regarding a patented 3D AS visualization system which, even if does not completely satisfy all the requirements of a "full immersive" VR, remains one of the most affordable system, in terms of cost and quality results.

The 3D monitor, offered by the Company, is based on the standard Full HD LCD and its feature back 8 points of view is called *MultiScope*. Each pixel of the LCD panel combines the three fundamental sub-pixel colour (red, green and blue) and the arrays of lenticular lenses (then Lenticular Imaging, see the schematization of Figure 2) cast different images onto each eye, since magnify different point of view for each eye viewed from slightly different angles (see Figure 3).

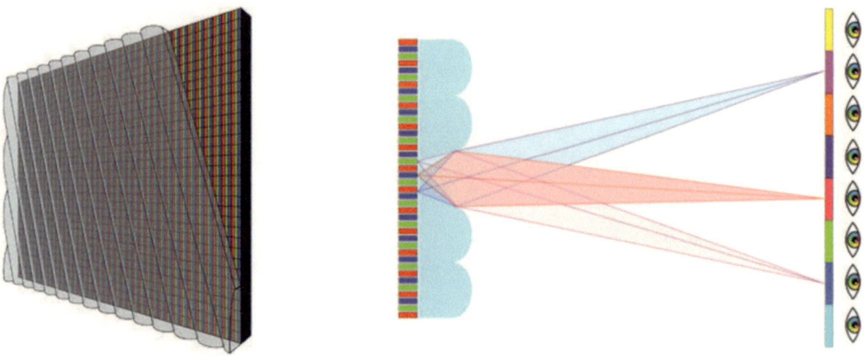

(a) (b)

Figure 3. (a) LCD panel with lenticular lenses, (b) Eight points of view of the same scene from eight cameras.

This results in a state of the art visual stereo effect, rendered with typical 3D software such as 3D Studio Max (www.autodesk.it/3dsmax), Maya (www.autodesk.com/maya), Lightwave (www.newtek.com/lightwave.html), and XSI (www.softimage.com). The display uses 8 interleaved images to produce the AutoStereoscopic 3D effect with multiple viewpoints.

We realized 3D images and videos, adopting two different approaches for graphical and real model. The graphical model is easily managed thanks to the 3D Studio Max Alioscopy plug-in, which is not usable for real images, and for which it is necessary a set of multi-cameras to recover 8 view-points (see Figure 4).

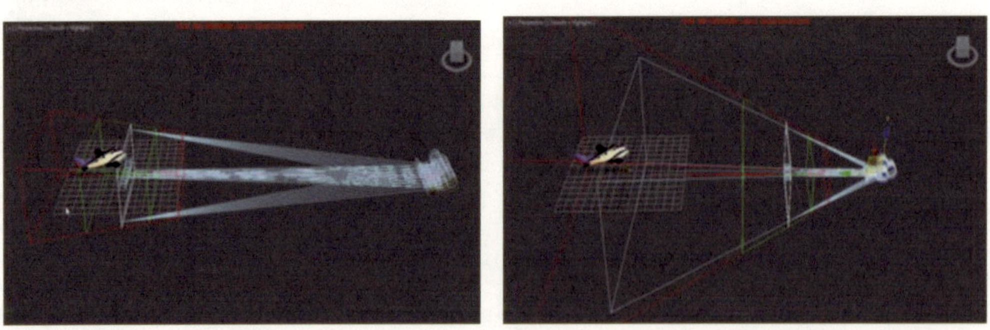

(a) (b)

Figure 4. The eight cameras with (a) more or (b) less spacing between them, focusing the object at different distances

The virtual images or real captured ones are then mixed, by means of OpenGL tools, in groups of eight to realize AutoStereoscopic 3D scenes. Particular attention must be paid in positioning the cameras to obtain a correct motion capture of a model or a real image, in particular the cameras must have the same distance apart (6.5 cm is the optimal distance) and each camera must "see" the same scene but from a different angle (see Figure 5).

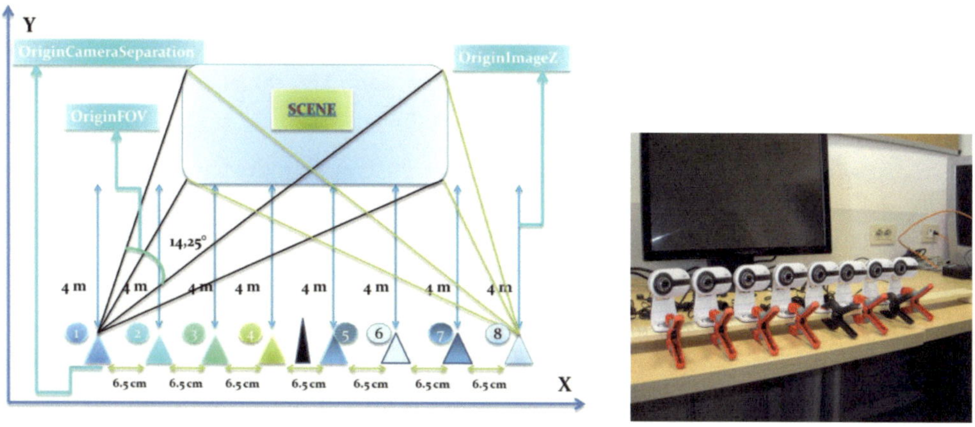

(a) (b)

Figure 5. (a) Schematization of the positions of the cameras among them and from the scene, (b) the layout we adopted for them

Figure 6 reports screen captures of three realized videos. The images show blur effects when reproduced in a non AutoStereoscopic way (as it happens in the Figure). In particular, the image in Figure 6c reproduces eight numbers (from 1 to 8), and the user see, on the AS monitor, just one number at time depending on his/her angular position with respect the monitor itself.

(a) (b) (c)

Figure 6. Some of realized images for 3D full HD LCD monitors based on lenticular lenses. Representation of (a) virtual and (b) real object, while the (c) image represents 8 numbers seeing one at time by the user depending from his/her angle of view.

The great advantage of the AS systems consists of an "immersive" experience of the user, with unmatched 3D pop-out and depth effects on video screens, and this is obtained without the uncomfortable eyewear of any kind of glasses. On the other end, an important amount of data must be processed for every frame since it is formed by eight images at the same time. Current personal computers are, in any case, capable to deal with these amount of data since the powerful graphic cards available today.

4.3. Transparent displays

Cutting-edge display technologies have brought us many new devices including thin and high-quality TVs, touchscreen phones and sleek tablet PCs. Now the latest innovation from the field is set to the *transparent technology*, which produces displays with a high transparency rate and without a full-size backlight unit. The panel therefore works as a device's screen and a see-through glass at the same time.

The transparent displays (TDs) have a wide range of use in all industry areas as an efficient tool for delivering information and communication. These panels can be applied to show windows, outdoor billboards, and in showcase events. Corporations and schools can also adopt the panel as an interactive communication device, which enables information to be displayed more effectively.

From research groups of Microsoft Applied Science and MIT Media Lab has been developed a unique sensor OLED (Organic Light Emitting Diode) transparent technology. It is the base of a "see-through screen".

Figure 7. A Kinect-driven prototype desktop environment by the Microsoft Applied Sciences Group allows users to manipulate 3D objects by hand behind a transparent OLED display (www.microsoft.com/appliedsciences)

Again from Microsoft Research comes the so called "HoloDesk", for direct 3D interactions with a Situated See-Through Display. It is basically an interactive system which combines an optical see-through display and a Kinect camera to create the illusion for the user to interact with virtual objects (Figure 7). The see-through display consists of a half silvered mirror on top of which a 3D scene is rendered and spatially aligned with the real-world for the user who, literally, gets his/her hands into the virtual display.

A TD is furnished by Kent Optronics Inc. (www.kentoptronics.com). The display contains a thin layer of bi-stable PSCT liquid crystal material sandwiched between either plastic or glass substrates. Made into a large size of meters square, the display exhibits three inter-switchable optical states of (a) uniform transparent as a conventional glass window, (b) uniform frosted for privacy protection, and (c) information display.

A transparent LCD Panel comes also from Samsung Electronics Co. Ltd (www.samsung.com) with the world's first mass produced transparent display product, designed to be used as a PC monitor or a TV. This panel boasts a high transmittance rate (over 20% for the black-and-white type and over 15% for the colour type), which enables a person to look right through the panel like glass. The panel utilizes ambient light such as sunlight, which consequently reduces the power required since there is no backlight, and it consumes 90% less electricity compared with a conventional LCD panel using back light unit.

The TDs are not so far-away to be used in every-day life.

Samsung announced to start mass production during the current year of a 46-inch transparent LCD panel, that features a contrast ratio of 4,500:1 with HD (1,366x768) resolution and 70% colour gamut. The company has been producing smaller 22-inch transparent screens since March 2011, but the recently-developed 46-inch model has much greater potential and wider usage.

LG Company (www.lg.com) is involved in the TD technology too. A 47 inch Transparent LCD display with multi-touch functionality has been realized with a full HD 1920×1080 pixel resolution. The Panel is an IPS technology with 10.000 K colour temperature. LG developed also a WVGA Active Transparent Bistable LCD which could be for future Head-up display (HUD).

4.4. HoloMachine

All the previously reported display systems are based on a solid support, generally a monitor or a projection surface. But a great improvement comes if the reproduction of a scene is realized with a *non-solid* support.

The holographic technique satisfies in principle this requirement. With the term of "holography" is generally referred the technique by which it is recorded the light scattered from an object and later reconstructed by a beam which restores the high-grade volumetric image of that object (see Figure 8). The result is that the image appears three-dimensional and changes as the position and orientation of the viewer changes in exactly the same way as if the object were really present. Unfortunately, the holography claims a technology that is still too complex and too expensive to find common applications in everyday life, so new possibilities are currently under investigation.

Figure 8. An example of hologram

A first new type of approach comes from the public lightshow displays, in which a beam of laser light is shone through a diffuse cloud of fog, but the results are not as good as a the reconstruction of a real scenario pretends, and the technique is limited to realize just written words or poor drawings.

The real new possibility is due to a new machine which realizes a screen made out of nothing but micro-particles of water. The HoloMachine (see Figure 9), that's the name of the innovation, is a patented technology (patent no. PCT/IB2011/000645), deposited by the authors of this paper, consisting of a holographic projection system which does not utilize solid screen but an air laminar flow, aerial, inconsistent, somewhat everybody can go through. The machine "creates" the illusion that the images are floating in mid-air.

Figure 9. The compact hardware of the HoloMachine. The woman indicates the slots from which the micro-particles of water are ejected. Courtesy of PFM Multimedia (Milan, Italy)

The heart of the system is an ultrasonic generator of "atomized" water, so that tiny droplets (few microns in diameter) are convoyed, sandwiched and mixed in a laminar airflow that works as a screen on which you can project (through a dedicated commercially available video-projector) images realized with a 3D-technology, Chroma-Key based. The subsequent holographic images you can obtain on this air laminar flow result suggestively aerial, floating in the air, naturally going-through by any spectator, disappearing and reappearing after have been passed through.

(a) (b)

Figure 10. (a) An image appears to be "suspended" in air and (b) a viewer can "pass through" the image with the hand Courtesy of PFM Multimedia (Milan, Italy)

This type of projection is very advantageous because it allows images to be reproduced where otherwise it would be very difficult to arrange a solid projection support due to space or light constraints or difficulties in installing conventional screens. Another advantage is because of absolutely absence of invasiveness with respect to the environment wherein the images are intended to be projected. Because of this, two of these machines have been adopted in the archaeological site of Pompeii, in Italy, one representing Giulio Polibio "talking" to the visitors and the second representing his pregnant wife swinging on a rocking chair and caressing her baby (see Figure 11).

Stands its characteristic, the HoloMachine can find application in museums, in science centres, in lecture theatres, in showrooms, in conference centres, in theme parks, in discotheques, in shopping malls, in fashion shows, etc., and for product launches, special event, entertainment purposes, advertising matters, multiplayer games, educational purposes, .. and in general for VR applications, or even Augmented Reality applications, for which "immersive" feeling for the user makes the difference.

From a mere technological point of view, this holographic projection technology takes advantage of the optical properties of water, indices of reflection and refraction, for generating a circumscribed volume of an nebulized air-water mixture, dry to the touch, that will behave like a screen adapted for image projection. This screen can be defined as "virtual" as it is only made of an nebulized air-water mixture, a turbulence-free "slice" of air-water a few millimetres thick, and once it is "on", it is possible to reproduce moving images on it, thereon using the more or less traditional methods such as the video projection, laser projection, live shot projection with video-projector, etc. (see Figure 12).

Since the light coming from the video-projector is reflected/transmitted with angles which depend on the position of the illuminated point of the air-water "slice" (the inner/outer point of the slice, the narrower/wider the reflection/transmission angle), the viewer experiences a sort of "holographic" view, since he/she has the illusion of the depth, having two offset images from the same source but separated to each eye.

(a) (b) (c)

Figure 11. 3D holographic scenes of Giulio Polibio and his wife in their domus at the archeological site of Pompeii in Italy (Courtesy by PFM Multimedia Company)

In principle this machine can generate images of any size. The limit is due to the technology adopted to eject the air-water mixture for which it depends the distance the air-water mixture keeps its consistency, before spreading all around. But, according to fluid-mechanic principles, a mixture of air-water which is denser than the surrounding air, could help to stabilize the system. Of course, if the machine is utilized in open space, the air-water mixture might be ruffled by a blast of wind but, when it occurs, the "slice" itself would refill with air-water and the images are reformed really very quickly, as well as it happens if a person goes *through* the screen.

The machine project design was conceived in a way that people would not get wet when *passing through* the "screen" and that the machine could operate within a broad range of environmental conditions, particularly thinking about the surrounding light conditions. The best viewing results are of course obtained in dark environments, but even under the direct rays of the sun, the images can still remain appreciably visible, the limit being due only to the light output capabilities of the projector (recommended 4500 ANSI lumen or higher), which can be any commercially available one.

In any case, the resulting definition and colour saturation of the projected images are not perfect (see Figure 11) and can still be improved, but this does represent a surmountable problem. It is mainly related to some parameters such as the type of fans that pump away from the machine the air-water mixture, the velocity the mixture reaches, the temperature, the real dimensions of the tiny droplets, their electrostatic charge, the Reynolds Number of the mixture flowing. So, a better image definition can be obtained with a better control of these parameters.

Also interactivity can be implemented, realizing an "immersive" touch screen, so expanding the application possibilities. The shown images can change, react or interact with the user as he/she changes the laminar air flow with his/her body (or even a simple blow!), also depending on the point/area where the laminar flow is deformed. Poke a finger at the screen, and the nebulized air-water mixture is interrupted, allowing the system to detect where you have "clicked".

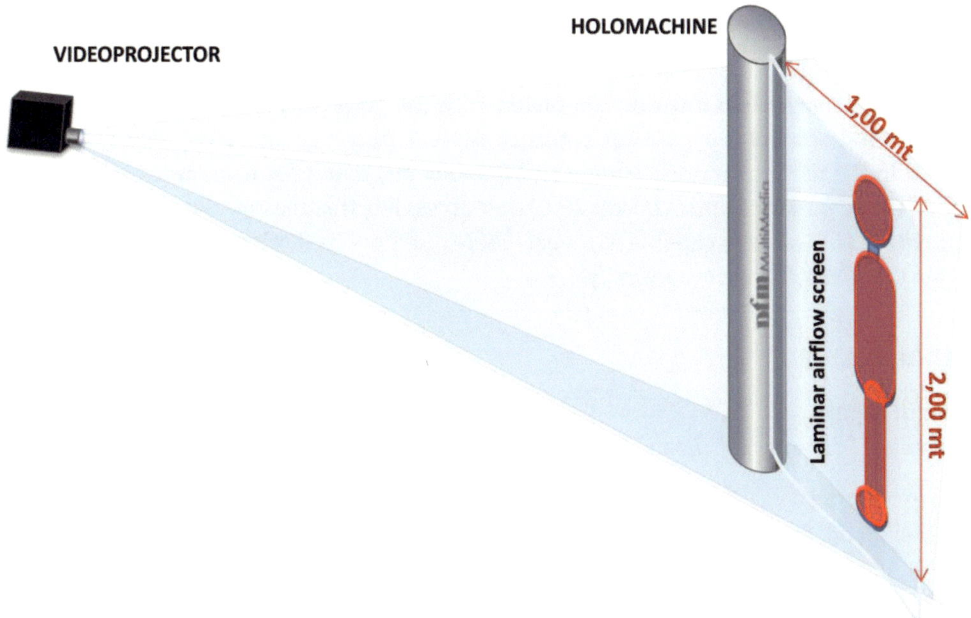

Figure 12. A scheme representing the HoloMachine. A Video Projector illuminates a screen made out of nothing but micro-particles of water

5. Conclusions

The final goal of VR is to deceive the five human senses in a way that the user can believe to live in a real environment. This means that the Real Environment and the Virtual Environment can be "confused" and the line of Figure 1 can become a circle so that the two extremes can result in only one point.

To this aim we have to develop systems to artificially create/recreate smells, flavours, tactile sensations, sounds and visions perceived to be physically real. After all, the Immersive VR can be thought as the science and technology required for a user to feel present, via perceptive, cognitive, functional and, even, psychological immersion and interaction, in a computer-generated environment. So, these systems have to be supported by commensurate computational efforts to realize computer-created scene, real-time rendered, and current computer machines can be considered reasonably adequate (also because they can work in cluster configuration with a high degree of parallelism). So, the main energies must be devoted to the development of new sensors, capable to better "measures" of the reality and, over all, new transducers, capable to convert an electrical signal into somewhat detectable by human senses in a way to be confused as "real", so that the user forgets that his/her perception is mediated by technology.

This chapter describes the new possibilities offered by the recent technology to obtain a virtual "vision" that has to be as "real" as possible. In such a view, panoramic 3D vision must be preferred and the better if the images can be "realized in air", i.e. without the adoption of a solid screen, as well as it happens in reality. So, details were furnished of the AutoMultiScopic for 3D Vision, in particular with the description of the Alioscopy screen, and details of the Holo-Vision for screen-less Vision, in particular with the description of the HoloMachine.

But an immersive system must be completed with the possibility of interaction for the user with the environment. So gestural controls, motion tracking, and computer vision must respond to the user's postures, actions and movements, and a feedback must be furnished, with active or passive haptic (Insko, 2001) resources. For this reason, the HoloMachine can be provided with sensors capable to reveal where and how its laminar flow is interrupted so that the scene can change accordingly.

Author details

Giovanni Saggio
University of "Tor Vergata", Rome, Italy

Manfredo Ferrari
PFM Multimedia Srl, Milan, Italy

6. References

Arthur K., (2000) Effects of field of view on performance with head-mounted displays, Ph.D. dissertation, Dept. Comput. Sci., Univ. North Carolina, Chapel Hill, 2000

Börner, R. (1999). Four Autostereoscopic monitors on the level of industrial prototypes. Displays 20, (pp. 57-64).

Bos P.J. (1993) Liquid-crystal shutter systems for time multiplexed stereoscopic displays, in: D.F. McAllister (Ed.), Stereo Computer Graphics and Other true 3D Technologies, Princeton University Press, Princeton, pp. 90-118

Huber J., Liao C., Steimle J., Liu Q., (2001) Toward Bimanual Interactions with Mobile Projectors on Arbitrary Surfaces, In Proceedings of MP^2: Workshop on Mobile and Personal Projection in conjunction with CHI 2011, 2011

Insko B.E., (2001) Passive Haptics Significantly Enhance Virtual Environments, Doctoral Dissertation, University of North Carolina at Chapel Hill, 2001

Milgram P., Kishino F., (1994) A Taxonomy of Mixed Reality Visual Displays, IEICE Transactions on Information Systems, Vol E77-D, No.12 December 1994

Mine, M. (1993) Characterization of End-to-End Delays in Head-Mounted Display Systems, The University of North Carolina at Chapel Hill, TR93-001

Okoshi, T. (1976). Three-Dimensional Imaging Techniques. Academic Press Inc (New York)

Pastoor, S. and Wöpking, M. (1997). 3-D Displays: A review of Current Technologies. Displays, 17 (1997), (pp. 100-110)

Watson, B., Walker, N., Hodges, L. F., & Worden, A. (1997). Managing Level of Detail through Peripheral Degradation: Effects on Search Performance with a Head-Mounted Display. ACM Transactions on Computer-Human Interaction, 4(4), 323-346

Woodgate G.J., Ezra D., Harrold J., Holliman N.S., Jones G.R. & Moseley R.R. (1998) Autostereoscopic 3D display systems with observer tracking, Signal Processing: Image Communication 14 (1998) 131-145

Chapter 2

The Virtual Reality Revolution: The Vision and the Reality

Richard M. Levy

Additional information is available at the end of the chapter

http://dx.doi.org/10.5772/51823

1. Introduction

1.1. Evolution of technology: Vision and goals

Like many technologies, virtual reality began as a dream and a vision. For example, the desire to fly had to wait for technology to progress before becoming a reality. Though the story of Icarus and Deadalus might have inspired a Leonardo to draw a bird-like flying machine, centuries past before science and technology set the stage for flight beyond mere kites and gliders. A high powered, light weight gas engine was one of many innovations required for heavier than air aircrafts to become a reality in the early 20th century. Over the course of a century, a series of innovations and inventions emerged that that were critical to the development of modern aircrafts. Although in principal today's aircrafts share much with their earlier predecessors, they have capability that far exceeds those early machines. Why it is now possible to fly at 30,000 ft in comfort, at speeds of over 500 mph, can best be understood as the culmination of a convergence in technological development over the last century.

The proposed replacement for the F16 fighter, the F35, was only possible with improvements in material technology. Being composed of carbon fiber material makes this jet a third lighter than its predecessor. With computer numeric control (CNC) the F35 is built to tolerances not previously achieved for carbon fiber aircraft. The engine built by Pratt &Whitney, today's most powerful engine, produces over 50,000 lbs at weight to power ratios much greater than could have been achieved even just a few years ago. Avionics and sensors give "situational awareness" and provide the F35 a level of virtual intelligence and awareness critical to mission success (Keijsper, 2007).

The piloting of these aircraft is assisted by the onboard computer capability. To assist the pilot in making critical decisions, a helmet mounted display gives information on targets and the aircraft's control systems. Today's modern jet aircrafts bear little similarity to the early predecessors made of wood canvas and wire and yet, both fly. The technology of flight has advanced beyond the dreams even of science fiction writers of just a century ago. Though the goals of flight have remained the same, the form of their technological solution has evolved in ways that could never have been imagined.

Virtual reality, in its development parallels that of flight. The simulators used in flight training during the Second World War share much in principal with those made today for military and passenger jets, even if they look like inventions out of retro-science fiction movies. Built in the day when mechanical lineages and analogue electrical gauges provided feedback in modern airplanes, these flight simulators could train air force pilots to fly in conditions of total fog or darkness. The desire to improve on the safety record of early pilots was the incentive for the Edwin Link to create simulators built from the same technology used to control pipe organs of the day. Yet even these crude devices incorporated much of what characterizes flight simulators today. With the link trainer, the student pilot was placed inside an enclosed cockpit mounted on a 360 pivot. Once inside the cockpit, the pilot would practice flying blind. With working controls and instruments, the pilot could practice flying in an immersive environment complete with feedback. The stick of the link-trainer worked like an actual airplane and allowed the trainer to turn and bank. Mimicking a real aircraft, artificial horizons and altimeter gauges provided the pilot with the feedback need to fly blind. Pilots would progress through a simulated mission with their route traced on a large table with a pen mounted on a small motorized carriage. Using radio headsets, communication between the trainer and the pilot simulated the actual sound between ground control and pilot. Advanced models featured the full instrumentation of the modern fighters of the day. With over 10,000 of these units built during the Second World War, they can still be found in many air museums in North America and Europe (Link Flight Trainer, 2000).

The link simulator provides two important lessons in the history of technology. First, virtual reality and the desire to have an immersive training environment preceded the computer revolution that began in the 1960's. Today's simulators, though similar in functionality and purpose, share little in the underlying technology used to accomplish their goal. Today's multimillion dollar simulators reproduce the view, sound and motion experience in a real jet cockpit. Built on top of a six degrees of freedom motion platform, the entire cockpit of a jet can bank, yawl and pitch as it flies under simulated conditions. When first developed, the computing requirements for these simulators were at the cutting edge of computer technology. Advanced graphic engines, parallel processing, high resolution graphic displays, motion controlled platforms, and a geographic database of the world's topographical features are all critical milestones in the history of computing and have contributed to the design of modern flight simulators (George, 2000). .

Second, VR as a simulation of reality has been instrumental in the advancement of the technology it simulates, in this case flight. The ability to fly an advanced fighter jet or one of the new generations of fly-by-wire passenger jets was dependent on the same technology used to create advanced simulators. For each advanced jet that flies today there is a simulator that prepares pilots for the actual experience of flight. Companies like Boeing, CAE and Lockheed Martin operate advanced simulators which utilize motion platforms, high resolution graphics systems and databases containing all the world's land features and airports at high resolution. In these simulators which mimic almost every aspect of flying in the cockpit, pilots can prepare themselves for such experiences as flying into bad weather or responding to a mechanical or electrical systems failure. The safety of an entire industry now depends on these advanced simulators and their capability to train pilots on how best to prepare for these extraordinary events.

Millions of dollars have been invested in creating simulators for the military that have proven indispensible for training pilots for all types of aircrafts. Simulated worlds are also valuable tools in many fields for exploration, testing and training. But, beyond flight simulators, advanced applications are rarely found in training and education. For example, there are a few advanced auto simulators used to in research on passenger and driver safety in US and Europe (NADS, 2012; Schwartz, 2003). However, given their great expense, it is doubtful they will be used to train a young teenage driver when the alternative, a practice permit and a shopping mall parking lot on a Sunday morning, is a simpler and less costly first introduction to the driving experience.

1.2. Simulators and the demand for high end graphics

When computing technology was first used in the development of simulators, the requirement for realistic simulation pushed the envelope of computing for the period. In the 1990's when simulators emerged as important training tools, displaying geographic detail in real time demanded high-end graphics mainframes. In part, SGI's early success resulted from the creation of the ONYX Infinite Reality engine, capable of rendering multiple views in high detail. Built for high-end rendering, an Onyx could contain up to 20, four 150 mhs processors. The Reality Engine2 Graphics system in 1998 (George, 2000; SGI) was capable of rendering up to 2 million mesh polygons and 320 M textured pixels per second, descriptions of these computers, which are still impressive by today's standards (NVIDIA, 2012), were critical to rendering the multiple views needed for each of the cockpit windows in a flight simulator. Pilots could view in details of cities on their flight path, and the landing and taxing to gates of any major international airport. When these virtual reality simulators were placed on a six degrees of freedom motion platform pilots had the experience of flying without ever leaving the ground. Today's consumers can have a taste of this experience by purchasing PC game programs like Flight Simulator (Microsoft, 2012) that put you in the cockpit of a Boeing 747 or WWII fighter. With multiple screen display, a PC with a gamer's video card and a dedicated yoke lets the average consumer achieve what the creators of the Link simulator could only have dreamed of half a century ago. Though inexpensive hardware has had a critical role in the history of VR, the demands for specific applications for work and play may be the force in promoting the diffusion of VR in the future.

1.3. Building the market for VR

Every technology benefits from an application that creates a growing demand. Without growth in markets, products remain in a niche supported by a few high-end users, e.g. the flight simulator. To drive down unit costs, products must appeal to a growing audience. Like the first computers built after the war, the demand for these costly goliaths served only a very small number of corporate and military users. For VR to grow beyond the use in the military and commercial aviation, a new group of potential users would have to be found. This would require the development of hardware and software solutions for medicine, architecture, urban planning and entertainment. Unlike flight simulators designed for a single task, the approach was to accommodate a range of applications in a multipurpose VR facility. Ultimately, this strategy could expand the number of potential users. CAVE's with multiple screens displaying content in 3D would seem to have offered a technological solution that would satisfy a range of users. With government research support, many universities and national labs established virtual reality centers, which were to offer engineers, design professionals, urban planners and medical researchers with a much needed facility for advanced visualization.

2. Applications of VR

2.1. The design of cities

In the 1990's, universities had sufficient funding to acquire sophisticated computing power. For example, UCLA obtained an SGI ONYX. In this facility Los Angeles city planners were given a first opportunity to visualize urban form in an immersive environment. Rather than crowding around a computer monitor to view data, specialized projection screens enabled planners and government officials to experience and evaluate development proposals within a life size 3D virtual world. The work of Jepson and Liggett at UCLA offered a glimpse into a future that promised public participation into the urban design process (Hamit, 1998; Jepson & Friedman, 1998; Liggett and Jepson, 1993). In their simulator, it was possible to see the impact of "what if questions" while driving down the city streets of Los Angeles.

VR had promising beginnings with several cities taking up the challenge of using VR as a tool in urban planning. Several universities would be in the vangard of this movement, following in the footpaths of Liggett and Jepson, including the University of Toronto and the New School for Social Science Research in New York. Creating VR environments with detailed virtual cities required the time and resources of CAD modelers and programmers (Drettakis, G., Roussou, M., Reche, A. & Tsingos, N., 2007; Batty, M., Dodge, D., Simon. D. & Smith, A., 1998; Hamit, 1998) . Since the 1990's many North American, European and Asian governments have created CAD models of their cities, but they are often used to produce animations, rather than used to enhance the planning process (Mahoney 1994; Mahoney 1997; Littelhales 1991) . Animations are important as part of marketing campaigns to promote, for example, a new train line, landmark commercial development or public space.

Without a driving interest by the professional planner to use VR in urban design and planning, its application over the last two decades has been limited to the exceptional case. Even today with GIS to easily show a city's buildings in 3D, models of a city are largely inaccessible to planners who often lack training and access to their corporate GIS.

Though planning has embraced the charette, open house and web-based survey, the discipline has yet to grab hold of design in real time. In part, this is a problem of logistics and cost. Finding facilities adequate to hold even half a dozen individuals is difficult. For those wishing to display 3D worlds in stereo, the price of glasses, special projectors or displays makes the technology out of reach for most city governments (Howard & Gaborit, 2007). Finally, there is a cultural dimension of planning practice which limits the adoption of VR. Planning is still largely done in a 2D world. Zoning maps and plot plans are easily stored, visualized and analyzed in 2D. Even for planners who have received their education during the last decade, an introductory course in CAD or GIS may not have been required. The older generations of planners, now in more senior positions, are even less likely to be knowledgeable GIS and CAD users (Mobach, 2008; Wahlstrom, M, Aittala, M. Kotilainen, H. Yli-Karhu, T. Porkka, J. & Nyka¨nen, E. 2010; Zuh, 2009).

Potentially, the impact of land use change on future development could be better understood using simulation tools of the kind used by transportation planners in designing and maintaining a road system for a city. Yet, most planning departments rarely use such modeling approaches. In contrast, the game world since 1985 has had a simulation tool, SIM City, which allows anyone with a PC to manage a city's budget and understand the impact of land use planning on the future development of the city (Simcity, 2012). Interestingly, a land use planning tool designed for professional city planners has yet to be become the norm in urban planning practice. Without the vision for what simulation can do for planning, serious tools have yet to appear in practice. Without the commitment to a vision of what potentially could be accomplished through the application of computer technology, these tools will await future development. Furthermore, land use policy can be implemented and enforced without the benefit of an advanced information system. In fact, VR and other advanced visualization technology may be counter productive to the planning process. Visualization of proposed development, if not carefully introduced to the political electorate, may incite adverse reactions from the public and create more work for the planners and their staff (Al-Douri 2010, Forester 1989; Mobach, 2008). Advanced modeling and simulation for this reason may not always be seen as a beneficial by practicing planners.

2.2. The rebirth of physical urban models

Recent innovation in 3D printing may actually reinforce the use of a physical model over that of the virtual world, when it comes to visualizing the future urban form of cities. With lower costs associated with 3D printing, it is now possible to create plastic models directly from CAD models. In the past, the expense of creating a model of a city with all of its buildings was not a simple task. Scale models of an entire city required teams of artists and cartographers to complete. Unlike paper maps and drawings, you would also need a large space for storage and examination. Brest, Cherbourg and Embrun are examples of a few cities for which scale models were commissioned by Louis XIV and constructed under the direction of Sébastien Le Prestre de Vauban (Marshall of France, b1663-d 1707) Known for his publications on siege and fortification, Vauban supervised the creation these models as important tools in the preparation of military defenses (de Vauban, 1968) Ultimately, more than 140 of these models were constructed for the King of France(Lichfield). In the 20th century, there are numerous examples of these types of large scale models. The most impressive include those representing Daniel Burnham's Plan commissioned for the Chicago Foundation in 1909, a model of Rome commissioned by Mussolini, the model of Los Angeles built under the WPA's in the 1930's and a model of Moscow completed in 1977(Itty Bitty Cities, Urbanist).

In the 1980's under Donald Appleyard, Director of the Environmental Urban Lab, University of California, Berkeley, College of Environmental Design, a full scale model of San Francisco was constructed(Environmental Simulation Laboratory). Prior to the use of computer modeling, this physical model served an important role in assessing the impact of new development on the immediate surroundings. By employing a video camera mounted with a model scope fixed to a moving gantry, it was possible to drive along roads and view the existing city and proposed developments. These models lit by an electric lamp were also capable of simulating the sun and shade at various times of the year. By examining alternative plans for development within this physical model it was possible to have a tool for facilitating public review of urban projects.

With the recent introduction of inexpensive 3D printing, it is now possible to create 3D models of entire cities. Like models of the past, such models of Tokyo, Toronto, and New York offer a bird's eye view of a large area (Itty Bitty Cities, Urbanist). Though the virtual version would offer greater flexibility in data retrieval, viewing alternative design concepts, understanding impact of zoning, and having physical representations are considered highly desirable by government officials, planners and architects. Like Lego Land and doll houses there is a strange attraction to such miniature worlds that is difficult to comprehend on a rational level.

2.3. Architecture and the art of image making

Advancements in BIM (Building Information Modeling) and CAD has given the architecture profession new tools for creating buildings. BIM can offer designers a completely interactive design space. Buildings can be designed from the ground up in a virtual environment. Using a host of simulation tools it is now possible to work collaboratively with the client and other consultants on the design of a building. Though it would appear to offer advantages over more traditional tools, it is yet to be an approach universally accepted by architects within their culture of design (Levy 1997; Novitski 1998). Since the Renaissance, it was through the art of drawing that architects distinguished themselves from the building trades. Even today architects differentiate themselves from engineers and urban planners by their artistic abilities and talents. Beginning in the 15th, architects of the stature of

Michelangelo, Sebastiano Serlio Palladio and Bramante employed the plan, elevation and section to create their designs(Kostoff 1977; Million 1997; Palladio, 1965). Knowledge of these drawing conventions, first mentioned in the oldest surviving architectural treatise by Vitruvius, Il Quattro Libri (1st Cent AD) are still considered essential skills for architecture students today (Kostoff 1977; Vitruvius 1960). One important aspect of orthographic constructions (plan, section, elevation) is the ability to take direct measurement from the scaled drawings. Borrowing from these established drawing conventions, CAD applications reflect the architect's preference for working in plan and elevation for determining design solutions. Visualizing the design in perspective occurs after the architect has created his concept in plan.

Perspective as a tool emerged during the Renaissance with the inventive work of Filippo Brunelleschi (1377-1456). Borrowing from the theory of optics and the mathematics of the period, Brunelleschi should be credited in creating the first augmented reality device. Using a set of mirrors, Brunelleschi was able to position a perspective drawing of the Baptistery of Florence onto a view of it in the Piazza Santa Maria, thus demonstrating that the new science of perspective drawing could simulate reality. The actual device consisted of two mirrors. The first of the two mirrors would be positioned in front of your eye. A small hole at the centre would allow you to view a second mirror, which was placed showing a perspective view of the Baptistery. When standing in front of the Baptistery in the exact same location from which the perspective was constructed (as a mirror image) the observer would see the image of the perspective reconstruction of the baptistery superimposed over its actual location. Varying the distance between the two mirrors would change the size of the perspective image relative to the actual surroundings. By removing the mirror furthest from the eye, the observer could compare the actual image with the perspective construction. Offered as proof that perspective was a tool for presenting how an architect's design would look when constructed, perspective would become a device for presenting both the real and the imagined (Collier, 1981; Edgerton, 1974). In the 16th and 17th century, perspective would become particular useful in the design of stage backdrops for fantastic architectural scenes used in opera and the theatre. Giovanni Maria Galli-Bibiena is perhaps one of the most important artist of this period whose work would grace the opera houses of Europe and would later be published as engravings by Christopher Dall'Acqua, and JA Ambrose Orio Pfeffel in 1731 (Pigozzi 1992).

Though a perspective drawing is an important visualization tool for architects, it is mostly relegated to the role of a presentation graphic. Often created for the client's benefit, perspective drawings are not the working tools of architects. Instead, it is the plan and elevation that serves the architect during the conceptualization and construction process. In published works by Andrea Palladio and Inigo Jones, their skillful use of plan and elevation is still studied by today's architects (Kostoff, 1977; Million 1997; Palladio, 1965). Later this approach to design would be adopted by the Ecole des Beaux Arts in Paris. With an emphasis on acquiring a high level of proficiency in creating high quality images in ink and color washes, the school's graduates would dominate the teaching ranks of architecture in the US and Europe during the period in the 20th century prior to emergence of modernism.

Even with the emergence of the Bauhaus in the 1920's, programs of architecture in the US or Europe would still demand expert draftsmanship from their graduates (Kostoff, 1977, Levy 1980).

Once a design is approved by the client, architects create the working drawings needed for the bidding and construction phase. In the past, working drawings were drawn in pencil or ink on velum to create the needed blueprints. The process of creating "working drawings" was a significant part of practice, consuming many hours of draftsmen's time. Photos of architects' offices from the last century often show junior architects working on drafting tables producing the drawings, which today would be printed on wide carriage plotters. In practice, changes and additions are part of the design process. With paper drawings, even a simple change, like the replacement of one window style with another could require hours of redrawing. Beginning with the introduction of CAD (computer aided design) in the 1980's, architects were relieved of the burden of having to make endless changes to paper drawings. CAD offered advantages over the traditional drawing methods used by architects since the Renaissance, but for many architects, the art of drawing distinguished them from engineers and technicians (Kostoff, 1977; Levy, 1997). Even when the interactive age of design seemed imminent, CAD was never widely adopted. Today, the culture of architectural design has yet to fully embrace the use of advanced CAD tools in design. Within an architectural firm, decisions rest with the senior partners; often, they are uncomfortable with the new CAD technology. For this reason, these new tools are the used primarily by technicians to create construction documents. Virtual reality design, a hopeful prospect in 1990's has yet to be fully developed or implemented.

With the advancement of BIM in recent years, architects have new tools for design and construction management. With BIM, an extension of CAD tools from the 1980's, it is possible to create integrated design solutions from concept to finished drawings. The design process begins with the development of a massing solution that responds to the urban context of zoning, adjacency of other buildings, and topography. Once a massing solution is produced, architects can move to the next phase of the interior space plan, which must respond to the needs of the program. At this stage, design becomes a multi-dimensional problem. BIM can provide both the senior and junior architect with a testing environment. BIM tools encompass the full range of design activities including the structural frame, HVAC system, and the electrical and mechanical systems. It can even analyze the flow of pedestrians responding to an emergency evacuation. Potential conflicts can be resolved early in the design process, rather than after the project begins, when changes and additions would need to be made to working drawings. In a virtual design environment, the production of documents for bidding is a matter of freezing the design solution. Unlike the past when drawings were inked on vellum, these virtual buildings can now be sent electronically to the general contractor responsible for the actual construction of the building. Using software like Autodesk's Navistar, it is now possible to plan for every aspect of the construction process. This includes the critical placement of cranes that accommodate the lifting of all materials to higher floors in the case of commercial buildings (Autodesk, 2012).

2.4. Accommodating the design process: The work environment and architecture

Design requires the participation and involvement of a team of professionals. For a large scale project, sharing and working with a large number of documents, drawings and CAD models requires a versatile and flexible work space. Traditionally, at the early stages in the development of a design, critical decisions are reviewed by sitting around a boardroom table with documents strewn on the table's surface. With drawings pinned to the walls, architects with notebooks and pens in hands, sketch, take notes, and exchange ideas about possible design solutions. The history of VR is one marked by the need for specially designed hardware and rooms needed to view a virtual world. This includes some of the earliest hardware, Sensorama in 1956, the work of Ivan Sutherland in 1960's, followed by more advanced hardware used for flight simulators and CAVE installations in the 1980's and 1990's. Hardware solutions required for interactive viewing has always been expensive and cumbersome to use in group settings. Imagine conducting a group design session with HMD's or wearing shutter glasses in a CAVE environment (Benko, Ishak & Feiner 2003, 2004; Coltekin 2003; Sutherland, 1965; Zhu, 2009). The cultural context of design always needs to be considered if VR technology is to gain greater acceptance among architects. If VR is to be used in the design, then it needs to support the culture of design. Visiting a dark room or isolating individual users with helmets and gloves will probably be never acceptable for architects.

Internet-based solutions for distributing work among collaborators may have had a greater impact on architecture design than VR. Today, a process of distributing work is becoming the norm in architectural practice. At the commencement of a project, a senior designer meets with the client to discuss objectives and concerns. Drawings, sketches or simple massing models created in a program like Sketchup may be used to establish the constraints, opportunities and context of the project. Commonly, many senior designers without education in CAD, provide their sketches or even models to staff for later conversion into CAD models. Frank Gehry, the architect of the Walt Disney Concert Hall and Guggenheim Museums in Bilbao and the Experience Music Project in Seatle is often cited as an architect who works from models which are later converted into CAD format by his staff architects. Once in CAD form, models can be shared between client, partners in other offices and consulting engineers (Kolarevic, 2003). For larger international firms distributing these tasks over several offices is the trend. By passing a project at the end of the day to associates in another part of the world at the beginning their day, a project can be completed more quickly by using a full 24 hour working day. This approach has two significant advantages. First, it allows firms to shorten the time required to complete a single design cycle. More important, firms can take advantage of lower wage scales abroad. Over the last decade architectural offices have employed designers, drafters, and CAD technicians in China and India, where the wages are significantly lower. By engaging firms that specialize in architectural design and production, a dramatic reduction is possible in the cost of working drawings, specifications and computer models used to produce high quality animations and renderings (Bharat, 2010; Pressman, 2007).

VR is making progress in changing the approach to design for interior design by major house ware retailers. IKEA now offers on-line a design tool that gives the prospective buyer an opportunity to layout a complete kitchen. The user can begin with the floor dimensions of their kitchen area and then add cabinets and appliances. Working in 3D they can alter styles for the cabinet, wood finishes, materials for the kitchen tops and the choice of appliances. By examining these designs in 3D, the client has an opportunity to create a virtual world of their future kitchen. Once completed, an order list and price sheet is generated for the store to complete the sales transaction with the client. Already, IKEA is experimenting with home design and will complete a major housing project in Europe in 2012. Perhaps the future of interactive design lies with manufacturers of homes where complete environments are delivered to the job site for quick assembly. (IKEA, 2012).

2.5. Archaeology and VR

Virtual Rome, developed under the direction of Bill Jepson at UCLA, was one of the first projects to take advantage of the rendering capability of the SGI ONYX reality engine. Using technology first developed for the film industry a computer model of the entire ancient city of Rome could be rendered in real time. A major attraction at conferences like SIGGRAPH and AEC (Architects, Engineering and Construction), this model of Rome was displayed on large panoramic screens in 3D. With the support of GOOGLE in recent years, the Virtual Rome Project can now be viewed in Google Earth, though the visual impact is much less on the small screen. The success of the Virtual Rome Project has fostered the creation of other virtual historic models including those of Jerusalem and Pompeii. More than models, these worlds can support virtual tours complete with guides that provide historical background and information. When viewed in 3D environments, on panoramic displays or in Geodes, like the one found in Paris, researchers and the public have a new venue for viewing and studying these ancient sites (Fore and Silotti, 1998; Frischer; 2004 Firscher, 2005; Rome Reborn; 2012; Ancient Rome, 2012)

With the appearance of long and short range scanners, archaeologist have been capturing data on historic sites and building. Once captured, it is possible to use this data to reconstruct these sites in their entirety by reproducing missing elements. One of the more notable projects involves the reconstruction of the Parthenon. Under the direction of Paul Debevec of UC Irvine, a team was assembled to scan both the Parthenon in Athens and plaster copies of the Elgin Marbles, which are preserved in Bern Switzerland. By adding the missing sculptures found in the pediment to the virtual model, it was possible to see for the first time in almost 200 years the Parthenon complete with all of its sculptural detail. Animations and images from this model were later used to promote the Olympics in Athens 2008. The ability to recreate an environment free of smog may be an additional benefit of viewing these models in virtual space (Addison 2000; Addison, 2001; Eakin, 2001; Levoy, 2000; Tchou, et al, 2004; Stumpfel, et al, 2003).

2.6. Medicine

Visualization technology has been instrumental in the advancement of medical science, beginning in the Renaissance with the printing of Vesalius, De Humani Corporis Fabrica Librie Septem in 1543 (Saunders, 1973; Vesalius, 1998). Though theory perpetuated by the Galen still persisted long after his death in 199 AD, the publication of this treatise would eventually transform medical science. The illustrations contained in this tome were based completely on human dissection, revealing all the organs and skeletal structure of the human body and transforming the study of medicine and anatomy. With the advancement of imaging and computing, this approach has been extended. It is now possible to transform an individual's MRI data into a virtual model of the individual patient, opening new doors to medical diagnosis. Using advanced 3D imaging, the "Lindsay Virtual Human" allows a student of medicine to examine the human anatomy at any scale: organs, tissues and cells. Furthermore, unlike the printed page, this virtual human is completely interactive. With the ability to simulate physiological processes, the virtual human can be used to help medical students understand life processes in real time. Viewed in stereo displays or mobile touch devices, "Lindsay Virtual Human" provides access to a virtual living being (Lindsay, 2012; Von Mammen, et al, 2010).

In the use of virtual models in surgery, a major challenge has been to develop haptic peripherals that allow the surgeon to have needed feedback to perform delicate operations. Without sensitive feedback from surgical instruments, the response of actual tissues and organs to incisions made by surgical tools would not be experienced realistically in the virtual world. In many areas of surgery, including removal of brain tumors, the virtual and the real have merged to create an approach for performing challenging surgical operations. In the 1980's during early days of robotic surgery, only pre-operative images were used to guide the surgeon. Robots compatible with MRI's in 1990's were developed that provided the surgeon with images reflective of the patient's condition throughout the surgery. Over the last two decades improvements to neurosurgical robots have included better imaging technology that can distinguish soft tissues, a robot with a full 6 degrees of freedom, and greater precision in the actual surgical instrumentation. Filtering out a surgeon's hand tremor has made for a much higher level of precision in these delicate procedures. Though robotic surgery is still far too expensive for general use, its continued development shows promise. With improvement in artificial intelligence, kinesthetic feedback and user interface, neurosurgery will see more robots assisting surgeons in the operating room (Greer, 2006; Howe & Matsuoka, 1999; Sutherland, 2006).

2.7. Games

VR has had the greatest universal impact on society in the merging of play and computing (Johnson 1999; Shaffer et al, 2004). Even in the early days of computing when all computing was done on mainframes, a first space war game created by Steve Russell at MIT in 1962 allowed the user to control a spaceship in a world where gravitational forces shaped the strategy for destroying adversaries. Later this game would be released as an arcade game in

1971 and became one of the first games to employ vector graphics. Interestingly, this early arcade game can still be purchased in its arcade form by game officinatos (Space Wars, 2012). With each improvement in graphics and computing power, games were able to attain a higher level of realism. Better shadows, real water, particles, photorealistic lighting, and more life-like characters provided gamers with experiences that mirrored those found in the real world. Today, games can simulate every aspect of life, real or imagined, on PC's or game consoles. Driving games, flight simulators, fantasy, role playing and war games are a few of the genres that have spawned from an industry that competes with the movie industry in size and value. With each new release, higher levels of graphics and realism are anticipated by gamers. It is now possible to simulate photo realistic lighting and architectural details as a game player drives through European cities while competing in the Grande Prix. In simulations of military combat, series like "Call of Duty" have re-created the war theatre for many of the famous engagements in Europe during the Second World War II (Call of Duty, 2012). More recently Activision, the developer of "Call of Duty', has turned to military engagements in the Middle East and wars placed in the future. Within these game environments, groups of combatants are able to play against each others (MMOG). Success in these MMOG's requires both time and dedication. The addictiveness and interest in war games has not been lost on the US Military(Johnson, 2004; Johnson, 2010; Stone, 2002). With America's Army 3, developers have created a game that that allows participants to experience life in the military in a massive on-line experience. In this world, you can fire weapons and participate in elite combat unites (US Army, 2012). Perhaps the military's most successful recruiting tool, America's Army Game, this virtual world allows you to assume roles and responsibilities of battle field soldiers and to train for a variety of missions.

Virtual worlds are not limited to recent historical events. In the Assassin's Creed series, the opportunity is given to engage enemies in worlds that mix historical fact and fantasy. In Assassin's Creed series the gamer is placed in 15th Florence and Venice. Strangely set in the 21st century, the central character Desmond Miles, having escaped from Abstergo Industries, is forced to relive past memories in a virtual past. Rendered in high detail, this world would provide a class in art and architectural history with a virtual classroom to view some of the greatest achievements of the Renaissance. Assassin's Creed with its open world play environment established a new level of visual accuracy in detail for a virtual world even if there is an occasional mixing of content from different historical periods.(Assassin's Creed, 2012) Unfortunately, time is of the essence in this game. The mission to avenge the murder of father and brothers leaves little time to gaze upon architectural wonders of the past.

Gamers who demand a high level of emersion in their visual filed of view can now purchase 3D TV's and 3D monitors that offer the quality of a 3D movie experience at a price only slightly higher than that of the average display. With movie theaters and production companies capitalizing on the 3D movie experience, this feature can now be added to most game experiences. Many games today are 3D ready and only require a video card that supports 3D, as well as either a 3D TV or a computer screen. By purchasing peripherals developed to support a specific game genre, a completely immersive experience is possible, whether flying a plane, driving a car or fighting off the enemy.

The Wii in 2006 introduced a new level of interaction and immersion to gamers. No longer did the user need to rely on a game controller that required hours of practice to master. Instead, the Wii controller uses motion sensing, a few buttons and gesture to control the virtual world. Using the Wiimote, a tennis rackets or a sword can be simulated and with purchased attachments, the action of a driving wheel and other devices can be imitated (Nintendo, 2012). Since the introduction of the Wii by Nintendo, Microsoft and Playstation have introduced game player controllers. Furthermore, the Kinect by Microsoft, employs real time mapping of the human form and gives gamers a sense of freedom by eliminating the need for any game controller (Microsoft, 2012). Even the youngest of game players quickly learn how to ski jump, play tennis or bowl in these virtual games. After several decades of experimentation, virtual reality has a universal audience of devoted gamers.

2.8. Military applications

The demonstrated value of flight simulators in training would spawn other applications of VR to the field of military training. Tank simulators are an example where VR would provide a valuable training environment. Inside an enclosed replica of an actual tank, gunners and drivers can maneuver and fire. Because tanks have a limited field of vision, simulating their view does not require high resolution graphic displays and expensive six degrees of freedom motion control platforms. Like a MMOG, tanks can be networked together. With coordination from central command, tank groups can practice field maneuvers. Today, the ability to link together training environments consisting of planes, tanks, and ships provides the military with opportunities to train and test strategies that require the coordination from central command of numerous combatants in the field, the air and on the sea (Johnson, 2004; Johnson, 2010; Stone, 2002).

Coordinated efforts of actual infantry on the ground in a true simulation of actual battles are the ultimate VR challenge. One solution which has been used for decades is to build mock villages for soldiers to practice their engagements. Still used today to prepare soldiers for conflicts in the Middle East, these towns and villages are inhabited by actors speaking the language of the countries where the troops are to be stationed. More recently, a completely virtual experience has been created using the most advanced motion capture and immersive technology. VIRTSIM, designed and developed as a joint venture between Ratheton Corporation and Motion Reality, Marietta, GA, is similar to the holodeck featured in Star trek from TV and film. In a space as large as a basketball court, a dozen soldiers wearing high resolution wireless 3D glasses can engage simulated combatants in a completely virtual world. Being able to view each member of the platoon as they engage virtual combatants provides the trainers with a unique perspective. In addition, it is now possible reconstruct actual troop engagements based on pervious battles logs from GPS transponders. To simulate battlefield conditions, each soldier wears electrodes that respond to virtual bullets and bomb blasts (Economist, 2012; Virtism 2012). Though perhaps the most expensive interactive video game environment ever created, these virtual training environments were outside the limits of computing and visualization until recently.

Not all simulated military training require the holodeck. In developing training environment to teach members of the US military Arabic and Farsi, an inexpensive PC based solution was deployed. In the Tactical Language Training System, students are introduced to Arabic, Farsi and Levantine languages and culture through participation in a virtual world. Like a video game, this role playing is used extensively. In these worlds, students have an opportunity to be immersed in a game space where they interact with animated characters in settings based on urban, rural and village life found in Iraq. An interactive story environment engages the learner; animated characters provide feedback on both pronunciation and dialogue. Speech recognition technology, which focuses on the most likely responses, gives the student feedback on appropriate responses with native speakers. This approach has shown promise even with students having limited prior experience in foreign language instruction (Johnson et al. 2004, Johnson 2010).

3. Augmented reality

From the early days of Virtual Reality and AR (augmented reality), researchers shared any of the same issues. Both required knowing where the user is relative to the scene in view. In AR, it is critical to superposition computer generated content accurately on the objects and architecture in the real world. In the early history of AR, a portable computer capable of generating even simple wire frames of models in 3D was no small feat. Then, projecting the content on to glasses worn by the user was an additional challenge. Cumbersome HMD (glasses) were expensive, heavy and difficult to wear for long periods of time. Making this a mobile solution would be almost impossible given the weight and size of laptops, batteries, video cameras and glasses. Not surprising, the early days of AR transformed the user into a borg-like image from Star trek. Finally, there was the need to access a database of places and associated attributes. The potential to store some information on a PC or PDA about a building or city existed, but a solution that would work in any locale would need to access the Internet. In the days before Wi-Fi and cell towers, access to the internet was not assured (Benko, Ishak & Feiner 2003, 2004; Coltekin 2003, Sutherland, 1965).

Within the last decade, AR has finally become a reality with the miniaturization of portable and wearable technology. The diffusion of inexpensive smart phones and tablets provide a platform capable of supporting AR based applications. With a video camera, GPS and compass, a smart phone can access a database of content and superimpose directly into the view of the touch screen. With the introduction of applications like Google Goggles and Layars, developers can use the power of an image search database. Though AR applications are still in their infancy, opportunities to apply this technology will be greatly expanded with the diffusion of tablet computers. With the potential for displaying a larger image in view, tablets with two video cameras, a powerful processor and access to the Internet will make AR applications exciting for a range of uses including, tourism, architecture, engineering, medicine, and education. Today, a foreign tourist can take a picture of a restaurant sign and gain access to the menu in his or her own language. It would also be possible to provide the specials of the day and the local critic's reviews all translated in real time. Similarly, AR could provide a tourist with a guided tour through an historic neighborhood and learn about the people and events that happened in the past. Filters could be added to confine the information to recent history or perhaps, to provide the architectural history of significant buildings in the area (Benko, Ishak & Feiner 2003, 2004; Bimber 2005; Gutiérrez, Vexo & Thalmann 2008a, 2008b).

One limitation of GPS is that it works only in open space. Furthermore, GPS will not provide precise superposition of content on the scene. Another strategy is to rely on object recognition. By capturing views and matching them against a library of known objects, it is possible to determine what the user is looking at and to provide the appropriate content overlayed or tagged to the object. However, even when image search is not feasible, it is possible today to use the camera in a smartphone to capture a QR Code marker, which links to web-based content. A perfect solution for educational institutions or museums, individuals with either a smart phone or a tablet can access text, images, video and 3D objects (Schneider, 2010).

If carrying and pointing devices at buildings and signs feels unnatural for some users, in the future, it may be possible to have a hands free AR environment by wearing contact lenses or light weight glasses. Research is already promising in this area. Companies like NOKIA can project web content onto lightweight stylish tinted glasses, complete with wireless earbuds and a haptic wrist controller. Ultimately, it will be the users who will decide if this approach is acceptable (Nokia, 2012).

4. Conclusions

In the 1980's, VR was only capable of producing a scene composed of wire frame images. Even finding a screen that could show graphics was beyond the reach of most researchers. In 1990's the development by SGI of high resolution real time graphics made simulators possible and met a critical need for the military and civil aviation. Over the last two decades, VR has been used to train pilots in simulators and provided surgeons with real time models of the human body. Since the beginning, building a market for VR has been a challenge. Other than commercial games, the audience for VR has been fairly limited. In creating applications for a narrow group of users, the cost of development has restricted its diffusion. The cost of application development includes building models, designing and animating characters, coding behaviors and responses and building the GUI interfaces. Even a modest virtual world requires considerable financial resources. If there are few users to bear the true cost of development, then the application's price will restrict it to a limited audience. If the use of virtual environments for training and education in the workplace, home or school is to have a promising future, reducing development costs is key.

With better scripting tools it may be possible to reduce the costs and time of developing a VR application. Software like FlowVR, now offers programmers an integrated solution. With FlowVR, it is possible to build worlds that merge the on-line worlds created in Second life with Layar Augmented reality (FlowVR, 2012). By using Microsoft Xbox Kinect and

Emotiv (thought controlled headset), inexpensive hardware can be used to view and control virtual worlds for training and education. For those who only require a simple navigation through a virtual world, Unity, an inexpensive game engine offers a cost effective solution for architects, planners and archaeologists to visit virtual worlds on a PC.

In the history of technology it is often difficult to predict the impact inventions will have on society. When computers were being used to solve business problems after WWII, the transformative power they would have on society would have been hard to imagine. Though the exact path VR has followed may not have been predicted, its development as a force owes much to those who had the vision and belief in its potential use to train, educate, and entertain. Hardware and software will always be a limiting factor in the development of VR. Similarly, an acceptable immersive solution for visualizing content will also be part of this equation. The need to wear cumbersome head mounted displays or visit a remote site to view a design in an CAVE has certainly limited the diffusion of VR. In creating VR solutions, the technology must accommodate the professional culture of the user. For architects sitting around a boardroom table or a surgeon in an operation room, the technology must do better in the context of professional practice. Perhaps the promise is portable personal devices like tablets and smart phones. The capability of these devices increases with each new model. With a projected world wide use of over two billion by 2015, this platform offers the greatest hope for the future of both AR and VR (Parks Associates, 2011). Everyone has one, and we carry them everywhere. Developers will finally have a market sufficiently deep to create applications that serve every market and profession. Perhaps VR is not dead, but merely ported over to a more universal accessible platform.

Author details

Richard M. Levy
Faculty of Environmental Design University of Calgary, Alberta, Canada

5. References

Addison A.C. (2001). Virtual Heritage – Technology in the Service of Culture. Proceedings of the 2001 *Conference on Virtual Reality, Archaeology and Cultural Heritage,* Nov. 2001, Glyfada, Greece, pp. 28-30.

Addison, A.C. (2000). Emerging Trends in Virtual Heritage. *IEEE Multimedia,* April –June, pp. 22-25.

Al-Douri, F. (2010). The Impact of 3D modeling function usage on the design content of urban design plans in US Cities, *Environment and Planning B: Planning and Design 2010,* Vol. 37, pp. 75-98.

Ancient Rome 3D (http://earth.google.com/rome

Assassin's Creed URL: http://www.1up.com/features/assassins-creed-historical-inaccuracies

Autodesk URL: http://usa.autodesk.com/

URL: http://usa.autodesk.com/revit/architectural-design-software/
URL: http://usa.autodesk.com/revit/structural-design-software/
URL: http://usa.autodesk.com/revit/mep-engineering-software/
URL: http://usa.autodesk.com/revit/mep-engineering-software/#document

Dave, Bharat (2010) On the Move…Bits of Practice *Source:Architecture, Australia;, Sep/Oct, Vol. 99 Issue 5, p71-72, 2p*

Batty, M., Dodge, D., Simon. D. & Smith, A. (1998). Modeling Virtual Environments, *Centre for Advanced Spatial Analysis, Working Paper 1*, January, ISSN: pp. 1467-1298.

Benko, H., Ishak, E. and Feiner, S. (2003) Collaborative Visualization of an Archaeological Excavation, *NSF Lake Tahoe Workshop on Collaborative Virtual Reality and Visualization* (CVRV 2003), October 26-28.

Benko, H., Ishak, E. W. and Feiner, S. (2004) Collaborative Mixed Reality Visualization of an Archaeological Excavation, *Proceedings of the 3rd IEEE/ACM international Symposium on Mixed and Augmented Reality* (November 02 - 05, 2004).

Bimber, O., & Raskar, R. (2005). *Spatial augmented reality: Merging real and virtual Worlds*, A K Peters Ltd. , Wellesley, MA.

Call of Duty (2012) URL: http://www.callofduty.com/

Collier, James, M. (1981). Brunelleschi's Perspective Demonstration Recreated, *Southeastern College Art Conference Review*, Spring 1981, Vol. 10 Issue 1, pp. 4-7.

Coltekin, A. (2003). Virtual Reality as an Interface to GIS: Focus on WWW, *In 21st International Cartographic Conference (ICC)*, Durban, South Africa.

de Vauban, Sebastien Le Prestre, (1968). *A Manual of Siegecraft and Fortification*, Translated from the French by George A. Rothrock, University of Michigan Press, Ann Arbor, M.

Drettakis, G., Roussou, M., Reche, A. & Tsingos, N. (2007). Design and Evaluation of A Real-world Virtual Environment for Architecture and Urban Planning, *Presence*, Vol.16, No. 3, pp. 318-332.

Economist, (2012). This is not a Game, *Economist, Technology Quarterly*, p. 10.

Edgerton, Samuel, Y, (1974). Florentine interest in Ptolemaic cartography as background for Renaissance painting, architecture and the discovery of America, *Journal of the Society of Architectural Historians*, Fol. 33, No. 4, 1974 pp. 274-292.

Eakin, E. (2001). Cybersleuths take on the mystery of the collapsing colossus. *The New York Times*, Saturday, October 27, 2001.

Environmental Simulation Laboratory, URL: http://laep.ced.berkeley.edu/simlab/serv.html

FlowVR, URL: http://flowvr.sourceforge.net/index.html

Maurizio F. & Siliotti, A. (1998 co). *Virtual Archaeology, Re-recreating Ancient Worlds*, Harry N. Abrams, Inc. Publishers, Thames and Hudson, Ltd. and Arnoldo Mondadori, Editors, London.

Forester, J. (1989), *Planning in the Face of Power*, University of California Press, Berkeley, CA.

Frischer, B. (2004) Mission and Recent Projects of the UCLA Cultural Virtual Reality Laboratory, *Proceedings of the Conference Virtual Retrospect* 2003, 6-7 November 2003, ed. by R. Vergnieux, C. Delevoie (Bordeaux, 2004) pp. 65-76.

Frischer, B. (2005) The Digital Roman Forum Project: Remediating the Traditions of Roman Topography, in *Acts of the 2nd Italy-United States Workshop, Rome*, Italy, November, 2003, edited by M. Forte, BAR International Series 1379 (Oxford 2005) pp. 9-21

George, G. (2000). The Army Aviation Collective Training Solution: AVCAT-A, 2000 URL: http://www.link.com/pdfs/ts-030.pdf

Greer A.D., Newhook P., Sutherland G.R. (2006) Human-machine interface for robotic surgery and stereotaxy, *International Journal of Computer Assisted Radiology and Surgery* Vol. 1 pp. 295-297.

Gutiérrez A., Vexo, M , & Thalmann, D. (2008). Cultural *heritage. Stepping into virtual reality*, Lausanne, Switzerland: Springer-Verlag London.

Hamit F. (1998). The Urban Simulation Lab's Image-Based Model of the Future of Los Angeles, *Advanced Imaging*, Vol.7, No. 13, pp. 32-36.

Howard, T. & Gaborit, N. (2007). Using Virtual Environment Technology to Improve Public Participation in *Urban Planning Process, Journal of Urban Planning and Development*, Vol. 133, No. 4, pp. 233-41.

Howe, R. & Matsuoka, Y. (1999). *Robotics for Surgery, Annual Review Biomedical Engineering.* 1999, Vol. 1, pp. 213.

IKEA, Plan your Kitchen in 3D,

http://www.ikea.com/ms/en_US/rooms_ideas/kitchen_howto/NA/plan_your_kitchen_in_3d.html#lnk-2-5

Itty Bitty Cities: 22 Models That Miniaturize the World, Web *Urbanist*
URL: http://weburbanist.com/2010/03/04/itty-bitty-cities-22-models-that-miniaturize-the-world/

Jepson, W., & Friedman, S. (1998). A real-time visualization system for large scale urban environments.
URL: www.ust.ucla.edu/bill/UST.html

Johnson, A., Ohlosson,T. & Gillingham, M. (1999). The Round Earth Project - Collaborative VR for conceptual learning, virtual reality. *IEEE Computer Graphics and Applications*, pp. 60-69.

Johnson, W., Beal, C., Fowles-Winkler, A. Lauper, U. Marsella, Narayanan, S, Papachristou , D. & Vilhjalmsson, H. (2004). Tactical Language Training System: An interim report, *Centre for Advanced Research in Technology for Education (CARTE)*, USC Information Science Institute, 4676 Admiralty Way, (Marina del Rey, CA, USA, pp. 1-10).

Johnson, W. (2010). Serious Use of a Serious Gem for Language Learning, *International Journal of Artificial Intelligence in Education*, Vol. 20, pp. 175-195.

Keijsper, G. (2007). *Joint Strike Fighter: Design and Development of the International Aircraft, F-25*, Pen & Sword Aviation Ltd, United Kingdom.

Kolarevic, B. (2003) *Architecture in the Digital Age*, Taylor & Francis, Oxon, UK.

Kostoff, Spiro, ed., (1977). *The Architect*, New York, Oxford University Press.

Levoy, M., K. Pulli, B. Curless, S. Rusinkiewicz, D. Koller, L. Pereira, M. Ginzton, S. Anderson, J. Davis, J. Ginsberg, J. Shade, & D. Fulk. (2000). The Digital Michelangelo Project: 3D scanning of large statues, *Proceedings SIGGRPAH 2000* (New Orleans, Louisiana, July 23-28, 2000), ACM SIGGRAPH, pp. 131–144.

Levy, R. (1997) Data or Image: The Influence of Professional Culture on Computing in Design, *Acadia* Quarterly, Fall, pp. 8-11,22-23.

Levy, R. (1980) *The Professionalization of American Architects and Civil Engineers, 1865-1917*, PhD Dissertation, University of California, Berkeley.

Lichfield, J, A very different perspective on French history Epic models built in 17th century of fortified towns and rural landscapes unveiled in Paris show.
URL: http://www.independent.co.uk/news/world/europe/a-very-different-perspective-on-french-history-6292613.html

Liggett. R. & Jepson, W. H. (1993). An Integrated Environment for Urban Simulation, *Third International Conference on Computers in Urban Planning and Urban Management*, pp. 565-583.

Link Flight Trainer, A Historical Engineering Landmark, (2000). Robertson Museum and Science Center, Binghamton, *ASME, International NW*, June 10, 2000.

Littlehales C. (1991). Revolutionizing the Way Cities are Planned, *IRIS Universe*, Vol. 19, 15-18.

Microsoft, URL: http://www.microsoft.com/games/flightsimulatorx/

Microsoft, URL: http://www.xbox.com/en-CA/Kinect

Million, H (1997). *The Renaissance from Brunelleschi to Michelangelo, The Representation of Architecture*, New York, Rizzoli International Publications, Inc.

Mobach, M. (2008). Do Virtual Worlds Create better Real Worlds?, *Virtual Reality*, Vol. 12, pp. 163-179.

Mahoney D. P. (1994). Cityscapes, *Computer Graphics World*, Vol. 17, No. 4, 36-43.

Mahoney D. P. (1997). Philadelphia 2000 Computer, *Graphics World*, Vol 20., No. 6, 30-33.

Parks Associates (2011). Smartphone hypergrowth - we'll be wading knee-deep by 2015, May 18, 2011.
URL: http://www.parksassociates.com/blog/article/smartphone-hypergrowth---we--ll-be-wading-knee-deep-by-2015

NADS (2012). URL: http://www.nads-sc.uiowa.edu/sim_nads1.php
URL: http://www.youtube.com/watch?v=RNHoaoWyq1k

Nintendo URL: http://www.nintendo.com/wii

Nokia URL: http://www.youtube.com/watch?v=A4pDf7m2UPE&feature=related

Novitski, B. (1998). An Architectural Awakening, *Computer Graphics World*, Vol. 21, No. 6, pp. 22-40.

NVIDIA URL: http://www.nvidia.com/object/product-quadro-4000-us.html

Palladio, A. , (1965 co.) *The Four Books of Architecture*, Dover Publications, Inc., New York.

Pigozzi, M. , Fagiolo, M. , ed, (1992). *Ferdinando Galli Bibiena : Varie opere di prospettiva : traduzione e diffusione di modelli e tipologie in centri e periferie*, Roma, Istituto poligrafico e Zecca dello Stato.

Pressman, A. (2007) New AIA Firm Survey Indicates that while Business is Good, the Profession Itself Changes Slowly, *Architectural Record*, March.
URL: http://archrecord.construction.com/practice/firmCulture/0703AIAfirm-1.asp

Rome Reborn (http://www.romereborn.virginia.edu)

Saunders, J. & O'Malley, C. (1973). *The Illustrations from the Works of Andreas Vesalius of Brussel*, Dover Publications, Inc., New York.

Schneider, The Best Tour Guide May be Your Purse, The New York Times, March 13, 2012. URL:http://www.nytimes.com/2010/03/18/arts/artsspecial/18SMART.html?_r=1&scp=1&sq=The%20Best%20Tour%20Guide%20May%20Be%20in%20Your%20Purse%20&st=cse

Shaffer, D., Squire, K. Halverson, R. & Gee, J. (2004). Video games and the future of learning. URL: http://www.academiccolab.org/resources/gappspaper1.pdf

Simcity URL: http://www.simcity.com/en_US

Space Wars, URL: http://www.davesclassicarcade.com/spacewars/spacewars.html

SGI, URL: http://www.futuretech.blinkenlights.nl/onyxgs.html

Stumpfel, J. , Tchou, C . Hawkins,T, Martinez, P., Emerson, B., Brownlow, M. Jones,A., Yun,N., & Debevec. P. (2003.) Digital Reunification of the Parthenon and its Sculptures, *Proceedings of the 4th International Symposium on Virtual Reality, Archaeology and Intelligent Cultural Heritage*, pp. 41-50.

Stone, R. J. (2002). Serious gaming. *Education and Training*, pp. 142-144.

Sutherland G., Latour I & Saunders J (2006). Intraoperative MRI: experience with 700 patients, *International Journal of Computer Assisted Radiology and Surgery* Vol 1, pp. 308-310.

Sutherland, I. E. (1965). The ultimate display, *Proceedings of IFIP Congress*, New York, USA., pp. 506-508.

Schwarz, C., Gates, T. & Papelis, Y (2003) Motion Characteristics of the National Advanced Driving Simulator, Document Number N2003-011.

Tchou, C., J. Stumpfel, P. Einarsson, M. Fajardo, and P. Debevec. (2004). Unlighting the Parthenon,

SIGGRAPH 2004 Sketch.

URL: http://www.ict.usc.edu/graphics/research/reflectance/

US Army

URL: http://www.goarmy.com/downloads/games.html

Wahlstrom, M, Aittala, M. Kotilainen, H. Yli-Karhu, T. Porkka, J. & Nyka¨nen, E. (2010). CAVE for collaborative patient room design: analysis with end-user opinion contrasting method, *Virtual Reality* Vol. 14, pp. 197-211.

Vesalius, A. (1998). Trans by W. F. Richarardson, *On the Fabric of the Human Body, Book I, Bones and Cartilages*, Norman Publishing, San Francisco, CA.

Virtism, 2012, URL: http://thesecretdesigncollective.com/virtsim/index.html

Von Mammen, Sebastian, Davison, T., Baghi, H & Jacob, C. (2010) Component-Based Networking for Simulations in Medical Education, IEEE Symposium, Computers and Communciations (ISCC) June 22-25, pp. 975-979.

Zhu, H. (2009). VEMap: A Visualization Tool for Evaluating Emotional Responses in Virtual Environments, *MS in Systems Design Engineering*, University of Waterloo, Ontario.

Chapter 3

High Fidelity Immersive Virtual Reality

Stuart Gilson and Andrew Glennerster

Additional information is available at the end of the chapter

http://dx.doi.org/10.5772/50655

1. Introduction

Virtual reality is now used as an aid to teaching and practice in a wide range of fields. In education, surgery, architecture and many other disciplines, virtual reality provides a tool that allows users to experience situations that could not be readily reproduced in the real world. As virtual reality technology becomes more pervasive, there will be a rising demand for improvements in the quality of VR displays, both in the accuracy with which they portray the location, shape and surface detail of objects and also the speed and fluidity with which the images on the display change in response to the observer's head movements, becoming ever closer to the visual feedback that observers experience in the real world.

The ultimate goal of virtual reality is to present to the user computer-generated scenes in such a manner that the user should not be aware that they are in a virtual reality system at all – a sort of Turing test [29] for VR. To achieve this, the images should be of such high resolution that the individual pixels cannot be distinguished, the display should change with the observer's head movements without perceptible lag and the rendered scenes should be exquisitely detailed with realistically rendered three-dimensional models.

Current capability in virtual reality falls some way short of this ideal. Nevertheless, recent advances in head tracking technology and pixel-drawing speed make this a useful point to pause and consider the state of the art in presenting high-fidelity immersive virtual reality. Issues that we will address in this chapter include approaches to minimise tracking latency; detection of and compensation for spatial distortions in head mounted displays and methods to check that a rendered scene corresponds well with the real-world rays of light that are being simulated (or 'virtualized'). These questions are, to a large extent, independent of the technology used.

To clarify terminology and lay a framework for subsequent discussion, we consider a virtual reality system to be comprised of three subsystems: tracking, rendering and display. Furthermore, we consider a 'data pipeline' to consist, broadly, of a real world event being sampled by the tracker, the generation of an appropriate scene on the VR graphics computer, and the final rendering of pixels in the display device. In this chapter we will examine the sources of error in each of these three subsystems, as data travels along the pipeline. First, though, we briefly consider the differences between 'virtual' and 'augmented' reality in the context of the VR Turing test.

1.1. Virtual and augmented reality

Given the speed at which computer graphics is developing and the increasing realism of films based on computer-generated scenes, there is a strong argument that augmented reality will be the first virtual technology to pass the VR Turing test and fool observers completely as to whether they are viewing a real or a virtual scene. Augmented reality – superimposing computer drawn graphics on the real world – is at present best achieved with a video see-through HMD, which uses small cameras to capture real-world images and displays them in the HMD. The digital images can have computer graphics overlaid, augmenting the real world scene. In practice, most systems suffer from an incorrect placement of the optic centres of the images – the optic centres of the two cameras do not coincide with the observer's eyes' optic centres, and thus lead to a mis-match between proprioception ('muscle sense') and vision. In practice, appropriately placed mirrors can minimize this mis-match [12] although most video-see-through augmented reality (AR) systems do not yet go to this trouble. There are distinct advantages to video-see-through AR. Because only a small portion of the entire scene is being computer-generated a great deal of computing power can be devoted to rendering the virtual objects accurately and in detail. Also, the problem of spatially aligning the virtual object so that it sits stably on a real surface is much easier to handle when both the real and virtual scenes are available in electronic form. Algorithms for ensuring that this alignment is correct can be run on each frame before display to the user, an option that is not possible in see-through augmented reality where the user sees the real world directly and virtual objects are superimposed, for example using a half-silvered mirror. Results in this area even for cameras with very rapid, jerky movements, are impressive [19].

On the other hand, a technology that is unlikely to fool observers completely is a CAVE. In a CAVE, the rendered VR scene is projected on up to 6 surfaces enclosing the observer. Their key advantage is that the observer need only wear a light-weight pair of shutter glasses, which provides the stereo signal to the observer's eyes. However, CAVEs suffer from various physical limitations, including the amount of space they require, and the fact that they can only really accommodate one observer at a time. But most significantly, the effective resolution of the VR scene is dependent on the distance of the projection surface to the observer and, for a freely-moving observer, this effective resolution will change. For our goal of virtualizing the rays an observer would see in the real world, a CAVE-based VR system will never suffice.

1.2. Head mounted displays

The majority of head-mounted displays – as the name suggests – involve miniature displays mounted to a helmet-like structure which rests on the observer's head, such that the displays lay in front of the eyes. Helmet designs range from fully-enclosed helmets, typically found in military applications, to bare-minimum ski-goggle like systems.

At present, all systems have non-negligible weight, which can be a problem for prolonged use. Even in the shorter term, having such a weight mounted on the head will restrict freedom of movement, and introduce rendering errors during high acceleration head movements – even when tightly strapped to the head, the weight of the headset under acceleration will 'twist' the scalp and the resulting non-rigid motion will appear as lag between the observer's movement and the viewed VR scene.

Furthermore, all present HMDs are tethered to some form of control box. This control box typically converts the video signal generated by the VR graphics computer, sent via VGA or DVI cable, into the proprietary-format signal required by the custom display in the HMD. To reduce damage from the continual usage, these tethering cables are generally sturdy, robust and comparatively inflexible. VR users will be aware of the cable, and may modify their behaviour to reduce any 'tugging' that the cable might cause on the HMD. This makes our ideal "freely moving" observer less free to move. Some HMD systems offer wireless HMDs, with the control box transmitting the video signal which is in turn detected by a battery powered receiver connected to the HMD. While this can alleviate many of the problems associated with thick tethering cables, the encode-transmit-receive-decode cycle of the video frames will introduce extra latency into the system (e.g. one contemporary wireless system adds "2 video frames latency"), which can be problematic in itself.

2. High fidelity virtual reality

Consider a VR application that attempts to virtualize a natural scene – consisting of a wide spectrum of colours, and numerous objects (e.g. trees, rocks) spanning a considerable distance in depth. While observing this scene, the user is free to move around the scene, turn their head, and to shift their gaze. At any moment in time, there will be an array of light rays hitting each retina, and it is these rays – their direction, intensity and wavelength – that we wish to duplicate in our VR system. If this is achievable for an object that is viewed from a wide range of viewpoints (in theory, all viewpoints), then it is justifiable to claim that the real object has been re-created in virtual reality, or 'virtualized'.

With this goal in mind, what are the obstacles preventing us from creating such an application with present-day hardware? Ultimately, these obstacles are issues of accuracy which we discuss here in terms of spatial, temporal and spectral components.

2.1. Spatial accuracy

Spatial errors are due to a misalignment of the real and virtual rays, and can arise from an incorrect estimation of the observer's head pose or location, or due to mis-calibration of the head mounted display. The first is a technology limitation, but the latter is a largely-soluble calibration issue.

2.1.1. Tracker accuracy

All tracking systems monitor movement by sampling changes of some continuous variable which is sensitive to motion. Magnetic systems sample the tiny current induced in sensors as they move through a (static) magnetic field generated by an emitter. Inertial systems use extremely sensitive accelerometers to sample changes in acceleration in any of the three planes of movement. Mechanical systems use articulated arms to modify potentiometers at the joints of the arms to produce a single 3D location. Finally, optical systems use three or more cameras to reconstruct movement in 3D from multiple 2D images.

All these systems have numerous advantages and disadvantages, and the choice for any given VR system will depend on many factors, including cost, the size of volume to be tracked, and the types of actions/movements that will be expected in the application (e.g. walking versus object manipulation by hand). Consideration should also be given to whether a given system needs to combine the signals from several sensors, which may lead to discontinuities as a tracked object moves between sensors [3].

For high-fidelity VR, we have found that optical systems offer the best attributes. Multiple cameras can be mounted to the perimeter of the tracked volume, and will track the position of passive markers on the observer (notably, on the HMD) and on tracked objects. Modern optical systems are real-time, using high-resolution, high-frame-rate cameras to sample the tracked volume to a high spatial and temporal accuracy (typically less than 1mm and 10ms respectively).

2.1.2. Spatial calibration of head mounted display

We consider the correct spatial calibration of the HMD to be one of the most critical components of a VR system. Without calibration, users can misinterpret the virtual world (for example, they often underestimate distances to objects which can be a symptom of an incorrect calibration [11]). Users can also experience premature fatigue and, with severely mis-configured HMDs, even nausea. [17, 18, 22].

Each of the HMD's displays are characterized by a frustum, which completely determines how 3D vertices in the VR world are transformed to pixel locations in the display (see figure 1). The frustum is determined from the HMD's resolution in pixels (w and h), and the horizontal and vertical field-of-view (FOV) in degrees (x and y). From these we can compute the centre pixel ($c_x = \frac{w}{2}$ and $c_y = \frac{h}{2}$) and the focal length ($f_x = \frac{c_x}{\tan(x)}$, $f_y = \frac{c_y}{\tan(y)}$), and then compute the intrinsic matrix:

$$\mathbf{P} = \begin{bmatrix} \frac{2\times\text{ncp}}{\text{right}-\text{left}} & 0 & \frac{\text{right}+\text{left}}{\text{right}-\text{left}} & 0 \\ 0 & \frac{2\times\text{ncp}}{\text{top}-\text{bottom}} & \frac{\text{top}+\text{bottom}}{\text{top}-\text{bottom}} & 0 \\ 0 & 0 & -\frac{\text{fcp}+\text{ncp}}{\text{fcp}-\text{ncp}} & -\frac{2\times\text{fcp}\times\text{ncp}}{\text{fcp}-\text{ncp}} \\ 0 & 0 & -1 & 0 \end{bmatrix}$$

where:

$$\text{left} = -\text{ncp} \times \frac{c_x}{f_x}, \qquad \text{right} = \text{ncp} \times \frac{w - c_x}{f_x},$$

$$\text{bottom} = -\text{ncp} \times \frac{c_y}{f_y}, \qquad \text{top} = \text{ncp} \times \frac{h - c_y}{f_y}$$

The near- and far-clipping planes (ncp and fcp) are application dependent. The intrinsic matrix, $\mathbf{P}$, describes how view-centric 3D coordinates are transformed to 2D pixel locations. The view-centric coordinates are obtained via the extrinsic matrix, $\mathbf{S}$, which transforms the 3D world coordinates relative to the position and orientation of the display:

$$\mathbf{S} = \begin{bmatrix} \mathbf{R} & \mathbf{T}^{\mathrm{T}} \\ 0 & 1 \end{bmatrix}$$

where **R** is a 3×3 rotation matrix and **T** is a 1×3 translation matrix.

Using the manufacturer's specification, it is possible to create a pair of intrinsic matrices for a stereo HMD. Conversely, the contents of the extrinsic matrix are entirely determined by the position of the 'tracked centre' – the point that is reported by the tracking system to the VR graphics computer – which depends on how the tracked markers are attached to the HMD. Unfortunately, manufacturer specifications are rarely of sufficient accuracy to qualify for high-fidelity VR display, and it can be very difficult to obtain accurate physical measurements from within the confines of a small HMD for the extrinsic matrix.

Instead, we need to calibrate the display. Yet, a thorough calibration is often neglected, perhaps understandably given the difficulties in obtaining suitable calibration values. We approach HMD calibration using a technique from camera calibration [27], called photogrammetry. If we treat the HMD displays as virtual cameras, we can use a modified version of this method to calibrate our HMD.

In Tsai's method [27], the objective is to take multiple pictures of a calibration object of a known geometry, and to pair the object's corners with their corresponding pixel locations in each of the images. Given sufficient images, these point correspondences can be used to constrain a minimization function, whose parameters are the intrinsic (five parameters: width, height, focal length and location of the centre pixel) and extrinsic properties (six parameters: 3D position and pose) of the camera.

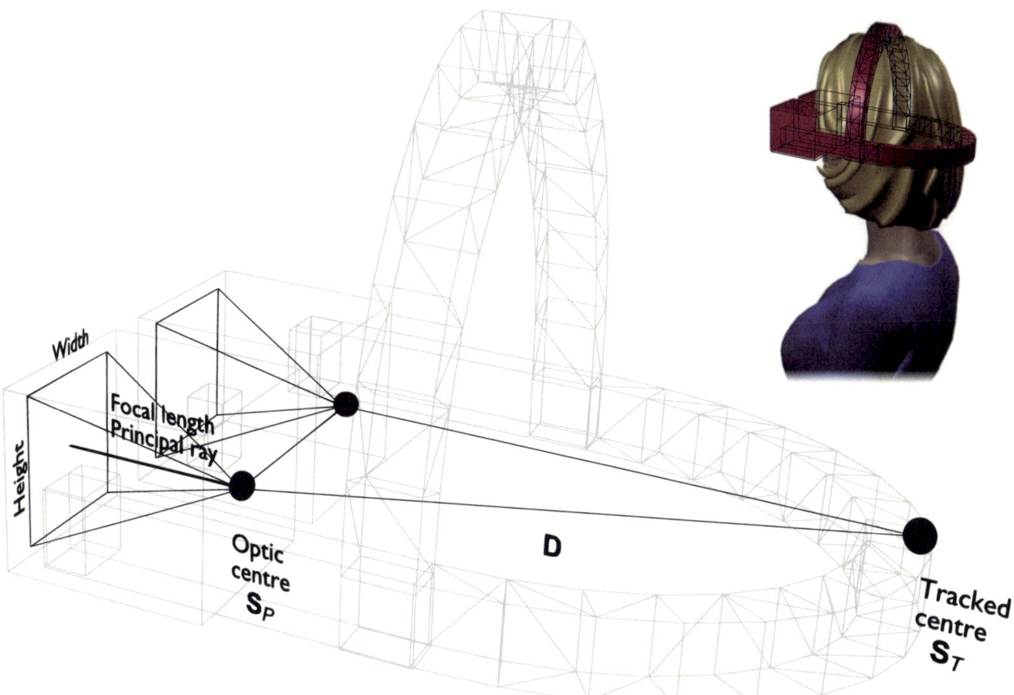

Figure 1. Intrinsic (width, height, focal length) and extrinsic (location of optic centre, and direction of principal ray, $\mathbf{S}_P$) shown relative to the tracked centre of the HMD ($\mathbf{S}_T$). **D** is the transformation between $\mathbf{S}_T$ and $\mathbf{S}_P$, i.e. $\mathbf{D} = \mathbf{S}_P \mathbf{S}_T^{-1}$.

Our method is as follows. A camera is mounted on a table in such a way that the HMD can be placed atop the camera and removed without moving or otherwise disturbing the camera. The HMD is positioned in such a way that the camera can 'see' as much of one of the displays as possible. A simple chequerboard grid is shown in this HMD display, and an image of this grid is captured and saved by the camera. Each of the vertices in this image (automatically extracted with image processing) can be paired with the known coordinates from the generated grid in the HMD display and, hence, we have a means of converting any camera image location to the corresponding HMD image location (see [4] for more details). We subsequently express all captured camera image coordinates in HMD coordinates and, crucially, we derive estimates of the HMD display frustum instead of the camera.

Ultimately, we need to know the display's extrinsic parameters relative to the tracked centre of the HMD. Yet, photogrammetry will give us the extrinsic parameters relative to the tracker's origin. If we record the HMD position and orientation at this time, we will be able to compute this relative transform (the component $\mathbf{D}$ in figure 1).

The next step is to record the image locations of a tracked calibration object. Somewhat counter-intuitively, this step must be carried out without the HMD in place. It is essential that the camera is not moved at this time, since this preserves the relationship between the recorded HMD chequerboard image and the corresponding 3D marker projections. Thus, we are able to relate any camera image features to the corresponding HMD display location, as if the HMD were in place and transparent.

Now we capture multiple images of a moving tracked marker. For each captured image, i, we will obtain 5 numbers – the marker's 3D location (in tracker coordinates, $\mathbf{X}_i$), and the 2D pixel coordinate of the marker projection in the camera. At this point (and henceforth in this section) the camera image coordinate are transformed into the corresponding HMD image location ($\mathbf{x}_i$).

The set of 3D coordinates $\mathbf{X}$ and 2D projections $\mathbf{x}$ are linked by a unique relationship – the 11 parameters which describe the frustum at the time the coordinates were recorded. The aim of photogrammetry is to find the 11 parameters that define this relationship. A proper treatment of this approach is beyond the scope of this chapter (see instead [5, 7, 27] for more information). Briefly, for any hypothesized frustum, we can compute the projection of $\mathbf{X}$ in the frustum image plane, to give $\mathbf{y}$. The difference between $\mathbf{x}$ (the original 2D projection) and $\mathbf{y}$ (the computed projection from $\mathbf{X}$) can be used as an error measure, and minimized to provide an estimate of the frustum's 11 parameters (see figure 2).

We thus obtain estimated values for the HMD display's intrinsic parameters, and its position and pose (denoted $\mathbf{S}_P$ in figure 1) relative to the tracker's origin. As we discussed earlier, since we also know the HMD tracked centre in the same coordinate frame ($\mathbf{S}_T$), we are now able to compute the transformation between the two ($\mathbf{D}$):

$$\mathbf{D} = \mathbf{S}_P \mathbf{S}_T^{-1}$$

Consequently, for any HMD position ($\mathbf{S}'_T$), we can now compute the appropriate optic centre and principal ray for the HMD display.

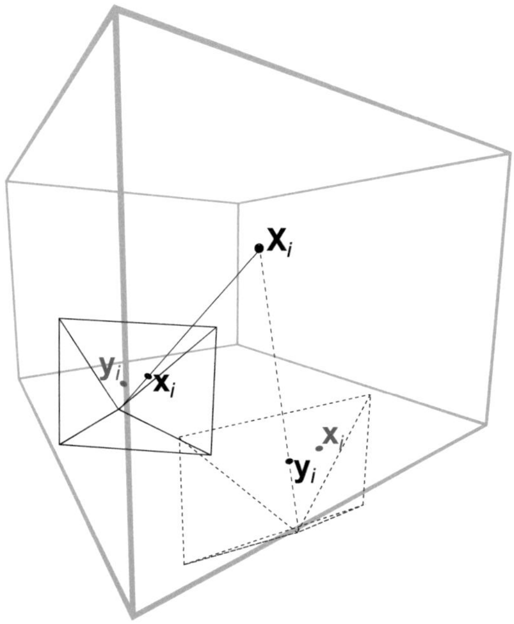

Figure 2. The ith 3D point ($\mathbf{X}_i$) projects to the camera image plane (solid lines) as pixel $\mathbf{x}_i$ (solid line). We estimate an HMD frustum (dashed lines) based on the projections for many i, and from this frustum are able to compute where $\mathbf{X}_i$ will project to in the new, hypothesised frustum ($\mathbf{y}_i$). Due to measurement errors, this estimate will be wrong, with an error of $|\mathbf{y}_i - \mathbf{x}_i|$ for all i. The difference in position and shape of the camera and frustum has been exaggerated here for illustrative purposes – after calibration, there is typically less than one pixel error per point, and the camera and frustum will almost be coincident.

For virtual reality applications, we can easily use the estimated frustum in common 3D graphics languages like OpenGL:

```
// Switch to intrinsic (projection) matrix mode.
glMatrixMode(GL_PROJECTION);

// Load intrinsic matrix, P.
glLoadMatrix(P);

// Switch to extrinsic (modelling) matrix.
glMatrixMode(GL_MODELVIEW);

// Load HMD_to_optic_centre transform.
glLoadMatrix(D);

// Incorporate the latest tracker transform.
glMultMatrix(S_prime_T);

// Draw the left-eye's scene.
drawScene();

// Repeat for the right-eye scene...
```

Values must be resolved for 11 parameters for each display. Inherent noise in the measurement systems (camera and tracker) means that many samples must be captured to allow robust estimation of these parameters. The method can be generalized to that of a single tracked point being dynamically moved within the field of view of the frustum. The camera, in 'movie mode', records the 2D locations of $\mathbf{x}_i$ in real time, permitting a high number of point correspondences to be gathered in a short period (see figure 3). We have found that 100 such correspondences are necessary for an accurate calibration, with 1000 or more being desirable [5].

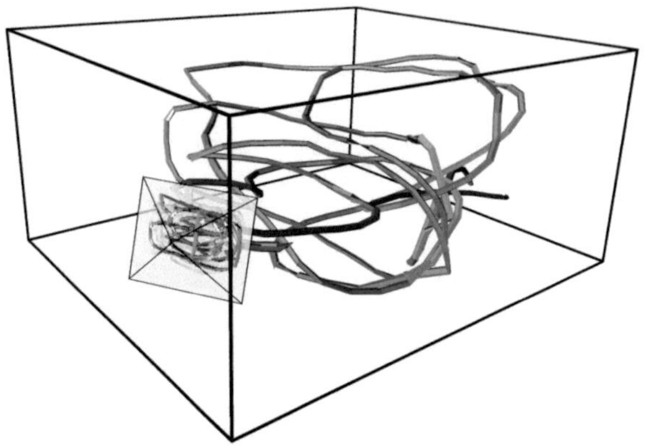

Figure 3. Graphical reproduction of one of the calibration trajectories and its projection into the frustum image plane (not all ≈3000 points are shown, for clarity).

With the modified photogrammetry method described above, we have obtained HMD display calibrations with a mean error less than one pixel. For reference, deriving intrinsic parameters from the HMD manufacturer's specifications, and extrinsic parameters by manual measurement yielded a mean error in excess of 100 pixels. This error would be very noticeable to the user, and is largely due to mis-measurement of the display's principal ray when measuring the extrinsic parameters. With trial and error this value could be reduced, but this is precisely the kind of error that proper calibration avoids. For example, keeping our calibrated extrinsic parameters but retaining the manufacturer's specifications for the intrinsic parameters gave an error of 13 pixels. In other words, an out-of-the-box HMD calibration will be at least this bad.

We believe this is a marked improvement over existing HMD calibration methods [15, 20, 28], although these papers did not provide pixel errors and so could not be compared directly with our method. These methods also require many judgments from a skilled human observer which, as we outlined above, would take a prohibitive amount of time to capture enough samples to robustly estimate the display parameters.

Note that the optic centre and principal ray obtained using this method are actually those of the camera, and not of the display. Our early constraint that the camera should be positioned in order to capture as much of the HMD display as possible will generally ensure that the difference between these two will be small. We return to this issue at the end of the chapter.

2.2. Temporal accuracy

To recreate natural viewing conditions, the latency between a head movement and the visual consequences of the movement should be minimized. Delays at any point of the VR pipeline will result in the perception of virtual objects lagging behind a hand or head movement, as if attached by elastic. At moderate levels of lag (≈300ms) users begin to disassociate their own movements from the VR movement [8, 13]. In the worst cases, latency can cause usability issues, including nausea [1, 10]. We consider now a procedure for measuring total system latency and discuss individual elements that contribute to this. Delays will primarily arise from the rendering system, and the tracker.

2.2.1. Rendering latency

Rendering typically involves reading coordinates from the tracker, positioning the virtual frustum accordingly, rendering the objects in the scene, and then swapping the freshly-rendered 'back' buffer to the 'front' buffer, which is controlled in hardware to coincide with the sending of pixel data to the display device. The rendering step must be repeated for the second display in a stereo HMD, and the whole cycle usually repeats at 60 Hz or more.

Thus, rendering time can be split into the following components: coordinate capture from the tracker; graphics pre-processing (e.g. determining what to draw based on the current coordinate); graphics rendering; swapping the 'back' buffer for the 'front' buffer (which will introduce a delay while the graphics hardware awaits the 'vertical sync' of the display device, in order to provide tear-free rendering). For a typical VR system, the HMD displays will be updated 60 times per second, which means the total rendering time must be less than 16.7ms if smooth animation is to be achieved (see figure 4, top).

Ultimately, the speed at which frames are rendered (and, hence, how smooth the VR scene moves) is determined by the swapping of the display buffers, which is the last event in the rendering cycle. This means that the tracker coordinate from which the current frame was rendered could be nearly 16.7ms old. For simple VR scenes, rendering may only take a few milliseconds (<4ms), and coordinate retrieval and processing could be less than a millisecond (measured using internal timestamps in the VR application). This would mean that there could be as much as 10ms delay introduced just waiting for the display device's vertical sync.

Dynamically monitoring the delays at each stage of the rendering cycle would allow the application software to alter an initial delay to accommodate a dynamically changing VR scene, where some frames will require more rendering time than others. To the VR user, this delayed rendering is not evident, except as reduced lag.

Specifically, the VR application software should inject time stamps into the rendering cycle, monitor how long coordinate retrieval, rendering, etc, take and introduce a small delay to the start of rendering each frame, before coordinates are retrieved from the tracker. In the above example, introducing a 10ms delay at the start of the rendering cycle means that the resulting graphics would have been rendered using a tracker coordinate that was only 6ms old, which is a significant reduction in latency (see figure 4, bottom).

For complex VR scenes, graphics rendering will consume more time, reducing the advantages obtained by this delayed rendering method. Even so, the speed of rendering of complex scenes can be improved using techniques like frustum culling, multiple-level-of-detail models, and GPGPU programming, a proper treatment of which is beyond the scope of this chapter. The reader is guided toward the multitude of real-time graphics books available.

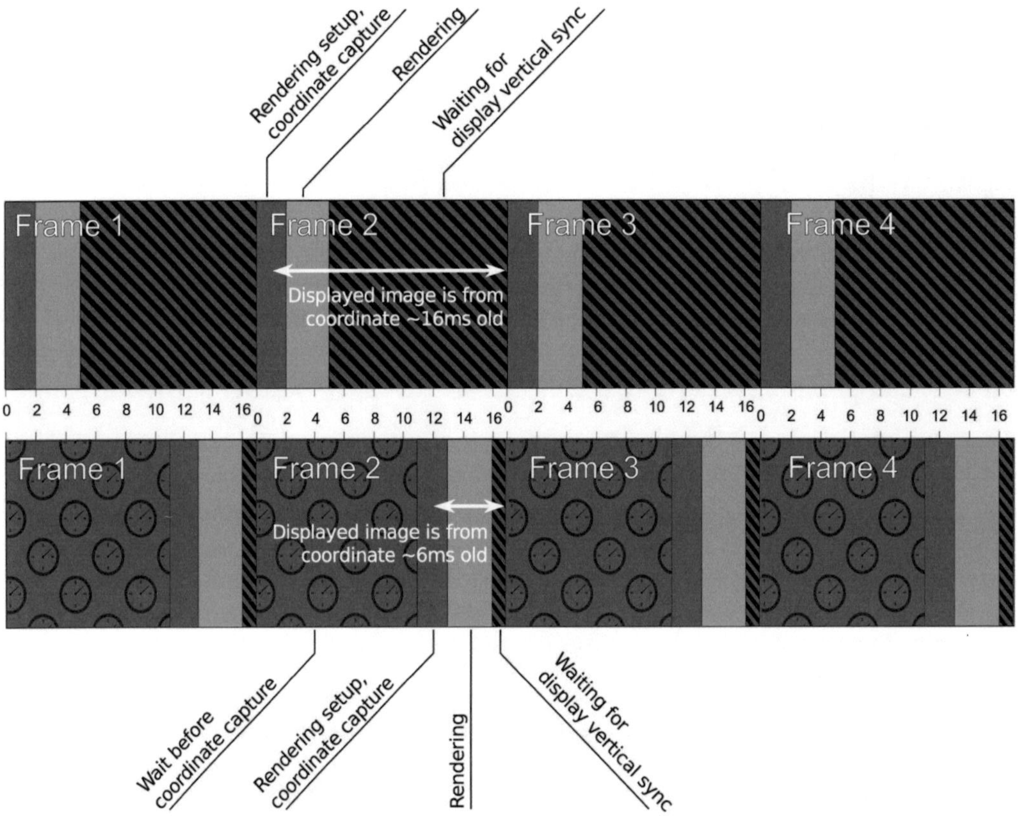

Figure 4. Minimizing tracker latency in a frame-rate limited VR application. Most of the computer's time is spent waiting for the display's vertical sync, which can mean that any given VR scene is from a tracked coordinate as much as 16.7ms old (top). By inserting a deliberate pause before capturing coordinates, the computer spends less time waiting for the display's Vsync, and the resulting VR scene is much younger (bottom).

2.2.2. Tracker latency

The tracking system will inevitably introduce a delay between a real world event (such as a head movement) and the corresponding movement of the VR scene in the HMD display. The real world event must be sampled using, for example, video cameras, which will have their own inherent frame rate and transmission time of the captured event to the motion processor. The motion processor must interpret the incoming signal, estimate the 3D structure of the tracked objects (e.g. from multiple camera images), apply filtering to reduce noise, and package the tracking data into a suitable data protocol before sending the data down the output medium (e.g. serial or Ethernet cable) to the graphics computer. Even on the very fastest hardware, this whole procedure takes a finite amount of time, and the latency – or lag – introduced will be ultimately manifest in the HMD display as a disassociation between movement and visual scene, especially for movements with high acceleration. Indeed, tracker latency has been described as "the largest single error source" in VR systems [9, page 134].

In the following section we describe a method for measuring the overall latency of the system. Computer graphics processing is now so fast that it contributes little to the overall latency, leaving the tracker as the largest source of delays.

2.2.3. *Measuring overall latency*

It is important to be able to measure the overall latency from head movement to image change for a VR system. It is not simple to deduce this value from manufacturers' specifications as there are several steps in series with potentially important delays between each.

An easy way to measure latency is to use a standard video camera to record a movie of a tracked object being moved in a roughly sinusoidal motion, fronto-parallel to the frustum. Also within the camera's field of view, is a computer monitor showing a VR scene of the tracked object. Using image processing, it is possible to extract the 2D coordinates (in pixels) of the tracked object, and its corresponding rendering on the computer monitor. This results in two streams of sinusoidal coordinates to which a root-mean-squared error (RMS) can be assigned to indicate the difference between the two streams. Minimizing the RMS error (e.g. with a gradient descent algorithm) yields the latency between the real-world event, and the commensurate changes in the HMD display (see figure 5).

Unfortunately, we are not just measuring the latency of the tracker, but also of the communication system between tracker and graphics PC, the decoding of tracked coordinates, the rendering of the 3D model, the delay before the rendered pixels appear on the monitor display, and the delay before those pixels are captured by the camera. However, we know the refresh rate of the monitor (60Hz, in this case, so a new image every 16.7ms) and of the camera (100Hz), and the amount of time the graphics PC spends on decoding coordinates and rendering (less than 1ms). We can thus assume the mean latency added by our measurement procedure to be $16.7/2 + 10/2 + 1 \approx 12$ms. We can subtract this number from the total measured latency to obtain the delays introduced by the tracker and communication protocol.

Using this method, we have measured latencies in three different tracking systems. An acoustic/inertial system added between 15 and 45ms depending on how many tracked devices were attached. A magnetic tracker showed latencies varying between 5 and 12ms for a single tracked object. A real-time optical tracker, with nine cameras tracking a single object with 4 markers, had a mean tracker latency less than 10ms.

Note that this method is independent of any possible latency introduced by the video camera. Since all coordinates are extracted from the frames of the recorded movie, latency in the camera's own image capture, compression, and storage do not impact the subsequent analysis.

Also note that the method does not include any additional delays that may be introduced by the controller for the HMD displays. Some HMDs may render the incoming video stream directly to the HMD displays resulting in no additional delay. Other systems, particularly those using digital wireless transmission, will need to decode the incoming signal to internal video store before forwarding to the HMD displays, adding at least one frame of latency. Such delays can only be measured by repeating the above procedure with the camera mounted inside the HMD, yet still able capture images of the real world. The compact nature of most HMD displays makes this a technical challenge.

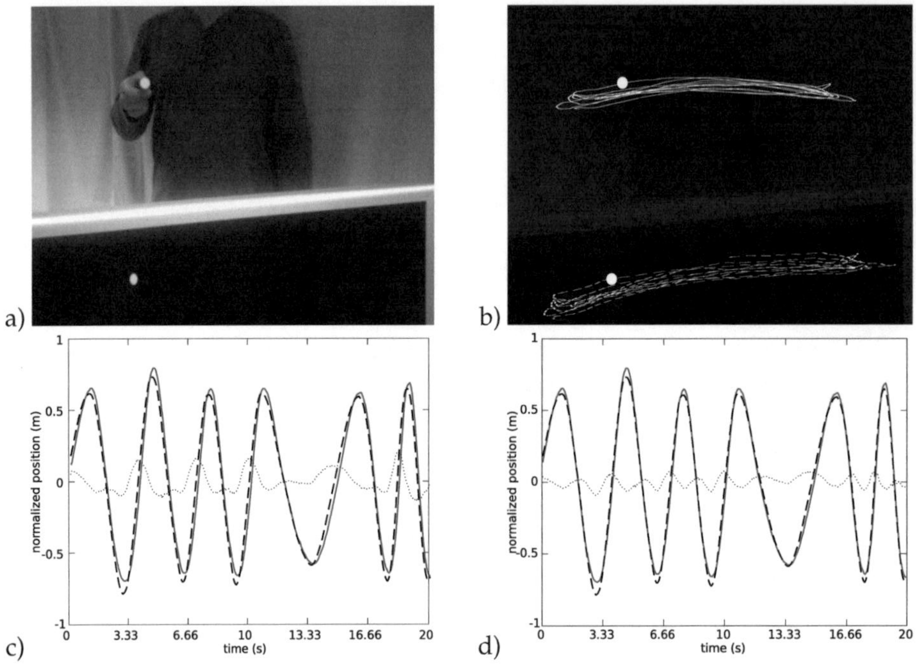

Figure 5. Measuring latency using a video camera to capture images of a hand-held tracked object and its VR representation on a computer monitor (a). Darkening and thresholding the image makes extraction of the centroids of the tracked object (solid line, overlaid onto camera image) and virtual object (dashed) easier (b). Plotting the lateral component of the two trajectories, aligned by camera frame, shows a small horizontal offset between the peaks (c). Finding the horizontal displacement of the tracked object which minimizes the RMS error (dotted line) between the two curves gives a measure of the latency in the system, about 60ms in this example (d).

2.3. Spectral

In our quest for true virtualization of light rays, we must consider the intensity and spectral composition (wavelength) of the rays, and how well modern HMD displays are able to produce such rays. Here, though, are numerous problems:

- display gamut – the displayable range of colours (gamut) of modern display technologies is significantly smaller than the gamut of the human eye.
- contrast – most modern HMD displays use some variation of liquid crystal display (LCD) technology. While these displays have many attributes making them suitable for HMDs, they do rely on back-lighting (illumination behind the crystals) to make the image visible. Unfortunately, the crystals can not be made completely opaque and will still allow some of the back-lighting to permeate through, so it is impossible to create a true black pixel. This can lead to contrast ratios (luminance of the brightest possible pixel to the darkest) as little as 100:1. At the time of writing, organic light emitting diode (OLED) displays are maturing rapidly and, as their name suggests, they emit light where needed, without the need for uniform back-lighting, and can achieve contrast ratios of 1000000:1.

- colour generation – some display technologies employ some 'tricks' to generate or improve colour appearance, but which can introduce artifacts. The authors have used a cathode-ray-tube (CRT) HMD, where the CRT itself was a greyscale unit, but a clever set of colour filters permitted colours to be displayed. While the gamut produced was on-par with other true-colour CRT systems, slight mis-alignment of the colour filters did introduce a distinct purple tinge toward the bottom of the display, which was not user-correctable. In another HMD based on liquid crystal on silicon (LCoS) technology, the display was only capable of displaying colours to 6 bits resolution per colour channel. It used a Frame Rate Control algorithm to create the appearance of more colours. While the end result was generally agreeable, such a display would be unsuitable for high-fidelity colour work.
- miniaturization – the desire to make the displays small and portable may lead to compromises in their construction, which may manifest as compromised colour fidelity.
- customer needs – For most VR users, colour fidelity is less of an issue than spatial and temporal accuracy. Manufacturers will therefore place less emphasis on colour fidelity when choosing displays for their HMDs.

Assessing the spectral properties of a conventional computer monitor would require pointing a spectrometer at a region of the display and recording the CIE 1931 xyY values for a set of test colours, and computing the gamut. Performing the same procedure for a given HMD display is made somewhat harder by the limited access to the HMD displays – quality spectrometers are large and will not fit within most helmet-based HMD designs. Furthermore, modern LCD-based HMD's are likely to be more difficult to calibrate satisfactorily [23]. Even so, it maybe possible to calibrate an HMD to some extent using a visual comparison technique [2].

3. Applications

One of the applications of virtual reality is in vision research. Immersive virtual reality allows experimental control of the visual scene in ways that would not be possible in the real world. This ability is critical for exploring the mechanisms of human vision in freely moving observers. Free movement is, of course, the normal, general case but vision is rarely studied in this state by comparison with the intensive investigation of static-observer vision. It is not just a practical issue. Many experiments are carried out in real-world scenes with parameters such as the direction of a pointer or the distance of a comparison object being changed physically and, of course, virtual reality circumvents these laborious aspects allowing data to be gathered in much larger quantities. In addition, though, virtual reality permits stimuli that would be, to all intents and purposes, impossible to create in the real world and yet which are critical in distinguishing between hypotheses about the workings of the visual system. We shall illustrate this with examples.

Before the results of experiments that use such 'impossible' stimuli can be considered, it is vital to establish that immersive virtual reality can recreate the conditions of the real world at least to the extent that performance on the task under investigation is similar to that in the real world when the virtual scene is designed to mimic a real scene. Hence, the emphasis on precise calibration that we have discussed here and on tests of performance in a variety of tasks under conditions that simulate, in relevant respects, the real world. For example, we have shown in our experiments that walking blind to previously-displayed objects has a similar accuracy to that in a real environment [26]; we have shown that biases in the judgment of distance [25] and object size [6, 21] are small, as is the case under real-world conditions.

Having established that participants behave as expected under 'normal' conditions, the implications of performance in manipulated environments should be taken seriously. The expanding room demonstration from our laboratory is a good example. As participants walk from one side of a virtual room to the other, the room expands by as much as fourfold but participants fail to notice that anything odd has happened (see figure 6). They believe they are in the same, static room and are amazed when told about the change in size. We have demonstrated the room to well over 100 participants and only one or two experienced stereo observers, who knew in advance about the phenomenon, reported being able to detect any change in room size. How can this be? The trick, which is only possible in virtual reality, is that the room expands about a point that is half way between the eyes (the 'cyclopean point' after the Cyclops, from Greek mythology, who had only one eye). What this means is that as each object in the room gets further away it also gets larger in such a way that the image (as seen by the cyclopean eye) remains the same. Given only the images that the cyclopean eye receives, the expanding room is indistinguishable from a normal stable room. But two cues that are usually thought of as providing reliable information about the 3D structure of the world, binocular disparity and motion parallax, are still present and should be just as effective at signalling the true size of the room as in a static room. We have investigated this phenomenon in a number of experiments [6, 21, 24, 25]. The important point here is that the isolation and manipulation of binocular disparity and motion parallax cues in this paradigm, independent of other depth cues and while still allowing observers to explore an environment freely, could not be achieved without virtual reality.

Another example from our laboratory shows how virtual reality can be used to test hypotheses about the signals people use when they are interacting with moving objects. Footballers running to head a ball could, in theory, compute the three-dimensional coordinate of football relative to their head and calculate how to move in order to intercept it. This is not considered a serious possibility in the neuroscience community; instead the argument in the literature is about what *type* of simple visual parameters might be used as control variables in determining how a player moves to intercept a ball. Many studies looking at players catching balls have analysed the curved trajectories they make as they run and fitted these using different models. However, a key test is to manipulate the variables in question during the flight of a ball and measure the effect that this has on the player's movement. We used virtual reality to do this using experienced football players as participants. Although they did not report noticing any difference between trials on which the ball travelled in a normal or manipulated trajectory, there were clear differences between the movements of players in these two conditions which could help discriminate between opposing hypotheses [16].

One heroic study by Wallach (1974) did *not* use virtual reality and serves as an illustration of what can be done by building elaborate physical apparatus instead. Wallach was interested in the mechanisms underlying visual stability. He arranged for a patterned ball to rotate so that on some trials it faced the participant as they walked while on other trials it would counter-rotate. The participant wore a headband that was attached via a series of pullies

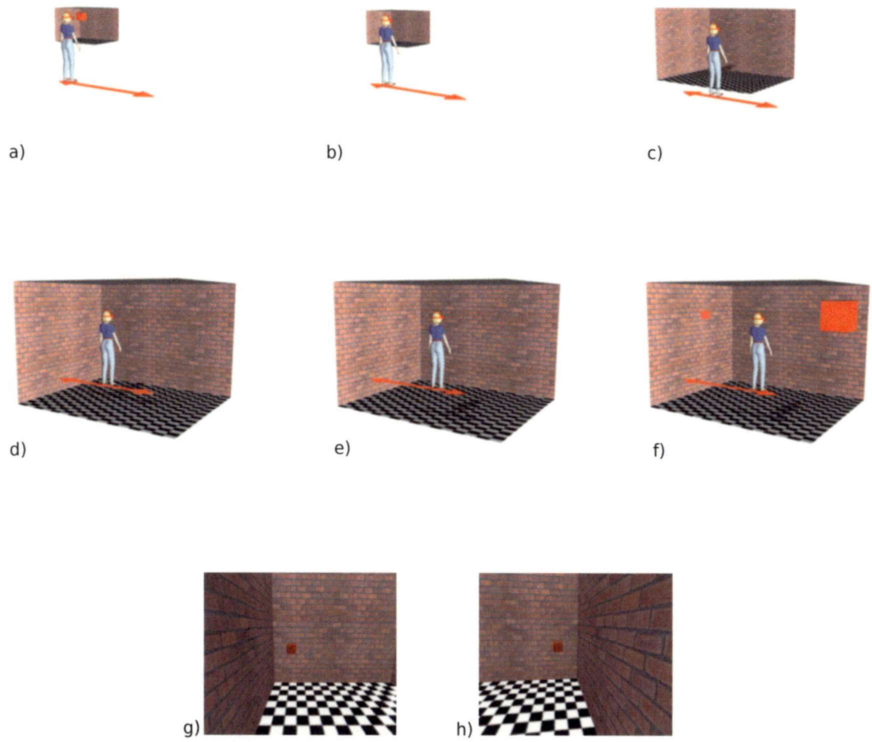

Figure 6. Schematic diagram of the expanding room experiment. In a), the observer views a reference cube in a 'small' room and makes some judgment of its size. b)–e) the observer walks to the right, and the room smoothly expands around their cyclopean point until it is four times bigger than the initial room. f) the observer sees another cube (possibly of a different physical size) and determines if it is bigger or smaller than the reference cube (shown semi-transparent for reader's benefit). In this example, the second cube is physically four times bigger than the reference yet, incredibly, most observers would call them the same size. g) and h) actual scenes from this trial.

to the ball, with a variable gearing affecting the ball's rotation. Generating a very similar stimulus in virtual reality, we were able to collect a significantly larger set of data and show that a static ball is reliably perceived as rotating away from them as they move (at least under these conditions, where the participant knows that the ball's rotation may be yolked to their own movement) [26]. Instead of building more elaborate mechanical devices, virtual reality allows the rotating-ball experiment to be extended to many different cases in which the visual change of a given object caused by an observer's movement (rotation, expansion, change in slant) can be manipulated independently from other features of the image (such as those that define the location of the object with respect to others in the scene). Such a systematic and comprehensive study of the parameters of visual stability has yet to be carried out, but it seems unlikely that it could be done in freely moving observers without using immersive virtual reality.

4. Future challenges

4.1. See-through augmented reality and eye tracking

We briefly touched upon augmented reality (AR) at the start of the chapter, and return to it here due to the inevitable fusion of AR and VR that is likely to take place as display technologies advance. With see-though OLED panels in early stages of development, it is likely that a "one-size-fits-all" HMD design will emerge which would be suitable for both AR (in see-though mode) and VR (in some form of black-out mode). Yet, an enduring problem with see-through HMD's is their inability to obscure rays from the real world. Creating truly opaque virtual objects is beyond current display technology.

However, such an HMD will present a new challenge which has not been met with existing video-based AR headsets, or conventional (non-see-through) VR HMDs. The challenge is that when the observer changes gaze direction, the eye does not rotate around its optic centre, but around some other point which will shift the optic centre. Thus, any static calibration (such as that obtained from our method described above) will fail to align virtual objects with their real-world counterpart. The misalignment will be worse for more extreme gaze angles. A possible solution would be to use a miniature, passive eye tracking system mounted within the HMD to track the gaze direction, report this to the graphics generating computer, which will modify the graphics frustums accordingly. Whether this can be done rapidly and unobtrusively remains to be seen.

4.2. High-resolution foveal rendering

While we wait for technology to catch up with our idealized VR system, and deliver the rich, high resolution scenes necessary to truly virtualize the real-world, there are ways in which the VR experience could be improved, for example using selective rendering. The human eye's fovea has a much higher spatial sensitivity than peripheral vision and, hence, rendering a high-detailed scene in regions of the HMD display that project to the eye's periphery is a waste of computational resources. Instead, eye tracking technology like that described above could be used to render a small, highly detailed sub region of the scene where the observer is fixating. The remainder of the display would comprise a low resolution rendering of the scene, which to peripheral vision is indistinguishable from highly detailed rendering. This type of technique has been used in reading research for many years [14].

5. Conclusions

Virtual reality is likely to have an increasingly pervasive influence on our lives in the future, driven in part by progressive advances in the realism of computer graphics and the ability, through augmented reality technology, to mix real and virtual objects seamlessly in the visual scene. Virtual reality technology still falls short of a full and accurate re-creation of the spatial, temporal and spectral properties of the rays arriving at the eye as an observer explores a real-world scene but, as we have discussed, great progress has been made towards this goal. Finally, we have emphasised the unique possibilities opened up by virtual reality for investigating the mechanisms of human vision and how, in this case, a rapid and faithful reproduction of the rays arriving at each eye is particularly important.

Author details

Stuart Gilson
Department of Optometry and Visual Science, Buskerud University College, Kongsberg, Norway.

Andrew Glennerster
School of Psychology and Clinical Language Sciences, University of Reading, Earley Gate, Reading, United Kingdom.

6. References

[1] Cobb, S., Nichols, S., and Wilson, J. (1995). Health and safety implications of virtual reality: in search of an experimental methodology. In *Proc. FIVE'95 (Framework for Immersive Virtual Environments)*, University of London, London, UK.
[2] Colombo, E. and Derrington, A. (2001). Visual calibration of crt monitors. *Displays*, 22(3):87 – 95.
[3] Gilson, S. J., Fitzgibbon, A. W., and Glennerster, A. (2006). Quantitative analysis of accuracy of an inertia/acoustic 6dof tracking system in motion. *J. of Neurosci. Meth.*, 154(1-2):175–182.
[4] Gilson, S. J., Fitzgibbon, A. W., and Glennerster, A. (2008). Spatial calibration of an optical see-through head-mounted display. *J. of Neurosci. Meth.*, 173(1):140 – 146.
[5] Gilson, S. J., Fitzgibbon, A. W., and Glennerster, A. (2011). An automated calibration method for non-see-through head mounted displays. *J. of Neurosci. Meth.*, 199(2):328 – 335.
[6] Glennerster, A., Tcheang, L., Gilson, S. J., Fitzgibbon, A. W., and Parker, A. J. (2006). Humans ignore motion and stereo cues in favour of a fictional stable world. *Current Biology*, 16:428–43.
[7] Hartley, R. and Zisserman, A. (2001). *Multiple view geometry in computer vision*. Cambridge University Press, UK.
[8] Held, R. and Durlach, N. (1991). Telepresence, time delay and adaptation. In Ellis, S. R., editor, *Pictorial Communication in Virtual and Real Environments*. Taylor and Francis.
[9] Holloway, R. L. (1995). *Registration Errors in Augmented Reality Systems*. PhD thesis, University of North Carolina at Chapel Hill.
[10] Kennedy, R., Lanham, D., Drexler, J., Massey, C., and Lilienthal, M. (1995). Cybersickness in several flight simulators and VR devices: a comparison of incidences, symptom profiles, measurement techniques and suggestions for research. In *Proc. FIVE'95 (Framework for Immersive Virtual Environments)*, University of London, London, UK.
[11] Kuhl, S. A., Thompson, W. B., and Creem-Regehr, S. H. (2009). HMD calibration and its effects on distance judgments. *ACM Trans. Appl. Percept.*, 6:19:1–19:20.
[12] Land, M. F., Mennie, N., and Rusted, J. (1999). The roles of vision and eye movements in the control of activities of daily living. *Perception*, 28:1311–1328.
[13] Liu, A., Tharp, G., French, L., Lai, S., and Stark, L. (1993). Some of what one needs to know about using head-mounted displays to improve teleoperator performance. *IEEE Transactions on Robotics and Automation*, 9(5):638–648.
[14] McConkie, G. W. and Rayner, K. (1975). The span of the effective stimulus during a fixation in reading. *Perception & Psychophysics*, 17:578–586.

[15] McGarrity, E. and Tuceryan, M. (1999). A method for calibrating see-through head-mounted displays for AR. In *Proceedings of the IEEE and ACM International Symposium on Mixed and Augmented Reality (ISMAR)*, pages 75–84.

[16] McLeod, P., Reed, N., Gilson, S., and Glennerster, A. (2008). How soccer players head the ball: A test of optic acceleration cancellation theory with virtual reality. *Vision Research*, 48(13):1479 – 1487.

[17] Mon-Williams, M., Plooy, A., Burgess-Limerick, R., and Wann, J. (1998). Gaze angle: a possible mechanism of visual stress in virtual reality headsets. *Ergonomics*, 41:280–285.

[18] Mon-Williams, M., Wann, J. P., and Rushton, S. (1993). Binocular vision in a virtual world: visual deficits following the wearing of a head-mounted display. *Ophthalmic & Physiological Optics*, 13:387–391.

[19] Newcombe, R. A., Lovegrove, S. J., and Davison, A. J. (2011). Dtam: Dense tracking and mapping in real-time. In *IEEE International Conference on Computer Vision (ICCV)*.

[20] Owen, C. B., Zhou, J., Tang, A., and Xiao, F. (2004). Display-relative calibration for optical see-through head-mounted displays. In *Proceedings of the IEEE and ACM International Symposium on Mixed and Augmented Reality (ISMAR)*.

[21] Rauschecker, A. M., Solomon, S. G., and Glennerster, A. (2006). Stereo and motion parallax cues in human 3d vision: Can they vanish without trace? *Journal of Vision*, 6:1471–1485.

[22] Regan, C. (1995). An investigation into nausea and other side-effects of head-coupled immersive virtual reality. *Virtual Reality*, 1:17–31. 10.1007/BF02009710.

[23] Sharma, G. (2002). LCDs versus CRTs – colour-calibration and gamut considerations. In *Proceedings of the IEEE*, volume 90.

[24] Svarverud, E., Gilson, S. J., and Glennerster, A. (2010). Cue combination for 3D location judgements. *Journal of Vision*, 10(1).

[25] Svarverud, E., Gilson, S. J., and Glennerster, A. (2012). A demonstration of 'broken' visual space (in press). *PLoS ONE*.

[26] Tcheang, L., Gilson, S. J., and Glennerster, A. (2005). Systematic distortions of perceptual stability investigated using immersive virtual reality. *Vision Res.*, 45:2177–2189.

[27] Tsai, R. Y. (1986). An efficient and accurate camera calibration technique for 3-D machine vision. In *IEEE Computer Vision and Pattern Recognition or CVPR*, pages 364–374.

[28] Tuceryan, M., Genc, Y., and Navab, N. (2002). Single point active alignment method (SPAAM) for optical see-through HMD calibration for augmented reality. *Presence-Teleop. Virt.*, 11:259–276.

[29] Turing, A. M. (1950). I. – Computing Machinery and Intelligence. *Mind*, LIX(236): 433–460.

[30] Wallach, H., Stanton, L., and Becker, D. (1974). The compensation lot movement-produced changes of object orientation. *Perception & Psychophysics*, 15:339–343.

Section 2

Virtual Reality in Robot Technology

Chapter 4

A Novel Rehabilitation Evaluation Method on Virtual Reality Based on RRR-I

Ying Jin, ShouKun Wang, Naifu Jiang and Yaping Dai

Additional information is available at the end of the chapter

http://dx.doi.org/10.5772/46405

1. Introduction

With the aggravation of the population aging in the world, more and more nations and communities attach importance to the research on the rehabilitation of the aging and the disabled. Nevertheless, the conventional rehabilitation apparatus dramatically have a number of problems, regardless of their good rehabilitation effects. For instance, the conventional training techniques require enormous physical therapists such as doctors, nurses and so forth to assist the patients in completing a series of activities, so that it would waste a lot of unnecessary expense and manpower. As a result, there is an increasing emphasis placed on the rehabilitation robot which may be a solution to the problems in conventional rehabilitation technique.

Some research job is about the lower-limb, and the researchers have designed many practical devices. Y. H. Tsoi and S. Q. Xie (2008) have invented a robot which could recover the patients' ankles. However, the training environment might be boring for most patients, for it lacks of a virtual game interface which may be full of entertainments. Meanwhile, there are also a lot of researchers who pay attention to the upper-limb rehabilitation robot. Koichi Kirihara, Norihiko Saga and Naoki Saito (2010) have designed a robot which has five degrees of freedom by virtue of its link mechanism. A pneumatic cylinder, arranged and integrated with the device, was used to operate it. Nonetheless, the safety could not be assured in this device, for the control of the pneumatic device often brings about fierce impulse which may do harm to the patients. Janez Podobnik, Matjaž Mihelj and Marko Munih (2009) also have made a HenRiE (Haptic environment for reaching and grasping exercises) device with two hemiparetic subjects. The HenRiE device is intended for use in a robot-aided neurorehabilitation for training of reaching and grasping in haptic environments. But the researchers fail to add an impedance environment to the patients who are being trained so that the patients' arm muscles could not be fully stimulated.

Ken'ichi Koyanagi, Junji Furusho, Ushio Ryut (2003) and Akio Inoue, T Kikuchi, K Fukushima, J Furusho and T Ozawa (2009) have developed a practical haptic device 'PLEMO-P1' ， in which adopts ER brakes as its force generators. Although, by using the ER brakes, it is safer and more convenient than other similar rehabilitation robots, the ER brakes still have some disadvantages such as the leakage of the inner liquid.

This chapter mainly gives a description of a new upper-limb rehabilitation robot using the magnetic particle brake (MPB), which is named RRR-I (Remote Rehabilitation Robot-I). The robot is shown in Fig.1. After the passive training technique in the rehabilitation field is applied to the design of the robot, the MPB is made full use of to generate an impedance environment for the patients. Furthermore, in order to make the training process more interesting and more attractive, a kind of virtual reality technique is put into training process. For example, a human-machine interaction interface is devised, so that the patients could play some particular computer games to enhance their arms' movement ability and then the researchers could assess their rehabilitation level. Finally, by using some correlative mathematical statistics methods, we create a kind of evaluation technique and basically obtain a good result.

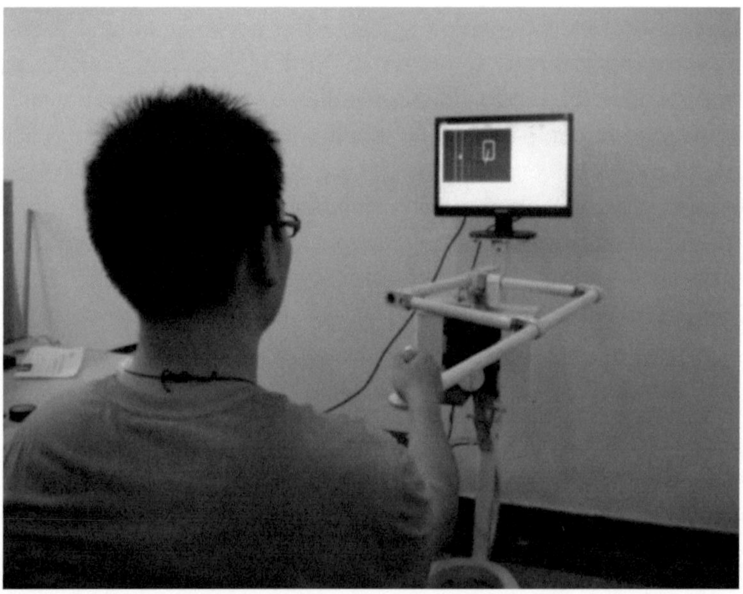

Figure 1. Experiment System of the RRR-I

2. The PNF technology in upper limb rehabilitation

PNF (proprioceptive neuromuscular facilitation) is a therapy which promotes the response ability of nerve and muscle through simulating proprioceptors. PNF was founded by Herman Kabat who was American physician and neurophysiologist in 1940s. It was originally used in cerebral palsy and multiple sclerosis patients, medical practice has proof that it also can apply to the stroke upper limb rehabilitation (2008).

According to common movement mode of human daily activities, PNF technology was founded based on the human body development learning and neurophysiology principle. One of the most commonly used PNF technology is diagonal mode (diagonal D), which is a kind of gross motor that can be seen in most function activities. It is the movement that formed by the interaction of three muscle in flexionandextension, internal and external exhibition, internal and external spin. Also diagonal mode is the last and highest form of normal development. All the diagonal movement is the merger of rotating component, which can promote the interaction of both left and right body sides because of the path across the body centre line. Common action: right hand touching left ear, resisted motion. The resisted motion was shown in Fig. 2.

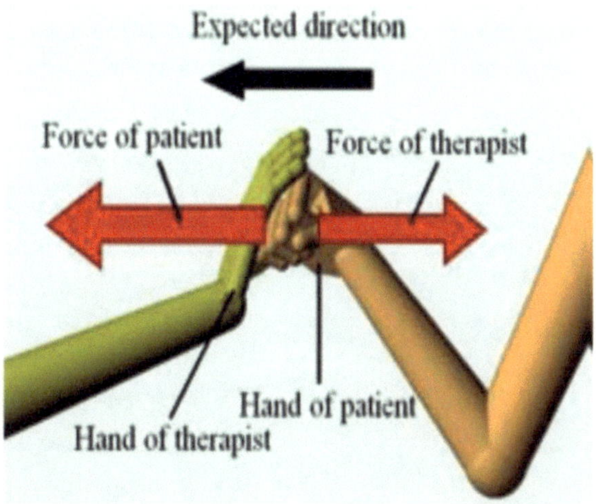

Figure 2. Resisted motion

The common promote method of PNF.

1. Command:

A short and concise command can stimulate patients to active force;

2. Visual cues:

Make patients take exercises by watching in order to help to exercising and coordinating;

3. The body location of therapists:

The therapists should be close to patients and move stable together with patients while providing resistance through their own weight;

4. Input of ontology sense:

According to the situation of patients, the resistance on the patients' sicken limbs should be suitable. The resistance will be ok while it allowing patients to do slow, stable and coordinated movement with no abnormal movement occurring.

3. Design of RRR-I

Fig. 3 shows the structure of the RRR-I. The robot mainly consists of robot arms, a handle, two balance blocks, a screen, a connection box, a computer box, a controller box and other parts. By referring to the Parallelogram Linkage Mechanism (PLM), we design the robotic arms which have balance blocks to keep the arm's balance. The absolute encoders are fixed in the connection box as well as the MPBs. But they have distinct functions. The encoders are used to attain the arms' rotation angles while the MPBs are applied to the resistance moment support. In order to control the pitching angle of the robot, which may change according to different patients, we make an attempt to design a rotation handle at the surface of the connection box. Meanwhile, the force of gripping is obtained through a force sensor on the handle. And the DSP in the controller box would receive the sensors' data information and then send the control information to the MPBs after a data analysis. In the end, a game interface would be displayed to the patients in the screen.

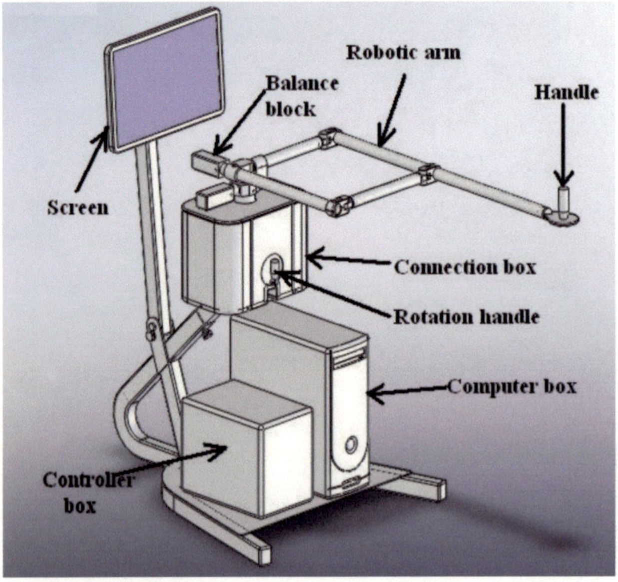

Figure 3. Overall Structure of the RRR-I

3.1. Upper limb rehabilitation robot system

The upper limb rehabilitation robot system and diagram of the whole robot system were respectively shown in Fig. 4 and Fig. 5. The hardware consisted of three parts: control unit, detect unit and execution unit.

3.2. Control unit

The micro control chip was one 32-bit fixed-point DSP TMS320F2812 made by TI, in charge of the control calculation of force feedback system, handle position and communication with PC; PC was responsible for the human-computer interaction.

3.3. Detection unit

Detection unit consisted of position detection and force detection.

The handle was a force sensor which can sense force in four directions and measure the force to limb. Because of the low moving speed of sicken limb, AD7705 with low working frequency was choose as A/D conversion chip. AD7705 can receive the weak signal directly came from sensors. Thus, error caused by the analog signal amplifier circuit can be avoided and the circuit was greatly simplified;

As the position detect unit, 14-bit accuracy absolute encoder ensured the movement tracking precision of patients' upper limb.

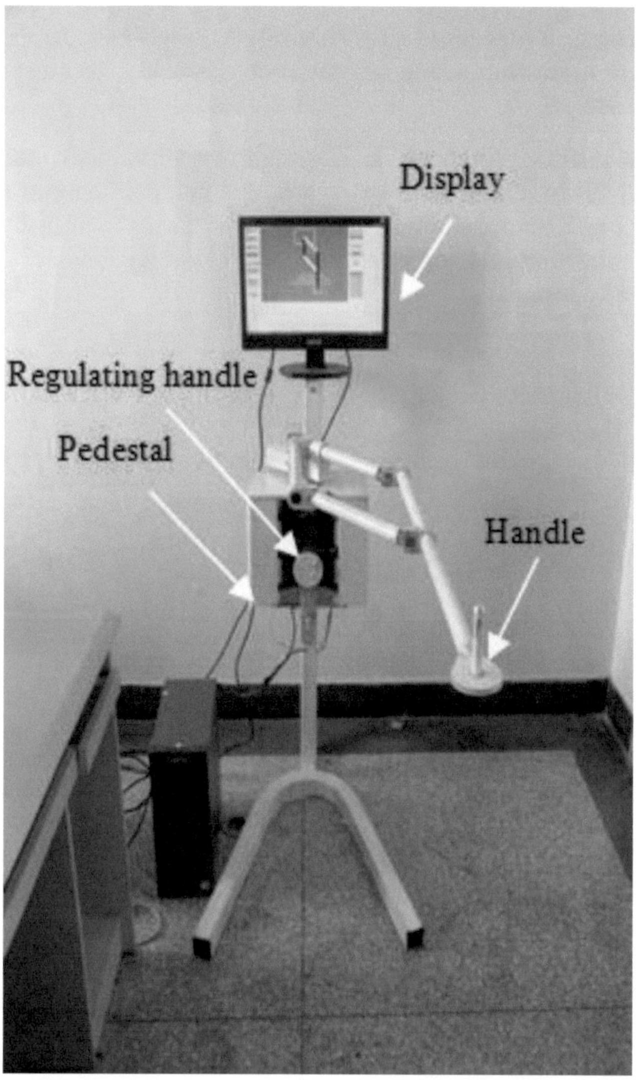

Figure 4. Upper limb rehabilitation robot based on magnetic powder brakes

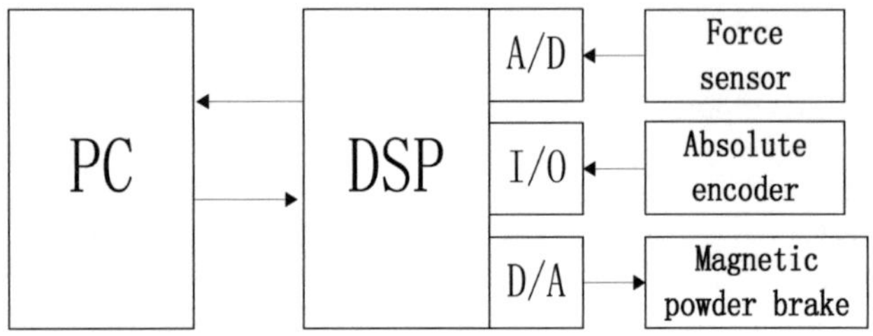

Figure 5. Diagram of upper limb rehabilitation robot system structure

3.4. Execution unit

As actuators, two magnetic powder brakes were responsible for the generation of resistance of 2 DOF. Two magnetic powder brakes were respectively linked to the inner and outer shaft through belt, so as to realize independent torque control of the inner and outer shaft of 2 DOF, as shown in Fig. 6.

Based on the principle of electromagnetic, magnetic powder brakes convey torque through magnetic powder, where relationship between torque and exciting current is linearity. So the torque can be easily controlled by changing exciting current. Normally, the relationship between exciting current and the conveyed torque is proportion linearity (2009) in the range of 5% to 100% of rated torque.

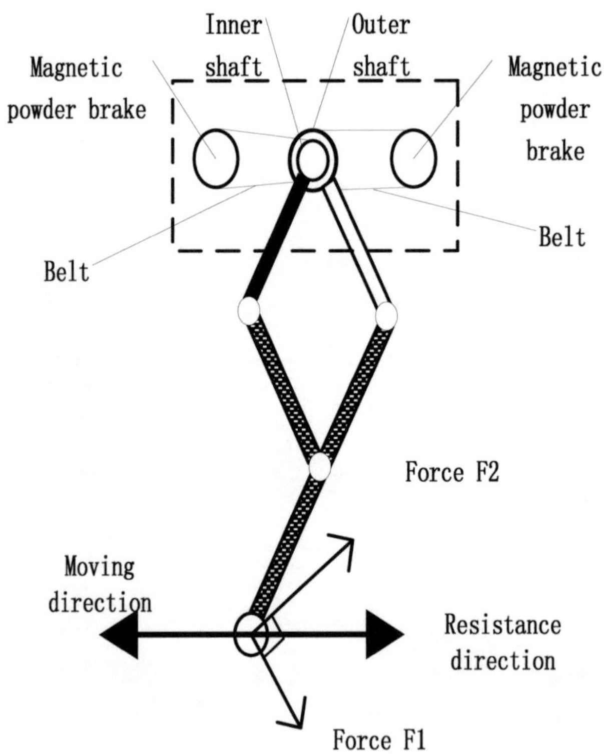

Figure 6. Braking force diagram of 2 DOF

When exciting current remain unchanged, the conveyed torque wouldn't be influenced by the differential speed between master driver and follower (sliding speed), i.e. there is no difference between static torque and dynamic torque (2004), so the constant torque can be stably conveyed. Then magnetic powder brakes only generate resistance torque result from its fixed follower. Magnetic powder brakes parameters were shown in table 1. Because of the feature above used in the handle force control, the required force to sicken limb can be achieved simply and effectively.

Rated voltage (V)	24
Rated torque (N. m)	12
Sliding power (W)	100
Max current (A)	0.6
Max rotate speed (rpm)	650
Diameter (mm)	150
Height (mm)	56

Table 1. Magnetic powder brakes parameters

3.5. Software

In this chapter, the man-machine interface of whole upper limb rehabilitation robot was realized by Visual C++. The interface consisted of virtual mechanical arm display and basic information display.

1. Virtual mechanical arm

This section displayed the real-time virtual mechanical arm, which gave patients more intuitive feelings. At the same time, path strategies, resistance strategies and command stimulating strategies were set in this section according to different mode, which would be mainly introduced in next chapter.

2. Basic information

This section recorded and displayed some information, e.g. running time, rehabilitation level, rehabilitation status and rehabilitation period, which would be the basis for doctor's diagnosis and rehabilitation plan.

4. Transformation of coordinate

Because the coordinate in the virtual reality has to be associated with the coordinate in the reality and the data obtained from the absolute encoders is just about the arms' angles, it is crucial for us to make a coordinate transformation in order to make an easier analysis on the arms' movement.

At first, it is necessary to set a coordinate system for the robot arms in the reality. Referring to the paper of Chieh-Li Chen, Tung-Chin Wu and Chao-Chung Peng (2011), we set the 2D rectangular coordinate system showed in Fig. 7.

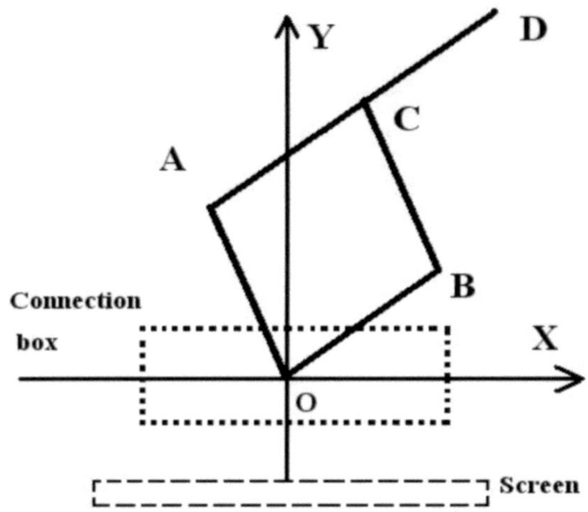

Figure 7. The Rectangle Coordinate System in which the Robot Arms Move

Since the arms' lengths in the virtual reality are not required to equal to the ones in the reality, it is assumed that the arms' lengths are all equal. It means

$$OA = OB = AC = BC = CD = l \tag{1}$$

Furthermore, in order to attain the coordinate figure of the handle (point D), we have to transfer the angle data got from the encoders to the position data in the XOY coordinate. However, because the range of the data from the encoder is from 0 degree to 360 degree and the positions of the 0 degree lines from two encoders are more likely to be different, it is a little complicated for us to deduce all situations. Thus, we initially consider only one situation showed in Fig. 8.

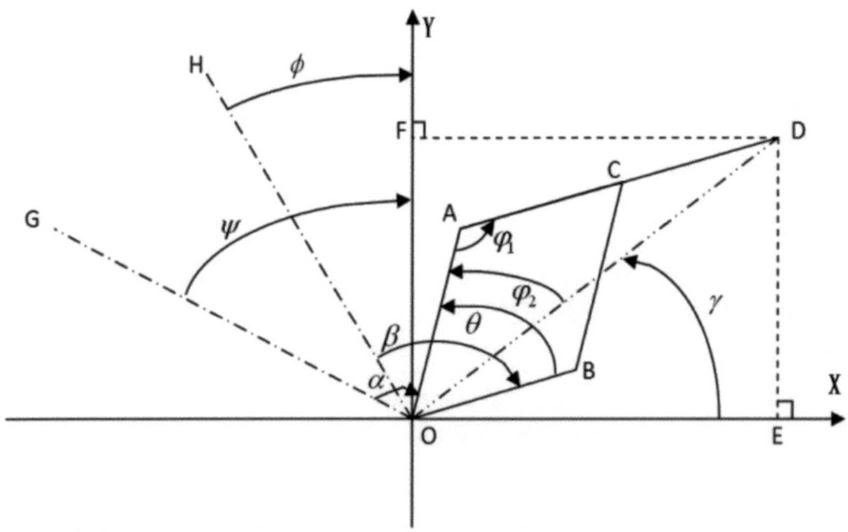

Figure 8. Coordinate transformation graph. OG and OH are the 0 degree lines from two encoders, OA, OB, BC and ACD are the robot arms.

According to Fig. 8, obviously, the position of D is:

$$\begin{cases} x = OE = OD \cdot \cos\gamma = l \cdot \cos\gamma \\ y = OF = OD \cdot \sin\gamma = l \cdot \sin\gamma \end{cases}, 0 < \gamma < \frac{\pi}{2} \tag{2}$$

Because the angle from the encoder is only measured clockwise, in Fig. 8, $0 \le \phi \le \psi \le \frac{\pi}{2}$, $0 \le \alpha \le \beta \le \pi$.

Therefore,

$$\theta = \beta + \psi - \phi - \alpha, 0 \le \theta \le \frac{\pi}{2} \tag{3}$$

$$\varphi_1 = \pi - \theta \tag{4}$$

$$OD = \sqrt{OA^2 + AD^2 - 2 \cdot OA \cdot AD \cdot \cos\varphi_1} = l \cdot \sqrt{5 - 4\cos\varphi_1} \tag{5}$$

$$\varphi_2 = \arcsin\left(\frac{AD}{OD} \cdot \sin\varphi_1\right) = \arcsin\left(\frac{\sin\varphi_1}{\sqrt{5-4\cos\varphi_1}}\right) \tag{6}$$

$$\gamma = \frac{\pi}{2} + \psi - \varphi_2 - \alpha, 0 < \gamma < \frac{\pi}{2} \tag{7}$$

After analyze other situations, we eventually conclude that (4), (5), (6) are the same while (3) and (7) are completely distinct.

In order to make calculation more convenient, we assume that:

$$\varepsilon = \beta + \psi - \phi - \alpha \tag{8}$$

$$\eta = \frac{\pi}{2} + \psi - \varphi_2 - \alpha \tag{9}$$

Thus, in connection with (3) and (7), we conclusively summarize four different situations.

Situation 1:

$$\text{if } -4\pi \le \varepsilon \le -3\pi, \text{ then } \theta = \varepsilon + 4\pi \tag{10}$$

Hence

$$\text{if } -2\pi \le \eta \le -\frac{3}{2}\pi, \text{ then } \gamma = \eta + 2\pi \tag{11}$$

Situation 2:

$$\text{if } -2\pi \le \varepsilon \le -\pi, \text{ then } \theta = \varepsilon + 2\pi \tag{12}$$

Hence

$$\begin{cases} \text{if } 0 \le \eta \le \frac{\pi}{2}, & \text{then } \gamma = \eta \\ \text{if } -2\pi \le \eta \le -\pi, & \text{then } \gamma = \eta + 2\pi \end{cases} \tag{13}$$

Situation 3:

$$\text{if } 0 \leq \varepsilon \leq \pi, \text{ then } \theta = \varepsilon \tag{14}$$

Hence

$$\begin{cases} \text{if } 0 \leq \eta \leq \pi, & \text{then } \gamma = \eta \\ \text{if } 2\pi \leq \eta \leq \frac{5}{2}\pi, & \text{then } \gamma = \eta - 2\pi \\ \text{if } -\frac{3}{2}\pi \leq \eta \leq -\pi, & \text{then } \gamma = \eta + 2\pi \end{cases} \tag{15}$$

Situation 4:

$$\text{if } 2\pi \leq \varepsilon \leq \frac{5}{2}\pi, \text{ then } \theta = \varepsilon - 2\pi \tag{16}$$

Hence

$$\begin{cases} \text{if } \frac{\pi}{2} \leq \eta \leq \pi, & \text{then } \gamma = \eta \\ \text{if } 2\pi \leq \eta \leq \frac{5}{2}\pi, & \text{then } \gamma = \eta - 2\pi \end{cases} \tag{17}$$

5. Strategies of upper limb rehabilitation

According to the introduction of PNF technology in the second section, some strategies of upper limb rehabilitation were presented. These strategies are just designed in ordinary frames and the detailed proposal will be described in the section 6.

5.1. Path strategies

In order to imitate diagonal movement form, such as resisted motion and right hand touching left ear, movement path of parallel lines and vertical lines was set. Before setting path, firstly, the current movement range of the patients' upper limb would be testing.

Push the handle to the foremost point;
Push the handle to the far left point;
Push the handle to the far right point.

The reachable zone of current sicken limb would be obtained through these three points above. The right upper limb movement path was shown in Fig. 9, which mainly consisted of horizontal lines. Three black points in Fig. 9 respectively represented the foremost point, the far left point and the far right point, which formed a triangle zone where patients' sicken limb can move safely. In Fig. 9, the solid line was specified path and the black dotted line in the middle was body center line.

The movement above was just in plane. Therefore, for the purpose of expanding the range of rehabilitation movement, the angle of pitch of pedestal can be changed through the regulating handle, as well as adjusting seat, so that patients had a relatively comfortable initial position, as shown in Fig. 10.

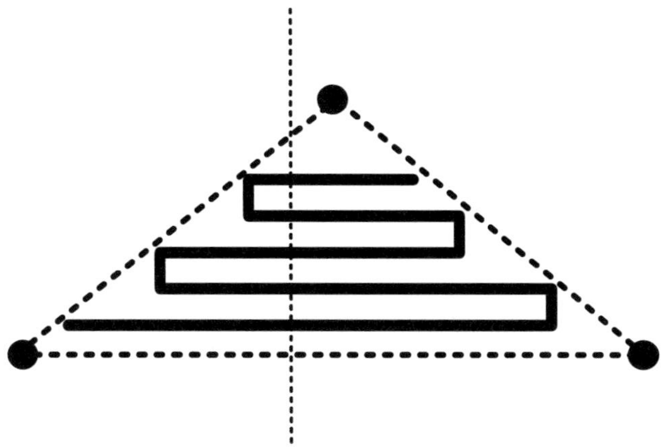

Figure 9. Schematic of right upper limb specified path

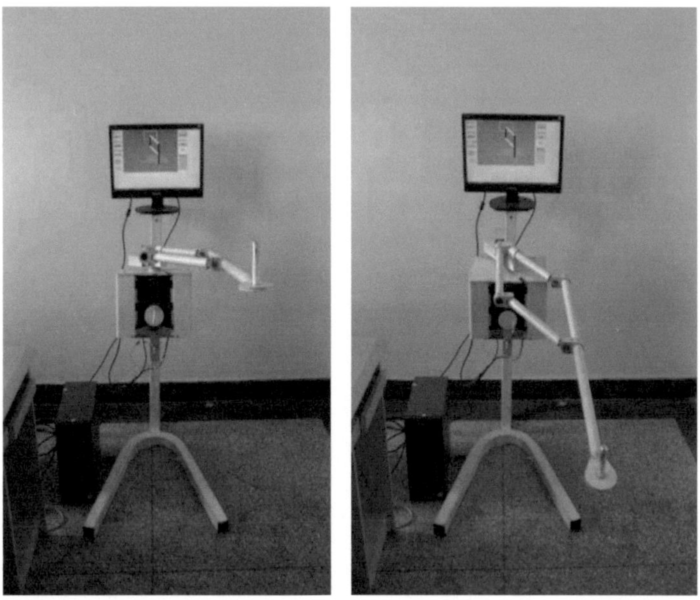

Figure 10. Rehabilitation robot under different angles of pitch

5.2. Resistance strategies

Resistance control was divided into two periods: basic period and improve period.

Basic period: the closer to the specified path, the smaller resistance was. This method can guide patients do movement along the specified path. The period should be changed into the improve period when the movement accuracy of patients' sicken limb was improved.

Improve period: the closer to the specified path, the bigger resistance was. This method can make patients do movement along the specified path more difficult, so as to further improve the flexibility and motion precision of patients' sicken limb.

A healthy people was made do the same path respectively in basic period and improve period, the result was shown in Fig. 11 and Fig. 12. The dotted line of two figures represented specified path. From these two curves of actual movement, we can see that the difficulty of tracking was bigger in improve period compared with basic period.

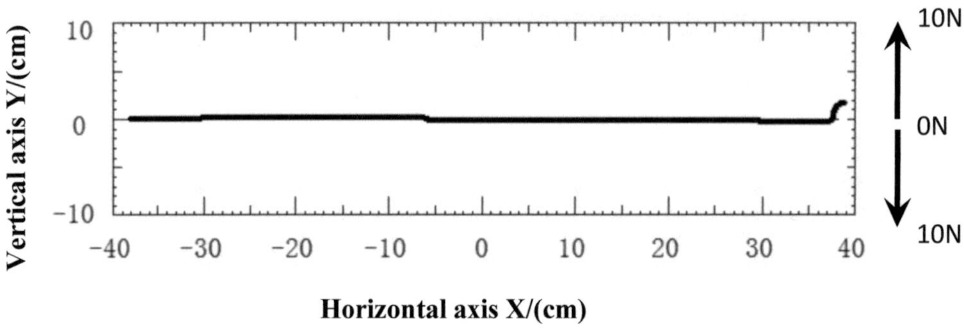

Figure 11. Movement curve in basic period

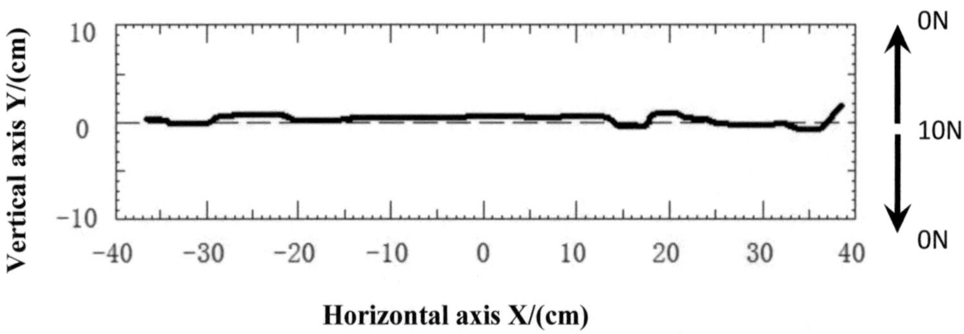

Figure 12. Movement curve in improve period

5.3. Command stimulating strategies

In the PNF promote method, command whose effect was important can stimulate patients to active force, also can give them encouragement and care.

When patients completed a movement in process, some suitable encouragements and praises can be given in speech way.

When the patients' sicken limb stopped moving in process, some encouragements should be given, e.g. "come on", "force", "you can do it".

When patients completed the whole process, some praises should be given, e.g. "very good", "such rapid process", "well done".

6. Medical training design and data analysis based on virtual reality

In this section, a medical training game, which is originated from the design in the section 5, will be presented. And, a novel data processing method will be introduced. All designs are based on a virtual game.

6.1. Virtual rehabilitation game design

According to the strategies presented in section 5, a game based on the virtual reality is designed, as showed in Fig. 13(a). The patient would hold the handle on the robot arm and move his or her hand along the trajectory in Fig. 13(a) in the virtual game. The trajectory is designed to move across human midline. It means the hand would move from the right of the human body to the left and then repeat circle again. Meanwhile, referring to the resistance therapy, we would apply three different resistance forces in trajectory OA, AB and BC to the patient's hand. Besides, $F_{OA} < F_{AB} < F_{BC}$.

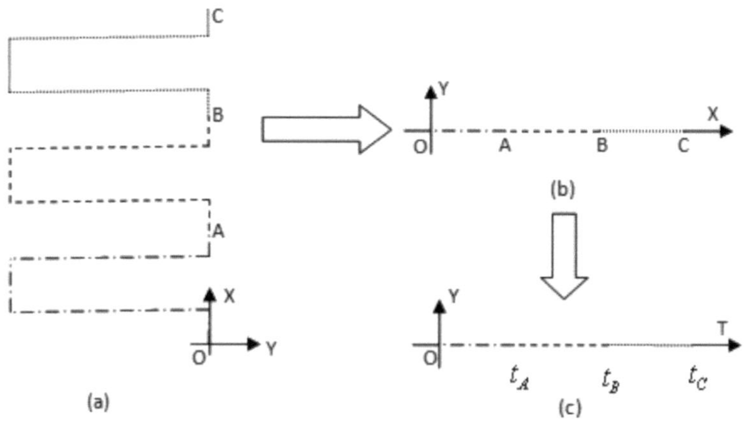

Figure 13. Virtual game's coordinate transformation graphs. The XOY coordinate system will move along the trajectory in (a), so it seems that the OABC rope is straightened to OX axis direction. (c) is obtained after the X axis in (b) is transferred to the time axis.

6.2. Data analysis method

In Fig. 13(b), the sample observation data $(x_{t_1}, y_{t_1}), (x_{t_2}, y_{t_2}), \ldots, (x_{t_n}, y_{t_n})$will be obtained according to the correlative observation time $t_1, t_2, \ldots, t_n$. If the horizontal axis is changed to the time axis, a new coordinate system showed in Fig. 13(c) would be set up. Then the sample observation data would become $(t_1, y_1), (t_2, y_2), \ldots, (t_n, y_n)$. Referring to the book written by Cook, R. Dennis (1998) and the book written by Irwin Miller, Marylees Miller (2004), it is appropriate to apply a variance function σ^2 to the rehabilitation evaluation.

Because the evaluation goal is to judge whether the trajectory of the patient's hand is the same with the expected one, we assume $\bar{y} = 0$. Then

$$\sigma^2 = E[(y - \bar{y})^2] = \frac{1}{n}\sum_{i=1}^{n}(y_i - \bar{y})^2 = \frac{1}{n}\sum_{i=1}^{n} y_i^2 \quad (18)$$

Considering that σ^2 may be zero and the time is a vital factor, we improve (18) to (19).

$$\chi = (1 + \sigma^2)t \tag{19}$$

Here the unit of the t is millisecond.

As a result of three different resistance forces, the variances and improved variances in OA, AB and BC should be calculated respectively. Then we obtain χ_{OA}, χ_{AB} and χ_{BC}.

Based on the AHP method by Lan Gan, Xuehu Wang, Rong Li (2009) and the importance of the three trajectories, we construct the judge matrix:

$$A = (a_{ij})_{3\times3} = \begin{bmatrix} 1 & 1/2 & 1/3 \\ 2 & 1 & 1/2 \\ 3 & 2 & 1 \end{bmatrix} \tag{20}$$

To solve the characteristic roots in (21)

$$(A - \lambda_{max} I)\omega = 0 \tag{21}$$

We attain that $\lambda_{max} = 3.0092$

And

$$C.I = \frac{\lambda_{max} - n}{n - 1} = 0.0046 \tag{22}$$

$$R.I = 0.58 \tag{23}$$

$$C.R = \frac{C.I}{R.I} = 0.0088 \tag{24}$$

Because the random consistency ratio $C.R < 0.10$, judge matrix will get a satisfactory consistency. Then value of ω would be got:

$$\omega = [\omega_{OA}, \omega_{AB}, \omega_{BC}]^T = [0.1634, 0.2970, 0.5396]^T \tag{25}$$

Therefore, finally, we define a rehabilitation evaluation function γ :

$$\gamma = \omega_{OA} \cdot \chi_{OA} + \omega_{AB} \cdot \chi_{AB} + \omega_{BC} \cdot \chi_{BC} \tag{26}$$

Theoretically, according to the properties of the time and variance, the same patient would become better, if the value of γ becomes smaller.

6.3. Experiment and results analysis

Through using Visual C++ and OpenGL, we eventually design a shovelboard 3D game interface showed in Fig. 14. The patient would move the robot handle of the RRR-I along the trajectory in the game. Meanwhile, the patient would feel resistance forces which are different in different area in the game. Moreover, the timer starts to record when the ball begins at the start line and ends in the finish line.

Figure 14. Shovelboard 3D game interface

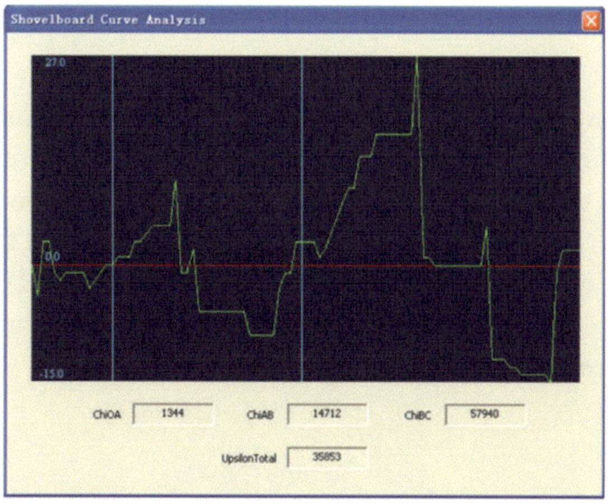

(a) $\chi_{OA} = 1344$, $\chi_{AB} = 14712$, $\chi_{BC} = 57940$ and $\Upsilon = 35853$.

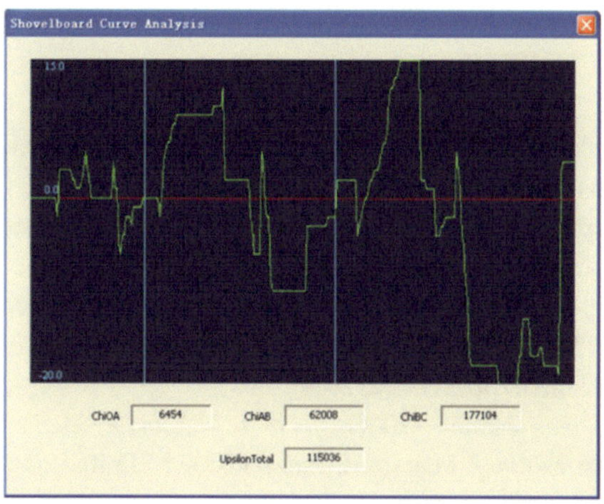

(b) $\chi_{OA} = 6454$, $\chi_{AB} = 62008$, $\chi_{BC} = 177104$ and $\Upsilon = 115036$.

Figure 15. Shovelboard curve analysis graph.

After a healthy individual plays this 3D game by using the RRR-I, a curve such as the one in Fig. 13(c) would be measured and then displayed. And the parameters such as χ_{OA}, χ_{AB}, χ_{BC} and Υ would be calculated and then showed. Although the proportions of the resistance forces in the three different areas always remain unchanged, the size of the forces under the circumstance showed in Fig. 15(b), it is three times larger than the one showed in Fig. 15(a).

In comparison with the two different curves and parameters' values in Fig. 15(a) and Fig. 15(b), it is obvious that, in Fig. 15(b), the values of every parameter become bigger. Meanwhile, the length of the time in every area also changes longer. It means the individual would spend more time to complete this game. Besides, the fluctuation of the curve in Fig. 15(b) is evidently fiercer. It means the movement of the individual's hand becomes harder. In a word, we could observe the changes by checking the variation of the value of every parameter.

7. Conclusion

In this chapter we realized an upper-limb rehabilitation robot named RRR-I and a new virtual 3D game used to recover patients. A new variance method and the AHP method are applied to the analysis on the rehabilitation level of the 3D game. Through an experiment on a healthy individual, a good consequence is obtained. In the future, the patients should be invited to participate in this experiment so that the effects of the RRR-I and other research could be proved more convincible. Besides, some new rehabilitation methods would be applied to the training on the patients.

Author details

Ying Jin, ShouKun Wang, Naifu Jiang and Yaping Dai
School of Automation, Beijing Institute of Technology, China

8. References

Cook, R. Dennis (1998). *Regression Graphics: Ideas for Studying Regressions through Graphics*, Wiley & Sons Press, New York, USA, 1998

Huang M T (1999). Application of magnetic powder brakes to tension control system for coiler. *Journal of Xi'an Mining Institute*, 1999, 6(19): 173-176

H. I. Krebs; B. T. Volpe; M. L. Aisen & N. Horgan (2000). Increasing productivity and quality of care: Robot-aided neuron rehabilitation, *Journal of Rehabilitation Research and Development*, vol.37, no.6, pp.639-652, 2000

Irwin Miller & Marylees Miller (2004). *John E. Freund's Mathematical Statistics with Applications(Seventh Edition)*, Pearson Education Asia Limited and Tsinghua University Press, Beijing, China, 2004

Kikuchi, T.; Fukushima, K.; Furusho, J. & Ozawa, T. (2009). Development of Quasi-3DOF upper limb rehabilitation system using ER brake, *Journal of Physics: Conference Series*, v 149, n 1, p 012015 (4 pp.), 2009

Kirihara, K.; Saga, N. & Saito, N. (2010). Design and control of an upper limb rehabilitation support device for disabled people using a pneumatic cylinder, *Industrial Robot*, v 37, n 4, p 354-63, 2010

Koyanagi, K.; Furusho, F.; Ryu, U. & Inoue, A. (2003). Rehabilitation system with 3-D exercise machine for upper limb, *Proceedings 2003 IEEE/ASME International Conference on Advanced Intelligent Mechatronics (AIM 2003) (Cat. No.03TH8670)*, p 1222-7 vol.2, 2003

Lan Gan; Xuehu Wang & Rong Li (2009). Research and implementation of AHP-based method base: model base application of hierarchical model, *Proceedings of the 2009 Pacific-Asia Conference on Knowledge Engineering and Software Engineering (KESE)*, p 107-10, 2009

Li Xing; Wang Jianhui; Fang Xiaoke & Ji Wen (2011). The Study of Virtual Simulation for 5dof Upper-limb Rehabilitation Robot, *Proceedings of the 2011 3rd International Conference on Advanced Computer Control (ICACC 2011)*, p 247-50, 2011

Nan D K & Huang X L (2009). *Practical Rehabilitation Medicine.* Beijing: People's Medical Publishing House, 2009: 719-744

Peter S. Lum; Machiel Van der Loos & Peggy Shor (1999). A robotic system for upper-limb exercises to promote recovery of motor function following stroke, *ICORR' 99: International Conference on Rehabilitation Robotics*, Stanford, CA

Podobnik, J.; Mihelj, M. & Munih, M. (2009). Upper limb and grasp rehabilitation and evaluation of stroke patients using HenRiE device, *2009 Virtual Rehabilitation International Conference*, p 173-8, 2009

Qin L & Huang X L (1997). PNF technology application. *Chinese Journal of Rehabilitation*, 1997

Ren G.H; Chen Z; Du P.Y; et al (2006). Measurement for mechanical characteristics of asynchronous motors using electromagnetic brake. *Electric Machines and Control*, 2006, 10(3): 275-277

Takehito Kikuchi; Kunihiko Oda; Shiro Isozumi; Yuuki Ohyama; Naoto Shichi & Junji Furusho (2008). Measurement of Reaching Movement with 6-DOF Upper Rehabilitation System "Robotherapist". *30th Annual International IEEE EMBS Conference Vancouver*, British Columbia, Canada, 4262-4265, 2008

Tsoi, Y.H. & Xie, S.Q. (2008). Impedance control of ankle rehabilitation robot, *2008 IEEE International Conference on Robotics and Biomimetics*, p 840-5, 2008

Wang S.H. & Zhang Y (2003). Constant Tension Control System Based on the Radius Feedback. *Information Technology and Information*, 2003, 1: 37-38

Xu Baoguo; Peng Si & Song Aiguo (2011). Upper-limb rehabilitation robot based on motor imagery EEG, *Jiqiren/Robot*, v 33, n 3, p 307-313, May 2011

Xu J L; Fan Y P & Li L (2008). The application of PNF Technology in Cerebral palsy rehabilitation. *Chinese Journal of Trauma and Disability Medicine*, 2008, 16(6)

Zhang G R (2004). The structure, properties and selection of magnetic powder clutch and magnetic powder brakes. *Machine Development*, 2004, 10(33): 77-79

Virtual Reality to Simulate Adaptive Walking in Unstructured Terrains for Multi-Legged Robots

Umar Asif

Additional information is available at the end of the chapter

http://dx.doi.org/10.5772/46404

1. Introduction

Walking robots posses capabilities to perform adaptive locomotion and motion planning over unstructured terrains and therefore are in the focus of high interest to the researchers all over the world. However, true adaptive locomotion in difficult terrains involves various problems such as foot-planning, path-planning, gait dynamic stability and autonomous navigation in the presence of external disturbances [1]. There is a large volume of research work that is dedicated to the development of walking robots that exhibit biologically inspired locomotion. In this context, an insect-sized flying robot [2], an ape-like robot [3], an amphibious snake-like robot ACM-R5 [4], for-legged robots like Big Dog and Little Dog, an ant-inspired robot ANTON [5] and LAURON [6], are some well-known examples of bio-mimetic robots. A related study [7] describes an implementation of a neurobiological leg control system on a hexapod robot for improving the navigation of the robot over uneven terrains.

However, the crucial problem that the general approaches suffer is the challenging task of achieving accurate transition between different gaits while maintaining stable locomotion in the presence of external disturbances [1]. In natural rough terrains, prior knowledge of the terrain information is not always available therefore, this chapter aims to make use of virtual reality technology to inspect adaptive locomotion over unknown irregular terrains for possible improvement in gait mobility and stability in the presence of unexpected disturbances.

In order to evaluate and inspect the dynamic characteristics of an adaptive locomotion over an unstructured terrain, it is difficult and time consuming to conduct real-world experiments often. Therefore, virtual prototyping technology serves a prime role that results in better design optimization and allows inspection and evaluation of the mathematical models specifically those which are complicated or impractical to estimate using real prototypes in real-world [16-18]. Virtual Reality Technology provides a rapid method of validating several characteristics of a mathematical model using dynamic simulations for the identification of potential errors in early design stages [8]. Possible defects can be identified and removed by modifying the simulation model itself which is less time consuming and practical if to be performed often. Thus, the complete control algorithm can be analyzed using the simulation model [8].

The chapter is structured as follows: second section describes the mathematical modelling of a hexapod robot using kinematics and dynamics equations. In the third section, gait generation is described for planning cyclic wave and ripple gaits. Fourth section is dedicated to the gait analysis over flat and uneven terrains. Finally, the chapter draws conclusion on the significance of using a simulation-based approach for rapid-prototyping of gait generation methods in multi-legged robots.

2. Mathematical modeling and design

The studies conducted in [8] & [9] use SimMechanics software to construct a simulation-based model of a six-legged robot which comprises of several subsystems interconnected to each other as described in Fig. 1. The physical robot is represented using a subsystem known as "plant". Another subsystem which represents the kinematic engine contains the forward and reverse kinematics of the robot. Other subsystems include a gait generation block and an environment sensing block as shown in Fig. 1. The aforesaid subsystems are further described in the following subsections.

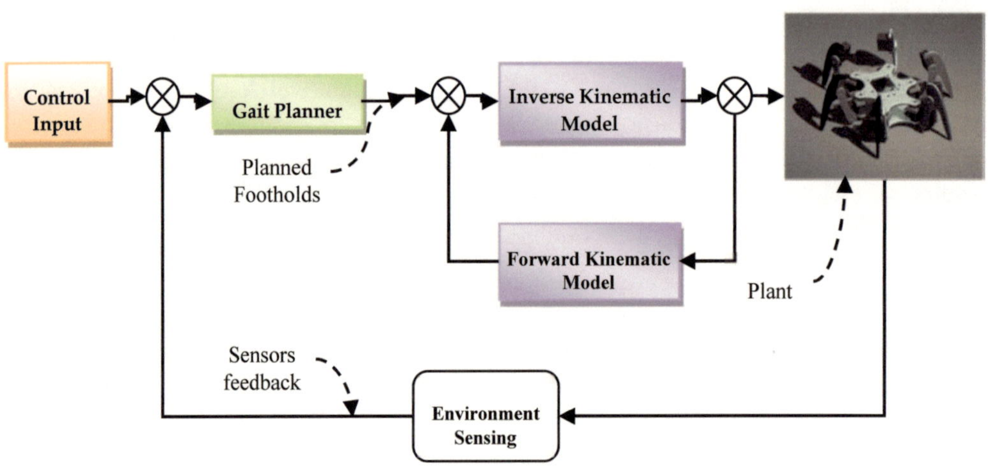

Figure 1. Overall control loop of the simulation model.

2.1. Plant subsystem

The "plant" is shown in Fig. 2 in the form of a block diagram that provides complete information about the mass, motion axes and moments of inertia of the bodies and their subassemblies. Each leg attached to the main body is considered as a 3-degree of freedom serial manipulator which acts as the actuating element in the overall simulation model. Furthermore, the block diagram shows joints to describe appropriate connections between the rigid bodies which provide an opportunity for actuation and sensing. Fig. 3 & Fig. 4 show the respective subsystems of a hexapod robot as investigated in [8, 9].

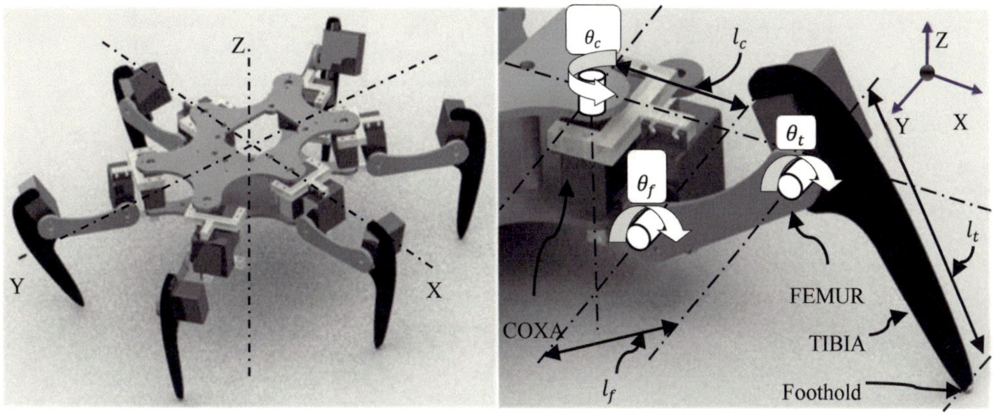

Figure 2. A six-legged hexapod robot and its leg kinematic representation.

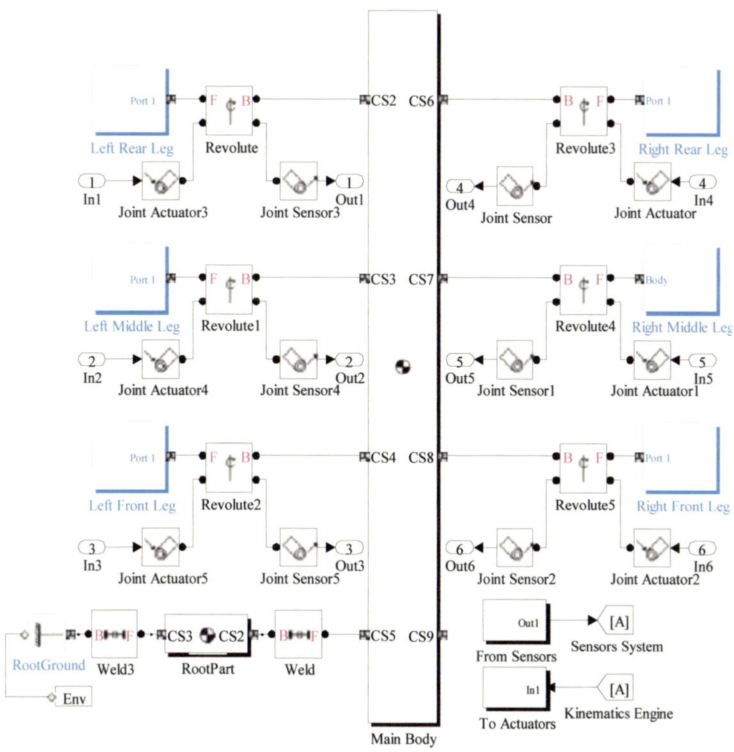

Figure 3. SimMechanics model representing the plant subsystem of a hexapod robot.

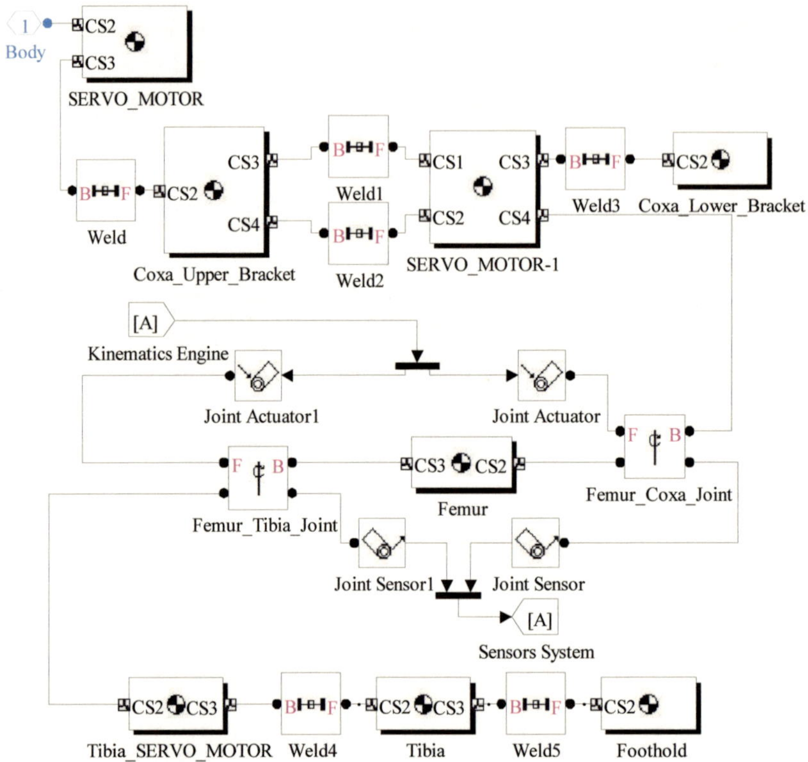

Figure 4. SimMechanics model of an individual leg as a 3-DOF serial manipulator.

2.2. Kinematics engine

The kinematic model of the robot reported here uses forward and inverse kinematic equations of a 3-DOF serial manipulator to control the foothold in 3D-space. The research studies [8 - 14] describe the mathematical modelling of a 3-DOF leg in 3D space in terms of a forward kinematic model. The details are given in the following subsections.

2.2.1. Forward kinematics

Each leg is modelled as a 3-DOF serial manipulator comprised of three members as: coxa, femur and tibia inter-related using pin joints. The joint connecting the body with the coxa (BodyCoxa-joint) is represented by θ_c, the joint connecting coxa with the femur (CoxaFemur-joint) is represented by θ_f, and the joint connecting the femur with the tibia (FemurTibia-joint) is represented by θ_t. The position of the foothold $[Xt\ Yt\ Zt]^T$ with respect to BodyCoxa-joint motion axis is obtained using Denavit Hartenberg convention and expressed as a general homogenous transformation expression as given by (1). Table1 enlists the D-H parameters of the robot leg shown in Fig.5.

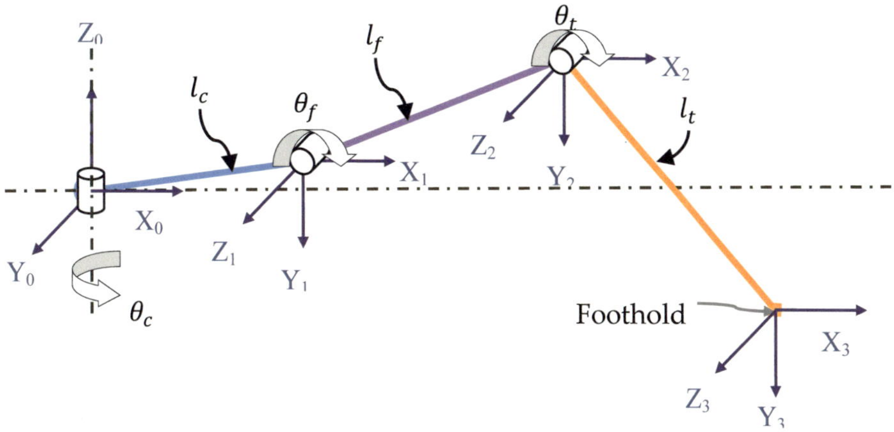

Figure 5. Kinematic Configuration of an individual leg.

i	α_i	θ_i	a_i	d_i
0	0	0	0	0
1	90	θ_c	l_c	0
2	0	θ_f	l_f	0
3	0	θ_t	l_t	0

Table 1. D-T parameters of leg shown in Fig. 5

$$\begin{bmatrix} Xt \\ Yt \\ Zt \end{bmatrix} = \begin{bmatrix} cos\theta_c & 0 & sin\theta_c & lccos\theta_c \\ sin\theta_c & 0 & -cos\theta_c & lcsin\theta_c \\ 0 & 1 & 0 & 0 \\ 0 & 0 & 0 & 1 \end{bmatrix} \times$$

$$\begin{bmatrix} cos\theta_f & -sin\theta_f & 0 & lfcos\theta_f \\ sin\theta_f & cos\theta_f & 0 & lfsin\theta_f \\ 0 & 0 & 1 & 0 \\ 0 & 0 & 0 & 1 \end{bmatrix} \times \begin{bmatrix} cos\theta_t & -sin\theta_t & 0 & ltcos\theta_t \\ sin\theta_t & cos\theta_t & 0 & ltsin\theta_t \\ 0 & 0 & 1 & 0 \\ 0 & 0 & 0 & 1 \end{bmatrix} \tag{1}$$

Solving (1) yields (2) which can be further simplified to (3).

$$\begin{bmatrix} Xt \\ Yt \\ Zt \end{bmatrix} = \begin{bmatrix} lccos\theta_c + lfcos\theta_c cos\theta_f + ltcos\theta_c cos\theta_f cos\theta_t - ltcos\theta_c sin\theta_f sin\theta_t \\ lcsin\theta_c + lfcos\theta_f sin\theta_c + ltcos\theta_f sin\theta_c cos\theta_t - ltsin\theta_c sin\theta_f sin\theta_t \\ lfsin\theta_f + ltcos\theta_f sin\theta_t + ltcos\theta_t sin\theta_f \end{bmatrix} \tag{2}$$

$$\begin{bmatrix} Xt \\ Yt \\ Zt \end{bmatrix} = \begin{bmatrix} cos\theta_c\,(lc + lt\ cos\theta_{f+t} + lf\ cos\theta_f) \\ sin\theta_c(lc + ltcos\theta_{f+t} + lfcos\theta_f) \\ ltsin\theta_{f+t} + lfsin\theta_f \end{bmatrix} \tag{3}$$

2.2.2. X-Y-Z (roll-pitch-yaw) body rotations

In order to obtain the position of foothold with reference to robot motion centroid, the body rotations in 3D-space must be brought into consideration. Body rotations (Roll-Pitch-Yaw) representation for orientation is given by (4).

$$\begin{cases} Roll = psi\ (\psi) = Body\ Rotation\ about\ X - axis \\ Yaw = gamma\ (\gamma) = Body\ Rotation\ about\ Z - axis \\ Pitch = phi\ (\varphi) = Body\ Rotation\ about\ Y - axis \end{cases}$$

$$Ft = R_{x,\psi} \times R_{y,\varphi} \times R_{z,\gamma} \tag{4}$$

Using general homogenous transformation matrices, the foot location with respect to body coordinate system can be obtained using (4) as given by (5)

$$\begin{bmatrix} Ft_x \\ Ft_y \\ Ft_z \end{bmatrix} = \begin{bmatrix} 1 & 0 & 0 & 0 \\ 0 & cos\psi & -sin\psi & 0 \\ 0 & sin\psi & cos\psi & 0 \\ 0 & 0 & 0 & 1 \end{bmatrix} \times \begin{bmatrix} cos\varphi & 0 & sin\varphi & 0 \\ 0 & 1 & 0 & 0 \\ -sin\varphi & 0 & cos\varphi & 0 \\ 0 & 0 & 0 & 1 \end{bmatrix} \times \begin{bmatrix} cos\gamma & -sin\gamma & 0 & 0 \\ sin\gamma & cos\gamma & 0 & 0 \\ 0 & 0 & 1 & 0 \\ 0 & 0 & 0 & 1 \end{bmatrix} \times \begin{bmatrix} T_x \\ T_y \\ T_z \end{bmatrix} \tag{5}$$

$$\begin{bmatrix} Ft_x \\ Ft_y \\ Ft_z \end{bmatrix} =$$

$$= \begin{bmatrix} T_z sin\gamma + T_x cos\gamma cos\varphi - T_y cos\gamma sin\varphi \\ T_x(cos\psi sin\varphi + cos\varphi sin\gamma sin\psi) + T_y(cos\varphi cos\psi - sin\gamma sin\varphi sin\psi) - T_z cos\gamma sin\psi \\ T_x(sin\varphi sin\psi - cos\varphi cos\psi sin\gamma) + T_y(cos\varphi sin\psi + cos\psi sin\gamma sin\varphi) + T_z cos\gamma cos\psi \end{bmatrix} \tag{6}$$

Where,

$$\begin{cases} T_x = LegOffsetX + Xt \\ T_y = LegOffsetY + Yt \\ T_z = LegOffsetZ + Zt \end{cases}$$

Thus, the forward kinematic model of the leg can be expressed by (6), also investigated in [13].

2.2.3. Inverse kinematics

In order to obtain the inverse kinematics solution, we solve the general homogenous transformation expression for a 3-DOF serial manipulator in 3D-space given by (7) as (8) & (9).

$$\mathrm{R} = \mathrm{T_1} \times \mathrm{T_2} \times \mathrm{T_3} \tag{7}$$

$$\mathrm{inv(T_1)} \times \mathrm{R} = \mathrm{T_2} \times \mathrm{T_3} \tag{8}$$

$$\mathrm{inv(T_2)} \times \mathrm{inv(T_1)} \times \mathrm{R} = \mathrm{T_3} \tag{9}$$

Where,

$$R = \begin{bmatrix} r_{11} & r_{12} & r_{13} & P_x \\ r_{21} & r_{22} & r_{23} & P_y \\ r_{31} & r_{32} & r_{33} & P_z \\ 0 & 0 & 0 & 1 \end{bmatrix}, T_1 = \begin{bmatrix} cos\theta_c & 0 & sin\theta_c & lccos\theta_c \\ sin\theta_c & 0 & -cos\theta_c & lcsin\theta_c \\ 0 & 1 & 0 & 0 \\ 0 & 0 & 0 & 1 \end{bmatrix}$$

$$T_2 = \begin{bmatrix} cos\theta_f & -sin\theta_f & 0 & lfcos\theta_f \\ sin\theta_f & cos\theta_f & 0 & lfsin\theta_f \\ 0 & 0 & 1 & 0 \\ 0 & 0 & 0 & 1 \end{bmatrix}, T_3 = \begin{bmatrix} cos\theta_t & -sin\theta_t & 0 & ltcos\theta_t \\ sin\theta_t & cos\theta_t & 0 & ltsin\theta_t \\ 0 & 0 & 1 & 0 \\ 0 & 0 & 0 & 1 \end{bmatrix}$$

Solving (8) yields (10)

$$\begin{bmatrix} cos\theta_c & sin\theta_c & 0 & -lc \\ 0 & 0 & 1 & 0 \\ sin\theta_c & -cos\theta_c & 0 & 0 \\ 0 & 0 & 0 & 1 \end{bmatrix} \times \begin{bmatrix} r_{11} & r_{12} & r_{13} & P_x \\ r_{21} & r_{22} & r_{23} & P_y \\ r_{31} & r_{32} & r_{33} & P_z \\ 0 & 0 & 0 & 1 \end{bmatrix} =$$

$$= \begin{bmatrix} cos\theta_f & -sin\theta_f & 0 & lfcos\theta_f \\ sin\theta_f & cos\theta_f & 0 & lfsin\theta_f \\ 0 & 0 & 1 & 0 \\ 0 & 0 & 0 & 1 \end{bmatrix} \times \begin{bmatrix} cos\theta_t & -sin\theta_t & 0 & ltcos\theta_t \\ sin\theta_t & cos\theta_t & 0 & ltsin\theta_t \\ 0 & 0 & 1 & 0 \\ 0 & 0 & 0 & 1 \end{bmatrix} \tag{10}$$

Comparing r_{34} elements of both sides of the (10) yields (11).

$$P_x sin\theta_c - P_y cos\theta_c = 0 \tag{11}$$

Thus, BodyCoxa joint angle θ_c can be determined from (11) as given by (12).

$$\theta_c = ATAN2(P_y, P_x) \tag{12}$$

Solving (9) yields (13)

$$\begin{bmatrix} cos\theta_f & sin\theta_f & 0 & -lf \\ -sin\theta_f & cos\theta_f & 0 & 0 \\ 0 & 0 & 1 & 0 \\ 0 & 0 & 0 & 1 \end{bmatrix} \times \begin{bmatrix} cos\theta_c & sin\theta_c & 0 & -lc \\ 0 & 0 & 1 & 0 \\ sin\theta_c & -cos\theta_c & 0 & 0 \\ 0 & 0 & 0 & 1 \end{bmatrix} \times$$

$$\times \begin{bmatrix} r_{11} & r_{12} & r_{13} & P_x \\ r_{21} & r_{22} & r_{23} & P_y \\ r_{31} & r_{32} & r_{33} & P_z \\ 0 & 0 & 0 & 1 \end{bmatrix} = \begin{bmatrix} cos\theta_t & -sin\theta_t & 0 & lt \times cos\theta_t \\ sin\theta_t & cos\theta_t & 0 & lt \times sin\theta_t \\ 0 & 0 & 1 & 0 \\ 0 & 0 & 0 & 1 \end{bmatrix} \tag{13}$$

Comparing r_{14}, r_{24} elements of both sides of (13) we get (14) & (15)

$$cos\theta_f(P_x cos\theta_c - lc + P_y sin\theta_c) - lf + P_z sin\theta_f = ltcos\theta_t \tag{14}$$

$$P_z cos\theta_f - sin\theta_f(P_x cos\theta_c - lc + P_y sin\theta_c) = ltsin\theta_t \tag{15}$$

Taking positive squares of both sides of (14) & (15) and summing them-up yields (16).

$$[cos\theta_f \times \Lambda - lf + P_z \times sin\theta_f]^2 + [P_z \times cos\theta_f - sin\theta_f \times \mathrm{A}]^2 = lt^2 \tag{16}$$

Where,

$$A = (P_x cos\theta_c - lc + P_y sin\theta_c)$$

Further solving (16) yields:

$$\frac{(A^2 + lf^2 + P_z{}^2 - lt^2)}{2lf} = cos\theta_f \times A + sin\theta_f P_z$$

$$G = cos\theta_f \times A + sin\theta_f P_z \tag{17}$$

Where,

$$G = \frac{(A^2 + lf^2 + P_z{}^2 - lt^2)}{2lf}$$

Using the trigonometry identities given by (18) & (19), (17) can be further solved to determine CoxaFemur angle as given by (20)

$$cos\theta_x \times a + sin\theta_x \times b = c \tag{18}$$

$$\theta_x = ATAN2(b, a) + ATAN2((\sqrt{a^2 + b^2 - c^2}), c) \tag{19}$$

$$\theta_f = ATAN2(P_z, A) + ATAN2(\left(\sqrt{A^2 + P_z{}^2 - G^2}\right), G) \tag{20}$$

Where,

$$a = A, b = P_z, c = G$$

Dividing (14) by (15) yields (21) which can be further simplified to obtain FemurTibia angle as given by (22)

$$\frac{ltsin\theta_t}{ltcos\theta_t} = \frac{P_z cos\theta_f - sin\theta_f(P_x cos\theta_c - lc + P_y sin\theta_c)}{cos\theta_f(P_x cos\theta_c - lc + P_y sin\theta_c) - lf + P_z sin\theta_f} \tag{21}$$

$$\theta_t = ATAN2((P_z \cos\theta_f - \sin\theta_f A), (A \times \cos\theta_f - l_f + \sin\theta_f P_z)) \tag{22}$$

2.3. Robot dynamics

Lagrange-Euler formulation is selected here to derive the dynamics of the robot leg. The Lagrange-Euler equations yield a dynamic expression that can be expressed as given by (23).

$$\tau_e - J^T F = M(q)\ddot{q} + H(q, \dot{q}) + G(q) \tag{23}$$

In (23), M(q) represents the mass matrix, H incorporates the centrifugal and Coriolis terms, and G(q) is the gravity matrix. τ_e contains active joint torques and F is a matrix representing ground contact forces estimated using force sensors embedded in each foot.

2.3.1. Foothold dynamics

The position of the foothold with respect to BodyCoxa joint motion axis is given by (3). Time derivate of (3) yields velocity of the foothold as given by (24) which can be expressed in form of Jacobean as given by (25)

$$\begin{bmatrix} \dot{X}_t \\ \dot{Y}_t \\ \dot{Z}_t \end{bmatrix} = \begin{bmatrix} -(lc \times sin\theta_c + lf cos\theta_f sin\theta_c + lt sin\theta_c cos\theta_{f+t}) & -(lf cos\theta_c sin\theta_f + lt cos\theta_c sin\theta_{f+t}) & -(lt \times cos\theta_c \times sin\theta_{f+t}) \\ lc \times cos\theta_c + lf cos\theta_c cos\theta_f + lt cos\theta_c cos\theta_{f+t} & -(lf sin\theta_c sin\theta_f + lt sin\theta_c sin\theta_{f+t}) & -(lt \times sin\theta_c \times sin\theta_{f+t}) \\ 0 & lf cos\theta_f + lt cos\theta_{f+t} & lt \times cos\theta_{f+t} \end{bmatrix} \times \begin{bmatrix} \dot{\theta}_c \\ \dot{\theta}_f \\ \dot{\theta}_t \end{bmatrix} \tag{24}$$

$$\dot{X}_t = J_D \dot{\theta}_t \tag{25}$$

Time derivate of (25) yields acceleration of the foothold as given by (26)

$$\ddot{X}_t = \dot{J}_D \dot{\theta}_t + J_D \ddot{\theta}_t \tag{26}$$

2.3.2. Femurtibia joint dynamics

The position of the FemurTibia joint with respect to BodyCoxa joint motion axis is given by (27).

$$\begin{bmatrix} X_f \\ Y_f \\ Z_f \end{bmatrix} = \begin{bmatrix} lc\ cos\theta_c + lf\ cos\theta_c\ cos\theta_f) \\ (lc sin\theta_c + lf cos\theta_f sin\theta_c) \\ 0 \end{bmatrix} \tag{27}$$

Time derivate of (27) yields velocity matrix as given by (28) which can be expressed in terms of Jacobean as (29)

$$\begin{bmatrix} \dot{X}_f \\ \dot{Y}_f \\ \dot{Z}_f \end{bmatrix} = \begin{bmatrix} -(lc\ sin\theta_c + lf\ sin\theta_c\ cos\theta_f) & -(lf\ cos\theta_c\ sin\theta_f) & 0 \\ lc\ cos\theta_c + lf\ cos\theta_c\ cos\theta_f & -(lf\ sin\theta_c\ sin\theta_f) & 0 \\ 0 & 0 & 0 \end{bmatrix} \times \begin{bmatrix} \dot{\theta}_c \\ \dot{\theta}_f \\ \dot{\theta}_t \end{bmatrix} \tag{28}$$

$$\dot{X}_f = J_D \dot{\theta}_f \tag{29}$$

Time derivate of (29) yields acceleration matrix as given by (30) which can be further expressed in form of Jacobean as given by (31).

$$\begin{bmatrix} \ddot{X}_f \\ \ddot{Y}_f \\ \ddot{Z}_f \end{bmatrix} = \begin{bmatrix} -lc\ cos\theta_c \dot{\theta}_c^{\ 2} - lf\ cos\theta_c cos\theta_f \dot{\theta}_c^{\ 2} - lf\ cos\theta_c cos\theta_f \dot{\theta}_f^{\ 2} - \ddot{\theta}_c lf cos\theta_f sin\theta_c - \ddot{\theta}_f lf cos\theta_c sin\theta_f - \ddot{\theta}_c lc sin\theta_c + 2\dot{\theta}_c \dot{\theta}_f lf sin\theta_c sin\theta_f \\ -lc\ sin\theta_c \dot{\theta}_c^{\ 2} - lf\ cos\theta_f sin\theta_c \dot{\theta}_c^{\ 2} - lf\ sin\theta_c cos\theta_f \dot{\theta}_f^{\ 2} + \ddot{\theta}_c lf cos\theta_f cos\theta_c - \ddot{\theta}_f lf sin\theta_c sin\theta_f + \ddot{\theta}_c lc cos\theta_c - 2\dot{\theta}_c \dot{\theta}_f lf cos\theta_c sin\theta_f \\ 0 \end{bmatrix} \tag{30}$$

$$\ddot{X}_f = \dot{J}_D\dot{\theta}_f + J_D\ddot{\theta}_f \quad (31)$$

2.3.3. Coxafemur joint dynamics

The position of the CoxaFemur joint with respect to BodyCoxa joint motion axis is given by (32).

$$\begin{bmatrix} X_c \\ Y_c \\ Z_c \end{bmatrix} = \begin{bmatrix} lccos\theta_c \\ lcsin\theta_c \\ 0 \end{bmatrix} \quad (32)$$

Time derivate of (32) yields velocity matrix as given by (33) which can be expressed in terms of Jacobean as (34).

$$\begin{bmatrix} \dot{X}_c \\ \dot{Y}_c \\ \dot{Z}_c \end{bmatrix} = \begin{bmatrix} -lc\ sin\theta_c & 0 & 0 \\ lc\ cos\theta_c & 0 & 0 \\ 0 & 0 & 0 \end{bmatrix} \times \begin{bmatrix} \dot{\theta}_c \\ \dot{\theta}_f \\ \dot{\theta}_t \end{bmatrix} \quad (33)$$

$$\dot{X}_c = J_D\dot{\theta}_c \quad (34)$$

Time derivate of (34) yields acceleration matrix (35) which can be expressed in terms of Jacobean as (36).

$$\begin{bmatrix} \ddot{X}_c \\ \ddot{Y}_c \\ \ddot{Z}_c \end{bmatrix} = \begin{bmatrix} -lc\ cos\theta_c\dot{\theta}_c^{\ 2} - \ddot{\theta}_c lcsin\theta_c \\ -lc\ sin\theta_c\dot{\theta}_c^{\ 2} + \ddot{\theta}_c lccos\theta_c \\ 0 \end{bmatrix} \quad (35)$$

$$\ddot{X}_c = \dot{J}_D\dot{\theta}_c + J_D\ddot{\theta}_c \quad (36)$$

2.4. Control algorithm

Dynamics of a robot as given by (23) can be further described using Lagrange-Euler formulations as given by (37).

$$Q = M(q)\ddot{q} + H(q,\dot{q}) + G(q) \quad (37)$$

Where,

$$M = \sum_{i=1}^{n} (J_{Mi}^T m_i J_{Mi} + \frac{1}{2} J_{Ri}^T I_i^0 J_{Ri})$$

The kinetic energy and potential energy of a link can be expressed as given by (38) & (39).

$$K = \frac{1}{2}\dot{q}^T M(q)\dot{q} \quad (38)$$

$$P = \sum_{i=1}^{n} m_i g^T r_{ci} \quad (39)$$

The mass matrix M of the robot leg can be written by assuming the leg as a serial manipulator consisting of three links as given by (40).

$$M = \sum_{i=1}^{3}(J_{Mi}^{T} m_i J_{Mi} + \frac{1}{2} J_{Ri}^{T} I_i^0 J_{Ri}) \tag{40}$$

The moments of inertia for each link (coxa, femur & tibia) of the leg can be determined from (41), (42) & (43).

$$I_c^0 = T_c^0 I_c^c T_c^T \tag{41}$$

$$I_f^0 = T_f^0 I_f^f T_f^T \tag{42}$$

$$I_t^0 = T_t^0 I_t^t T_t^T \tag{43}$$

The Jacobean terms of (40) can be determined from expressions (44), (45) & (46).

$$J_{Mc} = \begin{bmatrix} -lc\ sin\theta_c & 0 & 0 \\ lc\ cos\theta_c & 0 & 0 \\ 0 & 0 & 0 \end{bmatrix}, J_{Rc} = \begin{bmatrix} 0 & 0 & 0 \\ 0 & 0 & 0 \\ 1 & 0 & 0 \end{bmatrix} \tag{44}$$

$$J_{Mf} = \begin{bmatrix} -(lc\ sin\theta_c + lf\ sin\theta_c\, cos\theta_f) & -(lf\ cos\theta_c\, sin\theta_f) & 0 \\ lc\ cos\theta_c + lf\ cos\theta_c\, cos\theta_f & -(lf\ sin\theta_c\, sin\theta_f) & 0 \\ 0 & 0 & 0 \end{bmatrix}, J_{Rf} = \begin{bmatrix} 0 & 0 & 0 \\ 0 & 0 & 0 \\ 1 & 0 & 0 \end{bmatrix} \tag{45}$$

$$J_{Mt} = \begin{bmatrix} -(lcsin\theta_c + lfcos\theta_f\, sin\theta_c + ltsin\theta_c cos\theta_{f+t}) & -(lfcos\theta_c\, sin\theta_f + ltcos\theta_c sin\theta_{f+t}) & -(ltcos\theta_c\, sin\theta_{f+t}) \\ lccos\theta_c + lfcos\theta_c\, cos\theta_f + ltcos\theta_c cos\theta_{f+t} & -(lfsin\theta_c sin\theta_f + ltsin\theta_c\, sin\theta_{f+t}) & -(ltsin\theta_c\, sin\theta_{f+t}) \\ 0 & lfcos\theta_f + ltcos\theta_{f+t} & ltcos\theta_{f+t} \end{bmatrix}, J_{Rt} = \begin{bmatrix} 0 & 0 & 0 \\ 0 & 0 & 0 \\ 1 & 0 & 0 \end{bmatrix} \tag{46}$$

The velocity coupling vector H and the gravitational matrices are given by (47) & (48)

$$H_{ijk} = \sum_{j=1}^{n} \sum_{k=1}^{n} (\frac{\partial M_{ij}}{\partial q_k} - \frac{1}{2} \frac{\partial M_{jk}}{\partial q_i}) \tag{47}$$

$$G_i = \sum_{j=1}^{n} m_j g^T J_{Mj}^{i} \tag{48}$$

Using desired time-based trajectories of each joint, the robot can be commanded to follow a desired path with the help of a computed torque control law as given by (49)

$$D(q)(\ddot{q} - k_D \dot{e} - k_p e + H(q, \dot{q}) + G(q) = Q \tag{49}$$

The error vector "e" is given by (50)

$$e = q - q_d \tag{50}$$

Thus, the computed control law can be described by (51).

$$D(q)\ddot{q_d} + H(q,\dot{q}) + G(q) + D(q)(-k_D\dot{e} - k_P e) = Q \quad (51)$$

3. Gait generation

Gait generation is the main topic of investigation in the field of legged locomotion. Mobility and stability are two important factors which require specific attention while planning a gait for locomotion in natural environments. Generally, the gaits found in nature feature sequential

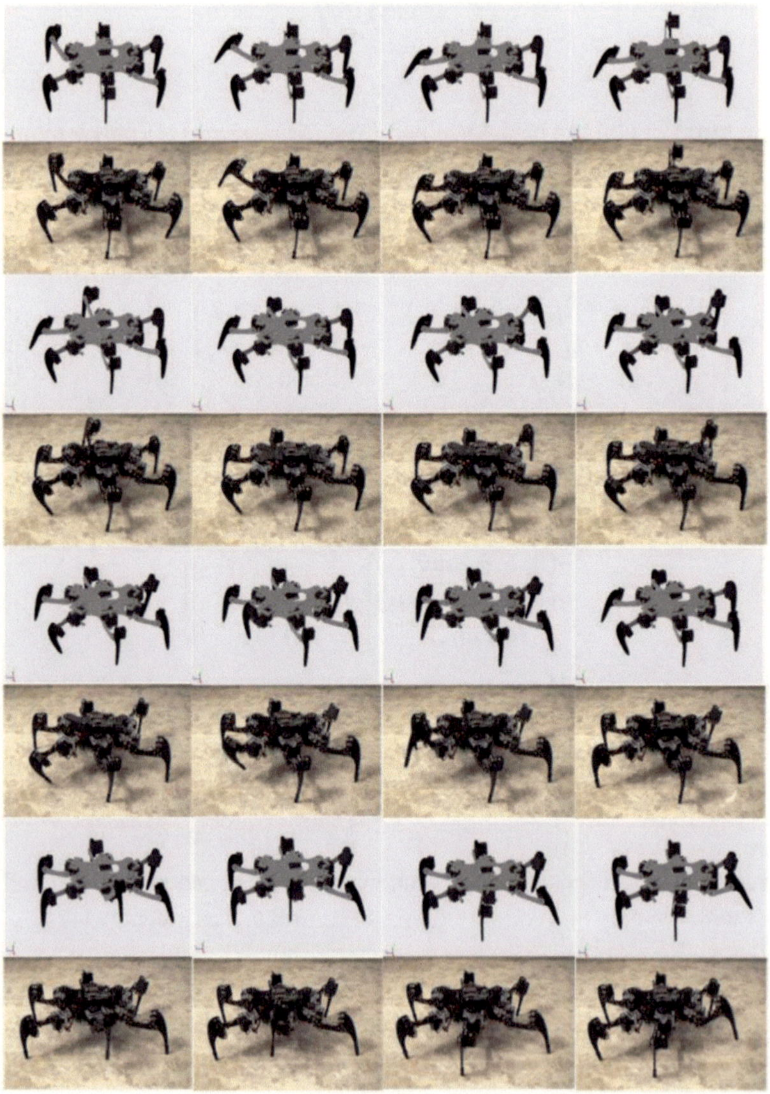

Figure 6. A comparative representation of wave gait generation in simulation model and actual prototype robot over a smooth flat surface.

motion of legs and the body. A large volume of work [5-14] deals with biologically-inspired gaits to replicate this sequential motion pattern found in insects into real robots. The gaits investigated here are cyclic periodic continuous gaits (wave gait & ripple gait) as investigated in [10 & 12]. Gait generation occurs in the gait planner shown in Fig. 1, where commanded foothold locations and orientations are combined with gait sequences to generate a sequential pattern of footholds in 3D-space. The computed leg-sequential pattern is submitted to the inverse kinematic model to determine appropriate joint angles to achieve the desired location. The motion of each leg is determined by the mathematical model. The sequential patterns of leg-lifts for a 12-step ripple gait and a 19-step wave gait are shown in Fig. 16 while, Fig. 6 shows a pictorial demonstration of the gait generation in simulation model and the actual prototype robot over a smooth flat surface.

SimMechanics provides a diverse library of software sensors to obtain information from the environment. These sensors mainly include rigid-body sensors and joint sensors. As shown in the figure, the sensors subsystem outlines a network of sensors employed at each leg and their respective joints. Sensors attached to the legs are used to obtain the absolute location and orientation of each foothold in 3D-space while the joint sensors provide information about each joint's linear and angular rates and accelerations. This sensory network acquires the information from each sensor, filters the data to reject noise. Motion planner, uses the feedback to compute corrections between the commanded data and the recorded data. A Butterworth high-pass 6th order digital filter is used to filter the sensor noise.

4. Dynamic simulations

The objective of carrying out dynamic simulations is to test the validity of the mathematical model and perform gait analysis over uneven terrains. In order to realize the first objective, the mathematical model is simulated first in forward dynamics mode and then in inverse dynamics mode. The robot is commanded to walk between two fixed points 2 meters apart. Straight line walking is achieved with an attitude control using GPS and Compass sensors feedback. Fig. 7 show respective views of robot straight-line walking achieved over flat surfaces using Microsoft Robotics Studio [15].

4.1. Test 1 – Forward dynamics mode

In forward dynamics mode, the objective is to analyze the torques produced at the joints provided each joint is actuated with a motion profile consisting of joint rotation, velocity and acceleration. The robot is steered with a periodic cyclic gait. The footholds planned by the gait generator are passed to the kinematics engine and appropriate joint angles are computed in return. The obtained joint angle profile of each joint is differentiated to compute joint rates and accelerations. Finally, the computed joint motion profiles are fed to the joint actuators to simulate the motion. Joint sensors are used to record the actual

Figure 7. A view of a hexapod robot being steered between two fixed points (2-meter apart) over a flat surface.

torque produced during the entire sequential motion. Actual torques data obtained from the simulation and those determined by the dynamic model are plotted as shown by Fig. 8 (D).

4.2. Test 2 – Inverse dynamics mode

In inverse dynamics mode, the objective is to analyze the joint motion profiles provided the joints are actuated using torques. Joint sensors are used to record joint rotations, velocities

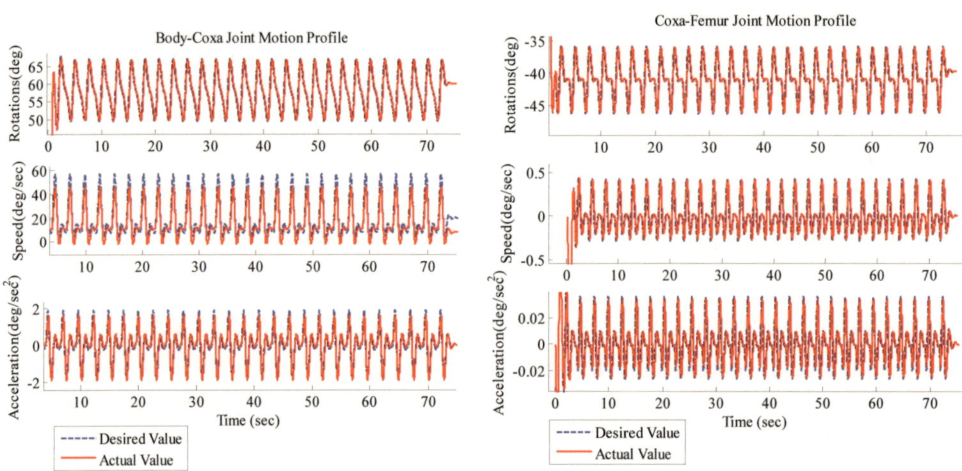

A B

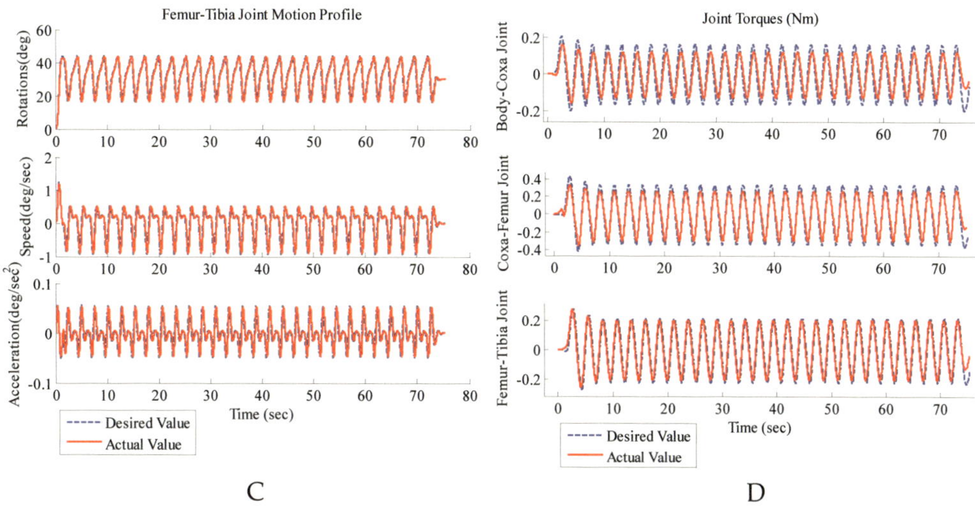

Figure 8. Comparative representation of sensors feedback and mathematical model results. (A) Motion profile of BodyCoxa joint. (B) Motion profile of CoxaFemur joint. (C) Motion profile of FemurTibia joint. (D) Joint torques.

and accelerations which are then matched with those determined by the dynamic model to study the errors. The comparative representation of actual motion data and desired data is shown by Fig. 8(A), Fig. 8(B) & Fig. 8(C). The close matching of the actual and desired data confirms the validity of inverse model for walking over flat surfaces.

4.3. Test 3 – Gait analysis over an uneven terrain

The objective of this test is to conduct a gait analysis in terms of robot speed, joint reaction torques and reaction forces at the foothold during robot-environment interactions.

4.3.1. Reaction forces at the foothold and reaction torques at the joints

In order to study an adaptive gait over an uneven terrain, we must first describe the joint reaction torques due to the reaction forces which arise at the footholds during the leg-terrain interactions.

4.3.1.1. Reaction torque at bodycoxa joint

Considering Fig. 9, the reaction torque about the BodyCoxa joint motion axis can be expressed by (52), further explained by (53) & (54).

$$\vec{\tau}_{BodyCoxa} = \{\vec{r}_1 \times \vec{F}_N + \vec{r}_1 \times \vec{F}_R + \vec{r}_2 \times \overrightarrow{W_{coxa}}\}Nm \tag{52}$$

$$\begin{cases} \vec{r_1} = \left\{(Ft_{x_i}^{G} - X_c)\hat{\imath} + \left(Ft_{y_i}^{G} - Y_c\right)\hat{\jmath} + (Ft_{z_i}^{G} - Z_c)\hat{k}\right\}m \\ \vec{r_2} = \left\{(COM_{x_i}^{G} - X_c)\hat{\imath} + \left(COM_{y_i}^{G} - Y_c\right)\hat{\jmath} + (COM_{z_i}^{G} - Z_c)\hat{k}\right\}m \\ \vec{F_N} = Nornmal\ reaction\ force\ vector\ at\ the\ foothold \\ \vec{F_R} = Friction\ force\ vector\ at\ the\ foothold \\ \vec{W}_{coxa} = Weight\ of\ the\ coxa\ link \\ \begin{bmatrix} X_c \\ Y_c \\ Z_c \end{bmatrix} = \begin{bmatrix} lccos\theta_c \\ lcsin\theta_c \\ 0 \end{bmatrix} = Position\ of\ Bodycoxa\ joint\ axis \end{cases} \tag{53}$$

$$\vec{\tau}_{BodyCoxa} = \left\{(Ft_{x_i}^{G} - X_c)\hat{\imath} + \left(Ft_{y_i}^{G} - Y_c\right)\hat{\jmath} + (Ft_{z_i}^{G} - Z_c)\hat{k}\right\} \times \{F_{Nx}\hat{\imath} + F_{Nx}\hat{\jmath} + F_{Nx}\hat{k}\} + \left\{(Ft_{x_i}^{G} - X_c)\hat{\imath} + \left(Ft_{y_i}^{G} - Y_c\right)\hat{\jmath} + (Ft_{z_i}^{G} - Z_c)\hat{k}\right\} \times \{F_{Rx}\hat{\imath} + F_{Rx}\hat{\jmath} + F_{Rx}\hat{k}\} + \left\{(COM_{x_i}^{G} - X_c)\hat{\imath} + \left(COM_{y_i}^{G} - Y_c\right)\hat{\jmath} + (COM_{z_i}^{G} - Z_c)\hat{k}\right\} \times \{W_{coxa}\hat{\jmath}\} \tag{54}$$

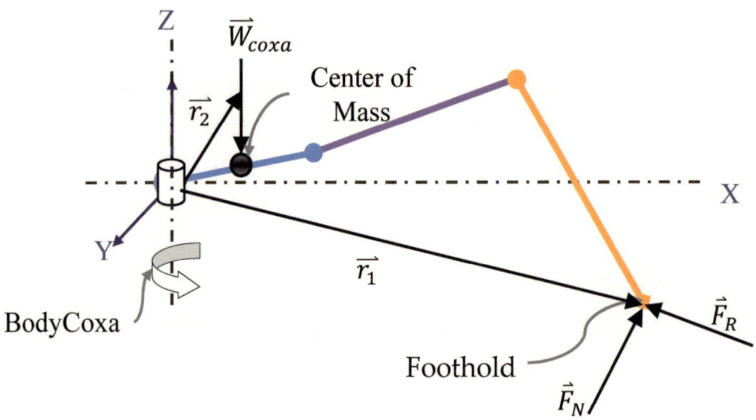

Figure 9. The total torque about BodyCoxa joint axis is equal to the sum of moments due to weight of the coxa link and moments due to friction force and normal reaction forces acting at the foothold.

4.3.1.2. Reaction torque at coxafemur joint

Considering Fig. 10, the reaction torque about the CoxaFemur joint motion axis can be expressed by (55), further explained in (56) & (57).

$$\vec{\tau}_{CoxaFemur} = \{\vec{r}_3 \times \vec{F}_N + \vec{r}_3 \times \vec{F}_R + \vec{r}_4 \times \overrightarrow{W}_{femur}\}Nm \tag{55}$$

$$\begin{cases} \vec{r_3} = \left\{(Ft_{x_i}^{G} - X_f)\hat{\imath} + \left(Ft_{y_i}^{G} - Y_f\right)\hat{\jmath} + (Ft_{z_i}^{G} - Z_f)\hat{k}\right\} m \\ \vec{r_4} = \left\{(COM_{x_i}^{G} - X_f)\hat{\imath} + \left(COM_{y_i}^{G} - Y_f\right)\hat{\jmath} + (COM_{z_i}^{G} - Z_f)\hat{k}\right\} m \\ \vec{F_N} = Nornmal\ reaction\ force\ vector\ at\ the\ foothold \\ \vec{F_R} = Friction\ force\ vector\ at\ the\ foothold \\ \vec{W}_{femur} = Weight\ of\ the\ femur\ link \\ \begin{bmatrix} X_f \\ Y_f \\ Z_f \end{bmatrix} = \begin{bmatrix} lc\ cos\theta_c + lf\ cos\theta_c\, cos\theta_f) \\ (lcsin\theta_c + lfcos\theta_f sin\theta_c) \\ 0 \end{bmatrix} = Position\ of\ CoxaFemurjoint\ axis \end{cases} \tag{56}$$

$$\vec{\tau}_{CoxaFemur} = \left\{(Ft_{x_i}^{G} - X_f)\hat{\imath} + \left(Ft_{y_i}^{G} - Y_f\right)\hat{\jmath} + (Ft_{z_i}^{G} - Z_f)\hat{k}\right\} \times \{F_{Nx}\hat{\imath} + F_{Nx}\hat{\jmath} + F_{Nx}\hat{k}\} + \\ \left\{(Ft_{x_i}^{G} - X_f)\hat{\imath} + \left(Ft_{y_i}^{G} - Y_f\right)\hat{\jmath} + (Ft_{z_i}^{G} - Z_f)\hat{k}\right\} \times \{F_{Rx}\hat{\imath} + F_{Rx}\hat{\jmath} + F_{Rx}\hat{k}\} + \\ \left\{(COM_{x_i}^{G} - X_f)\hat{\imath} + \left(COM_{y_i}^{G} - Y_f\right)\hat{\jmath} + (COM_{z_i}^{G} - Z_f)\hat{k}\right\} \times \{W_{femur}\hat{\jmath}\} \tag{57}$$

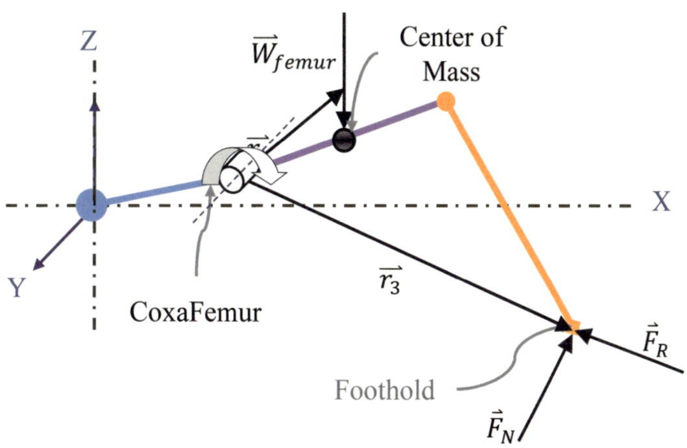

Figure 10. The total torque about CoxaFemur joint axis is equal to the sum of moments due to weight of the femur link and moments due to friction force and normal reaction forces acting at the foothold.

4.3.1.3. Reaction torque at femurtibia joint

Considering Fig. 11, the reaction torque about the FemurTibia joint motion axis can be expressed by (58), further explained in (59) & (60).

$$\vec{\tau}_{FemurTibia} = \{\vec{r}_5 \times \vec{F}_N + \vec{r}_5 \times \vec{F}_R + \vec{r}_6 \times \overrightarrow{W}_{tibia}\} Nm \tag{58}$$

$$\left\{\begin{array}{c} \vec{r_5} = \left\{\left(Ft_{x_i}^{\ G} - X_t\right)\hat{\imath} + \left(Ft_{y_i}^{\ G} - Y_t\right)\hat{\jmath} + \left(Ft_{z_i}^{\ G} - Z_t\right)\hat{k}\right\} m \\ \vec{r_6} = \left\{\left(COM_{x_i}^{\ G} - X_t\right)\hat{\imath} + \left(COM_{y_i}^{\ G} - Y_t\right)\hat{\jmath} + \left(COM_{z_i}^{\ G} - Z_t\right)\hat{k}\right\} m \\ \vec{F_N} = Nornmal\ reaction\ force\ vector\ at\ the\ foothold \\ \vec{F_R} = Friction\ force\ vector\ at\ the\ foothold \\ \vec{W}_{tibia} = Weight\ of\ the\ tibia\ link \\ \begin{bmatrix} X_t \\ Y_t \\ Z_t \end{bmatrix} = \begin{bmatrix} cos\theta_c\ (lc\ +\ lt\ cos\theta_{f+t}\ +\ lf\ cos\theta_f) \\ sin\theta_c(lc + ltcos\theta_{f+t} + lfcos\theta_f) \\ ltsin\theta_{f+t} + lfsin\theta_f \end{bmatrix} = Position\ of\ FemurTibia\ joint\ axis \end{array}\right. \tag{59}$$

$$\begin{aligned} \vec{\tau}_{FemurTibia} = & \left\{\left(Ft_{x_i}^{\ G} - X_t\right)\hat{\imath} + \left(Ft_{y_i}^{\ G} - Y_t\right)\hat{\jmath} + \left(Ft_{z_i}^{\ G} - Z_t\right)\hat{k}\right\} \times \left\{F_{Nx}\hat{\imath} + F_{Nx}\hat{\jmath} + F_{Nx}\hat{k}\right\} + \\ & \left\{\left(Ft_{x_i}^{\ G} - X_t\right)\hat{\imath} + \left(Ft_{y_i}^{\ G} - Y_t\right)\hat{\jmath} + \left(Ft_{z_i}^{\ G} - Z_t\right)\hat{k}\right\} \times \left\{F_{Rx}\hat{\imath} + F_{Rx}\hat{\jmath} + F_{Rx}\hat{k}\right\} + \\ & \left\{\left(COM_{x_i}^{\ G} - X_t\right)\hat{\imath} + \left(COM_{y_i}^{\ G} - Y_t\right)\hat{\jmath} + \left(COM_{z_i}^{\ G} - Z_t\right)\hat{k}\right\} \times \left\{W_{tibia}\hat{\jmath}\right\} \end{aligned} \tag{60}$$

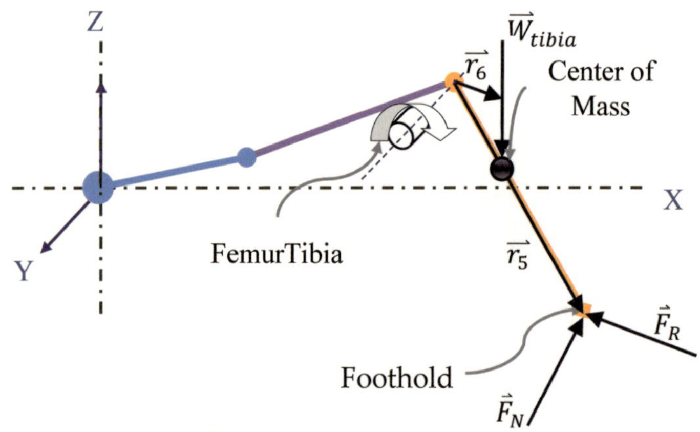

Figure 11. The total torque about FemurTibia joint axis is equal to the sum of moments due to weight of the tibia link and moments due to friction force and normal reaction forces acting at the foothold.

4.3.2. Gait analysis over an uneven terrain

The uneven terrain as shown in Fig. 13 is modelled in Microsoft Robotics Developer Studio. A terrain is modelled with random regions of depression and elevation so that the gait can be analyzed under the influence of unexpected disturbances. The robot is steered between defined waypoints and the joints torques are investigated with different gait patterns. Fig. 12(A) shows a comparative representation of torques computed by our mathematical model and those obtained through joint sensors provided by the simulation engine. The results shown in Fig. 12 are those obtained when the robot was steered with a fast-speed ripple gait. As evident from the forces plot shown in Fig. 12(B), friction force is close to the normal reaction point at some points and exceeds the normal reaction force at some other points which signifies that the robot experienced significant degrees of slip/drift which walking through those regions of the terrain. As a consequence, the mathematical model failed to determine adequate torques at the joints to counter the drift each foothold is experiencing while the locomotion. Therefore, the fast-speed ripple gait was found inefficient over an unexpected terrain due to the non-uniform distribution of payload about the two sides of the robot body in its support pattern.

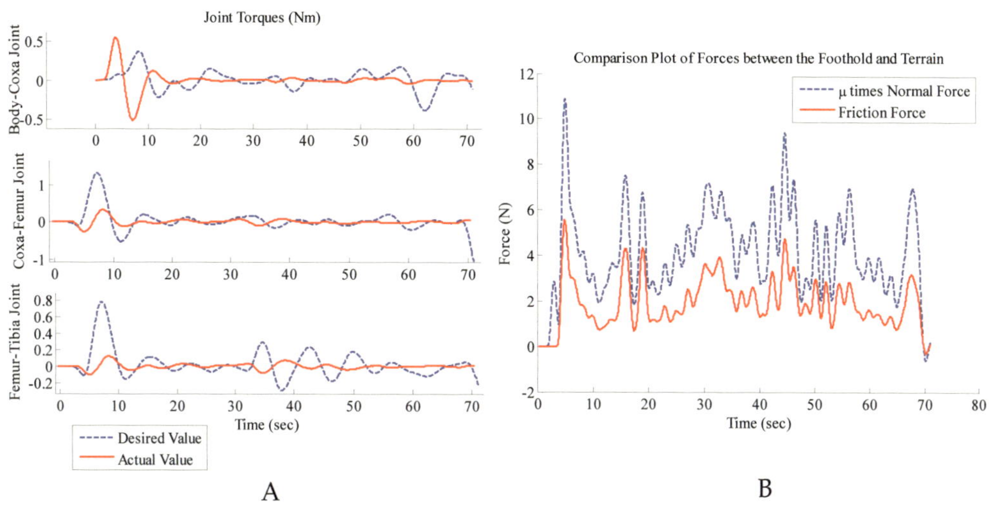

Figure 12. Results obtained when the robot was steered using a ripple gait. (A) Comparative representation of actual torques sensed at the joint and the torques data determined by the mathematical model. (B) Plot of normal reaction forces and friction forces at the footholds.

Figure 13. A view of the robot straight-line walking between desired waypoints over an unknown irregular terrain.

In the second run, the robot was steered with a slow-speed wave gait in which each leg is lifted whereas the remaining supports the body. This confirms an even sharing of payload on either side of the robot. The results of this simulation run are shown in Fig. 14 and Fig. 15. As evident from the Fig. 15(B) that the friction force data never exceeds the normal reaction force which confirms that the robot never experienced a slip/drift over the same track when using the wave gait. As a consequence, close matching of computed torques and the sensed torques during this simulation run as shown by Fig. 15(A) signifies the validity of our proposed mathematical model to realize adaptive walking over uneven terrains at slow speeds. Additional simulation results are exhibited in Fig. 14 which portrays the track of the centre of gravity of the robot and its speed profile. Fig. 15(C) & Fig. 15(D) show the profiles of body rotation angles and rates about x, y & z-axes. As evident from the Fig. 15(C), the roll and pith rotations of the body are minimal which confirms the validity of our attitude control for maintaining the body flat over an unknown irregular terrain.

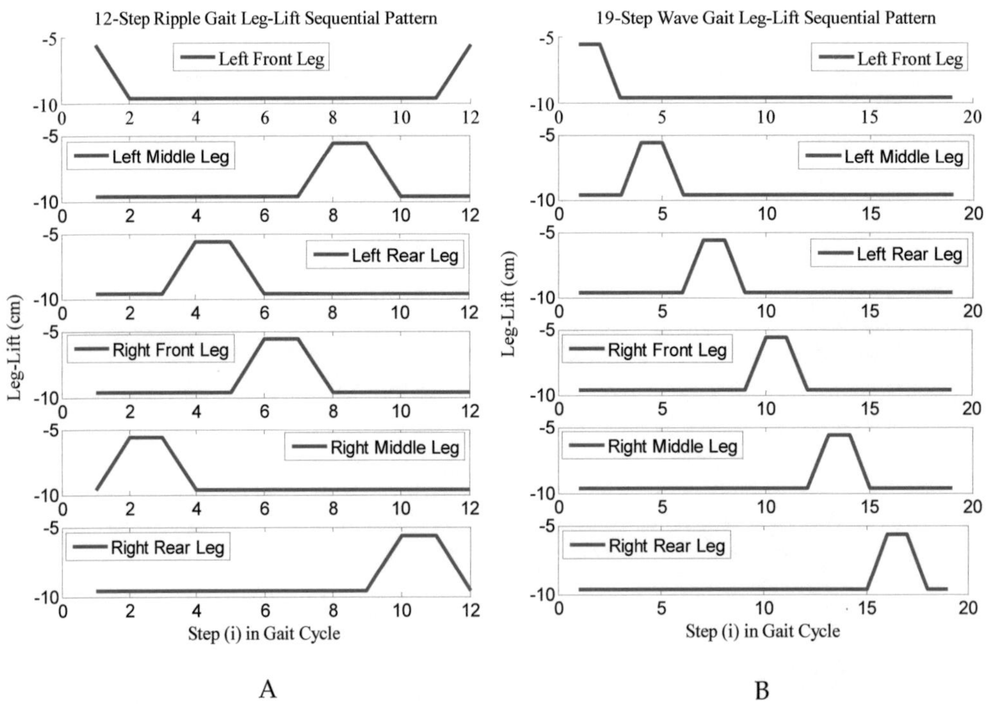

Figure 14. (A) 12-step ripple gait leg-lift sequential pattern. (B) 19-step wave gait leg-lift sequential pattern.

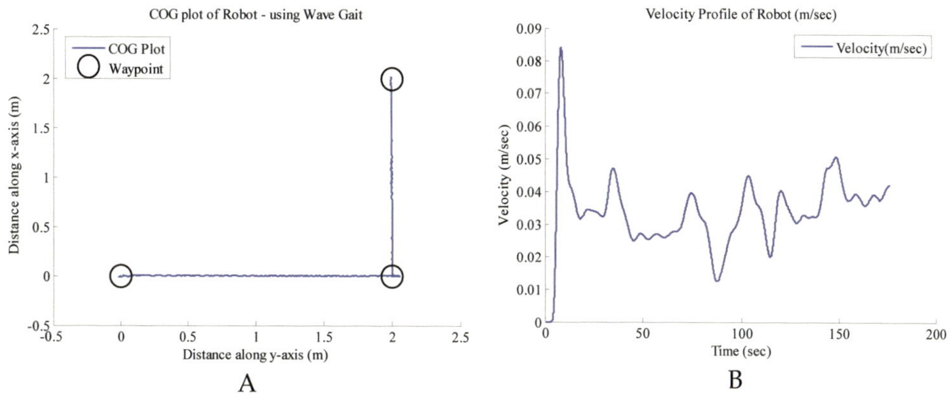

Figure 15. (A) Path outlined by the robot when using a wave gait. (B) Velocity profile of the robot during its locomotion.

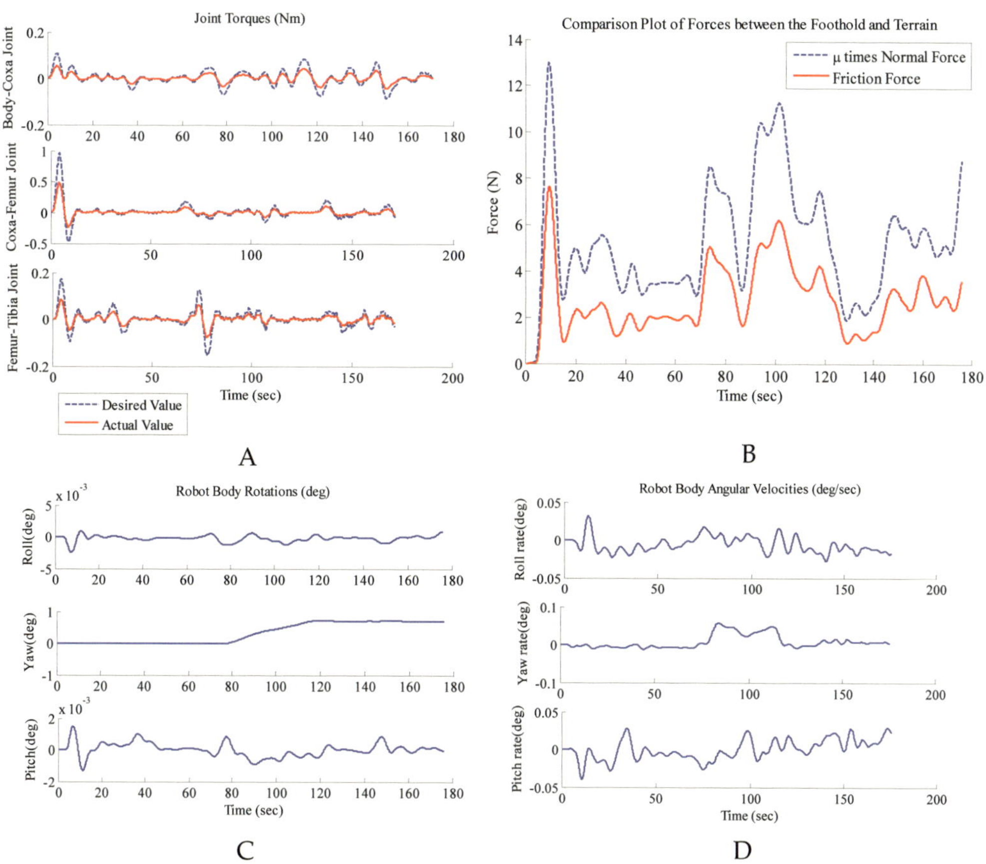

Figure 16. Results obtained when the robot was steered using a wave gait. (A) Comparative representation of actual torques sensed at the joint and the torques data determined by the mathematical model. (B) Plot of normal reaction forces and friction forces at the footholds. (C) Robot attitude tracking. (D) Angular velocity profiles of the robot's body.

5. Conclusions

This chapter outlines a study on signifying the importance of employing virtual reality technology in realizing legged locomotion over unknown irregular terrains. The objective is to emphasize that how virtual reality technology can serve a prime role in the improvement of legged locomotion by performing gait analysis over unstructured terrains which is often time intense and complex to conduct in real-worlds. The objective has been achieved by analyzing an adaptive gait of a six-legged hexapod robot with two unique support patterns namely: ripple and wave. A complete mathematical model of the robot is presented at the start of the chapter to equip the reader with the basic knowledge of forward and reverse kinematic equations used in robot kinematics. Robot dynamics is further described with a computed-torque control technique to incorporate the forces and moments at the feet. To validate the proposed mathematical model, simulation tests are first carried out in a constraint simulation environment using SimMechanics and results of mathematical model are compared with those obtained from on-board sensors. For gait analysis, the robot is steered over an unknown irregular terrain first using a fast-speed ripple gait and then using a slow-speed wave gait. Reaction forces at the footholds and the reaction torques about the joint motion axes in a leg are investigated which reveal that the wave gait is slow but more secure for adaptive locomotion over an unknown irregular terrain. This even sharing of active payload on either side of the robot body in wave gait results in greater stability especially in the regions of possible slip/drift. However, when using a fast speed ripple gait in which the force-distribution on either side of the robot body is not uniform, the support pattern fails to provide enough friction force against the normal reaction force that may prevent the slip/drift. As a consequence, ripple gaits provide high mobility and are effective over flat terrains however, wave gaits are more suited to walking over unknown irregular terrains.

Author details

Umar Asif
School of Mechanical & Manufacturing Engineering, National University of Sciences & Technology (NUST), Pakistan

Acknowledgement

The author would like to thank the editor for his detailed and pertinent comments.

6. References

[1] U. Asif, J. Iqbal, "Motion Planning using an Impact-based Hybrid Control for Trajectory Generation in Adaptive Walking", *International Journal of Advanced Robotic Systems,* Vol. 8, No. 4, pp. 212-226, 2011.

[2] Wood, R.J., "The First Take-off of a Biologically Inspired At-Scale Robotic Insect", in *IEEE Transactions on Robotics*, vol.24, no.2, pp. 341-347, April 2008.

[3] Kuhn, D. and Rommermann, M. and Sauthoff, N. and Grimminger, F. and Kirchner, F., "Concept evaluation of a new biologically inspired robot LittleApe", in *IEEE/RSJ International Conference on Intelligent Robots and Systems 2009* (IROS 09), pp. 589-594, 10-15 October 2009.

[4] Shumei Yu and Shugen Ma and Bin Li and Yuechao Wang, "An amphibious snake-like robot: Design and motion experiments on ground and in water", *in International Conference on Information and Automation* 2009 (ICIA 09), pp. 500-505, 22-24 June 2009.

[5] M. Konyev and F.Palis and Y. Zavgorodniy and A. Melnikov and A. Rudiskiy and A. Telesh and U. Sschmucker and V. Rusin, "Walking Robot Anton: Design, Simulation, Experiments", *in International Conference on Climbing and Walking Robots and the Support Technologies for Mobile Machines 2008* (CLAWAR 2008), pp. 922-929, 8-10 September 2008.

[6] A. Roennau, T. Kerscher and R. Dillmann, "Design and Kinematics of a Biologically-Inspired Leg for a Six-Legged Walking Machine", *in the Proc. of the 2010 3rd IEEE RAS & EMBS Int. Conf. on Biomedical Robotics and Biomechatronics,* The University of Tokyo, Tokyo, Japan, September 26-29, 2010.

[7] Willian A. Lewinger and Roger D. Quinn, "A Hexapod Walks Over Irregular Terrain Using a Controller Adapted from an Insect's Nervous System", *The 2010 IEEE/RSJ International Conference on Intelligent Robots and Systems,* October 18-22, 2010, Taipei, Taiwan.

[8] U. Asif and J. Iqbal, Rapid Prototyping of a Gait Generation Method using Real Time Hardware in Loop Simulation, "*International Journal of Modeling, Simulation and Scientific Computing (IJMSSC)*", vol. 2, no. 4, pp. 393-411, 2011.

[9] U. Asif and J. Iqbal, Design and Simulation of a Biologically Inspired Hexapod Robot using SimMechanics, "*Proceedings of the IASTED International Conference, Robotics (Robo 2010)*", pp. 128-135, Phuket, Thailand, November 24 - 26, 2010.

[10] U. Asif and J. Iqbal, A Comparative Study of Biologically Inspired Walking Gaits through Waypoint Navigation, "*Advances in Mechanical Engineering*", vol. 2011 (2011), Article ID 737403, 9 pages, DOI: 10.1155/2011/737403.

[11] U. Asif and J. Iqbal, "An Approach to Stable Walking over Uneven Terrain using a Reflex Based Adaptive Gait", *Journal of Control Science and Engineering,* Volume 2011 (2011), Article ID 783741, 12 pages, DOI:10.1155/2011/783741.

[12] U. Asif, J. Iqbal and M. Ajmal Khan, "Kinematic Analysis of Periodic Continuous Gaits for a Bio-Mimetic Walking Robot", *Proceedings of the 2011 IEEE International Symposium on Safety, Security and Rescue Robotics*, pp. 80-85, November 1-5, 2011, Kyoto, Japan.

[13] U. Asif and J. Iqbal, "Motion Planning of a Walking Robot using Attitude Guidance", *International Journal of Robotics and Automation,* pp. 41-48, vol. 27, no. 1, 2012. DOI: 10.2316/Journal.206.2012.1.206-3589.

[14] U. Asif and J. Iqbal, "On the Improvement of Legged Locomotion in Difficult Terrains using a Balance Stabilization Method", *International Journal of Advanced Robotic Systems,* Vol. 9, No. 1, pp. 1-13, 2012.

[15] Kyle Johns, Trevor Taylor, *Professional Microsoft Robotics Developer Studio* (Wiley publishing, Indianapolis, Indiana, 2008).

[16] U. Asif and J. Iqbal, Modeling, Control and Simulation of a Six-DOF motion platform for a Flight Simulator, "International Journal of Modeling and Simulation", vol. 31, no. 4, pp. 307-321, 2011. DOI:10.2316/Journal.20.2011.4.205-5587.

[17] U. Asif and J. Iqbal, Modeling, Simulation and Motion Cues Visualization of a Six-DOF Motion Platform for Micro-Manipulations, "International Journal of Intelligent Mechatronics and Robotics (IJIMR)", vol. 1, no. 3, pp. 1-17, 2011.

[18] U. Asif and J. Iqbal, "A Robotic System with a Hybrid Motion Cueing Controller for Inertia Tensor Approximation in Micro-Manipulations", International Journal of Advanced Robotic Systems, Vol. 8, No. 4, pp. 235-247, 2011.

Section 3

Industrial and Construction Applications

Chapter 6

Facilitating User Involvement in Product Design Through Virtual Reality

J.P. Thalen and M.C. van der Voort

Additional information is available at the end of the chapter

http://dx.doi.org/10.5772/48602

1. Introduction

The product development process *(PDP)* generally involves a sequence of gathering requirements, conceptual design, engineering, manufacturing and finally a market release. Successful product development depends on collaboration and communication between stakeholders (e.g. designers and engineers, but also end-users, marketeers or managers) throughout the phases in the development process. Tools that support this communication and collaboration primarily focus on *internal* communication. For instance, sketches and drawings facilitate communication between designers, CAD models facilitate communication between engineers and presentations or reports are used for communication between departments. Supporting *external* communication (i.e. communication between people inside the development process and people outside the process) is more challenging because external stakeholders (such as end-users or customers) are usually not trained in being involved in a PDP.

This chapter describes how Virtual Reality *(VR)* can facilitate the involvement of external stakeholders in the PDP. Stakeholder involvement can improve the information quality and quantity; end-user feedback for instance facilitates concept generation and selection, or identifies usability issues in an early stage. However, with only limited design information available it is difficult to provide stakeholders with a clear presentation of a product concept and future use context. We therefore propose to use VR technologies to create realistic concept representations in the early stages of the design process. VR technologies create an alternative reality in which worlds, objects and characters can be experienced that may not yet be available in reality. As such it allows stakeholders to not only see the future product (which could also be achieved with a concept sketch or mockup), but also experience the product and the interactions with its use context.

In this chapter we first elaborate on stakeholder involvement in the PDP, and highlight the importance of involving future end-users in particular. We also depict some of the characteristics that make VR suitable for facilitating stakeholder involvement. The main body of the chapter comprises a set of industrial case studies that illustrate how VR can be applied to achieve different levels of user engagement in various phases of the PDP. This overview and comparison of case studies leads to conclusions regarding the selection of appropriate VR techniques for specific types of user involvement in product design.

2. Background

Traditionally, the PDP is referred to as a problem solving activity in which the result is determined by a series of technical decisions [1, 2]. Recently, the product design process is more and more considered to be a group activity in which communication and collaboration between stakeholders plays a central role [3,4].

The importance of including these stakeholders, and in particular potential users, in the design process becomes clear when one considers the task-artefact cycle [5]. New products are designed to fulfill a certain task or activity, i.e. solve the signaled problem. However, the introduction of the new product will in return influence the identified problem. New problems may arise as well as new opportunities may be identified. As [6] explains: 'Design is always indeterminate, because design changes the world within which people act and experience' (p. 48). To support a continuous iterative design approach, a close and timely involvement of end-users in the design process is therefore required.

2.1. Facilitating user involvement

To successfully include end-users, a design process needs to have appropriate facilitating characteristics. In [7] the following set of conditions for effective and efficient participation of end-users is proposed.

- A direct and explicit communication between designer and end-user needs to be established. The way of communication should minimise the chance of misinterpretation on either side.
- End-users should be enabled to have a realistic interaction with the design information. They should be able to reliably assess the exact functioning and experience of the design under a wide range of circumstances.
- End-users should be enabled to reliably become conscious of and assess the consequences of design decisions. Consequences of design decisions should be made explicit and presented in a manner that is comprehensible regardless participant's training or discipline.

VR potentially provides solutions meeting all three conditions for successful user involvement. It supports a *realistic interaction* with design information: design information is presented in a way that is comprehensible regardless discipline or training, whereas consequences of design choices can be experienced rather than imagined [8]. The latter is especially beneficial when stakeholders (e.g. end-users) are unfamiliar with the product to be designed or with the technology that is suggested to be incorporated. The actual *experience of design information and consequences* will sincerely improve the reliability of the input provided by stakeholders to the design process. Furthermore, by using VR simulation, *misunderstandings* between human actors are less likely to occur compared to when using more abstract or symbolic representations of design information (such as natural language, sketches and CAD drawings). Another benefit of using VR simulation is that it eliminates the necessity to make physical prototypes. It not only saves money and time, but also allows for evaluation of candidate designs in an earlier phase of the design process [9]. Evaluation of candidate designs under dangerous or rare use circumstances is furthermore supported without compromising safety or efficiency.

While VR in principle meets all the proposed conditions, it is argued that VR is rarely a solution on its own. Integrating VR technologies with the PDP requires supporting principles to 'embed' the technology in the design process. In our case studies we primarily make use of *scenarios* and *gaming techniques* to do so.

Scenarios are explicit descriptions of hypothetical events concerning a product during a certain phase of its life cycle [10]. A scenario can be expressed by displaying a prototype (either real or virtual) in an environment (either real or virtual). Within design processes, scenarios are used to address problems, needs, constraints and possibilities. Like VR, the use of scenarios facilitates explicit communication of design information among involved stakeholders.

Gaming is generally described as a play with props following specific rules and often with an element of competition between players and decided by chance, strength, skill or a combination of these [11]. Within design, playing games is a way to generate ideas in a situated and participative way. Due to rapid developments in the gaming industry, the trend to use games as a design tool no longer means just board games and card games, but also computer games. Within a (computer) game, information is simultaneously generated, represented and evaluated. Therefore, design iterations can be performed very quickly. Furthermore, playing games helps to develop a common language between designers and users [12].

The majority of the case studies presented in this chapter use scenarios that were explicitly defined to serve as a frame of reference, whereas gaming techniques were added to trigger user participation.

3. Framework

This section introduces the framework through which the VR applications are presented and compared. The framework is based on the work of [13], who presents an overview of user involvement in product design methods. Each of our case studies will be positioned according to two dimensions, namely the *design phase* in which it is used and the intended *level of user engagement*.

The first dimension of the proposed framework represents the phase in the design process in which VR is applied. VR applications in product development (e.g. virtual prototyping, virtual assembly or virtual manufacturing) traditionally rely on CAD systems and consequently focus on advanced stages of the PDP, such as the engineering and manufacturing phase [14] for a survey). In this chapter however, we focus on the *early stages* (also known as the fuzzy front-end) of the PDP. The lack of concrete information in this stage of the PDP is challenging for designers, but also allows end-users to still have considerable impact on design decisions. The case studies will illustrate how the benefits of VR mentioned in the previous section facilitate various design activities in these early stages. To further characterise the case studies, the first two phases of the original framework (specification and conceptual design) are split into a *specification* phase, a *concept generation* phase and a *concept evaluation* phase. This allows for a differentiation between generative and evaluation applications that take place in the concept development phase.

The second dimension that is used to characterise the case studies is defined as the level of *user engagement*. User engagement is related to the extent to which a user is involved or participating in the design process. Interviews and surveys require a low level of user engagement, as the actual product development is on on behalf of the users (referred to as 'design for' in the original framework). A higher level of user engagement is achieved when users are allowed to try, evaluate and/or select proposed product concepts. This is referred to as 'design with' in the original framework. The highest level of user engagement is achieved through co-design activities, in which users actually generate product concepts themselves. This is referred to as 'design by' in the original framework.

Both dimensions have a continuous scale, meaning that there is no strict border between phases in the design process or level of stakeholder involvement. Some of the cases we present comprise an integrated design approach that spans the entire product development process, while other cases focus on a particular phase in the process.

4. Case studies

The case studies presented in this section originate from various research projects in which industrial partners participate by providing a design case. Consequently, there is a wide variety in application domains, ranging from automotive design and consumer electronics to healthcare and mechanical engineering. Furthermore, the industrial partners range from large multinationals to small or medium sized enterprises (SMEs). The involved industrial partners only had experience in the application of VR in the later design stages. Main reason was the unawareness of the involved industrial partners of the potential use of VR in the early stages of design; VR is associated with CAD applications, expensive user interfaces and technically complex tools. Showing demonstrations of early stage VR applications (often implemented using off-the-shelf technology) triggered the participants to explore new opportunities.

Each case study is placed in the framework according to the dimensions introduced in the previous section, as shown in Figure 1. As mentioned in the previous section, several case studies span multiple design phases. The detailed case study descriptions elaborate on this by explaining how some applications can indeed be useful across several design phases. Furthermore, the *application context, technical implementation* and the specific contribution to *user involvement* is explained.

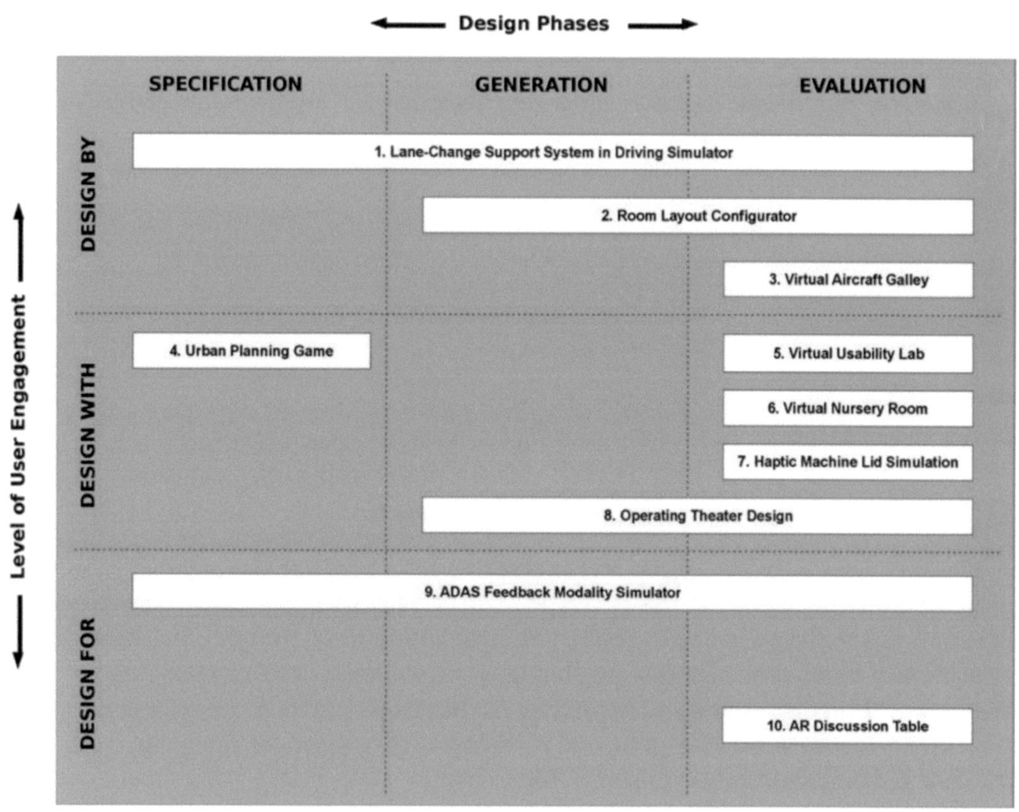

Figure 1. The framework in which case studies are positioned according to their place in the product development process and the achieved level of user engagement.

	Application Brief	Application Domain
1	A configurable user interface for lane-change systems, connected to an immersive driving simulator.	Automotive
2	An interactive virtual room connected to a multi-touch input table to discuss room layouts and visualise them in real-time.	Healthcare
3	An interactive virtual model of an aircraft galley, used to act-out scenarios and identify and discuss innovative concepts.	Aerospace
4	A serious game implemented on a multi-touch table to facilitate group decisions and visualise future urban planning scenarios.	Urban Planning
5	A virtual office environment in which current and future workflows can be experienced and evaluated.	Consumer Electronics
6	Evaluation of three future nursery room layouts by acting out use scenarios in a virtual room.	Healthcare
7	A low-cost and realistic model of a machine lid, involving haptic devices synchronised with a visualisation.	Machine Design
8	A virtual operating room connected to a multi-touch input table to cooperatively layout the room.	Healthcare
9	An immersive driving simulator extended with an emulation module that supports the design and evaluation of new interfaces for drivers support systems	Automotive
10	An augmented reality table for facilitating design review sessions with non-expert stakeholders.	Factory Layout

Table 1. Brief descriptions of the ten case studies and their application domains.

4.1. Lane change support system in driving simulator

Application Context – To investigate user preferences for a new *lane change support system*, an immersive driving simulator was developed [15]. A lane change support system helps a driver to safely change lanes on a highway, for instance by warning the driver about vehicles in a blind spot. The driving simulator allowed end-users to configure the user interface of this support system themselves, for instance by setting the level and type of support. In this case study a group of participants was asked to configure their ideal interface and evaluate it in a simulated traffic scenario.

Technical Implementation – The driving simulator uses a physical mockup of a car, positioned in front of a large semi-spherical display. The car mockup is equipped with configurable dashboard displays, audio speakers and actuators to provide various output modalities including visual cues, auditory cues and tactile feedback (see figure 2). The dashboard also features a Wizard-like application that guides participants through the dashboard configuration options.

Figure 2. The driving simulator used for testing lane-change support systems, also showing the configurable dashboard.

Figure 3. The room layout configurator. The foreground shows the surface table with tangible objects. The background shows the wall display with the virtual room.

User Involvement - The approach that was used in this case study supports designers in determining stakeholders' preferences and finding the best compromise between those preferences. This resulted in a hierarchy of information that is a detailed, consistent and reliable image of users' preferences. The hierarchy provides the designer insight in the relationship between user characteristics, use circumstances and desirable or undesirable product characteristics. The evaluation revealed that the new participatory design approach is viable in the sense that people understood their role in the design process, were able to perform the specified activities, and that these activities yielded actual results. Users were enabled to directly express their preferences and realistically experience the consequences of their decisions. Moreover, determining users' preferences has happened while immersing them in the relevant context, but without putting them in dangerous situations.

4.2. Room layout configurator

Application Context – This case study was carried out in cooperation with a design department particularly interested in *ambient experience design* [16]. Designers currently use physical replica rooms to test different lighting and sound concepts in various contexts. These physical rooms are not very flexible and cost efficient; a special room has to be built depending on the theme that is under investigation (e.g. hospital rooms, hotel rooms or living rooms). In this case study a VR application was developed to help designers with easily creating room layouts and evaluating the ambient experience.

Technical Implementation – The application consists of a Microsoft Surface Table (a table-size horizontal multi-touch display) connected to a large projection wall (see figure 3). The wall shows a 'first-person' view of a virtual room. The arrangement of furniture, as well as the first-person camera perspective can be controlled using tangible objects located on the Surface Table that are traced using visual tags underneath each object.

Figure 4. The virtual aircraft galley.

Figure 5. The virtual aircraft galley allows users to interact with the virtual model.

User Involvement – The setup is designed to facilitate multidisciplinary group meetings. The Surface Table interface enables a group (e.g. designers, end-users, experts, etc.) to collaboratively compose and review the layout of the room, regardless of the background and expertise of the group members. Each participant has an equal share in determining the room layout and everyone is able to explain his/her perspective on the design case. While group participants are able to create and change the layout of the room, the application primarily targets concept evaluation tasks; product concepts can be demonstrated and 'experienced' in different settings.

4.3. Virtual aircraft galley

Application Context – In [17] a synthetic environments consultancy approach is proposed that supports small and medium-sized enterprises in identifying VR opportunities for their product development process. To evaluate this approach, a case study for a design agency was performed that concerned the redesign of an aircraft galley. The redesign aims to achieve weight reduction, extra chairs in the cabin, easy exchangeable equipment and improved ergonomics. The consultancy approach guided the design agency through a series of workshops in which the designers identified potential bottlenecks in their development process. The approach used *scenarios* extensively to communicate the findings of these workshops between the researcher and the designers; for instance to describe potential implementations of VR in the design process.

Technical Implementation – In the end, the design agency decided to use an interactive walk-through model of the aircraft galley, projected on a large mutli-touch wall display (see figures 4 and 5). The application for instance allowed designers to virtually walk through the galley, and open doors or trays. The space in front of the multi-touch wall display is furnished such that it represents the space in the galley.

User Involvement – The case study illustrates how a 3D interactive visualisation can support multidisciplinary meetings for the design agency. The setup facilitates scenario visualisation but also triggers more interactive behavior in the group; session participants are encouraged to step in and show other participants what they have in mind in a particular situation.

4.4. Urban planning game

Application Context - 'Serious Games' facilitate decision making processes concerning complex problems. Urban planning is such a complex problem; developing cities, countries or regions is bound to involve many stakeholders and has many physical variables and constraints. This case study features the design of a serious game targeting the development of new city neighborhoods.

Technical Implementation – The resulting application is a multi-player collaborative serious game played on a Microsoft Surface Table. The table displays a top view of a city in which the neighborhood is to be developed (see figure 6). Game participants use tangible objects (e.g. bricks representing houses, trees, buildings, etc.) to modify the city design. The table responds to the bricks by immediately showing the results of a proposed solution. Game elements such as time restrictions and turn-taking are used to structure the game sessions.

User Involvement - The game eases communication about complex problems using simplified graphics and allows players to safely explore the solution space of various Urban Planning issues in a neighborhood planning project. Each player takes the role of a stakeholder (e.g. the mayor, an inhabitant or a housing corporation). Through this role, players are able to suggest and place solutions in the neighborhood (projected on the surface table) and see the effect. All players, as a team, have the opportunity to negotiate, discuss and decide which solution is most beneficial to the group (see figure 7). The primary aim of the game is not to

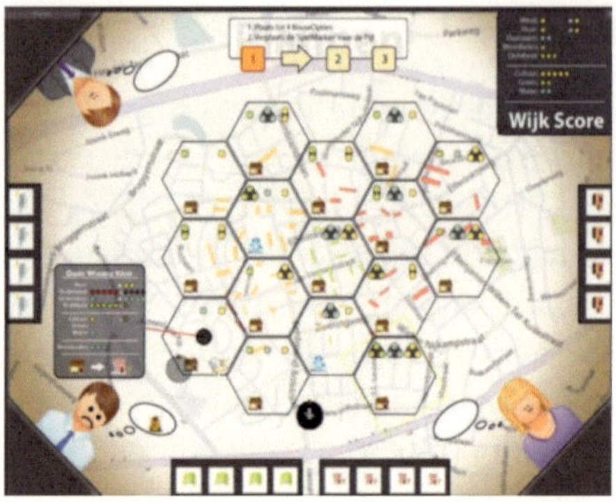

Figure 6. A top view of the urban planning game, showing a city region and three characters that play a role in the game.

Figure 7. Participants in an Urban Planning game session.

directly generate solutions, but rather to trigger discussions and explore new possibilities in early stages of an urban planning project.

4.5. Virtual usability lab

Application Context - The Virtual Usability Lab was created during a case study for a manufacturer of professional office machinery (primarily printers). The company had already achieved some level of user involvement in the early stages of their design process by asking future clients to evaluate new graphical user interface (GUI) prototypes. However, the reliability of these evaluations is reduced by the fact the GUI concepts were not evaluated in a realistic use context; the GUI concept is not connected to a physical printer, so evaluation participants have to imagine what the interaction with the real machine would be like. The Virtual Usability Lab addresses this shortcoming by providing a realistic virtual use context in which virtual office machinery can be evaluated by end-users.

Technical Implementation - During the case study two technical implementations for the Virtual Usability Lab have been developed and evaluated with company participants. Both implementations include a virtual office environment in which existing and future virtual printers can be operated (e.g. paper refill, start/stop printing, etc.). The first implementation uses hand-held *augmented reality* tablets to visualise the interactive virtual environment. Pointing the AR tablet on specific AR markers allowed users to see and interact with virtual objects. The second implementation provides the user with a first-person interactive walk-through on a wall display. The first implementation enables users to physically navigate the virtual office by moving between markers and pointing the AR tablet. The second implementation uses a more traditional interface, but does allow for a more immersive visualisation. After an evaluation of the two implementations (involving participants from the case study company) the fully virtual environment was considered more effective for representing the use context (see figure 8 and 9). While the augmented reality environment did allow for more physical interactions (e.g. really walking around an object), it failed to keep the designers 'immersed' in the virtual environment. The fully virtual environment was found to provide a more integrated experience.

Figure 8. A screenshot of the first-person perspective of the virtual usability lab.

Figure 9. Designers (on the right) using the virtual usability lab in a test case.

User Involvement – The case study showed that the application primarily helps with analysing high-level task flows, such as operator movement between different machines or locations in the office. Being able to track and analyse these movements, as well as the actions that take place at each location adds a lot of useful knowledge to the early design phases. The presented application allows designers to capture this knowledge (i.e. by letting real operators act out a 'day at work' in a future virtual office), but also to communicate this knowledge to other designers, engineers or marketeers who are usually not aware of certain real-life situations. Physical analyses, such as testing out different positions of paper trays on a virtual printer, were found to be less useful. Unless the virtual environment would also simulate weight, friction and other tactile aspects it is usually more effective to evaluate those aspects using physical prototypes.

4.6. Virtual nursery room

Application Context – The Virtual Nursery Room case study comprised the design of a *Neonatal Intensive Care Unit* (NICU) patient area [18]. A NICU houses premature babies in incubators and includes a large number of medical appliances to monitor and nurse the newborn. The involvement of end-users in the design process of such a room is important, since particularly in medical design few designers are familiar with and can therefore anticipate the specific use situations of the product and the demands that arise from it. Neither can the emotional situation of the parents that have their child lying at the NICU be envisioned to the full extend by persons that have not experienced a similar situation. A participatory design approach was used to evaluate room design concepts in a very early stage of the project.

Technical Implementation - For an optimal evaluation with regard to both emotional and usability aspects, it is essential that users can actually experience the room designs. Therefore, it was chosen to conduct a participatory session in a mixed reality setting: In an evaluation session hospital staff engaged with virtual representations of the candidate designs and judged them on usability as well as on emotional impact. The concepts were presented on a screen as pictures and in three similar animations. Afterwards, rendered pictures of the designs were projected life-size on a concave screen. A simple physical table was placed in front of the projection, representing the incubator. A baby dummy was placed on the table, fitted with medical material (see figure 10).

Figure 10. Participants acting out scenarios in front of a projected nursery room.

User Involvement - Participants, consisting of nurses and doctors were asked to play out nursing scenarios within the setup. The participants started with making a first concept choice based on how they estimated the emotional impact of the concepts. After playing out the nursing scenarios, the participants concluded that their first choice (based on emotional impact) had some usability issues. The case study illustrates how relatively simple mixed reality environments can help participants to better understand (future) situations, and review them from various perspectives. In this mixed reality sessions participants were able to evaluate concepts on both emotional and usability aspects.

4.7. Haptic machine lid simulation

Application Context – This case study aimed to demonstrate how VR can help with shifting design decisions regarding physical components to an earlier stage of the design process [19]. The case study features the design of the machine lid of which the hinges were to be chosen. The specification of these hinges (for instance their stiffness) affects the use experience of the whole machine. Instead of building several prototypes with various hinges a virtual prototype was created using a haptic feedback device.

Technical Implementation - For a realistic simulation of the lid hinges, an FCS-CS Haptic Master was used. A grip from a real machine was connected to the haptic arm. The haptic device was synchronised with a digital visualisation of the machine; moving the haptic device up and down allowed users and designers to open and close the virtual machine model (see figure 11). The haptic device could be configured to simulate various types of hinges.

Figure 11. A designer testing the haptic lid emulator. The display on the right shows a digital representation of the machine that is linked to the haptic device.

User Involvement – Unlike most of the other case studies presented in this chapter, this case study focused on simulating physical product aspects. The use of the haptic device allows designers to efficiently and realistically evaluate various hinges.

4.8. Operating theater design

Application Context - This case study comprises the design and evaluation of a VR design tool for operating theaters [20]. The application supports stakeholders of dedicated endoscopic operating theaters, such as surgeons, nurses and anesthetists, with the design of a ceiling mounted arm (CMA) systems in a virtual operating theater environment and gain insight in consequences of design decisions.

Technical Implementation – The VR application consists of a Microsoft Surface Table, a large wall display and miniature physical models of the CMA systems. The Surface Table displays a top down view of an operating theater, in which participants can create CMA concepts by placing the miniature CMA models (see figure 12). The models correspond to digital CMA systems in the virtual environment, projected on the large wall display. The wall display allows participants to walk-through the operating theater while still modifying it on the Surface Table (see figure 13).

Figure 12. The Surface Table with tangible CMA (Ceiling Mounted Arm) systems used for the operating theater design case study.

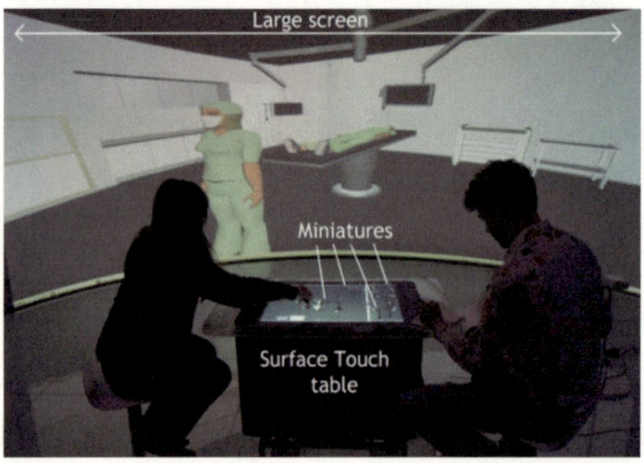

Figure 13. Operating theatre design; the surface table is used as an interface for the virtual theater (shown in the background)

User Involvement – The setup allows session participants to immerse into the environment by the use of movable virtual avatars and experience the consequences of the design decisions they have made. The effect of re-positioning a CMA system (which is difficult in real-life) is immediately visible for everyone on the wall display. As such the application can be used to evaluation CMA design concepts, but also to reenact use scenarios with future CMA systems, list priorities, etc.

4.9. ADAS feedback modality simulator

Application Context – The design of *advanced driver assistance systems* faces the challenge of providing automated support behavior that complements the human driver safely and efficiently. Driving simulators can be used to test these new systems, as illustrated in the Lane-Change Support case study. However, developing accurate virtual prototypes of these systems is time consuming. This case study therefore investigated the use of human emulation as a simulation alternative (known as the Wizard of Oz approach) [21].

Technical Implementation - An automated and an emulated version of a lateral support system were compared in a fixed-base driving simulator setup. Test participants are given a driving task (e.g. follow a preceding car). During this task they are given a cue on which they have to respond. The driver support was either generated by a predefined automatic version or by a human co-driver that emulated the support behavior. Co-drivers were seated behind a curtain and drivers were unaware of their presence and task. Co-Drivers controlled a secondary steering wheel which was connected to the drivers' steering wheel.

User Involvement – The case study addresses the same topic as the Lane-Change Support System case study, but provides users with predefined designs rather than asking users to generate solution concepts themselves. As a result, the technical complexity of this setup is reduced. The case study revealed that the behavior of a future driver support system can effectively and realistically be programmed as a human operator instead of a virtual prototype of the system. Consequently this approach is considered very useful for early concept selection.

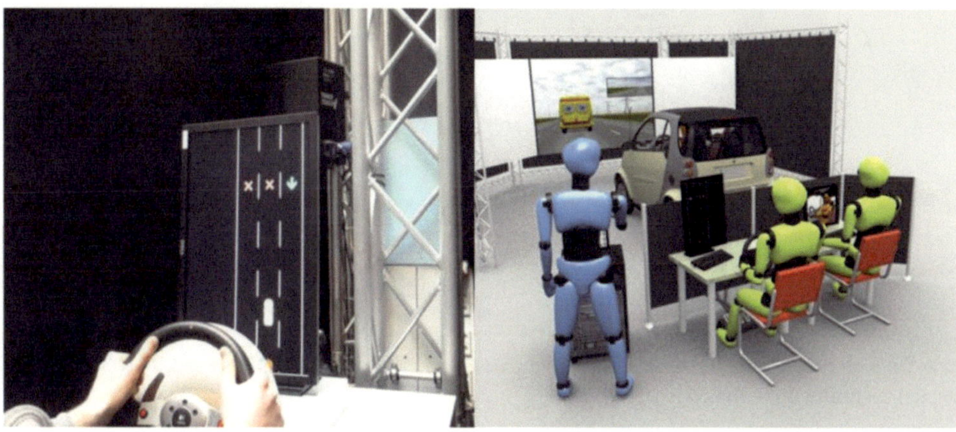

Figure 14. ADAS Feedback Modality Simulator: on the left, a human operator can send cues (e.g. haptic cue via steering wheel) to a test participant in the simulator (on the right)

4.10. AR discussion table

Application Context – The Augmented Reality (AR) Discussion Table was developed for a manufacturer of industrial dough processing machines. The client was interested in increasing end-user involvement in their product development process. The primary challenge in this case study was the communication between machine engineers, end-users (machine operators) and decision makers (customers). Especially when customers have to decide whether or not a proposed machine design meets their requirements it is sometimes difficult to reach an understanding between the stakeholders.

For this application an Augmented Reality (AR) table was developed to provide a more intuitive visualisation of machine design proposals. While the engineers currently use 2D technical drawings and sometimes renders of CAD models, the AR table provides an interactive 3D visualisation of an entire machine layout.

Technical Implementation – The AR Table uses an off-the-shelf web camera that is pointed on a table surface. The camera stream is sent to AR tracking software to identify and track specific *markers.* The position and orientation of each marker corresponds to a specific machine CAD model, resulting in a 3D interactive representation of the machine layout. Each machine can be rotated and re-positioned by moving the markers on the table, or by rotating the camera around the table. The entire 3D scene is projected on a large display next to the table.

User Involvement – Similarly to the *Room Layout Configurator* this application offers a low-threshold multi-user interface for manipulating 3D scenes. The AR table can be used to support meetings between the engineers, sales department and potential customers, allowing all participants to change or inspect the machine setup.

Figure 15. The Augmented Reality Table. The picture shows the markers and (inset) the virtual models projected on top of these markers.

5. Review

The overview of case studies illustrates the diversity of opportunities for VR applications in the early stages of the product development process and confirms the industrial need for this type of applications. Structuring the case studies according to their position in the PDP and the achieved level of user engagement provides several insights regarding the facilitation of user engagement through VR.

5.1. Application scope

The majority of the presented VR applications have a relatively narrow scope, meaning that they target a particular phase in the early stages of the PDP. Only the development of entirely new complex systems (such as driver assistance systems) benefits from VR support throughout the first three phases of its development: virtual prototypes can elicit product requirements, can be tested and improved by end-users, and serve as an evaluation or validation platform in the final stages of concept design. In return for a relatively high investment this offers a safe, flexible and time efficient development approach. For re-design or incremental innovation projects on the other hand, VR can be particularly useful for evaluating multiple concept directions. For instance, the re-design of office machinery does not usually involve radical modifications, but would benefit from being able to quickly evaluate several minor modifications to existing products.

As explained in section 2 of this chapter, scenarios and gaming techniques proved to be useful supporting principles in several case studies. Scenarios have been used to embed a specific VR technology in a more extensive approach, as illustrated in the Office Machinery and the Aircraft Galley case studies; participants act out predefined scenarios in a virtual environment. The use of the virtual environment strengthens the realism of the scenarios, while the scenarios add 'meaning' to the virtual environment. In the Urban Planning Game game elements made 'wicked problems' manageable for non-expert stakeholders, for instance by using metaphors and simplified scoring systems.

Specifying a proper balance between VR, supporting principles and other tools and methods turns out to be case dependent. In the automotive case studies for instance, the VR simulation and evaluation platform forms the basis of the method. The NICU case study on the other hand shows a more traditional participatory design process of which VR is a relatively small part.

5.2. User engagement

While it is not possible to strictly allocate an application to a certain level of user engagement, the majority of the early stage VR applications facilitates evaluation tasks, and aims to 'design with' end-users. A higher level of user engagement is possible, but often requires technically complex VR applications. With this level of engagement, the VR application needs to provide an appropriate user interface and flexible modeling features. Furthermore, end-users may need additional training or instructions to participate. In the ADAS interface configuration case study for instance, participants received instructions on how to create their personal user interface. However, emerging interface technologies such as multi-touch displays allow for more intuitive interactions, making it easier for end-users to participate in generating or at least modifying product concepts, as shown in the case studies that used a Surface Table as input device. When using VR to support the lower level of user engagement, it is obvious that VR facilitates the design process, but the added value with respect to user engagement is usually less obvious compared to the higher levels of engagement.

6. Conclusion

The case studies show how VR facilitates user involvement in various phases of the design process. While it should be noted that the review of case studies is currently limited to our own experience, the resulting insights could be valuable on a more generic level as well. The case studies were characterized based on the design phase application as well as the level of user engagement. The majority of the VR applications aims to 'design with users' in concept evaluations. From an industrial point of view, this type of application offers clear 'value for money'; they are not as complex as for instance the concept generation tools, yet offer clear benefits with respect to user engagement. Nevertheless, new interaction technologies more and more reduce the threshold for exploring concept generation and modification applications.

Successful deployment of VR in the early stages of a product development process is still very much case dependent. Incremental development seems to benefit from task specific applications while for new product development a wider scope of VR support could be worth the investment. Furthermore, supporting principles such as gaming techniques and scenarios can extend and strengthen the applicability of VR; VR can become part of a scenario based approach, or scenarios and gaming techniques can be used to give meaning to a VR application.

Author details

J.P. Thalen and M.C. van der Voort
Laboratory of Design, Production and Management, Faculty of Engineering Technology, University of Twente, the Netherlands

7. References

[1] Pahl G, Beitz W (1984) Engineering Design: a Systematic Approach. Springer, Berlin, Germany.

[2] Suh N.P (1990) The Principals of Design. Oxford University Press, New York, USA.

[3] Sohlenius G (1992) Concurrent Engineering. Annals of the CIRP, Vol. 41, No.2, pp. 645-655.

[4] Lu S.C.Y (2003) Engineering as Collaborative Negotiation: a New Paradigm for Collaborative Engineering Research. Whitepaper, Retrieved May 4th, 2006, from http://wisdom.usc.edu/ecn.

[5] Carroll J.M, Rosson M.B (1992) Getting around the task-artifact cycle: how to make claims and design by scenario. ACM Transactions on Information Systems, Vol. 10, pp. 181-212.

[6] Carroll J.M (2000) Five reasons for scenario based design. Interacting with Computers, Vol. 13, No. 1, pp. 43-60.

[7] Tideman M, van der Voort M.C, van Houten F (2008) A New Product Design Method Based on Virtual Reality, Gaming and Scenarios. International Journal on Interactive Design and Manufacturing 2, no. 4 (October 1, 2008): 195–205.

[8] Biocca F, Levy M.R (1995) Communication in the Age of Virtual Reality. Lawrence Erlbaum Associates, Hillsdale, NJ, USA.

[9] Tideman M, van der Voort M.C, van Houten F (2006) Haptic Virtual Prototyping for Design and Assessment of Gear-shifts. In: ElMaraghy, H.A., ElMaraghy, W.H. (eds.), Advances in Design, Springer, Berlin, Germany, pp. 461-472.

[10] Miedema J, van der Voort M.C, Lutters D, van Houten F (2007) Synergy of Technical Specifications, Functional Specifications and Scenarios in Requirements Specifications. In: Krause, F.-L. (ed.). The Future of Product Development: Proceedings of the 17th CIRP Design Conference, pp. 235 – 246, Springer

[11] Brandt E (2006) Designing Exploratory Design Games: A Framework for Participation in Participatory Design? In: Proceedings of the ninth Participatory Design Conference 2006, ACM, Trento, Italy, pp. 57-66.

[12] Ehn P, Sjögren D (1991) From system descriptions to scripts for action. In: Greenbaum, J. and Kyng, M. (eds.), Design at Work: Cooperative Design of Computer Systems, Lawrence Erlbaum Associates, Hillsdale, NJ, USA.

[13] Kaulio M (1998) Customer, Consumer and User Involvement in Product Development: A Framework and a Review of Selected Methods. Total Quality Management 9, no. 1 (1998): 141.

[14] Jimeno A, Puerta A (2007) State of the art of the virtual reality applied to design and manufacturing processes. In: The International Journal of Advanced Manufacturing Technology, Vol. 33, No. 9, 866–874

[15] Tideman M, van der Voort M.C, van Houten F (2008) A New Product Design Method Based on Virtual Reality, Gaming and Scenarios. In: International Journal on Interactive Design and Manufacturing 2, no. 4 (October 1, 2008): 195–205.

[16] Thalen J, van der Voort M.C (2011) User Centred Methods for Gathering VR Design Tool Requirements. Joint Virtual Reality Conference of EGVE-EuroVR, 75–81, 2011.

[17] Miedema J (2010) Synthetic Environments in Design Processes. PhD thesis, University of Twente

[18] Garde J, van der Voort M.C (2009) The Design of a New NICU Patient Area: Combining Design for Usability and Design for Emotion.

[19] Miedema J, Meijer F, Wang H, van der Voort M, van den Broek E, Vergeest S (2007) Synthetic Environments as Design Tool - A Case Study. Article in monograph or in proceedings, 2007. http://doc.utwente.nl/58730/.

[20] Huijing S, Garde J (2011) Applying Virtual Reality for Participatory Design: supporting end-users in the design process of an endoscopic operating theatre. In: Norbert Roozenburg, Lin-Lin Chen and Pieter Jan Stappers (eds), Proceedings of IASDR2011,

4th World Conference on Design Research, October 31 - November 4, 2011. TUDelft, 2011.

[21] Waterschoot B.M, van der Voort M.C (2012) Optimizing the design of driver support: Applying human cognition as a design feature. Proceedings of the 4th International Conference on Applied Human Factors and Ergonomics, *in press*, CRC press / Taylor & Francis.

Chapter 7

Construction and Maintenance Planning Supported on Virtual Environments

Alcínia Z. Sampaio, Joana Prata, Ana Rita Gomes and Daniel Rosário

Additional information is available at the end of the chapter

http://dx.doi.org/10.5772/46409

1. Introduction

The main aim of a research project (Sampaio and Gomes, 2011), now in progress at the Department of Civil Engineering of the Technical University of Lisbon, is to develop virtual models as tools to support decision-making in the planning of construction management and maintenance, PTDC/ ECM/67748/ 2006, *Virtual Reality technology applied as a support tool to the planning of construction maintenance*. A first prototype for the lighting system had already been completed (Sampaio et al., 2009). A second prototype concerning construction planning is now complete (Santos, 2010) and two Virtual Reality (VR) models concerning maintenance of the closure of interior (Rosário, 2011) and exterior (Gomes, 2010) walls are also finished. This chapter describes these three later models created as part of the overall research project.

Applications based on Virtual Reality technology for use in construction and maintenance planning of buildings were developed (Fig. 1).

- The first, applied to construction, is an interactive virtual model designed to present plans three-dimensionally (3D), connecting them to construction planning schedules, resulting in a valuable asset to the monitoring of the development of construction activity. The 4D (3D+time) application considers the time factor showing the 3D geometry of the different steps of the construction activity, according to the plan established for the construction.
- A second VR model was created in order to help in the maintenance of exterior closures of walls in a building. It allows the visual and interactive transmission of information related to the physical behaviour of the elements. To this end, the basic knowledge of material most often used in façades, anomaly surveillance, techniques of rehabilitation, and inspection planning were studied. This information was included in a database that supports the periodic inspection needed in a program of preventive maintenance.

- A third VR model is an application concerning the maintenance analyses of interior wall allowing the visualization of the degradation over time of the painted elements of a building. The virtual model support the inspection activity helping to choose the anomalies, the provable causes and the most adequate repair methodologies. In addition, a chromatic scale is created and associated with the walls covering elements to evaluate their degradation since they are painted until they reach their expected durability, and needed to be repainted.

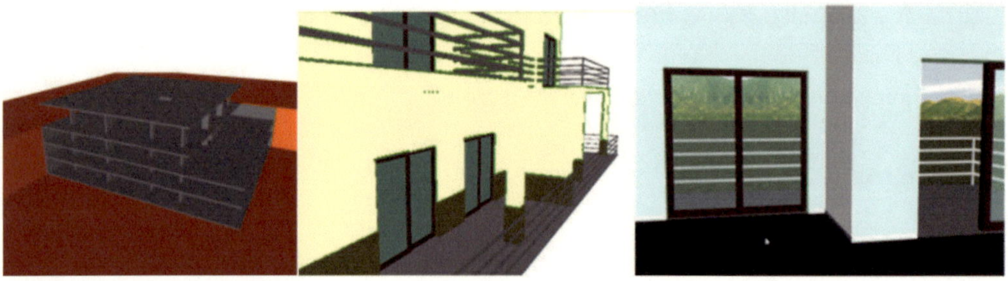

Figure 1. VR models of construction and coating elements of exterior and interior walls.

This work brings an innovative contribution to the field of construction and maintenance supported by emergent technology. The building lifecycle is in constant evolution, so require the study of preventive maintenance, though, for example, the planning of periodic local inspections and corrective maintenance with repair activity analysis. For this reason, the VR models facilitative the visual and interactive access to results, supporting the drawing-up of inspection reports. The focus of the work is on travelling through time, or the ability to view a product or its components at different points in time throughout their life. In maintenance, the time variable is related to the progressive deterioration of the materials throughout the building's lifecycle.

2. 4D and VR models in construction

These interactive models integrate VR technology and applications implemented in Visual Basic (VB) language. The models allow interaction with the 3D geometric model of a building, visualizing components for each construction. They are linked to databases of the corresponding technical information concerning the maintenance of the materials used as interior and exterior closures. The principal objective of the interactive VR prototypes is to support decision-making in the area of maintenance planning.

Currently, the management of information related to the maintenance of buildings is based on the planning of action to be taken and on the log of completed work. The capacity to visualize the process can be added through the use of three-dimensional (3D) models which facilitate the interpretation and understanding of target elements of maintenance and of 4D (3D+time) models through which the evolution of deterioration can be visually demonstrated and understood. Furthermore, the possibility of interaction with the geometric models can be provided through the use of VR technology.

Information technology, namely 4D modelling and VR techniques, is currently in use both in the construction activity and in education (Mohammed, 2007). At the Department of Civil Engineering, some didactic models have already been generated. The research project presented in this chapter follows on from that previous educational work: two 3D geometric models which support activity in the rehabilitation of buildings (Sampaio et al., 2006); and three VR models developed to support classes in Civil Engineering (wall, bridge and roof construction) in Technical Drawing, Construction and Bridge disciplines (Sampaio et al., 2010). The didactic VR models are in common use in both face-to-face classes and on an e-learning platform.

In construction industry, from the conception to the actual implementation, project designs are presented mostly on chapter, even though the two dimensional reading is often not enough, as mistakes can be introduced in early stages of conception or elements misunderstood on the construction site. 3D models present an alternative to avoid inaccuracies, as all the information can be included with the necessary detail. Computer systems used in construction for graphic representation have experienced a vast evolution, allowing new ways of creating and presenting projects. 4D models, also labelled as 3D evolutionary models, permit a better comprehension of the project throughout its life, minimizing the information loss through the chain of events. In addition VR technology can present a step-by-step guide in assembling complex structures in an interactive way. One of the benefits of VR in construction is the possibility of a virtual scenario being visited by the different specialists, exchanging ideas and correcting mistakes. Some applications are already offering the possibility of communication between different specialties while developing a mutual project (Yerrapathruni et al. 2003).

In construction management, over the years, technical drawings have played a crucial role in communication between the numerous partners in a project. Generally, drawings represent formal solutions, and often incompatibility mistakes are only detected at advanced stages, on site, accruing additional costs. In this field 4D models promote the interaction between the geometric model and construction activity planning, allowing immediate perception of the evolution of the work. In planning, in correct evaluation and the meeting of needs as they arise, 4D models constitute a positive contribution to decision-making when establishing planning strategies (Webb and Haupt, 2003).

Virtual Reality technology can support the management of data that is normally generated and transformed or replaced throughout the lifecycle of a building. This technology constitutes an important support in the management of buildings allowing interaction and data visualization. At present, the management of building planning can be presented in 3D form and various materials can be assigned to the fixtures and furnishing enabling the user to be placed in the virtual building and view it from inside as well as outside. This study contemplates the incorporation of the 4th dimension, that is, time, into the concept of visualization. The focus of the work is on travelling through time, or the ability to view a product or its components at different points in time throughout their life. In maintenance, the time variable is related to the progressive deterioration of the materials throughout the building's lifecycle. It is implicit that the incorporation of the time dimension into 3D visualization will enable the designer/user to make more objective decisions about the choice of the constituent components of the building.

The chapter describes both (interior and exterior walls) maintenance models, highlighting the constitution of the database supporting the models, and the organization of a user-friendly interface designed to be used by an inspection worker. During the construction of these models, the basic knowledge of the topics involved, such as aspects related to the materials, the techniques of rehabilitation and conservation and the planning of maintenance is outlined and discussed. In addition, methods of interconnecting this knowledge with the virtual model are explored. These prototypes were trailed in an actual project. The lifecycle aspects of the construction activity are in constant evolution, so require the study of preventive maintenance, through, for example, the planning of periodic local inspections and corrective maintenance with repair activity analysis. For this reason, the model facilitates the visual and interactive access to results, supporting the drawing-up of inspection reports.

The construction model brings an innovative aspect to 4D modelling as usually applied to construction planning, through the incorporation of pictures into the interface of the VR model, an important support element in the comparison between what is planned and what is in progress in situ after each construction task.

3. Construction planning model

Construction management can be defined as the planning, co-ordination and control of a project from conception to completion (including commissioning) on behalf of a client (Walker, 2002).

This requires the identification of the client's objectives in terms of usage, function, quality, time and cost, and the establishment of relationships between the people involved, integrating, monitoring and controlling the contributors to the project and their output, and evaluating and selecting alternative solutions in pursuit of the client's satisfaction with the outcome of the project. It is essential, therefore, that the project designer has the depth of knowledge to be able to correctly identify the different stages of the construction planning, as well as to take into consideration the logistics and resources involved in the project. The construction planning used in the implemented prototype is realistic and considers the graphic and written documentation, measurements and quantities map, specifications and regulations relevant to the project (Leinonen et al. 2003).

A prototype based on VR technology with application to these demands of construction planning, was created. This interactive virtual model presents the project in 3D, integrated with the construction planning schedule, resulting in a valuable asset in monitoring the development of the construction activity, compared to the construction planning already drawn up. The 4D application allows the time factor to be considered in conjunction with the 3D geometry of the different steps of the construction activity, according to the schedule established for the construction, thus offering a detailed analysis of the construction project.

Additionally, VR technology allows the visualization of different stages of the construction and interaction with the real-time construction activity. This application clearly shows the constructive process, avoiding inaccuracies and building errors, thereby facilitating better communication between partners in the construction process. This application was developed in three stages:

- Planning takes into consideration the final purpose of the presentation, and the definition of tasks; the details, therefore have to be in line with this idea. Using *Microsoft Project 2007*, the tasks are introduced and the relations between them defined;
- Geometric modelling needs to relate correctly to the tasks as defined at the planning stage. Using *AutoCAD 2010* as a modelling tool, the layers make the distinction between the different tasks and elements are created in enough detail to support correct comprehension. The application also presents a real-time illustration of the evolution of the construction through photographs of the site, taken at specific points in time;
- The third stage, integration of the first two stages, makes use of two programs. *EON Studio 5.0* (2010) and *Microsoft Visual C# 2008 Express Edition*, where the first takes the 3D model created with *AutoCAD* and introduces it in the application developed using the second.

3.1. Interface

The application, developed in C#, integrates all the components described with the interface as shown in Fig. 2. The application his organized as outlined below: Virtual model; pictures of construction site; planning task list; Gantt map.

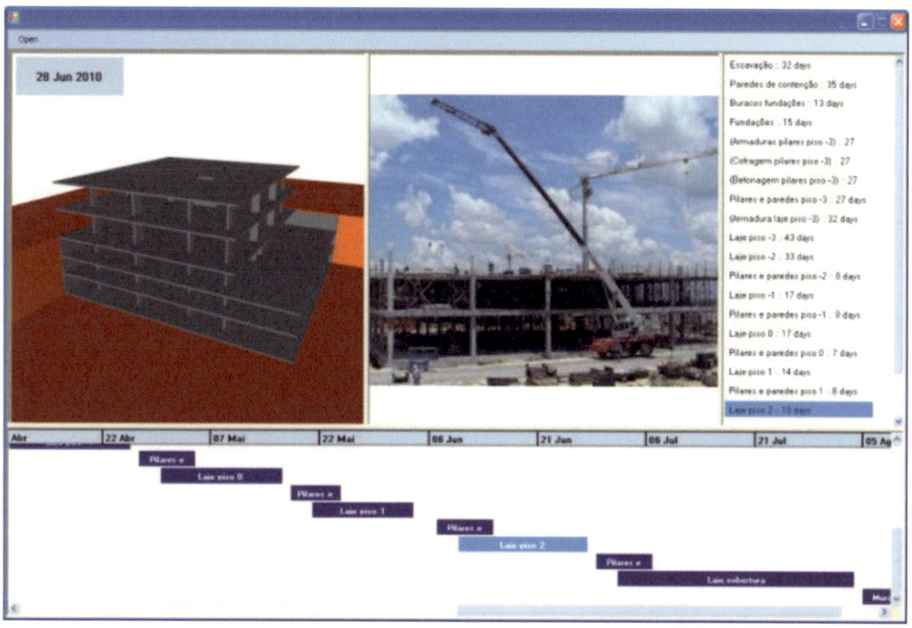

Figure 2. Application interface.

The interaction with the application is made through Planning task list and Gantt map. Both the task list items and Gantt map bars are buttons which, when pressed, send the information to the *EON* for the task selected, and in return *EON* presents the model in the current state, that is, it shows and hides specific elements depending on the specific stage of the construction.

EON can interact with the model in a number of different ways. In this prototype only the state of the elements and camera position is changed. The state of an element is presented by its Hidden property, whether it is selected or not, whilst the camera position is determined by translation and rotation coordinates. *EON Studio* also offers the possibility of changing the material associated with each element, creating a more realistic model.

Any new objects can be introduced into the application, just by modelling the new elements considering their positions relative to the ones already in the simulation and programming the associated action in *EON Studio.*

Likewise, the application accepts any kind of construction project, as long as its implementation imperatives are met. Additionally, with the appropriate models, it can also be used in construction site management.

3.2. Programming details

The weakness of this prototype lies in the time needed to carry out the preparation for the actual interaction with the application. Modelling a building may not be very extensive. The programming of the actions in *EON Studio,* however, can be time-consuming.

In the application, the geometric model of the building is presented in a sequence simulating the construction activity. For that, each modelled component of the building is connected to the programming instruction: hidden and unhidden (Fig. 3).

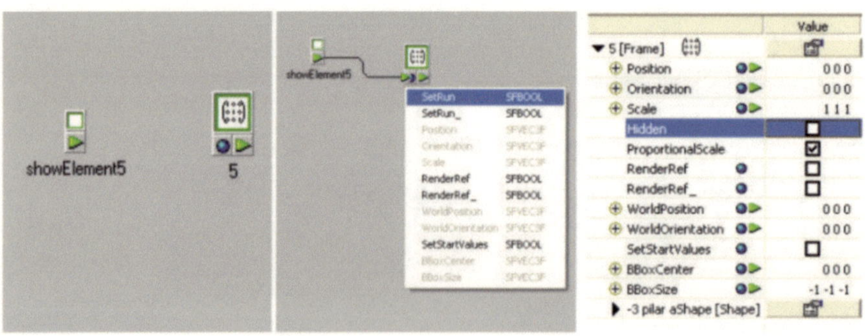

Figure 3. Hidden and unhidden instruction.

This is one of the capacities allowed by the *EON* software. The command of unhide is linked to each step (label of the list of activities and bar of the Gant map) and to each geometric model. The identification both in the list/map and the related geometric model is established by a number. The number corresponds to the sequence defined in the design project. An action will begin when the user click over a label or a bar.

Fig. 4 presents a tree of links connecting the command of interaction (executed by the user) and the instruction show of the respective element (see the instruction *showelement_n* linked to the geometric model identified by the *n* number).

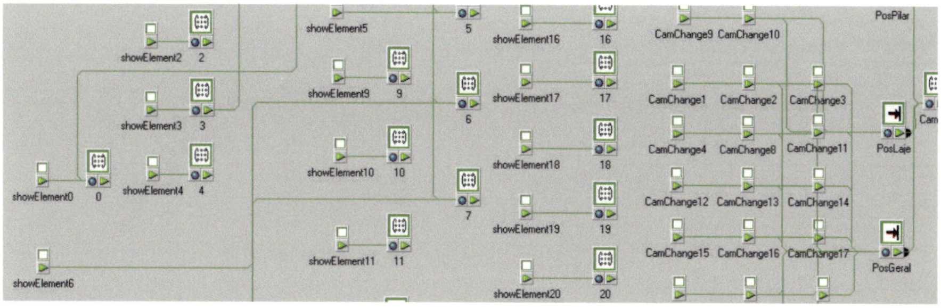

Figure 4. Diagram of actions hidden/unhidden for each element and the control of the camera.

In addition the control of the position and orientation of a camera (position, zoom and orientation of the model in relation to the observer) must be defined in accordance with the selected construction step. The position of the camera is controlled within the *EON* software as shown in Fig. 4. A first position of the camera is defined in order to allow the user to visualize adequately the selected detail of the building (Fig. 5). After that the user is free to walkthrough inside and around the model. For that the user must interact with the 3D model through the VR window of the interface.

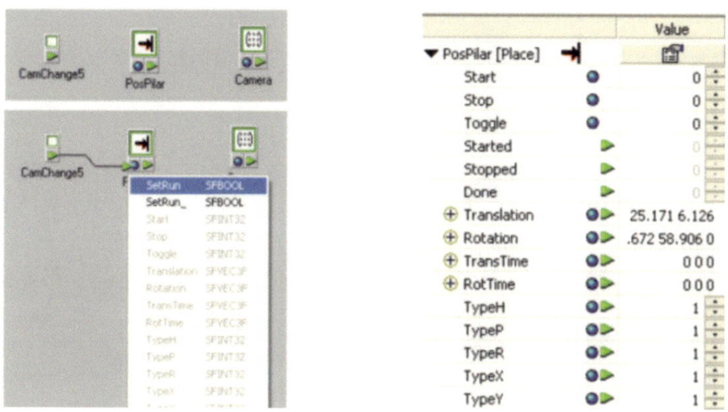

Figure 5. Control of the translation and rotation movements of the model.

3.3. Example of application

As a method of testing the application, a construction project was undertaken, more particularly, the structure of a building, using both its graphic documentation, that is, the architectural and structural blueprints, and the project description and construction planning (Fig. 6). The whole project was simplified to serve this chapter's academic purposes: the list of tasks was defined based on the more characteristic stages of a construction process, and a few tasks focused on the construction details of certain elements.

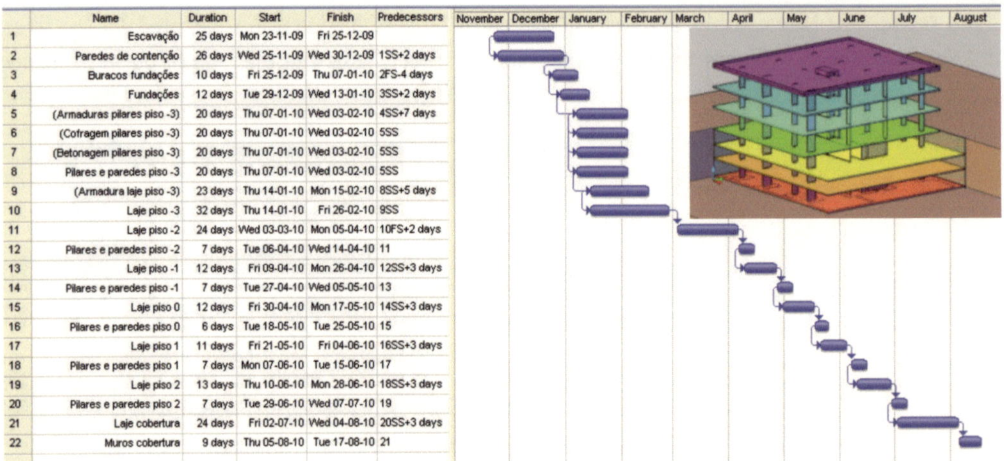

	Name	Duration	Start	Finish	Predecessors
1	Escavação	25 days	Mon 23-11-09	Fri 25-12-09	
2	Paredes de contenção	26 days	Wed 25-11-09	Wed 30-12-09	1SS+2 days
3	Buracos fundações	10 days	Fri 25-12-09	Thu 07-01-10	2FS-4 days
4	Fundações	12 days	Tue 29-12-09	Wed 13-01-10	3SS+2 days
5	(Armaduras pilares piso -3)	20 days	Thu 07-01-10	Wed 03-02-10	4SS+7 days
6	(Cofragem pilares piso -3)	20 days	Thu 07-01-10	Wed 03-02-10	5SS
7	(Betonagem pilares piso -3)	20 days	Thu 07-01-10	Wed 03-02-10	5SS
8	Pilares e paredes piso -3	20 days	Thu 07-01-10	Wed 03-02-10	5SS
9	(Armadura laje piso -3)	23 days	Thu 14-01-10	Mon 15-02-10	8SS+5 days
10	Laje piso -3	32 days	Thu 14-01-10	Fri 26-02-10	9SS
11	Laje piso -2	24 days	Wed 03-03-10	Mon 05-04-10	10FS+2 days
12	Pilares e paredes piso -2	7 days	Tue 06-04-10	Wed 14-04-10	11
13	Laje piso -1	12 days	Fri 09-04-10	Mon 26-04-10	12SS+3 days
14	Pilares e paredes piso -1	7 days	Tue 27-04-10	Wed 05-05-10	13
15	Laje piso 0	12 days	Fri 30-04-10	Mon 17-05-10	14SS+3 days
16	Pilares e paredes piso 0	6 days	Tue 18-05-10	Tue 25-05-10	15
17	Laje piso 1	11 days	Fri 21-05-10	Fri 04-06-10	16SS+3 days
18	Pilares e paredes piso 1	7 days	Mon 07-06-10	Tue 15-06-10	17
19	Laje piso 2	13 days	Thu 10-06-10	Mon 28-06-10	18SS+3 days
20	Pilares e paredes piso 2	7 days	Tue 29-06-10	Wed 07-07-10	19
21	Laje cobertura	24 days	Fri 02-07-10	Wed 04-08-10	20SS+3 days
22	Muros cobertura	9 days	Thu 05-08-10	Tue 17-08-10	21

Figure 6. Construction planning (list and Gantt map) and the 3D model of the building structure.

As a result, *AutoCAD* layers were created for each task defined and the 3D model constructed. When finished, the 3D model was exported to *EON Studio,* where a diagram of events was created, after which the application was ready to be used. As explained above, the task list and the virtual model are connected: when selecting a task, the relevant construction stage is presented (Fig. 7). The first scenario is the landscape and then the foundation work is shown. There being no picture associated, the camera symbol becomes visible instead.

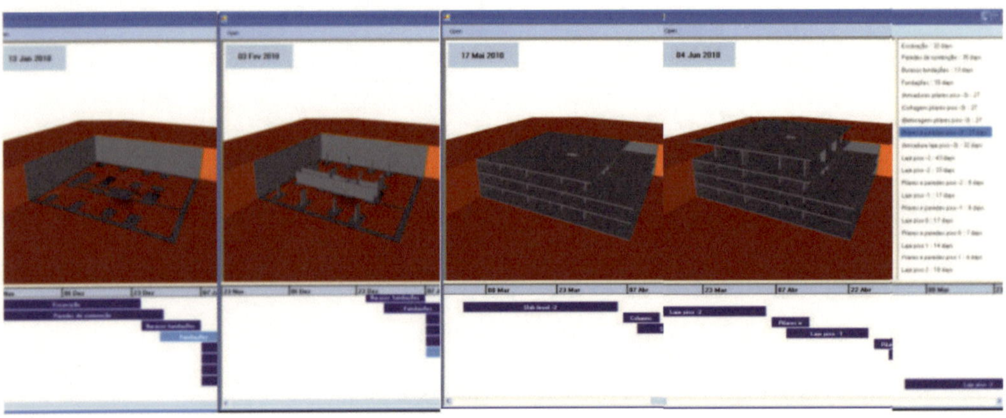

Figure 7. Application's virtual model and task list.

Some construction details have been modelled. Progress across three different stages, of one of the columns and a detail of the reinforcement and concrete of a slab, are shown in Fig. 8.

When constructing a building, the planning sometimes needs to be changed due to unexpected occurrences. Implementing these changes in the prototype is actually very simple, as the user has only attribute new start and finishes dates to the task in *MS Project* and load the new file into the application.

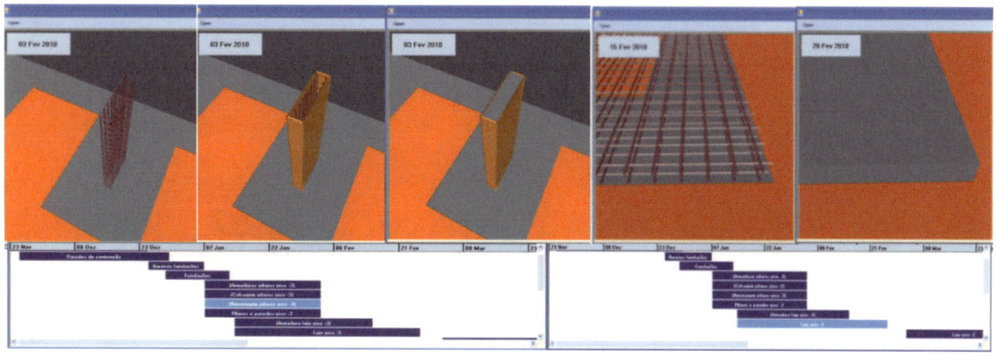

Figure 8. Column and slab construction: reinforcement, formwork and concreting.

All steps have been modelled and linked to the planning chart. Fig. 9 shows the details of the construction work. The date for each visualized task is shown in the upper left corner of the virtual model window.

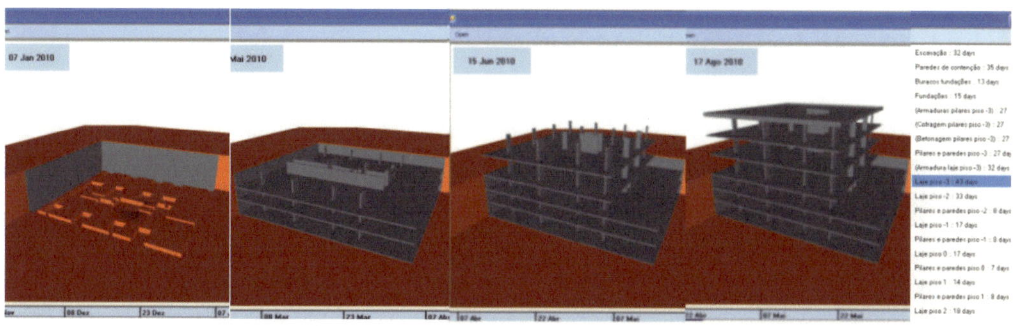

Figure 9. Sequence of the construction process.

When a task is selected in the construction planning chart the static position of the model is presented. A first view is always linked to a task. This was established to provide easier interaction with the 3D model, and to focus the attention of the user on the important sections of each task, guiding them through the proper course of development of the construction. Next, the user can manipulate the virtual model, in order to choose the identical perspective as that shown in the photo. So, with the visualization of what is planned and what has been done in the real building, the construction work can be better compared and analysed (Fig. 10).

In addition by manipulating the model the user can walk through the virtual building observing any construction detail he wants to compare. Comparing with other 4D models the interaction with the present model is not completed allowed and the pictures obtain in the construction place are not linked with the model (Casimiro, 2006). This VR model is more intuitive. So the principal innovative contribution of the model is the incorporation of updated pictures taken in situ. It helps designer to follow adequately the construction process and he can introduce the necessary changes in the construction plan previously established.

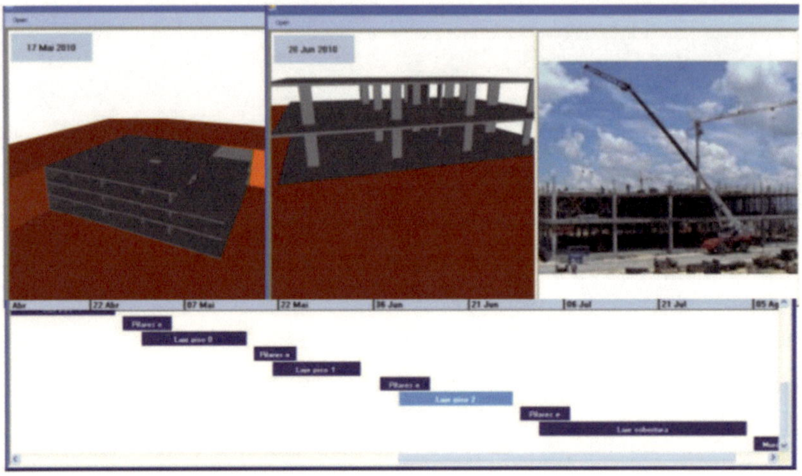

Figure 10. Rotation applied to the virtual model.

4. Interior wall maintenance model

The coating applied to building walls, naturally, performs an important aesthetic function: it is, however, essentially a protective element for the substrate on which it is applied as far as the action of environmental agents of wear and tear is concerned. The coating is fundamental to a proper overall performance of a building throughout its working life.

Materials frequently used in the coating of ordinary buildings are: paint, varnish, stone and ceramics (Eusébio and Rodrigues, 2009). In Portugal, where interior walls are concerned, the most commonly used coating is paint. It is a multi-purpose material, used under a variety of decorative effects, based on a widely-ranging palette of colours, patterns and textures and is easily applied on any type of surface. In addition, paint, compared to other materials, is less costly, not only as far as the product itself is concerned, but also in its application, since relatively non-specialized labour is required. Nevertheless, as deterioration is a given, maintenance is needed.

Factors such as the constant exposure of the coating to the weather, pollutants and the normal actions of housing use, linked to its natural ageing and, in some cases to the unsuitable application of systems of painting give rise to its deterioration and to the appearance of irregularities, which can negatively affect its performance as both an aesthetic and a protective element. According to Lopes (2004), in normal conditions of exposure and when correctly applied a paint coating can remain unaltered for about five years. Establishing suitable maintenance strategies for this type of coating is based on the knowledge of the most frequent irregularities, the analysis of the respective causes and the study of the most suitable repair methodologies.

The completed virtual model identifies the elements of the building which make up the interior wall coating so that monitoring can take place. The application is supported by a database, created for the purpose, of irregularities, their probable causes and suitable repair processes, which facilitates the inspection process. The information is recorded and associated to each monitored element, allowing subsequently, the inspection and repair activity log to be consulted, thus providing a tool for the definition of a rehabilitation strategy. In addition, the model assigns a colour to each of the coating elements, the colours defined by the time variable, so that the evolution of the deterioration of the coating material is clearly shown through the alteration in colour. The prototype is, then, a 4D model.

The model integrates a virtual environment with an application developed in Visual Basic programming language. This allows interaction with the 3D model of buildings in such a way that it becomes possible to follow the process of monitoring the coating elements, specifically, painted interior walls, in terms of maintenance, throughout the life-cycle of the building.

4.1. Maintenance

The General Regulations for Urban Buildings (RGEU, 1951) applied in Portugal, stipulates the frequency of maintenance work, stating that existing buildings must be repaired and undergo maintenance at least once every eight years with the aim of eliminating defects arising from normal wear and tear and to maintain then in good usable condition in all aspects of housing use referred to in that document.

The time-limit indicated is applicable to all elements of the buildings generally. It is clear, however, that the regulatory period is too long for some specific components and that, frequently enough, the time-limits for action are not respected. There are, too, inefficient rent policies, leading to long periods without rehabilitation, and that the prevailing culture is one of reaction on the part of the various parties involved in the maintenance process. To these aspects should also be added the defects sometimes registered during the construction of property developments, exacerbating the poor state of repair of the buildings. This gives rise to numerous irregularities which, in turn, frequently leads to inadequate safety conditions.

According to Cóias (2009), the purpose of maintenance is to prolong the useful life of the building and to encourage adherence to the demands of safety and functionality, keeping in mind the specific set of conditions of each case and its budgetary considerations. Satisfactory management of this activity is carried out by putting into practice a maintenance plan which must take into consideration technical, economic, and functional aspects arising with each case.

Collen (2003) points out that investment in the maintenance and rehabilitation sector in Portugal is still weak compared to that in the same sector in the construction industry in the other countries of the European Community. She makes it clear, however, on a more positive note, that some measures have already begun to be implemented here: some urban regeneration programs have been created, legislation, which focuses on the sustainability of buildings, has been laid down, and the revision of constructive solutions has been carried out, all with the objective of guaranteeing that the maintenance of built heritage be an integral part of the construction sector.

The maintenance of buildings, then, is an activity of considerable importance within the construction industry; its contributory aspects of conservation and rehabilitation work need to be supported by correct methodologies of action, underpinned by scientific criteria and by suitable processes for the diagnosis of irregularities and the evaluation of their causes. This chapter aims to make a positive contribution to this field using the new computer technology tools of visualization and interaction.

4.2. Pathologies in paint coatings

The technical document Paints, Varnishes and Painted Coatings for Civil Construction published by The National Laboratory for Civil Engineering (LNEC) (Eusébio and Rodrigues, 2009), defines paint as a mixture essentially made up of pigments, binder, vehicle and additives. It has a pigmented, pasty composition, and when applied in a fine layer to a surface, presents, after the dispersion of volatile products, the appearance of a solid, collared and opaque film (Farinha, 2010).

The durability of the painted coating depends on the environment in which it is used, and on the surface it is applied to as well as the rate of deterioration of the binder in the paint. The influence of the environment is the result of the action, in conjunction or alone, of a variety of factors such as the degree of humidity, the levels of ultraviolet radiation, oxygen, ozone and alkalis, variations in temperature and of other physical or chemical agents whose effect depends considerably on the time taken to apply it (Marques, 1985). When their influence is not counteracted or minimized, imperfections can arise in the coating film, such as, the appearance of defects in the layer or paint with the loss of functionality where the desired aim of the application is concerned.

These irregularities manifest themselves in various ways and in different degrees of severity. Based on the study made of the causes of the defects, specific methodologies for their resolution were established. Fig. 11 shows common defects in painted interior walls.

Figure 11. Swelling, efflorescence, cracking and blistering (Moura. 2008).

The information gained from the pathological analysis of this type of coating was used to draw up a database supporting the interactive application. These data support the creation of inspection files related to the elements which are monitored in each case studied.

In order to form a user-friendly database of relatable data, groups of pathologies, shown below in Table 1, were considered. This classification provides the required automatism of access to the database and supports the presentation of synopses of the causes and repair methodology inherent in each pathology.

Classification	Irregularity	Repair methodology
Alteration in colon	Yellowing	- Cleaning the surface and repainting with a finish both compatible with the existing coat and resistant to the prevailing conditions of exposure in its environment
	Bronzing	
	Fading	
	Spotting	
	Loss of gloss	
	Loss of hiding power	
Deposits	Dirt pick-up and retention	- Cleaning the surface.
	Viscosity	
Changes in texture	Efflorescence	- Removal by brushing scraping or washing; - repainting the surface; - When necessary apply sealer before repainting.
	Sweating	
	Cracking	
	Chalking	
	Saponification	
Reduction in adhesion	Peeling	- Proceed by totally or partially removing the coat of paint; - Check the condition of the base and proceed with its repair where necessary; - Prepare the base of the paint work.
	Flaking	
	Swelling	

Table 1. Classification of irregularities.

During the process of an on-site inspection, the user of the application can refer to the database in order to classify the abnormality being observed, consulting the list of defects, which includes, in addition to their identification, the most relevant characteristics and some of the causes that could be at the root of their development. Table 2 lists two of the irregularities from the classification: *Alteration in colour*.

Classification	Irregularity	Characteristics and causes
Alteration in colour	Yellowing	- A yellow colour caused by ageing of the film of the paint or varnish; - Action of environmental agents (solar radiation, temperature oxygen and humidity) on the binder in the paint provoking changes in its molecular structure.
	Discoloration	- Partial loss of colour of the film of paint coating; - Action of environmental agents (solar radiation, temperature, polluted atmosphere and chemically aggressive bases of application) on the binder and/or the pigments of the painted coating.

Table 2. Irregularities and Causes.

4.3. Interactive model

The completed application supports on-site inspections and the on-going analysis of the evolution of the degree of deterioration of the coating. The following computational systems were used in its development: *AutoCAD*, in the creation of the 3D model of the building; *EON Studio* (2010), for the programming of the interactivity capacities integrated with the geometric model; *Visual Basic 6* in the creation of all the windows of the application and in the establishment of links between components. All the systems were made available by the *ISTAR/DECivil* (2011), of the Technical University of Lisbon (TUL).

The main interface gives access to the virtual model of the building and to the inspection and maintenance modules (highlighted in Fig. 12). The first step is to make a detailed description of the building (location, year of construction, type of structure....., Fig. 13) and representative modelled elements of the interior wall coating, so that they can be monitored.

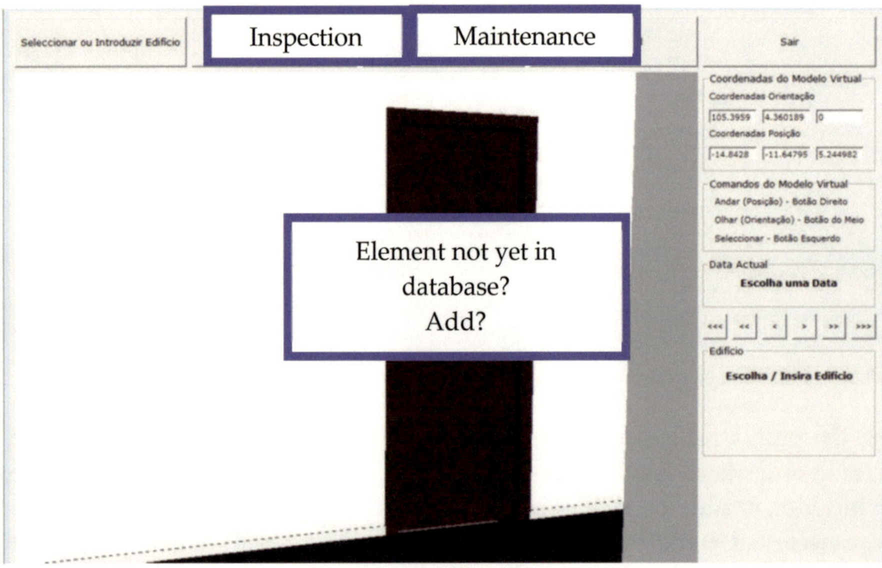

Figure 12. The main interface of the virtual application.

The model is manipulated in the virtual environment by using the mouse buttons (movement through the interior of the model and orientation of the camera, Fig. 13). The coordinates of the observer's position and the direction of his/her point of view are associated with the element during the process of identification. Thus, later, when an element in the database of the application is selected using the interface, the model is displayed in the visualization window so that the target coating can be observed.

Walking through the model with the aim of accessing all the elements of the building, the user needs to be able to go up and down stairs or open doors or windows. The virtual model has been programmed, using the *EON system*, in such a way that these capacities are activated by positioning the cursor over the respective objects, in that way, the user is able to walk through the whole model.

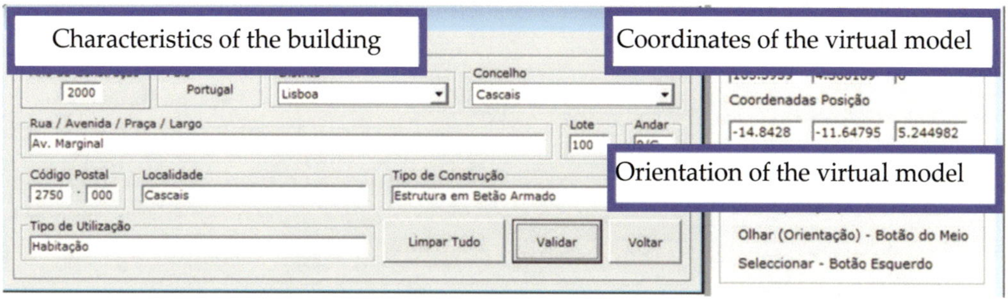

Figure 13. Interface for the detailed description of the building and coordinates and manipulation commands in the virtual model.

Each wall surface in each of the rooms of the house is a component which has to be monitored and, therefore, to be identified. Using the model, the user must click the mouse on an element, and the message New Element is shown (highlighted in Fig. 12). Associated to this selected element is the information regarding location within the house (hall, bedroom), wall type (simple internal masonry wall) and coating (paint).

4.3.1. *Making an inspection*

Later, on an on-site inspection visit, the element to be analysed it selected interactively on the virtual model. The inspection sheet (Fig. 15) is accessed by using the Inspection button which is found in the main interface (Fig. 12). The data which identify the selected element are transferred to the initial data boxes on the displayed page (Fig. 14).

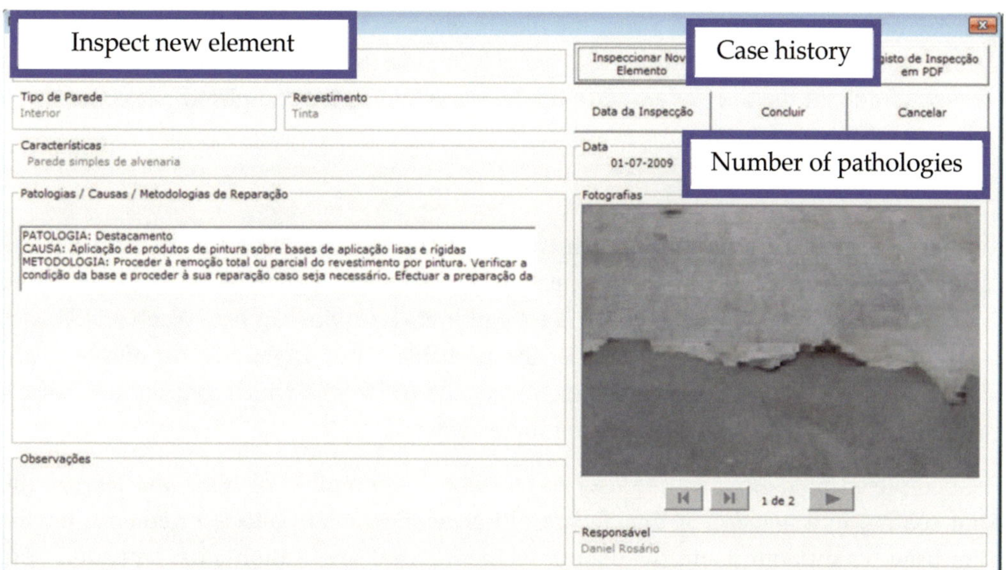

Figure 14. Presentation of the information introduced into the inspection sheet.

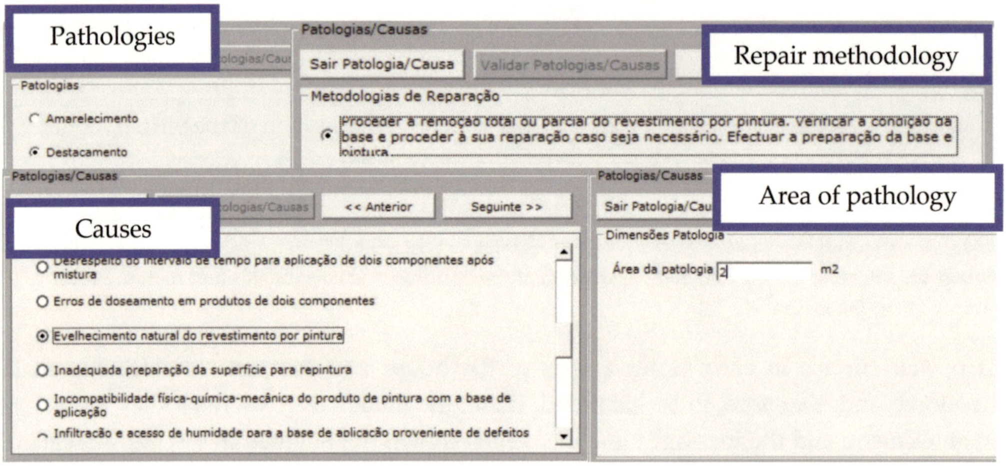

Figure 15. Interface for the selection of the irregularity, probable cause, area and repair methodology.

Next, using the database, the irregularity which corresponds to the observed defect, with its probable cause (ageing) and the prescribed repair methodology (removal and repainting) is selected (see highlighted area, Fig. 15). The current size of the pathology should also be indicated since it reveals how serious it is (*area of pathology*, Fig. 15). In the field *Observations*, the inspector can add any relevant comment (Fig. 14), photographs obtained on site can also be inserted into the inspection window and the date of the on-site visit and the *ID* of the inspector should also be added. Several different irregularities in the same coating can be analysed (field *Number of pathologies*, Fig. 14) and other elements can be analysed and recorded and defects observed. Later, the files thus created, associated to each of the virtual model elements, can be consulted (*Case history* button in the Interface in Fig. 14). This same window allows all the data referring to the building and to the completed inspection to be shown, in *pdf* format (Fig. 16).

4.3.2. Maintenance monitoring

How long the working life of any construction component might be is an estimate and depends on a set of modifying factors related to their inherent characteristics of quality, to the environment in which the building is set and to its conditions of use (Webb and Haupt, 2003). In maintenance strategy planning the probable dates when adverse effects might occur in each of these elements must be foreseen, and the factors which contribute to defects must be reduced and their consequences minimized.

The completed model allows the user to monitor the evolution of wear and tear on the paint coating in a house. For this, technical information relative to the reference for the paint used, its durability and the date of its most recent application must be added (Fig. 17) to each element through the Maintenance Interface (also accessed from the main interface, Fig. 12).

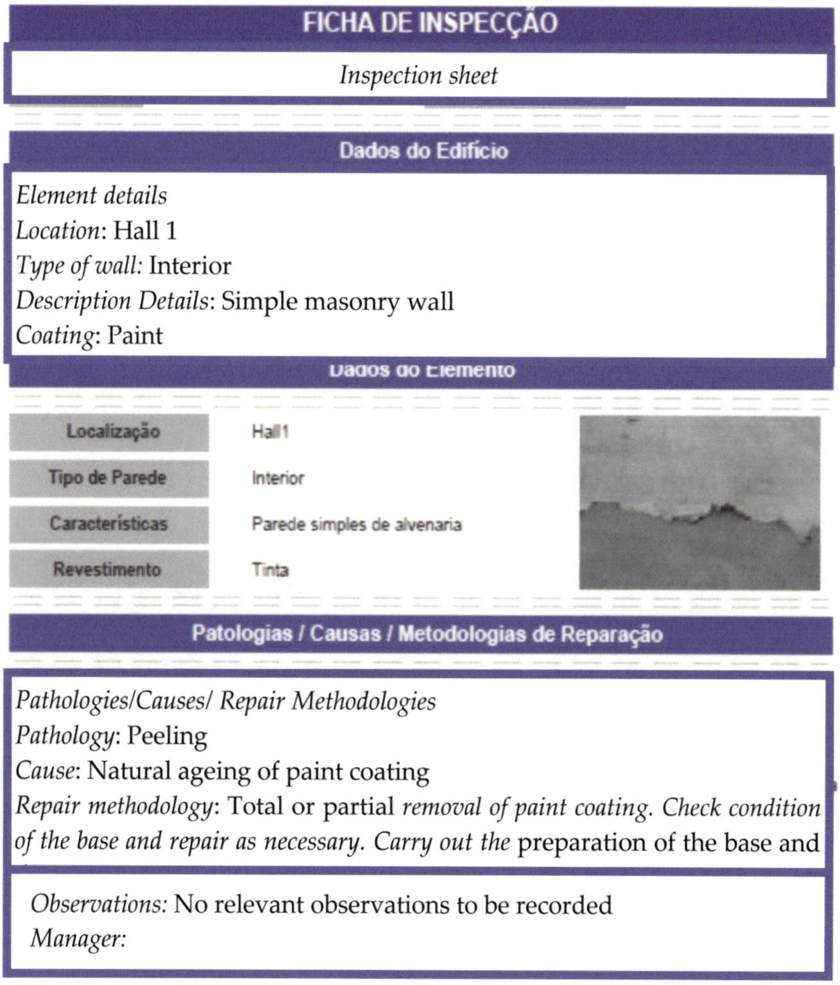

Figure 16. Inspection sheet.

Based on these data, it is possible to link in the date the virtual model is consulted and visualize, in the geometric model, the level of wear and tear as a function of time (see state of repair, Fig. 17). The period of time between the date indicated and the date when the paint was applied is compared to the duration advised, in the technical literature, for repainting. The value given for this comparison is associated to the Red, Green, Blue (RGB) parameters which define the colour used for wall in the virtual model (Fig. 18).

In this way, the colour visualized on the monitored wall varies according to the period of time calculated, pale green being the colour referring to the date of painting and red indicating that the date the model was consulted coincides with that advised for repainting (Fig. 18). The data for painting and repainting are saved to a list of coating elements to be monitored in the virtual model. When an element is selected from this list, the corresponding element is represented in the virtual model, through the preview window, in the colour that corresponds to the period of the consultation.

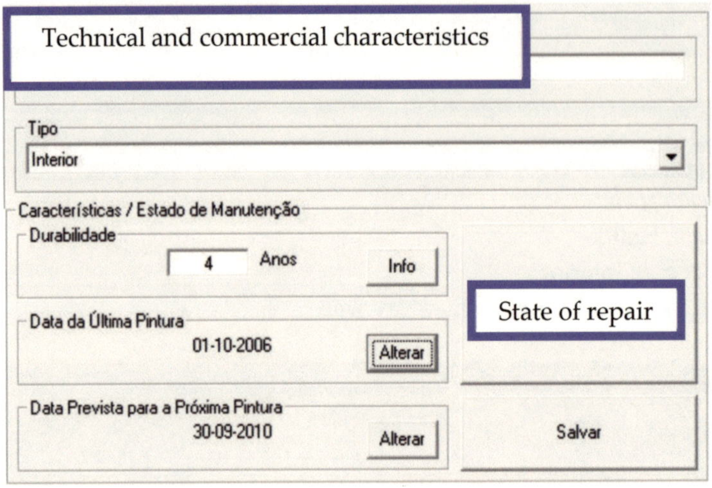

Figure 17. Technical characteristics and the durability of the paint-work.

Figure 18. Chromatic alteration of the coating according to its state of deterioration.

5. Façade maintenance model

Façade coatings play an important role in the durability of buildings, since they constitute the exterior layer that ensures the protection of the wall against the aggressive actions of a physical, chemical or biological nature. Naturally, they should also give the façade the required decorative effect. Since this building component is exposed to adverse atmospheric conditions it frequently shows an evident degree of deterioration, requiring maintenance work. In order to arrive at the best solution for eventual maintenance and repair work, a survey of defects and deterioration must be conducted.

In order to better understand the operation of façade coating, bibliographic research of materials usually applied to this type of material was carried out and a table of characteristics of these was drawn up. Subsequently, a survey was made of anomalies, probable causes, solutions and methods of repair for each of the coatings studied. The visualization of the maintenance data of a building and the impact of time on the performance of these exterior closure materials require an understanding of their characteristics (Gomes and Pinto, 2009) (Fig. 19):

- *Types of material*: painted surfaces, natural stone panels and ceramic wall tiles;
- *Application processes*: stones (panel, support devices, adherent products, etc.); ceramic tiles (fixed mechanism, procedures, ...); painted surfaces (types of paint products, prime and paint scheme surface, exterior emulsion paints, application processes);
- *Anomalies*: dust and dirt, lasting lotus leaf effect, covering power, insufficient resistance to air permeability or weather-proof isolation, damaged stones or ceramic tiles, alkali and smear effect, efflorescence, fractures and fissures and so on;
- *Repair work*: surface cleaning, wire truss reinforcing, cleaning and pointing of stonework joints, removing and replacement of ceramic wall tiles, removing damaged paint and paint surface, preparing and refinishing stone panels, etc..

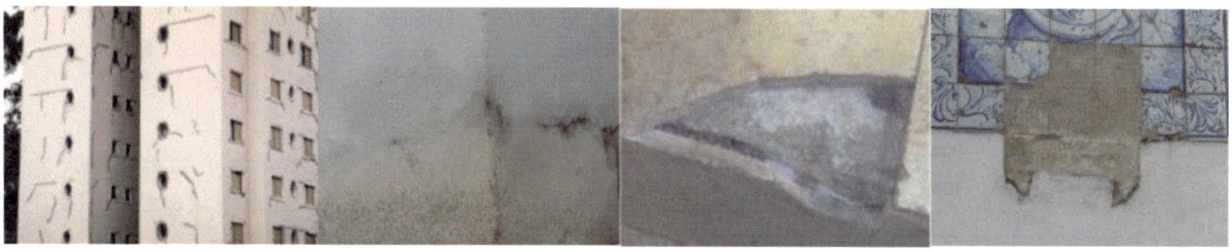

Figure 19. Different types of materials applied as façade coatings and some irregularities.

Depending on the role that the façade coatings play on the wall as a whole they can be classified as finishing, sealing or thermal insulation. The most frequent materials used as coating finishes are painting, tiling and, as sealing coating of the natural stone:

- Paint coating contributes to the aesthetic quality of the building and its environment and also protects the surface of the exterior wall against corrosion, deterioration and penetration of aggressive agents (Ferreira et al.,, 2009);
- The ceramic coating consists essentially of tiling panels, cement and adhesive and the joints between the slabs. The application of ceramic tiling to building façades has considerable advantages particularly as some degree of waterproofing is afforded by the glazed surface along with a great resistance to acids, alkalis and vapour (Veiga and Malanho, 2009);
- The use of natural stone in the coating of façade surfaces is a good solution both technically and aesthetically. The principal characteristics of the stones are: reduced water absorption, sufficient mechanical resistance to bending and impact, abrasion and shearing parallel to the face of the slabs.

5.1. Database

The most frequent anomalies that occur in the coated façades were analysed in order to create a database linked to the virtual model that could support the planning of inspections and maintenance strategies in buildings. This database contains the identification of anomalies that can be found in each type of material used in façades and the corresponding probable cause. For each type of anomaly the most adequate repair solutions were also selected and included in the database. The following example, concerning deficiencies in tiles, illustrates the methodology implemented in this virtual application (Table 3).

Anomaly	Detachment 	Cracking / Fracturing 
Specification of the anomaly	Fall in areas with deterioration of support	Failure of the support (wide cracks with well-defined orientation)
Repair solution	Replacement of the coat (with use of a repair stand as necessary)	Replacement of the coat (with repair of cracks in the support)
Repair methodology	1. Removal of the tiles by cutting grinder with the aid of a hammer and chisel; 2. Timely repair of the support in areas where the detachment includes material constituent with it; 3. Digitizing layer of settlement; 4. Re-settlement of layer and tiles.	1. Removal of the tiles by cutting grinder; 2. Removal of material adjustment in the environment and along the joint; 3. Repair of cracks, clogging with adhesive material (mastic); 4. Settlement layer made with cement in two layers interspersed with glass fibre; 5. Re-settlement of layer and tiles

Table 3. Example of anomalies and the associated repair solution.

5.2. Interface

The implementation of the prototype system makes use of graphical software programming, *Microsoft Visual Basic 6.0,* software to establish a suitable database, Microsoft office access, graphical drawing system, *AutoCAD* and VR technology based software, *EON Studio.*

Many potential users are not computer experts. Human perceptual and cognitive capabilities, therefore, were taken into account when designing this visualization tool with the result that the model is easy to use and does not require sophisticated computer skills.

It uses an interactive 3D visualization system based on the selection of elements directly within the virtual 3D world. Furthermore, associated with each component, there are integrated databases, allowing the consultation of the required data at any point in time.

The interface is composed of a display window allowing users to interact with the virtual model, and a set of buttons for inputting data and displaying results (Fig. 20).

For each new building to be monitored, the characteristics of the environment (exposure to rain and sea) and the identification of each element of the façades must be defined. The data associated to each element are the building orientation, the type of exterior wall (double or single), and the area and type of coating.

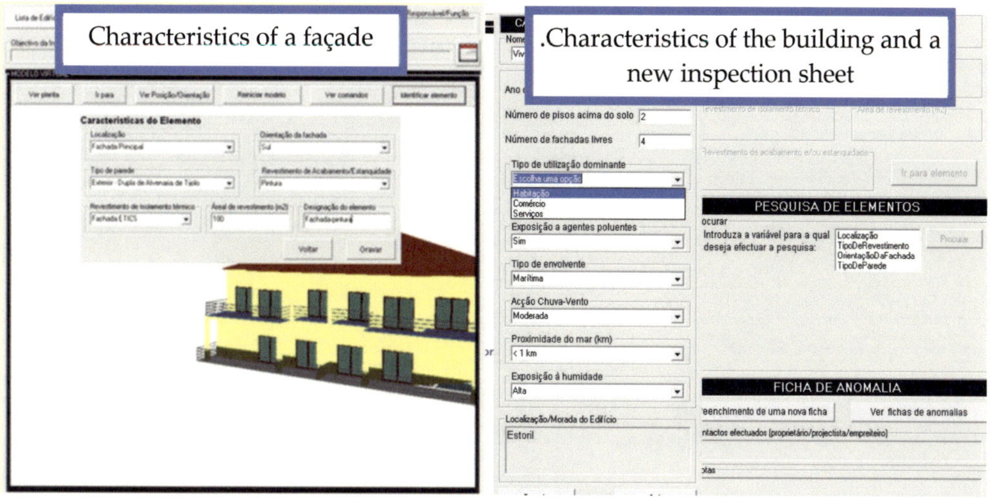

Figure 20. The main interface of the interactive application.

Once each monitored element has been characterized, various inspection reports can be defined and recorded and thereafter consulted when needed. An inspection sheet is accessed from the main interface (Fig. 21). The inspection sheet includes the type of covering (natural stone, Fig. 22), the anomalies (Cracking /Fracturing) and a list of possible causes to be selected and associated to the element. Several photos can be added.

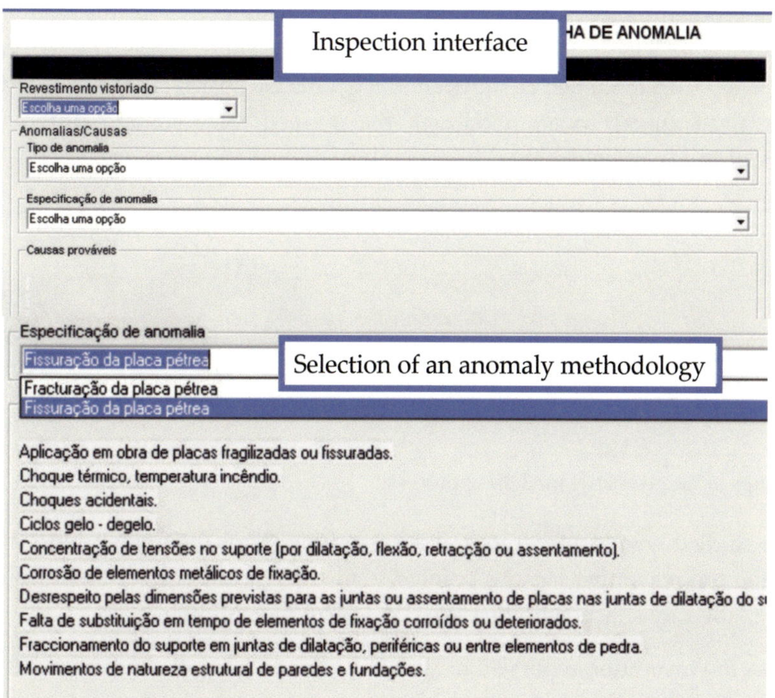

Figure 21. Inspection sheet interface.

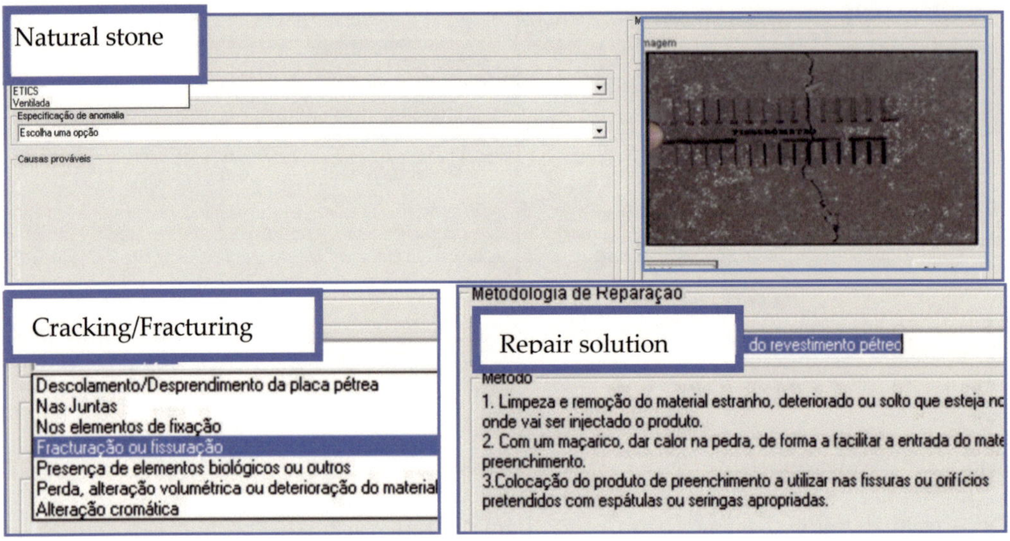

Figure 22. Selecting data in the inspection interface.

5.3. Case study

First, the 3D geometric model of a building was created (Fig. 23). In this case, the building consists of a ground-floor, a 1st floor and an attic with dwelling space. The coating elements of the walls were then modelled as independent geometric objects. In this way, each element can then support characterization data of the applied material and different kinds of information related to maintenance.

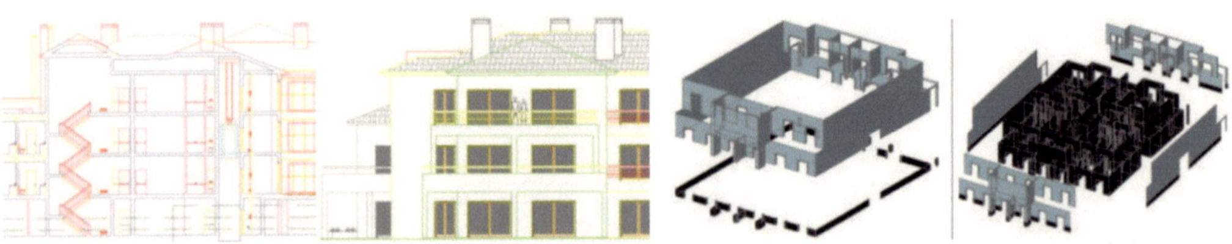

Figure 23. Steps in the geometric modelling process.

All coatings studied were considered in this case-study. Thus the main façade was assumed to be tiled and the remaining façades painted while hall façades are of natural stone. Fig. 24 shows how to identify a façade in the virtual model of the building.

Fig. 25 shows the inspection report of an anomaly. The developed software is easy to handle and transport for on-site inspections and comprises information of the causes, solutions and methods for repairing anomalies.

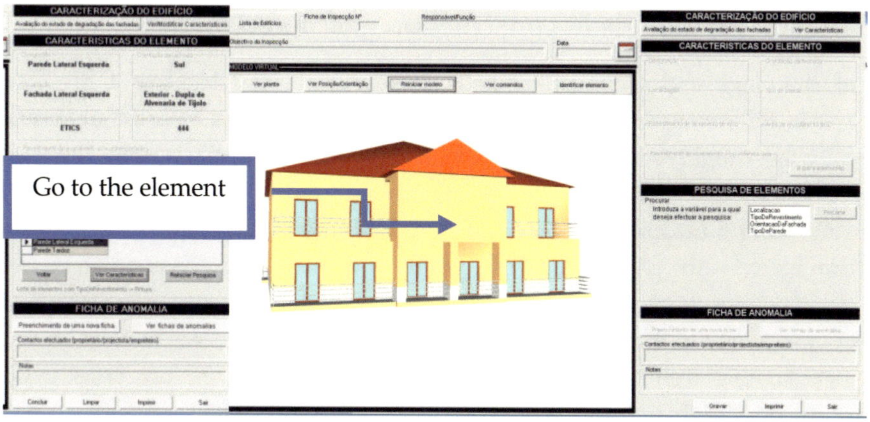

Figure 24. Identification of a façade element.

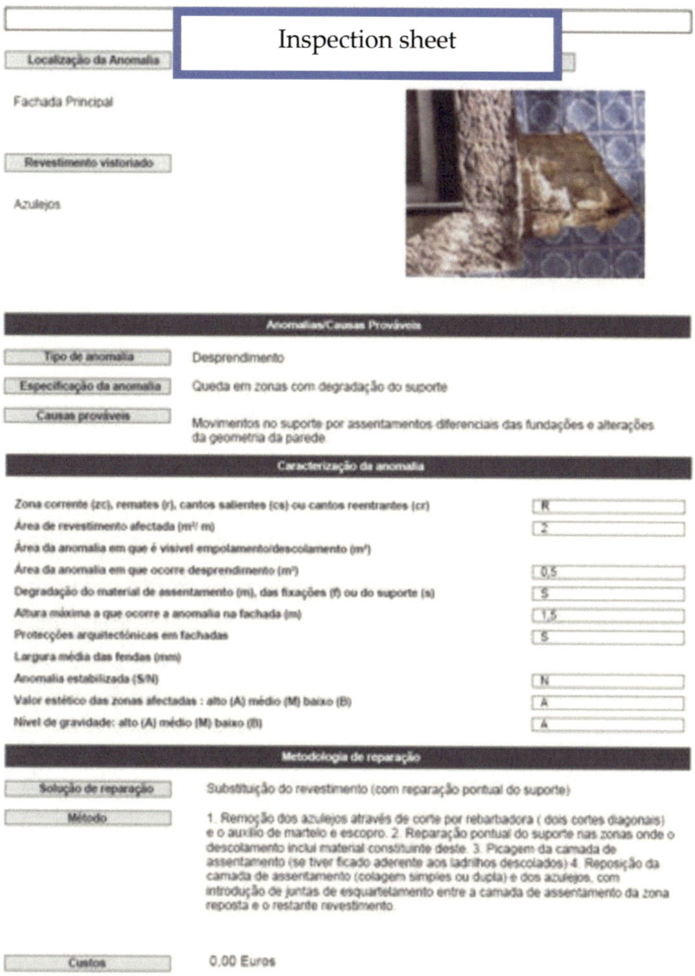

Inspection sheet

Localização da Anomalia

Fachada Principal

Revestimento vistoriado

Azulejos

Anomalias/Causas Prováveis

Tipo de anomalia: Desprendimento

Especificação da anomalia: Queda em zonas com degradação do suporte

Causas prováveis: Movimentos no suporte por assentamentos diferenciais das fundações e alterações da geometria da parede

Caracterização da anomalia

Zona corrente (zc), remates (r), cantos salientes (cs) ou cantos reentrantes (cr)	R
Área de revestimento afectada (m²/ m)	2
Área da anomalia em que é visível empolamento/descolamento (m²)	
Área da anomalia em que ocorre desprendimento (m²)	0,5
Degradação do material de assentamento (m), das fixações (f) ou do suporte (s)	S
Altura máxima a que ocorre a anomalia na fachada (m)	1,5
Protecções arquitectónicas em fachadas	S
Largura média das fendas (mm)	
Anomalia estabilizada (S/N)	N
Valor estético das zonas afectadas : alto (A) médio (M) baixo (B)	A
Nível de gravidade: alto (A) médio (M) baixo (B)	A

Metodologia de reparação

Solução de reparação: Substituição do revestimento (com reparação pontual do suporte)

Método: 1. Remoção dos azulejos através de corte por rebarbadora (dois cortes diagonais) e o auxílio de martelo e escopro. 2. Reparação pontual do suporte nas zonas onde o descolamento inclui material constituinte deste. 3. Picagem da camada de assentamento (se tiver ficado aderente aos ladrilhos descolados) 4. Reposição da camada de assentamento (colagem simples ou dupla) e dos azulejos, com introdução de juntas de esquartelamento entre a camada de assentamento da zona reposta e o restante revestimento

Custos: 0,00 Euros

Figure 25. An inspection sheet report.

6. Benefits of VR models in construction and maintenance

Technical drawings and explanatory texts often have little detail and are frequently insufficient in fully comprehending the object. Using VR models means that mistakes can more easily be caught before construction starts, which translates into time and cost reduction. The construction planning model can be used with any kind of construction project and, being a flexible application, accepts new data when necessary, allowing for a comparison between the planned and the constructed. The prototype can also be expanded to include other aspects of construction management, such as resource administration, or to have real-time access to the construction, through the use of cameras installed on site. The use of new mobile technologies could move the application to the construction site, clarifying any doubts about location or position of each component.

The developed VR models to support the maintenance of walls interior and exterior enables the visual and interactive transmission of information related to the physical behaviour of the elements. As the VR models are linked to each database in an interactive environment and have user-friendly interfaces with easily manipulation of the data, they engender collaborative systems. With these applications, the user may fully interact with the programs referring to the virtual models at any stage of the maintenance process and can analyse the best solution for repair work. They can also support the planning of maintenance strategies. The main aim of the application is to facilitate maintenance enabling the rapid and easy identification of irregularities, as well as the possible prediction of their occurrence through the available inspection record. This analysis has been shown as playing an important role in conservation and in the reduction of costs related to the wear and tear of buildings and contributes to the better management of buildings where maintenance is concerned. The developed software is easy to handle and transport for on-site inspections and comprises information of the causes, solutions and methods for repairing anomalies.

In addition to the inspection component, a maintenance component was developed which, being visualized in a VR environment, as well as being highly intuitive, facilitates the analysis of the state of repair of buildings. By means of a chromatic scale applied to the monitored elements, displayed in the walk-through of the geometrically modelled building, it is possible to identify the elements which, predictably, will need timely action. With the possibility of altering the time parameter freely, the user can carry out this analysis either for past instants or for future events, being able, in this way, to forecast future operations. This capacity of the model, therefore, contributes to the avoidance of costs associated to irregularities which, with the passage of time, become more serious and therefore more onerous.

The use of new mobile technologies could move the application to the construction site, clarifying any doubts about location or position of each component. As each 3D model is linked to a database in an interactive environment and has a user-friendly interface with easily manipulation of the data, it engenders a collaborative system. With these applications, the user may fully interact with the programs referring to each virtual model at any stage of the construction and maintenance processes and can analyse the best solution for alternative to construction plane and repair work. The maintenance applications can also support the planning of maintenance strategies and promote the use of IT tools with advanced graphic and interactive capabilities in order to facilitate and expedite the inspection process. The virtual model, moreover, allows users to see, in the virtual environment, the state of repair of the coating.

Two other VR models are now in progress, concerning the inspection activity of floors and roofs of buildings. With these two other modules the research project will be complete. Then the complete VR application will support different aspects of the maintenance process in buildings.

7. Conclusions

Virtual Reality technology with its capability of interaction and connectivity between elements was employed in the developed prototypes within a research project, offering several benefits both in presenting and developing projects and in supporting decision-making in the construction and maintenance domain.

The models support construction activity. The VR construction model allows the presentation of each step comparing what is planned with the real situation observed, the pictures taken in situ. The model, therefore, helps the designer and owner to redefine the early plan introducing changes to the work in progress. Thus, economic benefits of updating the planning schedule are achieved along with better, error-free construction with no unnecessary delays. The maintenance model supports the global analysis of the need for repair tasks in a building, helping the designer to define an adequate plan of rehabilitation work. The plan must incorporate the repair of all anomalies detected during an inspection visit, which are reported, with the help of the VR model, it, too, bringing economic benefits.

Both maintenance models show the characteristics of each element of the building in the model and the information related to inspection, anomalies and repair works. The information about pathologies, causes and repair methods, collected from a specialized bibliography, has been organized in such a way as to establish a database to be used as a base for the drawing up of a tool to support building maintenance.

Author details

Alcínia Z. Sampaio, Joana Prata, Ana Rita Gomes and Daniel Rosário
Technical University of Lisbon,
Dep. Civil Engineering and Architecture, Lisbon, Portugal

Acknowledgement

The authors gratefully acknowledge the financial support of the Foundation for Science and Technology, a Governmental Organization for the research project PTDC/ ECM/67748/ 2006, *Virtual Reality technology applied as a support tool to the planning of construction maintenance* (Sampaio and Gomes, 2011), still in progress.

8. References

Casimiro, J. (2006). *Integrated Planning of Deadlines and Costs in PME's Small and Medium Businesses*, M.S. thesis, Technical University of Lisbon, Portugal.

Cóias, V. (2009). *Inspections and essays on rehabilitation of buildings*, IST Press, 2nd Ed., ISBN: 978-972-8469-53-5, Lisbon, Portugal.

Collen, I. (2003). *Periodic Inspections in Buildings*, Planet CAD studies, March, 2003, Available from: http://www.planetacad.com/presentationlayer/Estudo_01.aspx?id=13&canal_ordem=04 03.

EON (2011). *Introduction to working in EON Studio*, EON Reality, Inc. 2011, May, 2011, http://www.eonreality.com/.

Eusébio, M.; & Rodrigues, M. (2009). *Paints, Varnishes and Painted Coatings for Civil Construction*, in report CS 14, National Laboratory for Civil Engineering, Lisbon, Portugal, ISBN: 9789724917627.

Farinha, M.B. (2010). *Construction of Buildings in practice: guide oriented to the development of processes and methodologies of construction*, Verlag Dashofer, Vol. 2. ed. Psicosoma, Lisboa. Available from: http://www.psicosoma.pt/

Ferreira, L.; Coroado, J.; Freitas, V. & Maguregui, I. (2009). *Causes of the fall of tiles applied to exteriors of buildings. Patterned tiling in buildings from 1850-1920*. Conf. Patorreb, 3rd Meeting on Pathology and Rehabilitation of Buildings, FEUP, Oporto, Portugal, March 18–20.

Gomes, A.M.; & Pinto, A.P. (2009). *Construction Materials*, Didactic text, Technical University of Lisbon, IST, Lisbon, Portugal.

Gomes, A.R. (2010). *Virtual Reality technology applied to the maintenance of façades*, M.S. thesis, Technical University of Lisbon, Portugal, 2010.

ISTAR (2011), *Architectural Laboratory of IST*, Lisbon, Portugal, May, 2011, Available from: https://fenix.ist.utl.pt/departamentos/decivil/lateral/o-ecivil/unidades-de-apoio/laboratorios-informaticos.

Leinonen, J.; Kähkönen, K.; & Retik, A. (2003). *New construction management practice based on the virtual reality technology*, in book:"4D CAD and Visualization in Construction: Developments and Applications", (Eds.) R. A. Raja, Ian Flood Issa, J. William O'Brien. A.A. Balkema Publishers, pp. 75-100.

Lopes, C. (2004). *Anomalies in Painted Exterior Walls: Technic of Inspection and Structural Evaluation*, Construlink Press, Monograph, 22(2004), Lisbon, Portugal.

Marques, M.I. (1985). *Durability of plastic tint*, in report ITMC 2, National Laboratory for Civil Engineering, Lisbon, Portugal.

Mohammed, E.H. (2007). *n-D Virtual Environment in Construction Education*, Proc. the 2nd International Conference on Virtual Learning, ICVL 2007, pp. 1-6.

Moura, A. (2008). *Characteristics and conservation state of painted façades: study case in Coimbra"*. M.S. thesis, Technical University of Coimbra, Coimbra, Portugal.

RGEU (1951) *General Regulations for Urban Buildings*, Decree-Law, nº 38 382, August 7, Lisbon, Portugal.

Rosário, D. P. (2011). "Virtual Reality Technology Applied on building maintenance: painted interior walls", M.S. thesis, Technical University of Lisbon, Portugal.

Sampaio, A. Z., and Gomes, A.M. (2011). "Virtual Reality Technology Applied as a Support Tool to the Planning of Construction Maintenance", research project report PTDC/ECM/67748/2006, FCT, Lisbon, Portugal 2008-2011.

Sampaio, A. Z., Ferreira, M. M. , and Rosário, D. P., and Martins, O. P. (2010). "3D and VR models in Civil Engineering education: Construction, rehabilitation and maintenance", Automation in Construction, 19 (2010), pp. 819–828.

Sampaio, A. Z., Ferreira, M. M., and Rosário, D. P. (2009). "Interactive virtual application on building maintenance: The lighting component", Proc. IRF2009, 3rd International Conference on Integrity, Reliability and Failure: Challenges and Opportunities, Symposium Visualization and Human-Computer Interaction, Porto, Portugal, July 20-24, abstract pp. 221-222, paper 11 pgs.

Sampaio, A. Z., Henriques, P. G., and Ferreira, P. S. (2006). "Virtual Reality Models Used in Civil Engineering", Proc. IMSA'06 - the 24th IASTED international conference on Internet and multimedia systems and applications Education, ACTA Press Anaheim, CA, USA, USA.,
http://portal.acm.org/ citation.cfm?id=1169188, [March, 2011).

Santos, J. P. (2010). "Construction Planning using 4D Virtual Models", M.S. thesis, Technical University of Lisbon, Portugal.

Veiga, M.; & Malanho, S. (2009). *Natural stone coating: methodology of diagnosis and repair of anomalies*. Conf. Patorreb 3rd Meeting on Pathology and Rehabilitation of Buildings, FEUP, Oporto, Portugal, March 18 - 20.

Walker, A. (2002). *Project Management in Construction*, Fourth edition, Oxford, Blachweel Publishing.

Webb, R.M., & Haupt, T. C. (2003). *The Potential of 4D CAD as a Tool for Construction Management*, Proc. 7th Int. Conf. on Construction Application of Virtual Reality, USA,.pp. 1011-1019.

Webb, R.M., & Haupt, T.C. (2003). *The Potential of 4D CAD as a Tool for Construction Management*, Proc. 7th Int. Conf. on Construction Application of Virtual Reality, USA.

Yerrapathruni, J.I.; Messner, A.J.; Baratta, & Horman, M.J. (2003). *Using 4D CAD and Immersive Virtual Environments to Improve Construction Planning*", Proc. CONVR 2003, Conference on Construction Applications of Virtual Reality, Blacksburg, VA, pp. 179-192.

Chapter 8

Virtual Simulation of Hostile Environments for Space Industry: From Space Missions to Territory Monitoring

Piovano Luca, Basso Valter, Rocci Lorenzo, Pasquinelli Mauro, Bar Christian, Marello Manuela, Vizzi Carlo, Lucenteforte Maurizio, Brunello Michela, Racca Filippo, Rabaioli Massimo, Menduni Eleonora and Cencetti Michele

Additional information is available at the end of the chapter

http://dx.doi.org/10.5772/51121

1. Introduction

The human exploration of the Universe is a real challenge for both the scientific and engineering communities. The space technology developed till now allowed scientists to achieve really outstanding results (e.g. missions around and landing on the Moon, the International Space Station as an outpost of the human presence, satellites and spaceships investigating and exploring Solar System planets as well as asteroids and comets), but at the same time further steps are required to both overcome existing problems and attain new and exceptional goals. One of the harshest trouble is the operative environment in which astronauts and rovers have to work in. Indeed, the outer space and extra–terrestrial planets have such different physical properties with respect to Earth that both space machinery has to be conceived selectively and manned crew has to be suitably trained to adapt to it. Nevertheless the entire product assembly integration and test campaign are made on Earth in 1G. Given so different ambient conditions, each phase in the whole life cycle of a space product is thorny and tricky and should be therefore carefully engineered. In particular, testing and operative phases could involve the most of risks because of the different product environmental conditions. Micro–or zero gravity environments are both impossible to be found and tough for a practical and realistic reproduction on Earth. In the past, for astronaut's tests, only parabolic flights and underwater conditions lead to some limited success, but their drawbacks – especially related to costs and dangerous situations – exceeded all the possible benefits and therefore, nowadays, they have a limited use.

The outstanding development of computer science techniques, such as virtual and augmented reality, has provided an interesting way to deal with such problems. Indeed, computer simulation of (portions of) real worlds is currently the best practice to feel one's concrete presence into a totally different environment, without being there physically. Virtual Reality

(VR in the following) high realism, immersion and easiness in interaction are the key ideas for such applications. Realism is to faithfully reproduce those environments, but not only from a graphical point of view: physical/functional simulation of objects presence and behavior/(mutual) interaction is fundamental too, especially for those disciplines (e.g. electrical, thermal, mechanical) heavily based on ambient reactions. Immersion is useful to enhance perception of the new environment and allows users (e.g. Astronauts, Engineering disciplines, Manufacturing) to behave as if it was their real world. At the end, interaction is the user's capability of communication with the simulation: the easier, the more effective and expressive the experience; the more intuitive, the less the amount of time required by (specialist and unskilled) users for practicing it; the more suitable, the better VR capabilities at one's disposal are exploited.

The space industry can largely benefit of the virtual simulation approach. In this context, the main help for aerospace disciplines is related to improve mission planning phase; its advantages are to allow realistic digital mock–up representations, provide collaborative multidisciplinary engineering tasks, and simulate both critical ground and flight operations. But benefits can arise in a number of other ways too. For instance, due to the one–of–a kind nature of space products, the only product after the spacecraft launch available on ground is its digital representation. Second, complex, scientific data can be successfully represented by VR applications. Indeed, data belonging to astrophysics and space mission domains are usually very hard to be understood in all their relationships, essence and meaning, especially those ones describing invisible properties such as radiations. In that sense, a suitable, graphical representation can help scientists (and not specialized audience too) to improve their knowledge of those data. Finally, VR laboratories can be organized to host virtual training of human crews, by exploiting their capability to direct interaction and physical behavior simulation ([26]).

Thales Alenia Space – Italy (TAS – I from now on) experience in virtual reality technologies is mainly focused on considerably enhancing the use of such tools. Two main research branches can be found there: user interaction with the virtual product/environment, and data cycle (that is from their production till their exchange among engineering teams) management. In the former case, the research is devoted to virtual reality technologies themselves – with an emphasis on the way to visualize different scenarios and large amounts of data – while in the latter case the focus is on the system data modeling. When put together, they shall converge towards a complex system architecture for a collaborative, human and robotic space exploration (see [2] for a more detailed insight). Our vision entails an unique framework to enforce the development and maintenance of a common vision on such a complex system. Therefore, recent advances in the entertainment and games domains coexist alongside the most up–to–date methodologies to define the most complete and reliable Model–Based System Engineering (MBSE) approach. This multidisciplinary view shall have an impact on the way each actor could conceive its own activity. For instance, engineering activity will benefit from such representation because the big picture could be at its disposal at any level of detail; it should be easier to prevent possible problems by detecting weakness and critical points; it should improve the organization of the entire system, and check whether all the mandatory requirements/constraints are met. Astronauts themselves find this is a worthwhile experience to gain skills and capabilities, especially from a training viewpoint. At the end, scientific missions could be planned more carefully because the simulation of several scenarios requires a fraction of time, can be easily customized by suitable set of parameters, and provides valuable feed–backs under several forms (e.g. especially simulation data and sensory perceptions). Collecting and analyzing data and information from there could help to diminish the crash and failure risks and consequently increase the chance the mission targets will be really achieved. For all the aforementioned reasons, the pillars of our research policy comprise, but they are not limited to: concurrent set–up and accessibility; several elements of 4D (space + time), 3D and 2D features for data manipulation and representation; exploiting immersive capabilities; easiness in interfacing with highly specialized tools and paradigms; user friendly capabilities; adaptability and scalability to work into several environments (e.g. from desktop workstations to CAVEs).

This chapter is organized as follows: paragraphs 2 and 3 will introduce the space domain context and the current state of art of VR systems in this field. The focus will be put especially on its requirements, the key points of view of our researches and the objectives we are going to meet. Progresses in VR field focused on the collaborative features and the interdisciplinary approach put in practice are described in 4. Section 5 is instead targeted on modeling complex space scenarios, while paragraph 6 some practical example of space applications are given. The chapter is ending up with section 7 illustrating both some final remarks and a possible road–map for further improvements and future works.

2. Motivation and goals

The aerospace domain embraces an enormous variety of scientific and engineering fields and themes. Given the intrinsic complexity of that matter, space challenges could be successfully tackled only when all the inputs from those disciplines are conveniently melt together in a collaborative way. The lack of both a common vision and suitable management tools to coordinate such several subjects can indeed limit the sphere of activity and the incisiveness of researches in space sciences. Computer science in general and VR in particular could really play an indispensable role for space scientists towards a significant qualitative leap.

To show up the previous assessment, we chose to discuss a specific theme from a practical point of view: the simulation of hostile environments. In this context, the term "hostile" is referring without loss of generality to those places where either stable or temporarily human presence is extremely difficult because of harsh physical conditions. Indeed, that is really the case of outer space and extra–terrestrial planets, but that definition could be extended to some environments on Earth too. In the latter case, it could even denote built–up areas after an outstanding event, such as natural disasters, and temporally unreachable, with limited communication links, or altered topography. Virtual reproduction of such environments is a particularly interesting activity according to several points of view. For that end, three main steps could be outlined. For each of them, examples will be discussed in detail aiming at presenting our *modus operandi* as well as some results we achieved. Given that practical stamp, this chapter has been outlined to highlight the following ideas. First of all, simulation of environments aids different disciplines to be complementary to each other. Indeed, we consider our virtual reality tools as connectors between apparently separated research areas. As connectors, we collect data coming from different disciplines, but describing similar phenomena, and visualize them as a whole. This multidisciplinary approach is intended to overcome partial views single disciplines could have and, at the same time, create new ways to make them interact and combine their knowledge. Practically speaking, the simulation of a specific environment in our case mainly involves research areas like astronomy, geology and meteorology which hardly overlap: the sight they have individually is usually staggered because they focus on different fields of investigation; their integrated sight, by spanning all possible features, allows a complete description of it. A similar case applies also to engineering disciplines, for instance, when space machinery models has to be conceived. They could be seen as a complex set of different sub-systems (e.g. mechanical, plumbing, energy), working together but designed separately from several group of people. People who typically have the know-how in their own field but could have some limitations in figuring out requirements from other engineering sources. Nevertheless, the real machinery has to work properly despite splits in engineering knowledge domains. In this context, VR supplies methodologies being able to simulate a portion of real world(s) according to its most relevant features (i.e. inputs from different fields of knowledge) and in an unified way. Second, for the sake of coherence with real operative environments, space simulations must reach the highest degree of realism as possible. In this field, realism gains a double meaning, referring to both visual appearance and correct physical behavior models. For that end, it is mandatory to deal with the most advanced techniques in computer graphics and engines for physical simulation. This double faced is the basic element for all the functional aspects of the simulation itself. Issues like aesthetics and photo–realism are especially very well polished when a thorough visual feedback is required, such as for training sessions, virtual assembly procedures and terrain exploratory missions. 3D models like terrain chunks, robotic machinery and/or natural elements are a natural mean to show huge collections of complex data and convey the right amount of information. Therefore, scientific and information visualization techniques should be carefully taken into account for informative simulation purposes. In this stage, advice and expertise from disciplines are fundamental to achieve the most plausible results, especially in modeling properly operational behaviors in such hostile environments and show related information. Last but not least, our discussion shall implicitly focus on interactions among several actors when they are dealing with virtual simulations. Indeed, we strongly trust in usefulness of such simulations for space disciplines, especially in terms of information flows and the gain each involved side could have by them. According to that point of view, virtual reality facilities could be potentially the natural way out for many disciplines. Indeed, its intrinsic way of conceiving multidisciplinary activities could lead to a novel way to think about (and maybe re–arrange) the engineering process itself. In this case, the aim of this part is to discuss our own experience in such a field. In that sense, we will introduce a typical example of complex scenario where lots of interactions between several actors are required. Possible case studies could be collaborative meetings, engineering briefings, training sessions and ergonomic and psychological surveys. The focus is to emphasize the virtuous cycle among participants and aiming at the improvement of both the simulation and all the engineering aspects of the represented product(s) (see Figure 1).

3. State of the art

The use of virtual reality (VR) and immersive technologies for the design, visualization, simulation and training in support to aerospace research have become an increasingly important medium in a broad spectrum of applications, such as hardware design, industrial control and training for aerospace systems or complex control rooms. VR applications provide a panorama of unlimited possibilities for remote space exploration, and their flexibility and power can impact many aspects of future space programs and missions. Modeling and interactive navigation of virtual worlds can provide an innovative environment which can

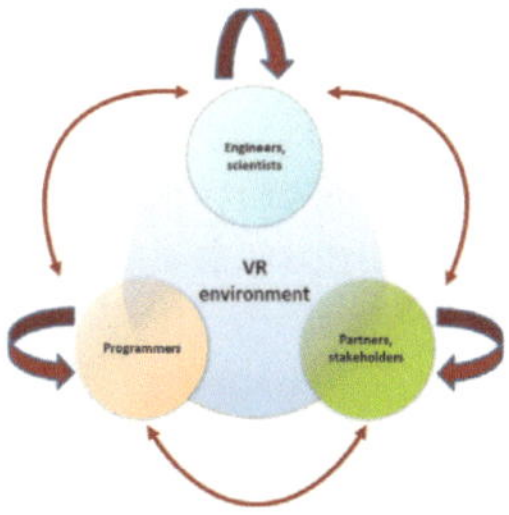

Figure 1. A pictorial representation of relationships happening into the VR simulation process. VR is the core of such a process and, by interacting with it, communications among all the actors shall generate added value, in term of both easiness in connections and knowledge acquisition / generation

be thought as an excellent medium for brainstorming and creation of new knowledge, as well as to synthesize and share information from variety of sources. Nevertheless, they can serve as a platform to carry out experiments with greater flexibility than those ones conducted in real world. In this section, a review of the projects and works related to the use of VR in the fields of (1) planet rendering (see section 3.1), (2) remote space exploration (see section 3.2) and (3) virtual prototyping (see section 3.3).

3.1. Planets rendering

Recently Google Earth, one of the most popular work related to the visualization of the terrestrial environment in 3D, has enabled users to fly virtually through Mars and Moon surfaces, providing a three-dimensional view that aid public understanding of space science. Moreover, it has given to researchers a platform for sharing data similar to what Google Earth provides for Earth scientists. The Mars mode includes global 3D terrain, detailed maps of the Mars rover traverses and a complete list of all satellite images taken by the major orbital camera. Likewise the Moon mode includes global terrain and maps, featured satellite images, detailed maps of the Apollo surface missions and geologic charts. Similar purposes and results are achieved by a number of 3D astronomy programs and planetarium software. The limited 3D modeling capabilities is their major drawback, nonetheless their usefulness in terms of public outreach has been definitively demonstrated by the increasing interest among the public audience in the space exploration.

In any case, they are somehow limited in providing suitable space industry services. The importance of supporting scientists and engineers work by highly–specialized, immersive facilities is a milestone at Jet Propulsion Labs and clearly described, among the others, in [35]. In this paper, the authors remark the contributions of 3D Martian soil modeling in the success in accurately planning the Sojourner rover's sorties during Mars Pathfinder Mission. The need for a well–structured and comprehensive reproduction of large amount of data, collected during Mars probes (especially Mars Pathfinder and Mars Global Surveyor missions) brought researchers to lay stress on VR coupled to astronomy and cartography applications ([29] [30] [31]). Indeed, frontiers of knowledge can achieve unprecedented and amazing results as coupled with tailored VR tools: new research directions spent their efforts both to increase the overall visual quality of the virtual scenes (e.g. see [3]) and improve the user's interaction with those VR facilities (e.g. [11] and [34]). In particular, the first real, immersive environment is the one described in Head's work [11]. His ADVISER system (Advanced

Visualization in Solar System Exploration and Research) was conceived as a new form of problem–solving environment, in which scientists can directly manipulate massive amounts of cartographic data sets, represented as 3D models. Its novelty was in integrating both hardware and software technologies into a very powerful corpus, being able to extend and improve scientists' capabilities in analyzing such data as they were physically on its surface. On the other hand, a first attempt to place side by side virtual and augmented reality tools was described in [33]. In order to enrich the users' experience, the authors created MarsView, where they added a force feedback device to a topographic map viewer. Thus, the haptic interface favors a more intuitive 3D interaction in which the physical feeling allows the users to actually touch the Martian surface as they pan around and zoom in on details. The golden age for Mars exploration from late 1990s onward has really generated an impressive data mole, whose main challenge is represented by its analysis tools. In this sense, examples above can illustrate how it could be efficiently faced by exploiting simulation and interaction capabilities. Nowadays, they are considered as unavoidable winning points for time saving, effectiveness, and catching complex interactions and relationships skills.

3.2. Virtual remote space exploration

Interactive 3D computer graphics, virtual worlds and VR technology, along with computer or video games technology support the creation of realistic environments for such tasks as dock landing, planetary rover control and for an effective simulation of the space–time evolution of both environment and exploration vehicles.

In [19] the major characteristics of the available virtual worlds are described, along with the potential of virtual worlds to remote space exploration and other space–related activities. Here, a number of NASA sponsored activities in virtual worlds are described, like 'NASA CoLab Island' and 'Explorer Island in second life' (the latter providing spacecraft models and Mars terrain surface model based on real NASA data), 'SimConstellation' that explores a broad range of lunar mission scenarios and 'SimStation', simulating the operation of the ISS, and training the astronauts to work on the space shuttle and space station. This work also describes some tools for virtual space activities, including Google Mars 3D and Google Moon. Landing on planets and their later exploration in space missions requires precise information of the landing zone and its surroundings. The use of optical sensors mounted to the landing unit helps to acquire data of the surface during descent. The retrieved data enables the creation of navigation maps that are suitable for planetary exploration missions executed by a robot on the surface. In [28] a Virtual Testbed approach is used to generate close–to–reality environments for testing various landing scenarios, providing artificial descent images test–data with a maximum of flexibility for landing trajectories, sensor characteristics, lighting and surface conditions. In particular, a camera simulation is developed including a generic camera model described by a set of intrinsic parameters distortions; moreover, further camera effects like noise, lens flare and motion blur can be simulated, along with the correct simulation of lighting conditions and reflection properties of materials in space. Besides these images are generated algorithmically, the known data in the Virtual Testbed can be used for ground truth verification of the map–generation algorithms. The work in [13] describes a Human Mars mission planning based on the Orbiter space flight simulator, where the authors have used Orbiter to create and investigate a virtual prototype of the design reference mission known as 'Mars for Less'. The Mission Simulation Toolkit (MST) [21] is a software system developed by NASA as a part of the Mission Simulation

Facility (MSF) project, which was started in 2001 to facilitate the development of autonomous planetary robotic missions. MST contains a library that supports surface rover simulation by including characteristics like simulation setup, controls steering and locomotion of rover, simulation of the rover/terrain interaction, power management, rock detection, graphical 3–D display. In another work carried out by NASA Ames Research center [7], a visualization and surface reconstruction software for Mars Exploration Rover Science Operations is analyzed and described. It is based on a 'Stereo–pipeline', a tool that generates accurate and dense 3D terrain models with high–resolution texture–mapping from stereo image pairs acquired during Mars Exploration Rovers (MER) mission. With regard to lunar environment modeling, a realistic virtual simulation environment for lunar rover is presented in [36], where Fractional Brown motion technique and the real statistical information have been used to modeling the lunar terrain and stones, forming a realistic virtual lunar surface, where main features may be easily expressed as simulation parameters. In this work a dynamics simulation model is developed considering the mechanics of wheel–terrain interaction, and the articulated body dynamics of lunar rover's suspension mechanism. A lunar rover prototype has been tested in this environment, including its mechanical subsystem, motion control algorithm and a simple path planning system.

3.3. Virtual prototyping

Prototypes or mock–ups are essential in the design process [25]. Generally a mock–up involves a scale model, more frequently full size, of a product. It is used for studying, training, testing, and manufacturability analysis. Prototyping, which is the use of mock–ups for designing and evaluating candidate designs, can occur at any stage of the design process. In a later stage, mock–ups are already completed in every detail and can be used for testing ergonomic aspects. However, physical prototypes can be expensive and slowly to be produced and thus can lead to delays in detecting eventual problems or mismatches in the solution under development.

Computer science offers the opportunity to reduce or replace physical prototypes with virtual prototypes (VP). A VP is a computer–based simulation of a physical prototype and having a comparable degree of functional realism than a physical prototype but with the potential to add some extra functionality. By using VP, different design alternatives can be immediately visualized, allowing users to give real-time feedback about the design alternatives and their use. Furthermore, changes to the solutions can be made interactively and more easily than with a physical prototype, which means that more prototypes can be tested at a fraction of time and costs required otherwise. The last feature is particularly crucial for the development of 'one–of–a–kind' or 'few–of–a–kind' products.

The use of VR can contribute to take full advantage of Virtual Prototyping. In order to test the design optimization of a VP product in the same way as the physical mock–up, a human–product interaction model is required. In an ideal way, the VP should be viewed, listened, and touched by all the persons involved in its design, as well as the potential users. In this scenario VR plays a meaningful role since it can allow different alternative solutions to be evaluated and compared in quite a realistic and dynamic way, such as using stereoscopic visualization, 3D sound rendering and haptic feedback. Therefore VR provides a matchless and more realistic interaction with prototypes than possible with CAD models [17].

By using VR tools, not only aesthetic but also ergonomic features could be evaluated and optimized. There are several approaches for the ergonomic analysis in a VR scenario. The first involves having a human operator interacting with the VE through haptic and/or tactile interfaces and the second is based on human virtual models that will interact with the VP, in a pure simulation technique. These human virtual models can be agents, that are created and controlled by the computer, or avatars, controlled by a real human.

4. VR for collaborative engineering

Model Based System Engineering (MBSE) is the term currently used to represent the transition between system data management through documents (e.g. specifications, technical reports, interface control documents) to standard–based semantically meaningful models, to be processed and interfaced by engineering software tools. MBSE methodologies enable a smoother use of VR in support to engineering teams, representing one of the most interesting applications.

The core of a MBSE approach is the so–called system model, that is the collection of different models, representing one of the possible baselines of the product, and formally describing the different, characterizing features throughout the product life cycle. In particular MBSE provides a consistent representation of data from the system requirements to the design and analysis phases, finally including the verification and validation activities. With respect to a more document–centric approach, the different characteristics of a product are defined more clearly, from its preliminary definition up to a more detailed representation. This shall ensure less sensitivity to errors than the traditional document–centric view, still widely used for system design. MBSE methodologies have highlighted the capability to manage the system information more efficiently compared to the existing approaches. This process allows introducing advantages that draws attention particularly for commercial implications. Indeed, since the last decade many industrial domains have been adopting a full–scale MBSE approach through their research, developments and applications, as demonstrated by INCOSE (International Council of System Engineering, [41]) initiatives in that sense. There is not a unique way to approach MBSE. The main discriminating factor is the definition of concepts, as a semantic foundation derived from the analysis of the system engineering process. The resulting conceptual data model shall be able to support the product and process modeling, with a particular emphasis on the data to be exchanged during the engineering activities, considering both people and computer tools. The selection or definition of the modeling and notation meta–models is specific to the needs of a particular domain, and even engineering culture, but it shall be compatible with current efforts, so to assure compatibility between tools and companies. A joint team from TAS – I and Politecnico di Torino is currently involved in researches focusing on the latest developments in this domain, with a particular emphasis on active participation on the related European initiatives. For instance, worthwhile experiences are: the Concurrent Design Facilities for the preliminary phases (lead by ESA experience in its CDF [38], but also in the ASI CEF&DBTE [23] and in industrial practices inside TAS – I); the ESA Virtual Spacecraft Design on–going study for more advanced phases [8]. The current developments have the objective to summarize the above mentioned initiatives, giving the possibility to be in line with the ongoing standardization and language definition efforts (e.g. ECSS–E–TM–10–25, ECSS–E–TM–10–23 ([37]), OMG SysML [45], Modelica [44]). The definition of a system model generally involves several engineering disciplines in a deeper way with respect to the traditional approach. The project team is composed by experts belonging to engineering and/or scientific areas that are very different among them. In this context the VR definitely becomes a useful tool in the management of data available, providing the technology necessary for effective collaboration between different disciplines. The VR allows viewing directly data and information that are often difficult to read for those who may not have technical background but who are otherwise involved in the design process of a given system.

The MBSE methodology is commonly characterized by the definition of all the processes, methods and tools that allow supporting and improving the engineering activities. In particular it is possible to consider some of experiences that are evolving within various organizations' system engineering structure and procedures and that are spreading through technical publications and studies. For instance Telelogic Harmony–SE® represents a subset of a well-defined development process identifiable with Harmony® [6]. In this case activities as requirements analysis, system functional analysis and architectural design are properly related each other within the context of life cycle development process. Another example may be expressed with INCOSE Object–Oriented Systems Engineering Method (OOSEM). The model–based approach introduced is characterized by the use of OMG SysML™ as an instrument to outline the system model specification. This language enables a well-defined representation of the systems, supporting the analysis, design and verification activities [20]. IBM Rational Unified Process for Systems Engineering (RUP SE) for Model–Driven Systems Development (MDSD) may be considered an interesting methodology similarly to the examples considered above. In particular this process is derived from the Rational Unified Process® (RUP®) and it is used for software development in the case of government organizations and Industrial [16]. Vitech Model–Based System Engineering (MBSE) Methodology is another example where a common System Design Repository is linked to four main concurrent activities defined as: Source Requirements Analysis, Functional / Behavior Analysis, Architecture / Synthesis and finally Design Validation and Verification [32]. The elements that characterized the methodologies presented above as other similar initiatives are particularly suitable for the management of complex situations, which are difficult to handle when the product development progresses over time. For instance the study of hostile environments, such as the analysis of certain space mission scenarios, generally leads to the definition of high complexity systems. In this case the management of a considerable amount of data through a coherent and flexible way has expedited the spread of model–based methods. The growing complexity of systems that are analyzed often becomes increasingly too difficult to realize a proper collaboration, avoiding at the same time potential design errors. The MBSE provides the necessary tools to formally relate the possible aspects of a given system. A representation through the techniques of VR about hostile environments, as well as a similar view of the data generated, points out many advantages. The VR allows, in relation to the structure data available through MBSE approach, to define in an extended manner the system architecture, while ensuring greater availability of information. Another benefit is also linked to the clarity with which the VR allows to report for instance the development phases of a given system. Virtual model directly connected to the network of information of a unique data structure also ensures access to the most current representation of the system.

Based on the progress made in recent years VR allowed to generate an ever more faithful representation of the reality about the possible physical phenomena that are analyzed. In this manner it is therefore possible to consider the generation of virtual environments where to conduct realistic simulations of possible scenarios in which the system can potentially operate so making use of the time variable (the 4D). The advantages related to this capability are highlighted in the ability to reproduce situations for which the construction of a real mock–up requires substantial economic investment. This becomes evident especially in the aerospace industry where both the complexity of the systems involved, the high amount of changes to manage and the possible operational scenarios require a limitation of the physical prototypes that are built. Today space domain is becoming a free worldwide market so there is a clear trend towards a reduction of economic costs that are incurred during the project and that most affect the tests that are made on real physical systems. The generation of virtual models has also the advantage to be able for example to analyze directly different possible design alternatives. Through the use of VR in fact more people may be involved at the same time in project activities for which there are discussions about equivalent system configurations. Generally the development of virtual environments becomes necessary when there is the need to face critical situations. VR in fact allows considering environments that commonly are not possible to reproduce on Earth, as for instance in the case of space mission scenario: gravity, dust. In a virtual model it is possible instead to recreate some of the characteristic features that we can potentially find during these situations. Moreover it is possible to manage the system variables to proper modify the scenario, considering in this manner other different conditions for the system under analysis. This capability could be difficult to reproduce with real physical elements mainly because of the economic investment that would require. The simulations that can be realized in VR environment allows also to avoid all the possible unsafe situations for the possible user. This characteristic becomes of particular interest for human space activities where often certain actions may lead to harmful situations.

MBSE techniques applied to space projects are often associated to 2D diagram–based models (e.g. an activity diagram in SysML, a control loop visualized in Simulink), or to 3D virtual models (e.g. a virtual mock–up built with a CAD application, multi–physics analysis visualized with CAE tools). These visualization techniques reached a high degree of maturity in the last decade, deriving from different experiences performed at discipline level. Just as an example, a SysML–like representation is closer to a software engineer than to a mechanical engineer. In a multidisciplinary team, the integration of discipline–level defined data in a system–level Virtual Environment represent an effective way to assure the full understanding by the whole team of the key system issues, representing a WYSIWYG at product level, such as a modern word processor is for a document. Figure 2 shows a simplified example of integration of tools in VR. The CAD model is used to define the physical configuration, and retrieve the related drawing. Current applications allow the user to calculate and/or store in the same CAD model also relevant properties, such as mass, moments of inertia (MOI), center of gravity position. Such values are of interest of the whole team and through dedicated interfaces those properties may be extracted and related to the system architecture (product structure, interfaces between elements). If in the same integrated environment the CAD model is linked with the system model providing input for simulations (e.g. mass properties for spacecraft dynamics) then the Virtual Environment allows a project team to visualize them in the same place.

The above mentioned approach may be used to visualize products and their properties (with precise values, such as mass properties or nominal values). As far as the product elements are linked with the virtual reality elements, also their behavior may be associated through the related parameters (e.g. instantaneous position). Behaviors are represented by functions (e.g. Provide Locomotion, with related ports with the Distribute Electrical Energy function, and the Environment functions for the terrain). Each function (or composition of functions) can be represented by a model able to provide simulation capabilities. Figure 3 shows an example at data level of linking between virtual reality and Modelica code through the system model. The integration of simulation models allow the Virtual Environment to be the collector of engineering discipline analysis, but a complete system level simulator is still far to be implemented in such way and it is subject of our current research. The integration of several simulations requires a simulation process manager and a revision of the simulation models to be able to include the multi–effects. As explained in previous sections, the virtual environment may contain own simulation capabilities, thanks to an embedded physical engine, able to simulate e.g. collisions, dynamics, soft bodies. These features may be used for a rapid prototyping of the simulation, providing rapid feedback during concept and feasibility studies, as well as during the evaluation of alternatives.

Product and operational simulations does not saturate the VR support capabilities for a project team. The use of the VR with embedded simulation capabilities may also be used to validate part of the AIT (Assembly Integration and Test) planning, supporting the definition and simulation of procedures, or for training purposes. Procedures can be created in VR, they can be validated and then made available using Augmented Reality (AR) format so that to guide hands free assembly task execution (see Figure 4).

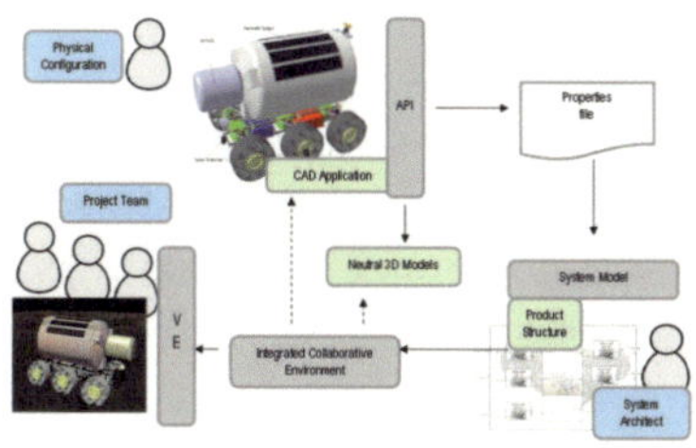

Figure 2. A scheme showing the connection between MBSE approach and VR environment seen as a natural finishing line to improve all the designing phases and to support teams during their work.

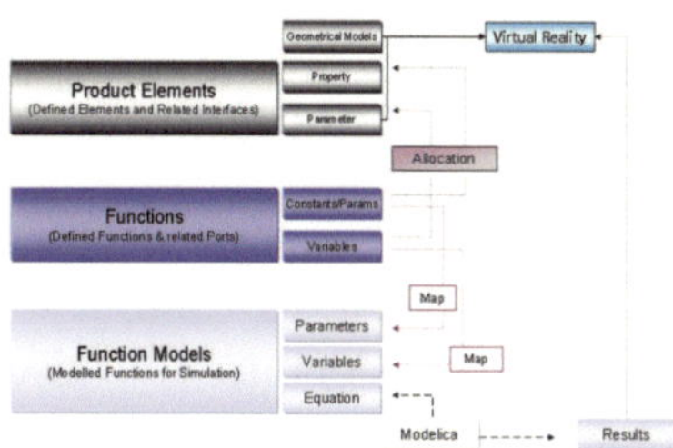

Figure 3. VR association to the system model at data level (modeled by Modelica language), where each object in a virtual world has a formal description at a higher level.

5. Modeling environments

Since space environments are extreme with respect to Earth's ones, a careful model of them is mandatory before undertaking any scientific mission. The study of real operative conditions

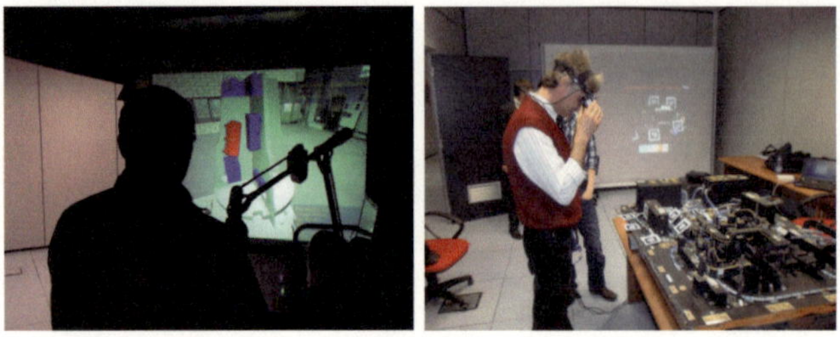

Figure 4. Current experiments performed in TAS–I focusing on the evaluation of the potential benefits of a VR / AR approach: user feed–backs are encouraged to improve their implementation.

spans from understanding physical laws to defining geological composition of the surface, from measuring magnetic fields to analyze natural phenomena. Of course, the better the knowledge, the greater the likelihood to succeed in a mission. That is, failure factors such as malfunction, mechanical crashes, accidents and technical unsuitability are less likely to happen, while crew safety, support decision optimization, costs reduction and scientific throughput and outcome will increase consequently. The added value of VR in this context is its ability in supporting this need for realism in a smart and effective way.

5.1. Physic laws

Technically speaking, a physic engine is a software providing a numerical simulation of systems under given physical laws. The most common dynamics investigated by such engines comprise fluid and both rigid and soft bodies dynamics. They are usually based on a Newtonian model and their contribution to virtual worlds is to handle interactions among several objects / shapes. This way it is possible to model object reactions to ambient forces and therefore create realistic and complex software simulations of situations that might be hardly reproduced in reality: for instance, by changing the gravity constant to the Moon one (that is more or less one sixth of the terrestrial value), it is possible to handle objects as they were really on Earth's satellite; similarly, precise space module conditions could be achieved in order to train astronauts in a (close to) zero gravity environment. The great advantages of these solutions are cheapness, flexible customization and safety. Indeed, with respect to other common solutions usually adopted, such as parabolic flies, they do not require expensive settings to work - a modern PC with standard hardware, graphical card and processing power is more than enough to perform simulations of medium complexity. At the same time, setting–up virtual world behaviors relies mainly on customizable parameters as inputs for the simulation algorithms. Lastly, digital mock–ups can be stressed out till very extreme conditions without their breaking physically occurs. And also final users are not subject to any risks while they are facing a simulation.

The two main components a modern physics engine typically provide, concern rigid body dynamics, that is a collision detection/collision response system, and the dynamics simulation component responsible for solving the forces affecting the simulated objects. More complex cores allow engines to successfully deal with particle/fluid, soft bodies, joints and clothes simulations. Given all those features, it appears clear why a physic engine allows studying natural and artificial phenomena with ambient conditions that are different from the Earth ones: for example, testing dust behavior at gravity conditions on Mars (natural phenomena), or driving a Martian rover acting on velocity, friction and external forces (artificial phenomena). Virtual reality simulations are so flexible that specific and reiterated tests could be performed several times in a row. This could be accomplished for a variety of scenarios: for instance, training crew in performing particular difficult actions could lead to find the best practice for a given task; simulating different terrain conformations could help in finding possible troubles on the way of an autonomous, robotic vehicle; pushing the use of some mechanical component to the limit could suggest how resilient it is to external stresses, its risk threshold and so on.

When physic engine results are connected to suitable input/output devices being able to return perceptions to the user, then the realism of the simulation is definitely increasing. Therefore, feedbacks making the user feel lifelike forces and sensations (e.g. bumps of an irregular terrain while driving a rover or the weights in moving objects) push further specific studies in complex fields. For example, by means of haptic feedback device and motion capture suite it is possible to perform ergonomic and feasibility studies (i.e.: reachability test to check if an astronaut is able to get to an object and then to perform a particular action like screwing a bolt). On the other side, a primary limit of physics engine realism is the precision of the numbers representing the positions of and forces acting upon objects. Direct consequences of this assertion are: rounding errors could affect (even heavily when precision is too low) final computations and simulated results could drastically differ from predicted ones, if numerical (small) fluctuations are not properly taken into account in the simulation. To avoid such problems, several tests on well-known phenomena should be performed before any other simulation in order to detect the margin of error and the index of trustfulness to count on.

5.2. Terrain modeling

To model planetary surfaces like the Moon and Mars ones, a Digital Elevation Model (DEM) is required. Technically speaking, it looks like a grid or a raster-graphic image where elevation values are provided at regularly spaced points called posts. Reference DEMs come from NASA High Resolution Imaging Science Experiment and Lunar Reconnaissance Orbiter missions (HiRISE [39] and LRO [42] respectively) and represent the most up-to-date and precise advances in space geology measurements and cartographic imagery. In general, ground data can be derived at a post spacing about 4X the pixel scale of the input imagery. Since HiRISE images are usually between 0.25 and 0.5 m/pixel, each pixel describes about 1-2 m. Vertical precision is then also very accurate, being in the order of tens of centimeters. The altitude computation is a very time intensive procedure and requires several stages as well as careful pre–and post–processing data elaboration, sophisticated software, and specialized training. During this process, image elaborations techniques could inherently introduced some artifacts but despite this fact, a near-optimal reconstruction satisfy modeling constraints is largely possible. For more detailed information about the complete (Mars) DEM computation process, see [9] and the on-line resources at [40]. Instead, for a visual reference, look at Figure 5.

Inserting a terrain model into a virtual scene is only the first step we perform to achieve environmental reconstruction. Indeed, the description of a planet could be more complicated than it appears at a first glance. In the next sub–sections, we will describe how to enrich the simulation of a planetary terrain by inserting more typical landscape elements and modeling natural phenomena occurring on their surfaces.

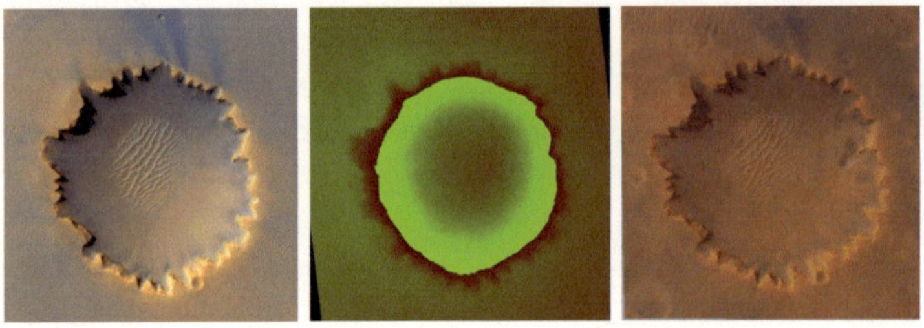

Figure 5. Examples of DEM processing on Victoria Crater pictures. From left to right: High resolution photo (from http://photojournal.jpl.nasa.gov/catalog/PIA08813); The original DEM computed as described in [22]; A front view of our final 3D model (raw model + texture)

5.2.1. Rocks

Almost every image taken from astronauts and/or robotic instrumentation shows Mars (and somehow the Moon too) to be a very rocky planet. But those details do not appear into reference DEMs, despite their astonishing resolution. Even if those small details cannot (still) be caught by advanced laser instrumentation, the presence of rocks and stones poses a severe challenge for robotic equipment because they increase the chance of a mechanical crash in case of collisions. Then, for the sake of a better plausibility, we have to add rock models on the so far reconstructed surface. In that sense, studies made for Mars, like [10] and [4], are really useful because they describe a statistical distribution of them, with a particular emphasis of those terrains visited during rover missions, like the Pathfinder site. Moreover they can estimate both the density and rock size-frequency distributions according to simple mathematical functions, so that a complete description of the area is furnished. Those data turn to be really useful especially during landing operations or when a site has to be explored to assess the risks in performing exploration tasks. For instance, those model distributions estimate that the chance for a lander impacting a >1 m diameter rock in the first 2 bounces is <3% and <5% for the Meridiani and Gusev landing sites, respectively.

Our 3D rock models are inserted onto the terrain by following that statistical approach and according to specific site parameters such as the total number of models, size and type. During simulation sessions, that distribution could change. The aim is clearly at forcing operational situations in order to analyze reactions of the simulated equipment in hardly extreme conditions. In particular, thanks to the collision detection engine, it is possible to evaluate impact resistance factors to guarantee the highest level of safety ever. From a modeling point of view, the rock generation procedure could be summarized as follows: i) generate a random set of points (rock vertices) in a given 3D space; ii) compute the convex hull in order to create the external rock surface; iii) compute the mesh of the given volume; iv) adjust and refine the model (e.g., simulate erosion or modify the outer appearance with respect to shape and roundness) in order to give it a more realistic look; v) statistically compute the site on the planet surface where the rock will be laid; vi) put the rock onto that site according to the normal direction in that point. Examples of rock skeletons (that is after the first three steps of the previous algorithm) are shown in figure 6, while complete rocks can be seen in many figures spread across this paper.

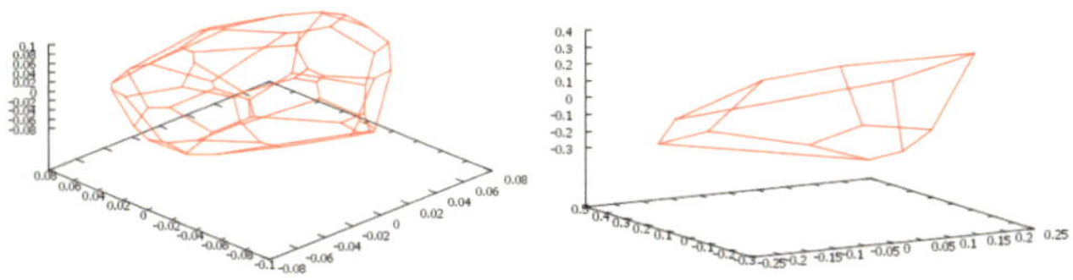

Figure 6. Examples in generating rocks having both different shapes and number of vertices.

5.2.2. Dust

Another issue is represented by the presence of an huge quantity of dust laying down on the soil. When any perturbation of the stillness state occurs (such as the rover transit or an astronaut's walk), a displacement of an huge amount of small, dusty particles is caused: they could form big clouds raising up quickly and being in suspension for a long time period after (because of the lower gravity). Scientific literature describes this phenomenon mainly for the Moon because of the several lunar missions undertaken in 70s and 80s. For instance, studies like [1], [15] and [5] show in details the typical behavior of dust when its particles are emitted by a rover wheel: schemes and formulas are then given (for instance, to determine the angle of ejection or the distance a particle covers during its flight) with the aim of characterizing this unavoidable effect, which should definitely modeled in our simulations since it affects any operational progress. Indeed both the visual appearance and the physical behavior of dust have to be carefully represented. In the former case, to test driving sessions under limited conditions in the vision field or to find a set of man-oeuvre being able to lift the smallest quantity of dust as possible. In the latter case, because avoiding malfunctions, especially for those modules directly exposed to dust interaction (e.g. solar panels, radiators and wheels joints), is still a high-complex engineering challenge.

5.2.3. Atmosphere events

A thin atmosphere is surrounding Mars. Even if it could not be compared to the Earth's one, some weak weather activities happen all the same in it, so that winds blow and seasons rotate. The presence of winds in particular could be considered as an issue, especially during some thorny task performance, like a capsule landing. Therefore even this new factor should be simulated efficiently.

The Mars Climate Database (MCD, [43]) offers an interesting set of data particularly suitable for that purpose. Indeed, it collects several observations (e.g. temperature, wind, chemical composition of the air and so on), caught at different sites and over periods, and focusing towards the definition of a complete 3D Global Climate Model (GCM) for Mars. In [24] and [14] further details on such models can be found. A complete predictive model for Martian atmosphere behavior is still far to come to a complete end, but some good approximations could be achieved through a simplified version of the Earth's weather models. In particular and without loss of generality, a simpler version of equations described in [24] have been considered throughout our experiments[1]. Technically speaking, they are Navier-Stokes

[1] Where the simplification comes after considering Martian atmosphere distinctive features, such as extreme rarefaction, (almost) absence of water vapor and heat exchange, lower gravity and so on

equations describing the 3D wind directions and changes in pressure and temperature. Since our interest is on being able to describe the weather situation at a given interval of time and with respect to a limited area of the planet (that is a landing site typically), they are used to define a Local Area Model for which the input data come from the MCD itself. In other words, the goal is to adapt global models to a smaller scale (meso-scale) for which both precision and accuracy might be guaranteed at most for short-term forecasts. However, caution in initializing data has to be undertaken because even small errors in them could potentially have a huger impact for those reduced area.

First results made on the Pathfinder site showed a good approximation in describing the wind activity, compared to different MCD entries. Visualizing them in a 3D environment (see Figure 7) represent therefore a first step towards a fully definition and integration of a Martian weather 'forecast' predictor. When this result will be achieved robustly, missions definition will gain another powerful tool to ensure reliability and safeness.

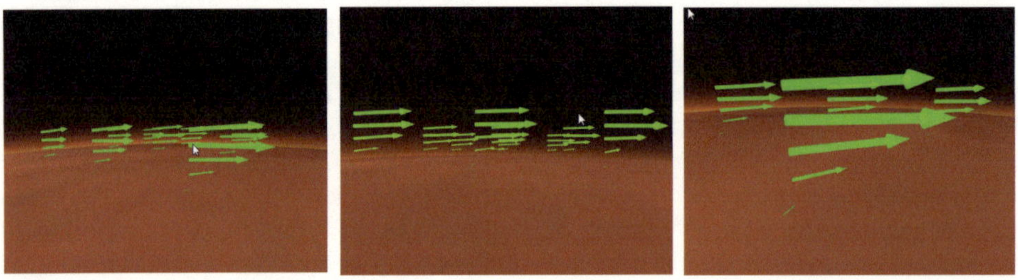

Figure 7. Representation of winds in the Martian atmosphere at several time intervals. Arrows points to the blowing directions while their size encodes their strength.

6. Scenarios

The goal of this paragraph is to show how virtual reality paradigm can be adopted for real applications into the space industry domain. Case studies described in the following represent only a small part of the most innovative activities undertaken at TAS – I. Nevertheless they are really representative of how flexible and effective VR simulations are for several challenging and practical problems.

6.1. Rover driving

This is maybe the best example to explain the tight collaboration among several scientific disciplines when there is the need to represent several data into a visualization application only. Indeed, it comprises contributions from: astronomy and geology (high–resolution planet surfaces and rocks modeling); physics (to handle the behavior of objects according to specific environmental conditions); technical engineering disciplines (to set–up the 3D rover model as a logic set of layers and sub–systems, considering for each of them its working functionality as both a stand–alone and in collaboration with all the other ones); ergonomic (to understand astronauts' requirements about a comfortable and safe life on board and therefore design suitable tools); human–computer interaction (to design interfaces to help crew in understanding the surrounding environment and take actions accordingly).

Figure from 8 to 13 shows many of the features aforementioned. We present two different scenarios: on Mars (Figure 8–10) and on the Moon (Figure 11–13). In the former case, we

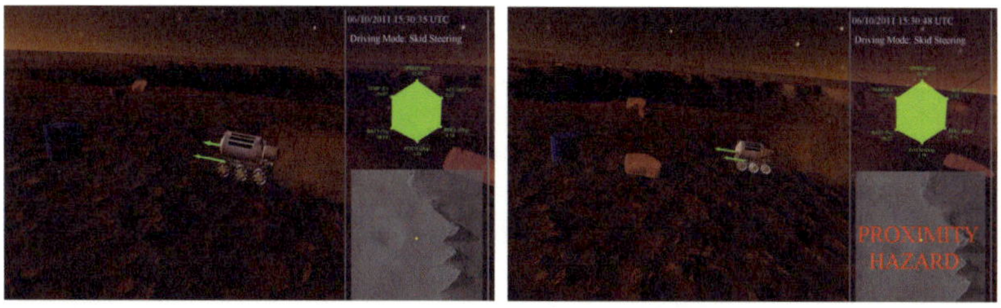

Figure 8. The interface for rover driving: Mars scenario. When possible accidents are likely to occur, a red hazard alert is shown to the driver (picture below).

Figure 9. Danger: the rover is falling down into the crater and crashing against a rock. Another hazardous man-oeuvre: the rover is rolling over after going around a bend

reconstructed an area of approximately 1 km^2 where the Victoria Crater, an impact one located at 2.05°S, 5.50°W and about 730 meters wide, stands. Instead in the latter case, our attention is paid to Linnè Crater in Mare Serenitatis at 27.7°N 11.8°E. The goal is to drive a (prototype of a) pressurized rover –that is an exploratory machine with a cabin for human crew –onto those surfaces, avoiding both to fall down into the pits and crashing against natural hindrances (mainly massive rocks, such as those ones depicted in Figures 8 and 9). The task is made more difficult by the presence of huge clouds of dust which, according to the specific planets conditions, are usually thicker, broader and take more time with respect to the Earth to dissolve completely. Since in those situations the visibility could be extremely reduced, the importance of being able to rely on secure instrumentation, prior knowledge of the terrain to be explored and accurate training sessions is essential, because indeed, any error could have wasting consequences on crew and equipment. Therefore, astronauts should be able to fully understand all the risks, the policies to avoid them and how to approach every step in such missions. In this context, a VR simulation offers a reliable tool to safely undertake such training. To help the crew to perform their duty, a suitable, basic interface has been built. It stands on the rightmost side of the screen where a double panel is shown. In the first one, at the top right corner, parameters such as roll, pitch and yaw angles, level of battery, speed, acceleration and outside temperature, are mapped onto a deformable hexagon, to keep them always under control. Their values are continuously updated during the simulation to suddenly reflect the current situation. If all of them are kept under a pre–defined safety threshold, the whole hexagon is green. When an alert occurs, the respective parameter turns to red: in this case, the crew should take appropriate countermeasures to face that danger (for instance, by reducing the rover speed). In the second control panel, a small bird's–eye–view map of the surroundings is depicted. On this map, small red circles represent potential hazards, such as huge rocks. As the rover is reducing too much its minimum safety distance (that is, it could run into collision with a rock), a red alert appears, so that a correct man-oeuvre could be undertaken in time. To help the drivers a blue cylinder is projected facing the engine too. In this case, it points out where the rover will be after a configurable, small amount of time (e.g., 20 seconds) if any change in the march occurs. The driving commands are given through a suitable interface aiming at reproducing the corresponding mean to be mounted on the rover (e.g. control sticks, levers, steering wheel and so on). They could be either some haptic interfaces (with or without the force feedback impulse) or, as in our case, wii–motes. The direction as well as the intensity of the strength applied to the rows is shown by a couple of green arrows.

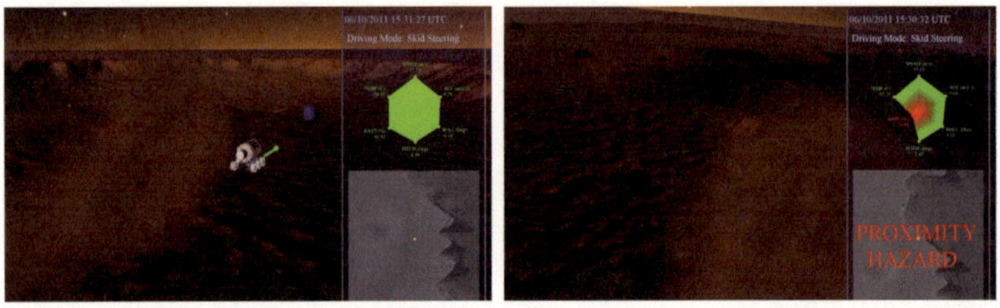

Figure 10. The Martian dust. Since Mars is a rocky and sandy planet, ejecting dust is really likely to happen. Thickness and density of dust clouds depend on several factors, including the speed the rover is traveling. The presence of dust could be a problem for safe driving, building–up on solar panels, and unpredictable effects by intruding in exposed mechanical parts.

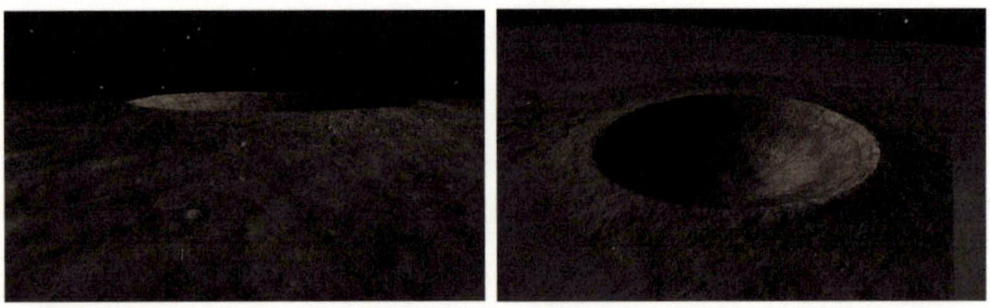

Figure 11. The Lunar scenario. A close look to the surface of the Lunar Linnè Crater. The surface reproduced here is only a small portion of the whole Lunar soil. Indeed Lunar DEM do not cover yet the whole surface of the terrestrial satellite.

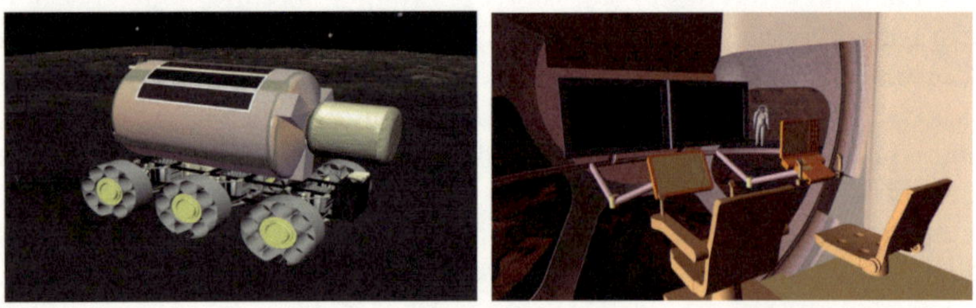

Figure 12. A possible look for a scouting expedition rover, with both the external and inner views. The ergonomic in designing machines and tools to explore planets is a crucial aspect in the whole scientific mission setting–up, beside its operational functionalities. Among the main requirements needed for that, we can cite comfortableness, habitability and safety.

6.2. Planet landing

Another essential task (and another typical example where cooperation among disciplines is strictly essential) is to bring onto the extra–terrestrial surface all the machinery required for

Figure 13. Dust behavior modeling: in a physical environment (leftmost image) and on Moon, where it is lifted up by rover transit. Dust emitters are positioned on rover's wheels. In principle, only a small number of dust particles are modeled. The dust cloud is then rendered for realistic simulations by adding some visual effects and simulating the presence of more particles around the original ones. All the equations used to simulate particles trajectories have been taken by [15]. Similar works for Mars are still missing at the best of our knowledge. Therefore, we adapted the Lunar ones to match the Martian environment.

the scientific mission. This operation is usually performed by a lander. It could be thought as a composition of at least three distinct parts: the capsule, the propulsion system, and the anchoring units. The first module carries all the machinery to settle on the ground; the second part is used during both the take–off and the landing and it aims at balancing loads and thrusts and avoiding sharp and compromising movements; the last one is the first one to touch the soil and has to soften the landing and provide stability. This kind of operation is really ticklish because in case of failure, the equipment is very likely to be lost or damaged or having malfunctions. To avoid such a possibility, carefulness in choosing the landing site is mandatory: interesting sites from the scientific point of view could be landing targets if in the surroundings a flat terrain, almost rock–free and without any other obstacle is present. Therefore, an accurate research should be performed prior the implementation of the mission itself. During the VR tests, different landing sites could be tested, till the most appropriate one is detected (see the first two pictures in Figure 14). Those trials are suitable for another couple of things. First of all, to test endurance, impact absorption, breaking and tensile strength and some other mechanical properties of lander legs. In this case, series of physical simulations should be set up to test changes in parameters and find the right combination of them to guarantee the maximum of safety in real operative environments. (see the last picture in Figure 14) Then, since dust clouds are a major challenge, blind landing should be taken into account. In this case, both automatic and manual landing operations have to deal with complementary sensors (e.g. sonar and radar) integrating previous knowledge of the targeted site. In this case, VR simulations can help scientists to find the best descent plan according to the supposed hypothesis and the real operative situations, which can be surprisingly different from the first ones. Therefore, plan corrections should be undertaken to face problems such as malfunctions, higher speed, error in measuring heights, winds (on Mars) and other unpredictable events.

6.3. Visualizing radiations

Scientific visualization is an interdisciplinary field whose objective is to graphically represent scientific data so that scientists could understand and take a more detailed insight of them. It usually deals with 3D structures and phenomena coming from several science branches such as astronomy, architecture, biology, chemistry, medicine, meteorology and so forth. Computer

Figure 14. Preparing a landing mission. From left to right: a scale model of the targeted terrain; its 3D elaboration (from a scanned cloud of points) for VR applications; physical tests on landing legs. Legs are composite models with many joints connecting all the parts whose mechanical properties are the subject of several researches undertaken at TAS-I. The red and green arrows display strength and direction of applied forces.

graphics plays a central role because of its techniques in both rendering complex objects and their features (among the others volumes, surfaces, materials and illumination sources) and dealing with their evolution in time (see [18]). The importance of visualization is essential to manage complex systems and when events to be displayed are invisible (i.e., they could not be perceived because of either micro–or even lower scales or they happened outside the optic frequency band). In those cases, visual metaphors should be used to show such phenomena and therefore keep the audience aware of their existence, effects and consequences. This approach has been successfully applied to projects aiming at investigating how radiations will affect human health and electronic components during space missions. In particular, we focused on representing the Van Allen radiation belt surrounding the Earth. This area is located in the inner region of the magnetosphere and mainly composed by energetic charged particles coming from cosmic rays and solar wind. The purpose of this study is to show how radiations will spread and amass on and all around the whole spaceship volume, given the significant time spaceships spend in orbit. This way, it will be possible to design suitable countermeasures to shield against all the potential risks. As shown in Figure 15, the belt has been represented as a ball of threads enveloping Earth, getting thicker and thicker as time flows and spaceships orbit our planet. At the same time, a color scale gives to the observer the feeling of danger, by ranging from cold (that is, low risks) to warm colors (highest damages) (Figure 16).

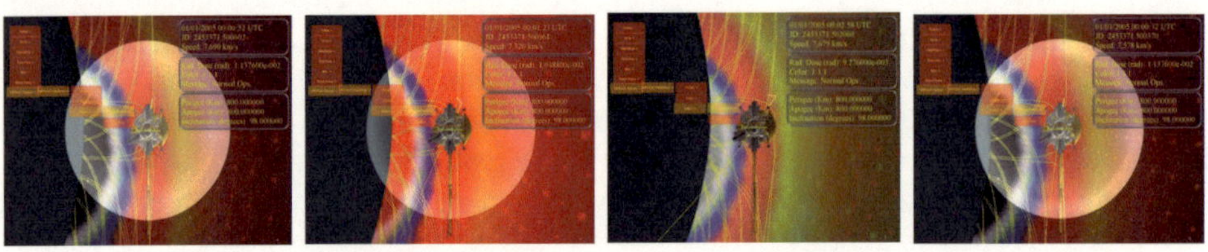

Figure 15. Radiations hitting a spaceship as it orbited around the Earth (first two images: cumulative amount of electrons; last two images: protons)

6.4. Cargo accommodation

The International Space Station (ISS) is the farthest outpost of the human presence in space and can be thought as an habitable satellite. Since 1999, its pressurized modules allowed the presence of astronauts whose main goal is to conduct experiments in several fields

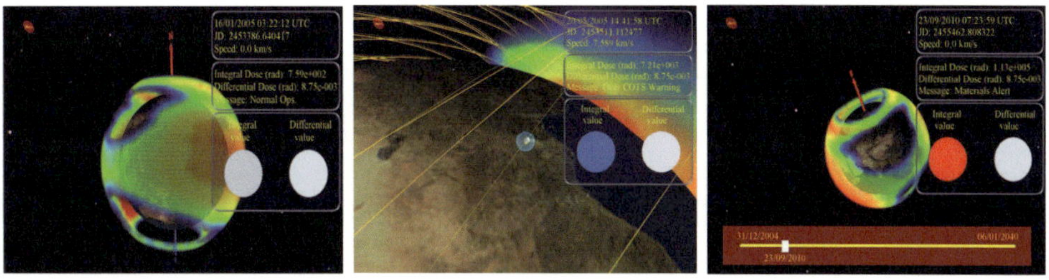

Figure 16. Other representations of Van Allen's belt, showing the integral and differential radiation doses. As they exceed tolerance limits, an alert message is shown in red.

by exploiting its micro–gravity and space environment research facilities. Shuttle services provided in years a continuous turnover of astronauts as well as supplies, vital items and scientific equipment. Anyway, carrying provisions and other stuff back and forth is far from being a simple task, at least in its designing phase. Indeed, the most difficult challenge is how to put the greatest amount of items into a cargo so that time, money and fuel could be saved and providing at the same time the best service as possible. In other words, it means facing the well–known knapsack problem on a larger scale. The CAST (Cargo Accommodation Support Tool) program has been established to work out that problem by optimizing the loading within transportation vectors such as Columbus and ATV (Automated Transfer Vehicle). Practically speaking, it has to find the optimal disposal for items (usually bags) into racks, that is the main focus is on properly balancing the loading. This means finding the best center of mass position for each rack into the vector, such that resource wasting is minimal, any safety issues will occur and it will take the smallest number of journeys as possible. The balancing problem can be solved algorithmically through an interactive, multi–stage process, where problems such as items–racks correlation, rack configuration and item, racks and cargo accommodation have to be addressed. The result is a series of 3D points, whose final configuration corresponds to how bags have to be stored into racks according the given constraints. A visual representation of them is particularly useful if it could be conceived as a practical guide to help people during load/unload phases. In order to allow users to test several configurations at run–time and analyze how they will affect the final cargo accommodation, direct interaction has been guaranteed through wii–motes, data gloves and force–feedback haptic devices. Moreover, in order to guarantee the best simulation as possible, physical constraints have been added too. So, easiness in picking and moving objects will be affected by object masses and weights; collision detection among bags and racks will limit movements in changing object positions and guarantee at the same time the consistency of results (that is, impossible positions cannot occur).

6.5. Understanding natural risks

Although TAS–I experience in modeling 3D terrains is principally devoted to reconstruct extra–terrestrial soils, we can present here an example of an application involving Earth territories. The work comes after Alcotra–Risknat (Natural Risks) project. Alcotra is an European Commission approved program for cross–border cooperation between Italy and France. In the context of improving the quality of life for people and the sustainable development of economic systems through the Alpine frontier between the two countries, a special care towards enforcing public and technical services through a web–based platform in the natural risk protection field is given. Among the objectives, we can remind the need to

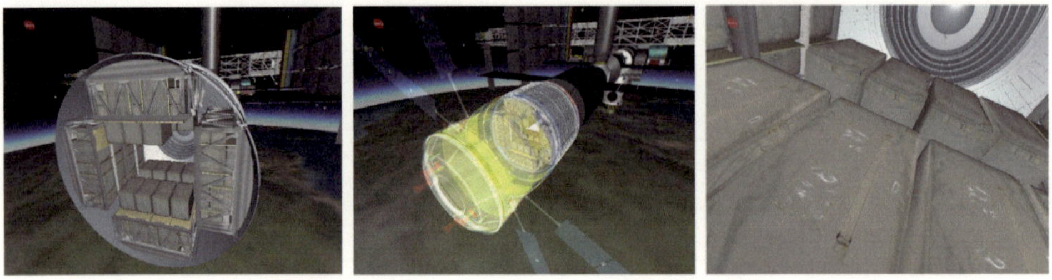

Figure 17. Visualizing bags disposal into ATV cargo racks. From left to right: the bags inside their container as they arrived at ISS; ATV module (in transparency) after docking the ISS station; a close look to bags to see the photo–realistic textures describing them. Such an application could be used as a guide helping during load/unload operations and to recognize single bags.

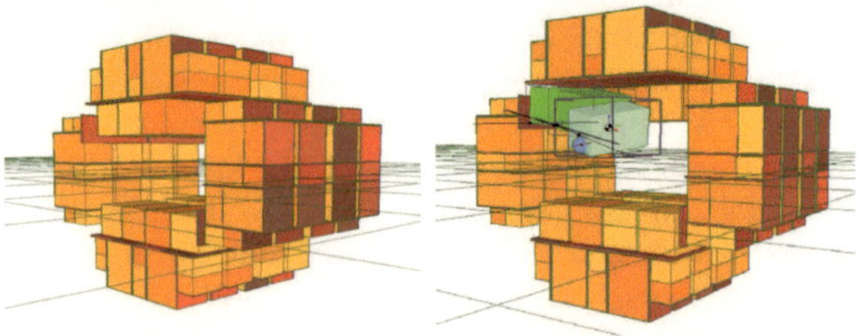

Figure 18. A schematic view of bags and racks to solve the balancing problem in a graphical way. Moving a bag (in green) will change the center of mass position and therefore the balance optimization. Physical constraints can limit the bag movements. The center of mass position is graphically updated after every new change.

provide innovative technological strategies to manage territory policies efficiently; develop an environmental awareness depending on sustainability and responsible management of resource use paradigms; coordinate civil defense facilities and equipment in the cross–border areas. Given this context, our main contribution consisted in a 4D physically–realistic simulation demo of a landslide occurred at Bolard in the high Susa Valley. Thanks to stereoscopic vision and 3D sound effects, we developed interactive and highly immersive scenarios for citizen risks awareness purposes. The demo consists of a 3D model simulating the physical propagation of debris and rocks slides in a mountain site (see Figures 19 and 20). The simulation has been built on real geological data coming after *in situ* measures and given the local terrain morphology and orography at that time. Photos and videos of that period have been used to both reproduce the slide path along the interested mountainside and reproduce the likely appearance (e.g., color, density, speed and so on) of the slide itself.

Figure 19. Scenario for RiskNat simulation: a landslide in the Susa Valley (Piemonte, Italy). From left to right: the mountain raising up the village of Bolard; three different views of the mudslide. The cartographic data have a resolution of about 5 meters. The slide run has been modeled according to density, viscosity and speed parameters very close to the original ones.

Figure 20. Scenario for RiskNat simulation: the village of Bolard. From left to right: the village before the arrival of the landslide; the flow of mud, rocks and debris at the village gate; all the buildings submerged just after the flood.

7. Conclusions and future work

The COSE Center facility is an innovative and highly technological equipped laboratory, currently involved into developing both VR and AR applications to support inner research at TAS-I. After being successfully used in several fields such as the entertainment industry, they have been satisfactorily introduced also in the management of complex production projects with the aim of improving the quality of the whole engineering steps chain, from the collection and validation of requirements till to the final realization of the product itself. TAS-I proficiently application to its products is double-folded. First, as a new, integrating tool in all the decision making phases of a project, by supporting manual engineering tasks and other well-known instruments (e.g., CAD) and overcoming their limitations. Second, as a set of interactive simulation tools, being able to realistically reproduce hostile, extra-terrestrial environments and therefore supporting disciplines to properly understand operational behavior under extreme conditions. The VR facilities could be considered as a center of attraction to improve knowledge, technical skills and know-how capability. This enables the COSE Center research activities to have reached several positive results in the policies of simplifying the team approach to complex products and projects. Among them, we could cite a better interaction with customers and suppliers and among multidisciplinary experts too; improving the effectiveness of evaluation/assessment by the program teams according to a tightly collaborative approach. The good results achieved thank to the VR-lab have been reached because the system structure and behavior are shown in a more realistic way to the team. Running several simulation sessions by stressing virtual models under different conditions is a fast and economic way to collect data about product requirements, limitations and strong points. Practically speaking, the set of virtual tools adopted at TAS-I and the current research results has lead in some cases engineering disciplines to rethink about both their relationship to the implementing system and the necessity to focus on new critical aspects, emerged during interactive sessions. In some other cases, engineers decided to optimize their internal process given the results obtained through virtual tool analysis. In the future, we are aiming at improving the capabilities of our VR facility in several research directions. First of all, by implementing new features / applications according to the engineering fields needs and allowing a more natural interaction with them through specific devices (e.g., new tracking devices, touch-screen devices, improved AR interfaces and so on). Second, by involving a higher number of disciplines in order to achieve the most complete vision as possible of the environment to be simulated. A complete simulator of hostile environments is still far from being implemented, but our efforts tend towards that end. This shall mean that physical engine features would be extended to encompass a wider range of possible dynamics to be reproduced. This shall also mean that a tighter cooperation with scientist is mandatory to enforce the realism of a simulation.

Acknowledgments

The realization of such a work comes after several years of researches. The authors gratefully thank all the people from COSE Center being involved to enrich our experience into the Virtual Reality fields. This work is also the result of several projects such as: Astro–VR, STEPS, Manu–VR and Alcotra–RiskNat.

Author details

Piovano Luca, Lucenteforte Maurizio, Brunello Michela, Racca Filippo and Rabaioli Massimo
Department of Computer Science, University of Torino, Torino, Italy

Basso Valter, Rocci Lorenzo and Pasquinelli Mauro
Thales Alenia Space–Italia SpA, Torino, Italy

Bar Christian, Marello Manuela, Vizzi Carlo
Sofiter System Engineering SpA, Torino, Italy

Menduni Eleonora
Department of Mathematics, University of Torino, Torino, Italy

Cencetti Michele
Politecnico di Torino, Torino, Italy

8. References

[1] Agui J.H. and Nakagawa M. (2005) Dust on the Moon and Mars, 43rd AIAA Aerospace Sciences Meeting and Exhibit, Reno, NV, USA.

[2] Basso V., Pasquinelli, M., Rocci L., Bar C., Marello M. (2010) Collaborative System Engineering Usage at Thales Alenia Space–Italia, 4th International Workshop on System and Concurrent Engineering for Space Applications –SECESA 2010, Lausanne (CH)

[3] Beeson B., Lancaster M., Barnes D., Bourke P., and Rixon G. (2004). Visualising Astronomical Data using VRML, Proc. of the SPIE Digital Library, Vol.5493, pp. 242-253, International Society for Optical Engineering.

[4] Bernard D.E., Golombek M. (2001) Crater and rock hazard modeling for Mars landing, Space 2001 Conference and Exposition, Albuquerque, New Mexico, USA.

[5] Carrier W.D. III, Olhoeft G.R. and Mendell W. (1991) Physical properties of the lunar surface, In Lunar Sourcebook, G.H. Heiken, D.T. Vaniman, and B.M. French (eds.), Cambridge University Press, Cambridge.

[6] Douglass B.P. (2005) The Harmony Process, I–Logix white paper, I–Logix, Inc.

[7] Edwards L., Sims M., Kunz C., Lees D., Bowman. (2005) Photo–realistic Terrain Modeling and Visualization for Mars Exploration Rover Science Operations. In Systems, Man and Cybernetics, 2005 IEEE International Conference on, Vol. 2, pp. 1389–1395.

[8] Eisenmann H., Basso V., Fuchs J. and De Wilde D. (2010) ESA Virtual Spacecraft Design, 4th International Workshop on System and Concurrent Engineering for Space Applications –SECESA 2010, Lausanne (CH).

[9] Eliason E., Castalia B., Mattson S., Heyd R., Becker K., Anderson J. and Sides S. (2009) Software Interface Specification for HiRISE reduced data record products, Mars Reconnaissance Orbiter, JPL Document Number D-32006, Version 1.2.

[10] Golombek M.P., Haldemann A.F.C., Forsberg-Taylor N.K., DiMaggio E.N., Schroeder R.D., Jakosky B.M., Mellon M.T. and Matijevic J.R. (2003) Rock size-frequency distributions on Mars and implications for Mars Exploration Rover landing safety and operations, Journal of Geophysical Research, Vol. 108, 8086, 23 pp.

[11] Head J., van Dam A., Fulcomer S., Forsberg A., and Milkovich G. R. and S. (2005). ADVISER: Immersive Scientific Visualization Applied to Mars Research and Exploration, Photogrammetric Engineering and Remote Sensing, Vol. 71(10), pp. 1219-1226.

[12] Heim M. (1993) The Metaphysics of Virtual Reality, Oxford University Press, New York.

[13] Irving B., Sorley A., Paton M. and Bonin G. (2006) Virtual prototyping of human Mars missions with the Orbiter space flight simulator. Mars Society Conference, Washington, DC.

[14] Kass D.M., Schoeld J.T., Michaels T.I., Rafkin S.C.R., Richardson M.I. and Toigo D. (2003) Analysis of Atmospheric Mesoscale Models for Entry, Descent and Landing, Journal of Geophysical Research, Vol 108, pp 1–31.

[15] Katzan C.M. and Edwards J.L. (1991) Lunar dust transportation and potential interactions with power system components. NASA Contractor Report 4404.

[16] Kruchten P. (2003) The Rational Unified Process: An Introduction, Third Edition, Addison–Wesley Professional: Reading, MA.

[17] Miedema J., van der Voort M.C. and van Houten F.J.A.M. (2009) Advantageous application of synthetic environments in product design. CIRP Journal of Manufacturing Science and Technology, Vol. 1, pp. 159-164.

[18] Nielson G.M., Hagen H. and Müller H. (1997) Scientific Visualization: Overviews, Methodologies, and Techniques. IEEE Computer Society.

[19] Noor A. K. (2010) Potential of virtual worlds for remote space exploration. Advances in Engineering Software, Issue 41, pp. 666–673.

[20] Object Oriented System Engineering Method (2006) OOSEM Descriptive Outline for INCOSE SE Handbook Version 3, Annotated Update, Sect. 6.4.2, pp. 6–1 to 6–6.

[21] Pisanich G., Plice L., Neukom C., Flückiger L. and Wagner M. (2004) Mission Simulation Facility: Simulation Support For Autonomy Development. AIAA Conference, Reno, Nevada.

[22] Piovano L., Brunello M. M., Rocci L., and Basso V. (2010) Representing planetary terrains into a virtual reality environment for space exploration. In Proceedings of 10th International Conference on Pattern Recognition and Image Analysis: new Information Technology (PRIA 2010).

[23] Portelli C., Belvedere G., Basso V., Davighi A., Del Vecchio Blanco C. and Rosazza Prin P. (2008) ASI CEF&DBTE: Future applications of concurrent engineering methodology integrated with knowledge based economic analyses, 3rd International Workshop on System and Concurrent Engineering for Space Applications SECESA 2008, Rome, Italy.

[24] Rafkin Scot C.R., Haberle R.M., Michaels T.I. (2001) The Mars Regional Atmospheric Modeling System: Model Description and Selected Simulations, Icarus, Vol. 151(2), pp. 228–256, Elsevier.

[25] Rebelo F., Duarte E., Noriega P. and Soares M.M. (2011) Virtual Reality in Consumer Product Design: Methods and Applications. In: Human Factors and Ergonomics in Consumer Product Design: Methods and Techniques, CRC Press.

[26] Rönkkö J., Markkanen J., Launonen R., Ferrino M., Gaia E., Basso V., Patel H., D'Cruz M. and Laukkanen S. (2006) Multimodal Astronaut Virtual Training Prototype, International Journal of Human–Computer Studies –Interaction with virtual environments, Vol. 64(3), pp. 182–191.

[27] Rossmann J. and Sommer B. (2008) The Virtual Testbed: Latest Virtual Reality Technologies for Space Robotic Applications. In Proceedings of the 9th International Symposium on Artificial Intelligence, Robotics and Automation in Space, Hollywood, USA.

[28] Rossmann J., Wantia N., Springer M., Stern O., Müller H. and Ellsiepen M. (2011) Rapid Generation of 3D Navigation Maps for Extraterrestrial Landing and Exploration Missions: The Virtual Testbed Approach. In: 11th Symposium on Advanced Space Technologies in Robotics and Automation (ASTRA), ESA/ESTEC, pp. 1–7.

[29] Stoker C.R., Blackmon T., Hagen J., Kanefsky B., Rasmussen D., Schwehr K., Sims M., Zbinden E. (1998). Marsmap: An Interactive Virtual Reality Model of the Pathfinder Landing Site, Proceedings of Lunar and Planetary Science Conference (LPSC'98), Lunar and Planetary Institute.

[30] Stoker C.R., Zbinden E., Blackmon T., and Nguyen L. (1999). Visualizing Mars Using Virtual Reality: A State of the Art Mapping Technique Used on Mars Pathfinder, Proceedings of the 5th International Conference of Mars, Lunar and Planetary Institute.

[31] Stoker C.R., Zbinden E., Blackmon T., Kanefsky B. et al.(1999). Analyzing Pathfinder data using virtual reality and super-resolved imaging, Journal of Geophysical Research - Planets, Vol. 104(E4), pp. 8889- 8906.

[32] Vitech Announces Participation in INCOSE's 17th Annual International Symposium, Delivering Five Key Systems Engineering Presentations, Papers and Panels, Vitech News Release, Vitech Corporation, Vienna, VA.

[33] Walker S. and Kenneth J. (2003). Large haptic topographic maps: MarsView and the proxy graph algorithm, Proceedings of the ACM SIGGRAPH, Symposium on Interactive 3D Graphics, pp. 83-92. ACM Press.

[34] Wang S., Damon M., and Yuen D. (2005). Visualization in the Earth Sciences: A Discussion on Various Visualization Methods using Amira, Proceedings of the 16th IEEE Visualization Conference (VIS 2005), p. 112, IEEE Society Press.

[35] Wright J., Hartman F., and Cooper B. (1998) Immersive Environments for Mission Operations: Beyond Mars Pathfinder, Proceedings of Space Operations, Tokyo, Japan.

[36] Yang Y., Bao J., Jin Y., Cheng Y. (2008). A virtual simulation environment for lunar rover: framework and key technologies. International Journal of Advanced Robotic Systems, Vol. 5, No. 2, pp. 201–208.

[37] European Cooperation for Space Standardization: http://www.ecss.nl.

[38] ESA Concurrent Design Facility: http://www.esa.int/cdf.

[39] HiRISE: http://hirise.lpl.arizona.edu/

[40] HiRISE DEM Home Page: http://hirise.lpl.arizona.edu/

[41] http://www.incose.org.

[42] Lunar Reconnaissance Orbiter: lro.gsfc.nasa.gov.

[43] The Mars Climate Database: www-mars.lmd.jussieu.fr/mars/access.html

[44] Modelica Association –"Modelica –A Unified Object–Oriented Language for Physical Systems Modeling –Language Specification", v. 3.2, March 2010.

[45] OMG –"System Modeling Language –SysML Specification", v. 1.2, June 2010.

Chapter 9

A System Engineering Perspective to Knowledge Transfer: A Case Study Approach of BIM Adoption

Yusuf Arayici and Paul Coates

Additional information is available at the end of the chapter

http://dx.doi.org/10.5772/3333

1. Introduction

The building industry is under great pressure to provide value for money, sustainable infrastructure, etc. and this has propelled the adoption of Building Information Modelling (BIM) technology (Mihindu and Arayici, 2008). Owners can anticipate greater efficiency and cost savings in the design, construction and operation of facilities with the adoption of BIM. From an architectural point of view the consequences of BIM depends on how the technology is implemented and integrated into the firm's business model. BIM offers many new financial and creative opportunities for most construction related organizations (e.g. architectural companies), but to realize these benefits firms will need to embrace the integration of design and construction that BIM will promote. This will require changes in project delivery methods and in the composition of the firm's staff. Properly implemented, BIM may also change the role of professions (e.g. architectural) an expanded role in the AEC/O industry. To realize the BIM benefits, an active role in guiding its implementation must be taken (Arayici et al, 2009) (Bernstein and Pittman, 2004).

There is enough evidence to suggest the architectural profession is beginning to come under pressure to adopt BIM. This information management technology has existed in some form for over 20 years. However during last few years, building owners are becoming aware that BIM promises to make the design, construction and operation of buildings much more streamlined and efficient (Coates et al, 2010). Owners are starting to enforce that architects and other design professionals, construction managers and construction companies adopt BIM. This trend gained enormous momentum when the General Services Administration (GSA) of USA announced that it would require all schematic design submittals to be in BIM format starting in 2006 (US-GSA, 2008). Many other similar uptakes from Europe and Australasia have followed (Mihindu and Arayici, 2008).

The productivity increases promised by BIM would seem to make it attractive to architects and other design professionals, contractors as well as to owners. The intensely competitive nature of building industry makes it likely that most if not all of any productivity gains realized by BIM will be passed through to owners and clients. This is what happened with CAD (Oakley, 2007).

In some countries such as Finland, Denmark, Norway and the USA, the use of BIM has been endorsed (Aouad & Arayici, 2010) by the government of these states for the state project, while some other countries have progressed toward it. A fuller analysis of the external influences which have promoted BIM adoption in these countries may provide an indication of how development of the use of BIM in the UK might be stimulated. Such factors in the UK might include the attitudes of market constituents affecting adoption and standards such BS16001 and the use of BIM in compliance.

2. The construction industry and its features

In the past decade, construction companies spent a great deal of effort and resources in improving their business processes. New forms of innovative project management, supported by recent IT developments, appeared in response to ever-growing pressure from owners to complete projects on time and deliver high quality buildings. Although many sectors such as automotive, manufacturing and the service sectors have improved their competitiveness from IT, the construction industry has had some difficulties, resulting in the construction industry lagging behind the other sectors. The constraints the construction industry has experienced can be outlined as follows (Aouad and Arayici, 2010):

The Nature of Information and its Flow: Construction projects consist of many interrelated processes and sub-processes, often carried out by different professionals at different locations. Most of the tasks involved in construction processes are mainly about exchanging information between project stakeholders. All construction researchers addressed the need to improve the poor cross-disciplinary communications.

The Fragmented Supply Chain of the Construction Industry: One of the main features of the construction industry is the high fragmentation in its supply chain. However, despite the increasing trends towards multi-disciplinary practical arrangements between construction firms, such as partnering, the construction industry still consists of hundreds of small and medium size firms that offer undifferentiated products and services.

The Culture of the Construction Industry: The widespread culture of the construction industry is a claiming, confrontational one, which has underpinned the inefficiency and the ineffectiveness of its processes. The strong resistance to change could be partly attributed to the strong and rigid culture of the construction industry.

Lack of Long-Term Strategic Management Thinking: The absence of sophisticated management techniques and methods is a dominant feature of common practices in the construction industry. Many researchers highlighted the coherent lack of management expertise and the poor applications of strategic management in the construction industry.

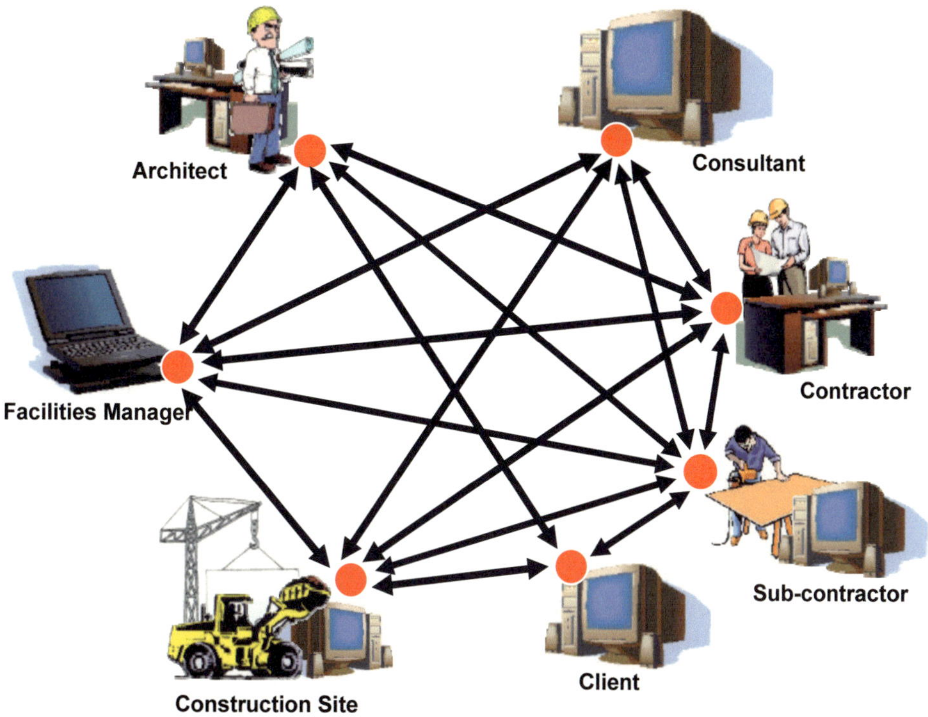

Figure 1. Illustrates the current work environment in the construction industry (Aouad and Arayici, 2010)

Figure 1 above depicts the traditional practices in construction projects. The construction industry is fragmented by nature. Added to this fragmentation between the construction stakeholders, a high level of complexity of the work flow resulting from a high number of companies working on the same project increases the inefficiency of construction projects. For example, repeated processes or functions and duplications due to the lack of communication and standardisation that causes waste and lead times in the project lifecycle, and extra cost to the client for non value added activities.

For example, clients and some stakeholders such as local authorities and residents have an incorrect perception, or lack of understanding the 2D architectural and engineering drawing. The design team cannot fully understand the client's needs due to a lack of communication, a shared platform, and an understandable Virtual Reality (VR) tool by both the client and the architect. Eventually these constraints will bring about client dissatisfaction (Aouad and Arayici, 2010).

3. Building Information Modelling and its benefits

In the past, researchers used IT tools for providing numerous decision support systems for the professionals of the industry. However, these systems have created islands of automation and are far from achieving an acceptable level of integration across disciplines and across the design and construction processes. It is recognised that greater benefits can be obtained and the constraints can be considerably reduced if a complete integration based on VR tools is achieved. In this respect, major benefits of a desired integrated VR environment are considered as follows (Aouad and Arayici, 2010);

- Improving the coordination and communication between the client, design team members, and construction professionals, by using standard formats, and intuitive VR tools that ease communication and information sharing.
- Since VR tools allow the design team to have quick and high quality feedback on the project, in terms of architectural, technical, financial and environmental aspects, the design may be evaluated at the very early stages of the project lifecycle.
- Looking at "what if" scenarios at the detailed design stage, to assess the design solution in lighting, acoustic and thermal aspects.
- Closing the gap between the design team and the construction team and providing them with an integrated platform through which they can collaborate for the best buildability and appropriate construction planning.
- The use of past project knowledge and information for new developments.

Furthermore, visualisation in conjunction with integrated model driven construction systems can be expected to:

- Enable designers, developers and contractors to use the VR system and virtually test a proposed project before construction actually begins.
- Offer "walk-through" views of the project so that problems can be found and design improvements can be made earlier.
- Provide a free flow of information between CAD systems and other applications work packages, in order to minimise misinterpretation between project participants.
- Facilitate the selection of alternative designs, by allowing different plans to be tested in the same virtual world.

Due to its potential, Building Information Modelling has become an internationally recognized concept. BIM can be described as the use of the ICT technologies to streamline all the processes that require a building infrastructure and its surroundings, to provide a safer and more productive environment for its occupants; and to assert the least possible environmental impact from its existence; and more operationally efficient for its owners throughout the life cycle of the building infrastructure (Aouad and Arayici, 2010).

BIM in most simple terms is the utilisation of a database infrastructure to encapsulate built facilities with specific viewpoints of stakeholders. It is a methodology to integrate digital descriptions of all the building objects and their relationships to others in a precise manner, so that stakeholders can query, simulate, and estimate activities and their effects of the building process as a life cycle entity. Therefore, BIM can provide the required value judgments that create more sustainable infrastructures, which satisfy their owners and occupants (Aouad and Arayici, 2010).

BIM as a lifecycle evaluation concept seeks to integrate processes throughout the entire life cycle of a construction project. The focus is to create and reuse consistent digital information by the stakeholders throughout the life cycle. Some advantages are (i) model based decision making, (ii) design and construction alternatives, (iii) costs, energy and lifecycle analysis, the automated building code checking (Cheng, 2005) or thermal load calculations (Kam et al, 2003) or environmental impact assessment (e.g. CO_2 emission), etc. can be performed by using these models for design changes and use of alternative material types over the infrastructure life cycle.

Some attributes of BIM include; robust geometry, comprehensive and extensible objects properties, semantic richness, integrated information and ability to support the infrastructure life cycle (Schevers et al, 2007).

BIM incorporate a methodology based around the notion of collaboration between stakeholders to exchange valuable information throughout the life cycle. Such collaboration can be seen as the answer to the fragmentation that exists within the building industry which has caused various inefficiencies. The above scenarios show the expected stakeholder collaboration and the aim of using BIM. Although BIM is not the salvation of the construction industry, a great deal of effort has gone into address those issues which have remained unattended far too long (Jordani, 2008).

The Implementation of BIM systems requires dramatic changes in current business practices, which will lead to the development of new and sustainable business process models. The rest of the chapter discusses the BIM implementation from the systems engineering perspective through best practices and a case study of the BIM implementation.

4. The priory scoping study for the BIM adoption

Finland is seen as a leader in BIM use and implementation in the construction sector. They have a clear vision of BIM implementation at both governmental and operational levels. In order to capture the best practices in Finland, interviews were conducted with three academics and five industrialists in Finland to obtain the in-depth understanding about many years of experience in BIM adoption, challenges, barriers and also strategies for solutions against these challenges and barriers.

The interviews in Finland were carried out in an unstructured manner, as each company and institution had a unique experience of BIM and varying viewpoints on their activities. The unstructured approach to the interviews was adopted in order to capture their uniqueness as well as commonalities in their BIM experiences. However, all the interviews had the same aim and goal, which is to understand their views and strategies for BIM use and implementation in practice. As a result, these interviews enabled the perception of every company's experience about BIM use and implementation from their research and practical projects in the last 15 years not only in-depth but also in a broad manner. In order to carry out comprehensive exploration and analysis, the data collected from the interviews was documented and compiled together through mind mapping (Novak and Canas, 2008) shown in figure 2.

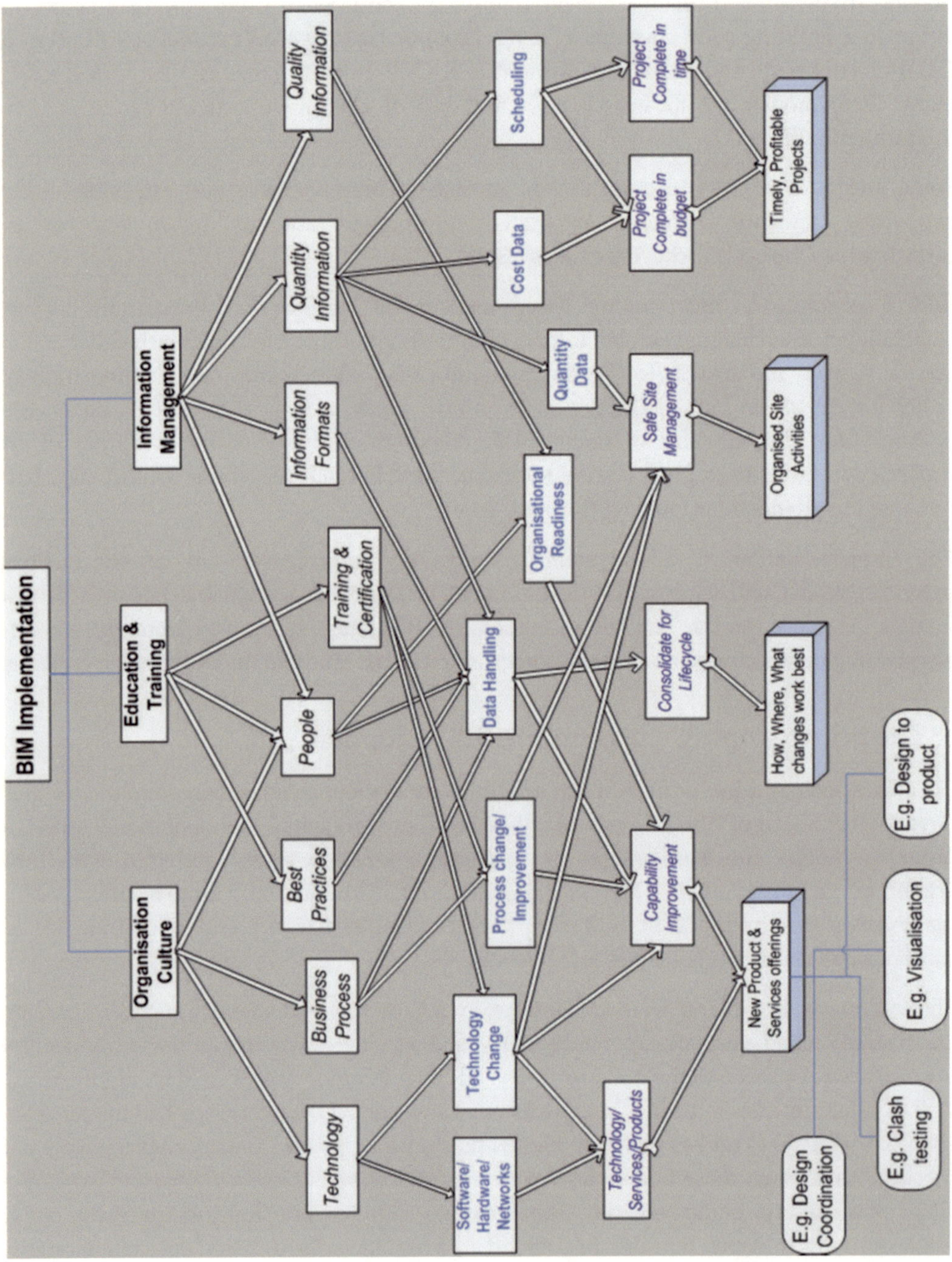

Figure 2. BIM implementation concept map from the interviews

Findings from the interviews have provided a focus on three predominant themes; organisational culture, education and training, and information management. This shows that the BIM implementation for an organisation should fundamentally address its impact on culture, personnel, and the organisation's use of technologies. That is to say, the focus is not only on technology but also on process and people.

4.1. Organization culture

As noted the organisational culture is predominantly created and practiced by everyone involved in the organisations. Further it is an aspect that is inherited as the organisation changes, grows and merges. Its effects can be identified within the business process, technologies used and people's work practices. While these aspects ultimately contribute towards the organisational readiness to accept BIM, peoples' ability, their understanding of the new process, and the availability of the required support including governance are to provide the necessary environment for achieving a successful implementation process. BIM implementation has forced technology change and process change within the organisations, which will force much improvement of the organisational capabilities or services offered. In most cases, this also involves integration or discontinuation of software and hardware systems within the organisation.

New systems can also provide challenges in data handling, which require training within the whole organisation. Due to the nature of BIM, consolidation of data throughout the lifecycle of a given project will be a reality. Therefore many other applications will be able to access such data streams to provide further services, e.g. asset management and demolition management during the lifecycle. In addition, such changes will create new opportunities and improvements, e.g. design coordination, clash testing, virtualisation services and streamlined design to product workflows, which can become a part of the core business process model of the organisation.

4.2. Education and training

Education and training has become an important part of BIM implementation due to the process and technological changes within the organisation. In order for the implementation to be successful, all affected people require up skilling. Those who are in specific positions may need to gain certain standards of education and training. This is noted as 'certification' on the concept map. Those who are trained will engage and administer organisational process and technological changes that are initiated through BIM implementation appropriately. Learning the best practices through professional training is the other important aspect. BIM technology is linked with many other sources of data, e.g. costing, scheduling, and materials flow. However depending on the tools being used such links may or may not be available to a great extent. When the BIM technology is used appropriately most of the links that show data from the building lifecycle become visible.

4.3. Information management

BIM is seen as an efficient information management methodology within construction projects. It heavily involves people's perspectives, firstly as creators or collectors of data from the site and other sources, and secondly as users of processed data, i.e. information or knowledge from the building models. Different BIM technologies available to date may provide different organisational capabilities and hence the stakeholders are required to assess currently available technologies on the market with necessary concerns. This will allow the organisation to select the suitable technology with a futuristic vision, perhaps further services that the organisation is willing to provide in the future. Similarly in some circumstances multiple tools may be required to achieve specific outcomes. Due to the variety of software and tools being used many different types of files formats are involved. Here, greater simplicity can be achieved by using integrated products, e.g. Vicosoft and Tocosoft (Tocoman, 2008), (Tekes, 2008). Since such tools provide various features with different complexities stakeholders should investigate their recommendations with appropriate future goals. Quantity and quality management has been an important part of such product listings. Quantity data can also assist the appropriate site management feature, e.g. site safety and minimising onsite storage. Costing and scheduling can provide timely project completions with maximum profits/savings.

Overall, successful adoption of BIM should incorporate strategies considering technology, process and people. As indicated in the concept map, technology, process and people aspects can be covered under i) organisation culture, ii) education and training and iii) information management headings. However, each category implies different strategies to the BIM implementation. Therefore, complementary strategies should be adopted coherently, which can be characterised as people oriented, information and process driven.

5. The case study project of BIM adoption

This case study BIM adoption and implementation has been undertaken under a DTI funded Knowledge Transfer Partnership (KTP) scheme. It aims not only to implement BIM and therefore assess the degree of the successful implementation, but rather to position this within the context of value-add offerings that can help the company place itself at the high-end knowledge-based terrain of the sector. Therefore, it adopts a socio-technical view of BIM implementation in that it does not only consider the implementation of technology but also considers the socio-cultural environment that provides the context for its implementation.

5.1. The case study company: John McCall's Architects (JMA)

The company was established in 1991 in Liverpool in the UK, and has been involved in architecture and construction for more than 17 years designing buildings throughout Northwest England. Focusing primarily on social housing and regeneration, private housing and one off homes and large extensions, the company is known for good quality, economical, environmentally sustainable design. JMA works with many stakeholders from the design through to building construction process and the associated information is very fragmented. Projects in which JMA are involved are typically of 2½ years duration, involving many stakeholders and requiring considerable interoperability of documentation and dynamic information.

5.2. BIM implementation and adoption strategy for JMA

Based on the vision in the KTP project and taking into considerations in the scoping study in section 2 for successful BIM implementation and reengineering JMA's processes, the following strategies are employed;

- Soft system methodology, for user led system implementation
- Information engineering, predominantly data driven
- Process innovation, driven by processes and technology

The priorities and focus in the BIM implementation change through the BIM adoption process. Further, from the scoping study, it is confirmed that the BIM implementation strategy should be comprehensive enough to coherently consider people, process and technology parameters. Therefore, a combination of human centred, information and process driven system implementation strategies have been employed in the project.

5.2.1. Soft System Methodology (SSM)

SSM comprises seven steps, which underpin the methodology (Checkland and Poulter, 2010). These are

Step 1. a problem situation is acknowledged in its unstructured form
Step 2. the problem situation is expressed (this often entails the development of a 'rich picture')
Step 3. root definitions of relevant system are provided
Step 4. conceptual models of the purposeful activities are developed
Step 5. the conceptual models are compared with the real world
Step 6. changes are proposed- these should be systematically desirable but culturally feasible and
Step 7. action to improve the situation is taken

5.2.2. Information Engineering (IE)

Information engineering is a methodology to successfully indentify the underlying nature and structure of an organisation's data as a stable basis from which to build information systems. In other words, IE approach is to arrange the data in a structured framework and store them in a data bank which provides an easy means to access the data. However, that does not mean that IE does not take into account processes. In fact, it does recognise that processes have to be included in detail in the development of information systems. It balances the modelling of data and processes as appropriate (Betts, 1999).

This methodology commences with a top-down approach and begins with a top management overview of the enterprise as a whole. This enables an overall strategic approach to be adopted. As the steps are carried out in an iterative manner, more and more details are derived and decisions are made for continuous development (Finkelstein, 1992).

5.2.3. Process Innovation (PI)

Process innovation is a methodology which ties Business Process Redesign (BPR) with Information Systems (IS) or Information Technologies (IT). Importantly, PI is an approach to information systems which takes into account strategic aspects of BPR. The essence of BPR is a radical change in the way in which organisations perform business activities (Voss, 2006).

The fundamental rethinking and radical redesign of business process to achieve dramatic improvements in critical, contemporary measures of performance, such as cost, quality, and service and speed. Redesign determines what an organisation should do, how it should do, and what its concerns should be as opposed to what they currently are. Emphasis is placed on the business processes and therefore IS/IT enables the change, and also encompasses managerial behaviour, work patterns and organisational structure (Grint & Willcocks, 2007). The following steps of process redesign are crucial to the success of re-engineering processes with IT (Betts, 1999).

Step 1. the organisational strengths and weaknesses need to be identified, along with the market analysis for opportunities and threats.

Step 2. identification of the processes to be reengineered. Processes, which are of high impact, of great strategic relevance or presently conflict with the business vision, are selected for consideration and a priority attached to them.

Step 3. understanding and measuring existing processes. The present processes must be documented. This will help to establish shared understanding and also help to understand the magnitude of change and the associated tasks. Understanding the existing problems should help ensure that they are not repeated. It also provides measures, which can be used as based for future improvements.

Step 4. identification of IT levers that will help push the changes: This methodology proposes that an awareness of IT capabilities can influence process redesign and should be considered at the early stages.

Step 5. Design and build prototype of the new process: in this final stage, the process is designed and the prototype built through successive iterations.

5.3. BIM adoption and implementation process

BIM implementation and adoption is planned through the stages summarized in Table 1 below. However, in practice these stages are carried out in accordance with the aforementioned strategies.

Stages	Activities	Implementation Strategy
Stage 1: Detail Review and Analysis of Current Practice	Production of Current Process Flowcharts	**Soft System Methodology** (Steps 1,2,3 and 4 of the methodology via contextual inquiry and contextual design techniques, SWOT analysis)
	Review of overall ICT systems in the company	
	Stakeholder Review and Analysis	
	Identification of competitive advantages from BIM implementation	
	Review of BIM tools for the company	
Stage 2: Identification of Efficiency gains from BIM implementation	2.1.Efficiency gains from BIM adoption	**Process Innovation** (Steps 1,2, and 3 of the methodology via SWOT analysis and balance scorecard)
Stage 3: Design of new business processes and technology adoption path	3.1. Identification of Key Evaluation Metrics	**Soft System Methodology** (Step 4 of the methodology via brainstorming and interviews)
	3.2. Production of detail strategies and documentation of Lean Process and Procedures	**Process Innovation** (Step 4 and 5 of the methodology via A3 method)
	3.3.Development of the Project Support Information Management System	**Information Engineering** via evolutionary prototyping
	3.4.Documentation of BIM implementation plan	**Soft System Methodology** (Step 5 and 6 of the methodology via contextual design technique and communication to stakeholders)
Stage 4: Implementation & roll-out of BIM	Piloting BIM on three different projects (past, current, and future)	**Soft System Methodology** (Step 6 and 7 of the methodology via prototyping and testing on piloting projects)
	4.2. Training the JMA staff and stakeholders	
	4.3. Devising and improving companywide capabilities	**Process Innovation** (Step 5 of the methodology via A3 method and prototyping and check listing with KPIs)
	4.4. Documentation and integration of process and procedures	
Stage 5: Project review, dissemination and integration into strategy plan	5.1. Sustaining new products and processing offerings	**Process Innovation** (all the steps in revision via measuring against the KPIs and check listing)
	5.2. Evaluation and dissemination of the project	

Table 1. The Stages of BIM implementation Process

The stages and the activities within those stages are mapped out with the implementation strategies in the table below and explained accordingly.

5.3.1. Detail review and analysis of current practice

1. Production of Current Process Flowcharts

Firstly the methods of communication in the organization were analyzed and flow diagrams produced. The main methodology for mapping the current process workflow was the contextual design technique (Beyer & Holtzblatt, 1998), which prescribes modelling techniques such as flow diagrams, sequence diagrams, artefact modelling, and physical environment modelling and culture modelling to understand and examine the current practice, needs and requirements for improvement via contextual inquiry. For example, the communication flow diagrams in pictorial nature were made easily legible and formed a good basis for discussions and interviews with the members of staff and obtained feedback from them. As part of the contextual design approach as a methodology, storyboarding technique was adopted to find out how the members of staff carried out their activities at John McCall Architects and identify the correct needs and user requirements through contextual inquiry: This was undertaken by a series of interviews of members of staff in their working situation where possible examples and demonstrations were asked for. Flowcharts and rich picture diagrams by storyboarding were produced from the investigations (Aouad & Arayici, 2010).

2. Review of overall ICT systems in the company

The IT System at John McCall Architects is integral with the production processes undertaken by the practice. The standard server PC (Personal Computer) model was adopted with intranet connections. The software adopted can be broken up by usage such as document production, presentation production and drawing and graphic production. Bespoke software is used for accounting and resource monitoring processes. All the different software result in a lot of duplication of data in different file formats. In some cases the data is fragmented such as reference files to allow multiple members of staff to contribute to one drawing or brochure.

Unifying all activities is a standard electronic filing system. Packaging and transmission of information represents a time consuming activity for many of the staff, who are generally proficient software users. The IT System is overseen by the computer manager and CAD management is devolved to the team members. The IT system is on a rolling program of upgrade subsequently staff skills are upgraded while hardware and software is upgraded.

With the adoption of BIM and the use of larger files the network transfer capabilities will need to be reviewed as the individual processing power of the individual PCs will increase. Most of John McCall Architects work is within the housing sector. This raises certain criteria that will be required by the BIM system chosen. Multiple house types should be able to be inserted into a single site model. Ease of creating site terrain is also important. Also the ease of working with brick dimensions would be a real bonus. In evaluating the appropriateness of the BIM tools to be adopted, it is important to understand the present skill set of the staff.

The level of presentational output from the BIM system will be expected. Additional rendering engines may be used. The way multiple users interact with a single model is also important. The methods of sharing outputs and interaction with other consultants within the building team are also critical. How models can be recombined and clash and warning mechanisms are also important. The level of support and training provided by the software vendor also needs to be considered. The other question is whether to adopt a BIM system that runs on top of 2D software or to purely adopt a BIM system. Another consideration is the level of bidirectional interoperability the BIM software has.

3. Stakeholder Review and Analysis

An important part of the success of the project has been the buy-in by senior member of staff. However, the BIM implementation will affect both internal and external stakeholders. Using contextual design techniques how the existing stakeholders interact with the present process was observed. An area of particular interest was how internal stakeholders maintain the consistency of the drawing set. An area where BIM could make considerable saving in maintaining the dimensional consistency of between representations (drawings) was noted.

External stakeholders may demand intelligent or non intelligent outputs from the BIM system. In this sense there should be a flexibility of output, but this does not degrade the output to the stakeholders compared with the output from the existing CAD systems. The primary need of the external stakeholders is to facilitate the built objective. Though the multifaceted forms of output and analysis from the BIM model is possible, new and more appropriate artefacts can be created and tailored to the building design process. The stakeholder review and need analysis has involved discussion with clients, consultants and contractors. A simplified questionnaire was produced and discipline specific presentations have been given. At this stage, it is recognized that the full benefits of this project will only be realized if the BIM process is integrated and utilized by the other disciplines in the building process.

4. Identification of competitive advantages from BIM implementation

As a background for the BIM implementation project, a SWOT (Strength, Weaknesses, Opportunities, and Threats) analysis was undertaken to realize the competitive advantages for JMA. Since the BIM implementation is a fundamental change, it is sensible to undertake a SWOT analysis at this time. Through the SWOT analysis, both internal and external positions of JMA at the current time and in the future have been examined; looking into the company's strengths, weaknesses, opportunities and threats. The analysis included looking at emerging technology and changing methods of procurement. By understanding the strengths of the company it is possible to understand those factors that are important for JMA to maintain competitive market share. By looking at the companies weaknesses and undertaking a review against lean principles (Koskela, 2003) it was possible to reveal areas of waste.

By envisioning the future trends, it is possible to better predict how BIM will be used in the company. It is also possible to predict for what type of project the BIM process will be used. The competitive advantages in the SWOT report were identified as cost leadership, differentiation, cost focus, differential focus and collaboration. BIM has the potential to provide advantages in all of these areas. By reducing both the time and the effort to generate architectural information, BIM may give John McCall Architects or its team the opportunity to offer the most competitive bids for projects. By avoiding errors and reducing the need for information requests from site John McCall Architects has the potential to differentiate itself by providing a better service by using BIM.

Cost Focus competitive advantage is gained by carrying out specific parts of the process cheaper than competitors. Sustainability issue is becoming more and more important for housing design. By adopting BIM, John McCall Architects should be able to analysis environmental factors at a lower cost. BIM offers several potential areas for differential focus. For example, using BIM virtual preconstruction analysis and project production storyboarding become more feasible. Secondly the BIM system has a major potential for use in facility management and life cycle management. The major advantage of BIM is by providing a central focus on the collaboration between the building team and through integration and alignment of all the participants within the building process, savings will be made on cost, quality and time.

Whilst the major gains from this KTP project are only be realized in the later stages of the project, several initial gains have already been identified. One of the potential gains coming out of the SWOT analysis is the use of BIM models for rapid prototyping via 3D printers. This has the potential to give yet another understanding of a scheme as it develops. The SWOT analysis also demonstrated how saving could be made through the adoption of Lean principles (Koskela & Ballard, 2006). Initial seminars have been given in the office on "quality" and "lean principles". The discussion about lean principles; avoiding waste and focusing on value adding processes has provided a good counter balance to the ISO 14000 principles which are also been reviewed by the practice. Meetings have also been setup to discuss how the adoption of BIM can assist in the drive for sustainable design projects. On the other hand, members of staff need to be trained how to use the BIM system and guideline and procedures will be developed. But the important thing is to engender the staff with the attitude of looking for better ways of working and the team mentality of discussing new ideas as an ongoing process development and improvement.

5. Review of BIM tools for the company

Continuous evaluation of alternative BIM systems took place for a period of three months. Software vendors have visited the office to give presentations or webinars to discuss the benefits of their particular software platform. This has proved to be an effective way to generate interest and awareness in the office to BIM and its terminology and associated ways of working. It has been a good way to reduce the reservations of many staff in the office to the adoption of BIM, which has been described as a paradigm shift in the way architects work. The more exposure members of staff become more knowledge about the new concepts, the easier the transition will be.

5.3.2. Identification of efficiency gains from the BIM implementation

The main characteristics of BIM implementation strategy and the subsequent efficiency gains are clarified after the stage 1: detail review and analysis of current practice. Completion of these diagnostic activities has led to make some decisions to identify the scope and the characteristics of the actual BIM Implementation and adoption strategy. Making these decisions is best facilitated with the use of a scorecard (Malmi, 2001). These decisions have helped determine the roadmap and the resources required for the BIM adoption and subsequently the identification of the efficiency gains from the BIM adoption, which are listed below (Arayici et al, 2009). BIM adoption and implementation will re-engineer the operational and IT processes and broaden the knowledge of existing staff and stakeholders up and down the supply chain

- Significant competitive edge over similar sized practices resulting in increased turnover of at least 10%; increase of 20% more work utilizing a staffing growth of below 10%.
- Improved management of the client/contractor/consultant relationships, essential to support the sales growth, leading to enhanced partnering/framework options.
- Better co-ordination, better quality data production and information exchange across the wide spectrum of information sources utilised and exported to others, including the building model, technical drawings, schedules and specifications.
- Enhanced design solutions developed at an earlier stage due to more time and effort being available to the design team. Improvements in dealing with design changes and change control enabling the practice to react efficiently and proactively to changing client aspirations throughout the design stages.
- Savings through improved internal efficiencies and better service delivery to clients enabling John McCall to position itself at the forefront of international trends.
- Development of staff to increase the visible expertise and reputation of the company. Increased technical staff job satisfaction by the removal of inefficient and repetitive tasks which detract from the core task of the design process.

5.3.3. Design of new business processes and technology adoption path

1. Identification of Key Evaluation Metrics

In order to derive the KPIs, it is necessary to understand the organizational inputs, outputs, and desired outcomes and these KPIs should be as closely linked as possible to the top-level goals of the business. Specifically with BIM, there has been a lack of consistent fiscal benchmarking to evaluate the business improvements and gains from BIM adoption (Gerber & Rice, 2009). Using the diagnostic material from stage 1 and 2 of the BIM implementation approach, the following attributes are sought for the definition of KPIs:

- Does the KPI motivate the right behaviour?
- Is the KPI measurable?
- Is the measurement of this KPI affordable (cost-effective)?
- Is the target value attainable?
- Are the factors affecting this KPI controlled by the company?
- Is the KPI meaningful?

The following steps have been undertaken in the KPI identification.

Step 1. conducting brainstorming sessions in JMA and interviewing the external stakeholders JMA collaborates:

Step 2. Filling out the KPI design form for all the potential KPIs collated from the brainstorming sessions and the interview with the external partners

Step 3. Evaluation and assessment of the potential KPIs from step 2 to filter them against the checklist above recommended by Gerber & Rice, (2009)

This process has led to finalized identification of the KPIs for the evaluation of the business improvement in JMA and subsequently the assessment and measure the extent of the success of BIM adoption. The following list of KPIs has been identified for JMA's business.

- Man hours spent per project - efficiency with cost per project
- Speed of Development
- Revenue per head
- IT investment per unit of revenue
- Cash Flow
- Better Architecture
- A better product
- Reduced costs, travel, printing, document shipping
- Bids won or win percentage
- Client satisfaction and retention
- Employee skills and knowledge development

2. Production of detail strategies and Documentation of Lean Process and Procedures

The main approach used for lean improvement in the project is A3 method, which is a proven to be a key tool in Toyota's successful move towards organisational efficiency and effectiveness and improvement (Durward and Sobek, 2008), (Koskela, 2003). For example, it has been used for i) improvements achieved via storing project support information in the new knowledge database, ii) improvements achieved in email handlings, iii) improvements achieved in mail scanning and digitisation, iv) Improvements achieved via BIM based product information documentation, etc. The Figure 3 and subsequent table 2 show an example for BIM based product information documentation and for storing project support information in the new knowledge database.

The Figure 4 and subsequent table 3 also show another example of A3 Lean exercising for Improvements via knowledge Management system at organisational level.

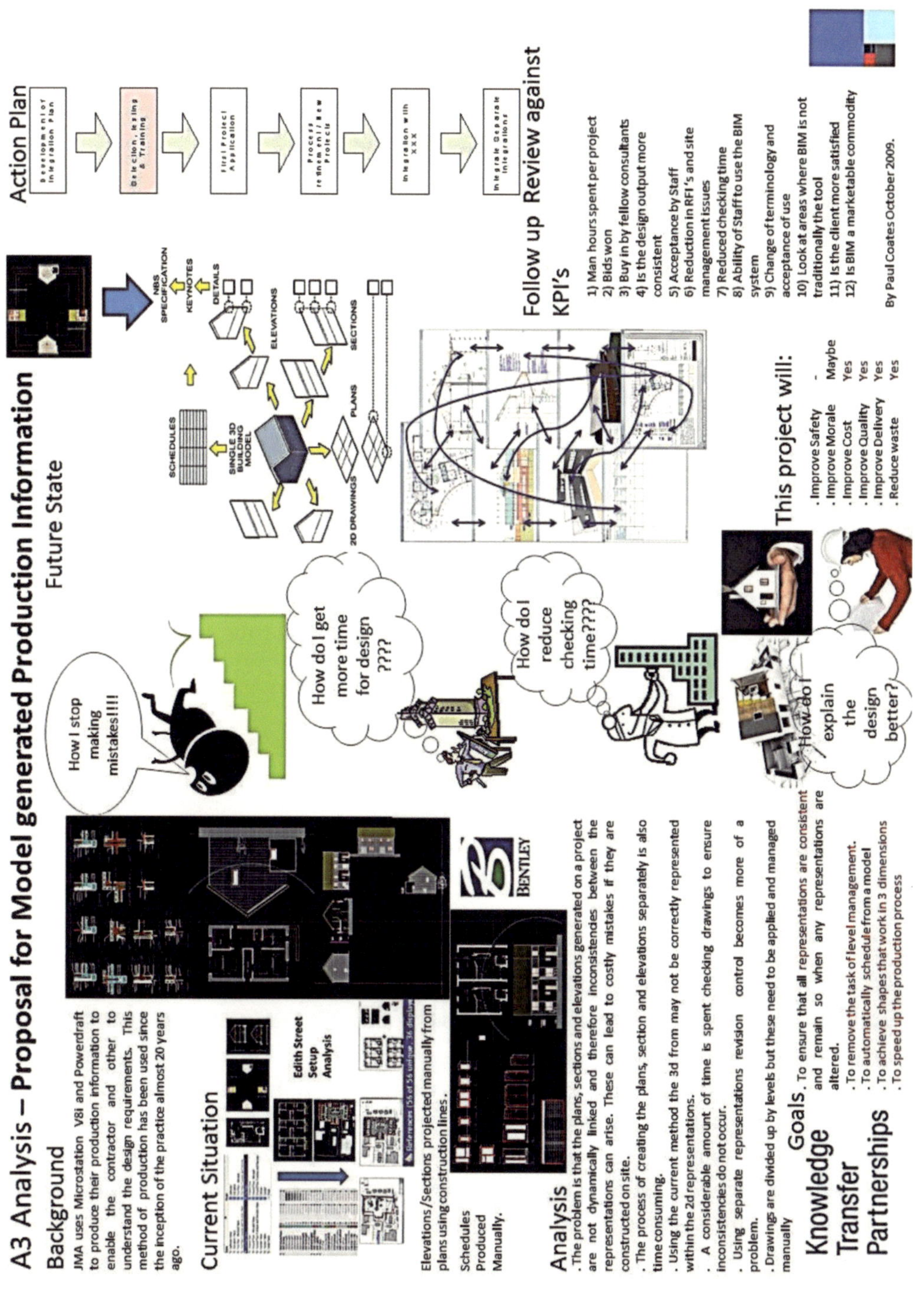

Figure 3. Improvements via BIM based product information documentation at project levelThis figure 3 above is further explained and elaborated below in table 2

1.Background
JMA uses Microstation V8i and Powerdraft to produce their production information to enable the contractor and the stakeholders to understand their design requirements. This method of production has been used since the inception of the practice almost 20 years ago. 2D representations are created to illustrate 3D forms.
Situation before the BIM tool Adoption
Elevations/Sections projected manually from plans using construction lines. Schedules produced manually.
Analysis
The problem is that the plans, sections and elevations generated on a project are not dynamically linked and therefore inconsistencies between the representations can arise. These can lead to costly mistakes if they are constructed on site. The process of creating the plans, section and elevations separately is also time consuming. Using the current method the 3D from may not be correctly represented within the 2D representations. A considerable amount of time is spent checking drawings to ensure inconsistencies do not occur. Using separate representations revision control becomes more of a problem. Drawings are divided up by levels but these need to be applied and managed manually.
Goals
To ensure that all representations are consistent and remain consistent and accurate when any representations are altered. To remove the task of level management. To automatically generate schedules from the BIM model. To achieve shapes that work in 3 dimensions. To speed up the production process.
Situation after the BIM tool Adoption and the Lean Efficiency Gains Achieved
Using BIM software to create 3D models from which 2D representations and schedules can be generated automatically. Furthermore, construction planning, costing, energy and thermal analysis, daylight and acoustic analysis can be carried out in a fast and accurate to ensure sustainable design outputs. Efficiency gains are 1) The consistent and better quality design outputs, 2) reduction in RFI (Request For Information) and site management issues 3) Reduced checking time 4) Ability of Staff to use the BIM system and capacity improvement 5) pinpointing other areas where BIM is not traditionally the tool for improvement but still requires improvement, 6) Reduced costs, travel, printing and document shipping.

Table 2. A3 exercise for process improvements via BIM tool adoption (Arayici et al, 2011)

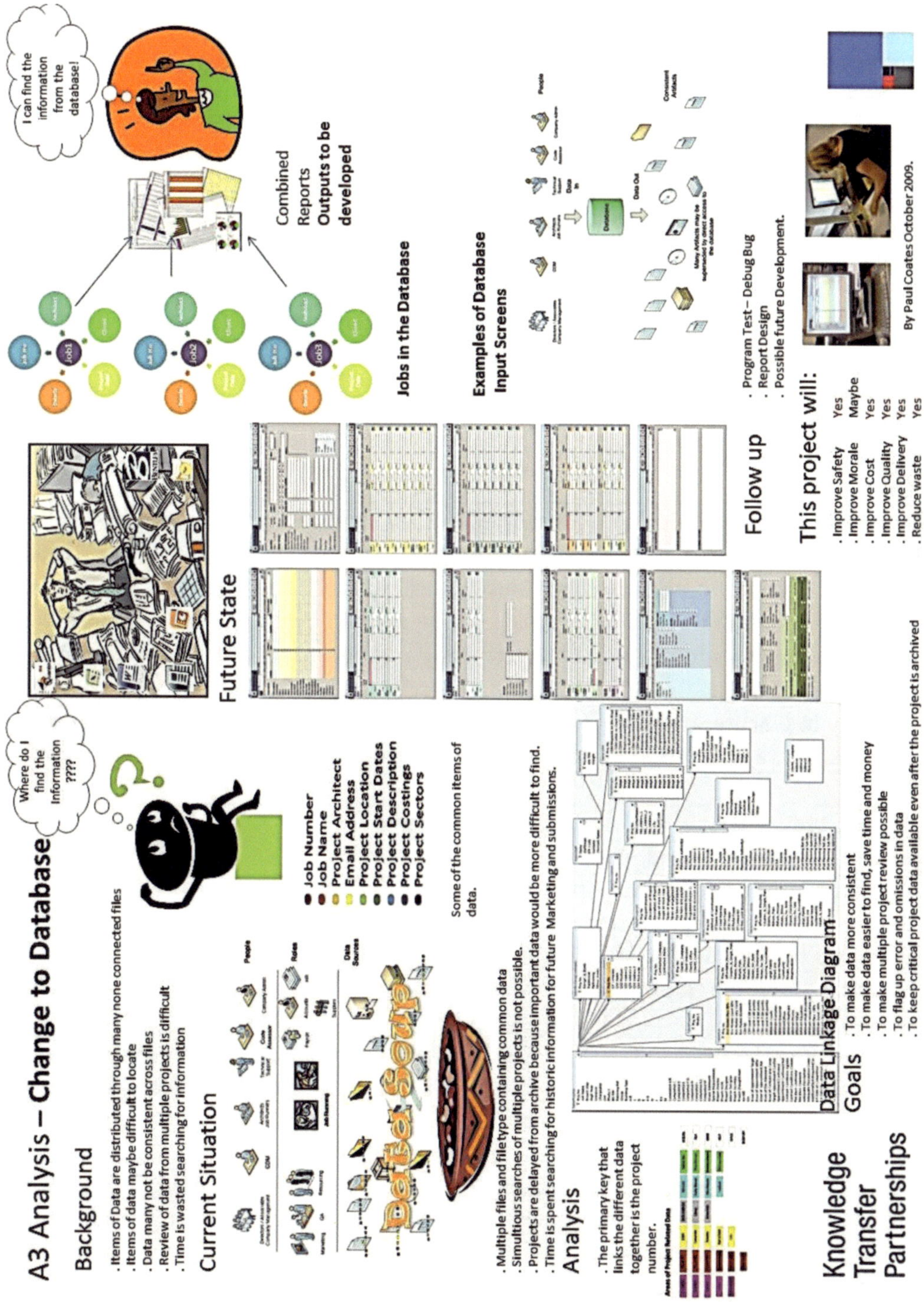

Figure 4. Improvements via knowledge Management system at organisational level

Background
Items of information that are distributed through many none connected files Items of information that are difficult to locate Some information is not consistent across the files in the company Review of data from multiple projects is difficult Time is wasted searching for information scattered across the company
Situation before the knowledge database development
Duplications and multiple files with different file types but containing common data Simultaneous searches of multiple projects are not possible. Projects are delayed from archive because important data would be more difficult to find. Time is spent searching for historic information for future marketing and submissions is painful and lengthy Knowledge and experience from past projects remains only with the individuals not as a company knowledge and experience
Analysis
Some primary project support information has been identified as commonly reoccurring such as project number, project name, project architect, email address, project start dates, project description, project castings, and project sectors. The database structure was developed around these fields. The scope to be covered by the database came out of interviews with most of the staff in the company and discussion on how different stages of the projects are addressed at John McCall Architects. Tasks that currently cause the difficulty in practice were identified and the structure and the front-end of the database were design to address these deficiencies in the current system.
Goals
To make project support information more consistent To make data easier to find, save time and money To make multiple project review possible and obtain lessons learnt from past projects To flag up error and omissions in data To keep critical project data available even after the project is archived
Situation after the knowledge database development and lean efficiency gains achieved
Database can be accessible to all JMA staff to input and obtain project related information. The JMA staff can also refer to past projects in similar kinds to learn and apply to their current and future projects. In addition, lean efficiency gains obtained are 1) reduced waiting time, 2) improved quality in dealing with project support information and external stakeholders, 3) facilitating audit and reviews, 4) improved quality of service to JMA partners and clients, and 5) allows archiving and learning from past projects 6) retaining key knowledge and experience from projects for the company not only with individual JMA staff.

Table 3. A3 exercise for process improvement via the development of a knowledge database (Arayici et al, 2011)

3. Development of the Knowledge Database

The major advantage of BIM is to input to a single information model and the multiple representations and extraction of that single information model. In the project, it was decided to apply these principles for the project support information residing outside of the BIM graphical model such as client names, address, dates etc. For this purpose, critical data that is commonly duplicated in spreadsheets, word documents and emails has been reviewed and developed into a relational database used by all members of staff in the company. This has provided a platform to record, share and interrogates project support information internally across the company. The particular benefits of this knowledge database are that information is retained in the same database even when projects are archived.

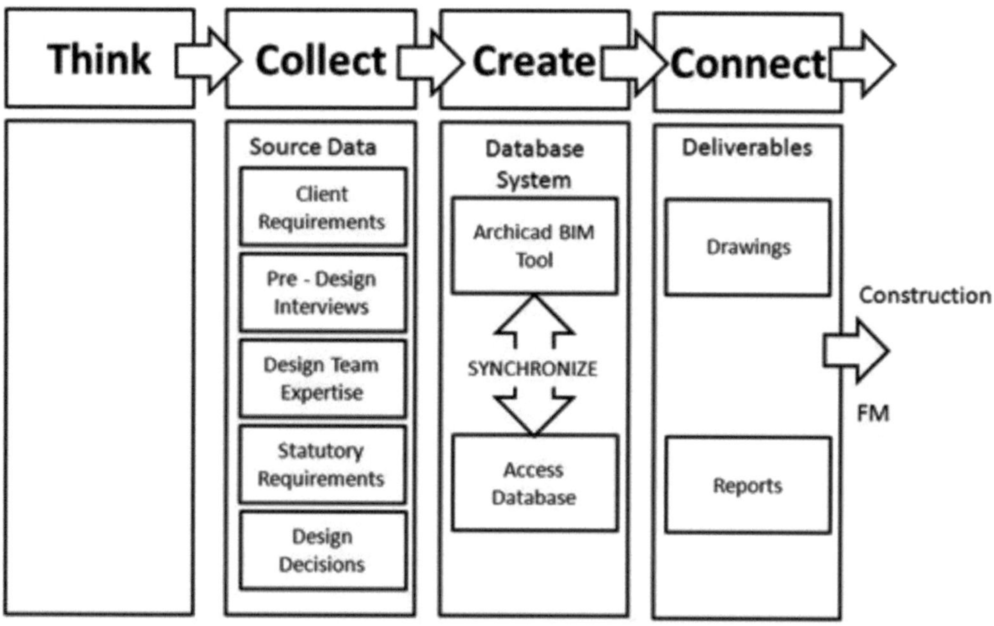

Figure 5. Combined model for project information with BIM and project support information with the knowledge database

Also the database has become particularly useful for marketing purposes. Further links with the graphical BIM model and other processes at John McCall Architects are also being investigated as illustrated in figure 5. The resultant schema that is being worked towards is as to capture knowledge and experiences from past projects and from experienced staff via this knowledge database in the future.

4. Documentation of BIM implementation plan

This stage is the preparation and planning of the actual implementation of the new BIM system and the processes on to past, present and future projects. In addition, training and up skilling staff is also planned at this stage. The preparation and planning of the actual BIM implementation is primarily prescribed by three factors; i) the financial restrictions on the speed with which the BIM software could be purchased, ii) finding appropriate projects on which to use the BIM orientated approach and iii) the speed with which members of staff could be trained to use the BIM authoring software. Particular consideration in the planning process was given to when and how the BIM object libraries and also office BIM standards were to be developed.

5.3.4. Implementation and roll out of BIM

1. Piloting BIM on three different projects (past, current, and future) and Training

The adopted BIM software was experimented on the "Grow Home" project; an award winning design previously produced by JMA. This exercise proved positive in some respects. For example, reproducing this project in BIM has highlighted the specific order of decisions that are required to produce BIM models. The Grow Home project had not been taken through the production information phase, which resulted in some materials used and the construction methods remained undefined in BIM modeling for the Grow Home project. This raised issues about the requirements for accurate and complete information when developing BIM models. Figure 6 below shows some example views from the BIM models.

The other project undertaken was the Millachip Phase 3 project; a series of sheltered housing bungalows. A 2D set of CAD drawings had already been developed on this project and BIM models with associated plans sections and elevations were rapidly produced. Objects were built from scratch on this project. It helped to match the generated 2D drawings from the BIM model with the previously produced 2D drawings to observe the accuracy, consistency, speedy and timely maintenance of such drawings and finally to establish a good communication with the client. Finally this project will form the basis of the BIM object libraries for JMA in its practice in housing and regeneration. However, future piloting projects will be defined once the core training activities for the JMA staff are fully completed. Furthermore, it will be determined on a project which can benefit from eco analysis in line with the sustainable design vision being developed as a result of new BIM led infrastructure in the company.

Those benefits below are also realized from those projects above via BIM adopted in JMA.

- Avoidance of Data Atrophy
- Move towards Integrated Project Delivery
- Use of Clash Detection and Constrains in Design
- Models allowing GPS use on site
- Analysis of Site Safety and Site Logistics
- Linking the models to Bills of Materials
- Output to virtual environments
- Better analysis against Code for Sustainable Homes
- Production for models for post completion services

Figure 6. Illustrates various projects undertaken with BIM, demonstrating different assessment and analysis tasks in design

Overall, four areas of training were organised and conducted. These are: 1) Basic Operation Skills, 2) JMA modelling standards, 3) JMA methodology of model construction, 4) How to work with external parties. These are illustrated in figure 7.

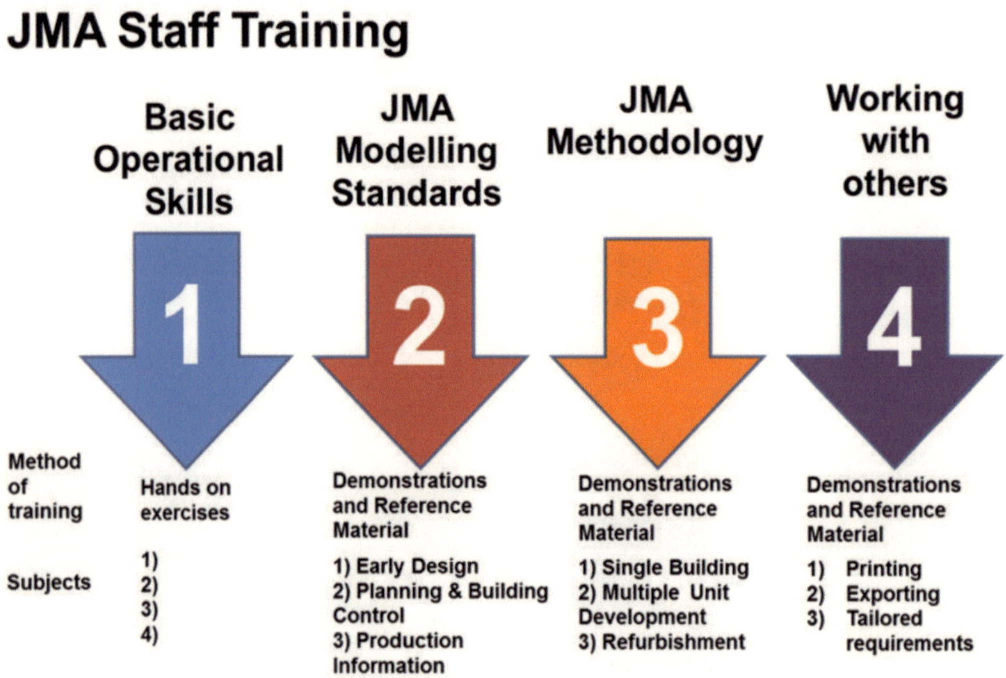

Figure 7. BIM Implementation Training programme

2. Devising and improving companywide capabilities & documentation of process and procedures

Continuous improvement is a facet built into JMA's quality system. But with such a radical change in BIM adoption, it makes sense to continually review and benchmark the new process. BIM opens the door to many possibilities. Working with 3D models facilitates the generation of 3D visuals, 3D printing and linking with virtual environments. Part of improving the companywide capabilities is maintaining the BIM dialogue so BIM knowledge and best practice is disseminated around the practice. The BIM enabled process and procedures were developed. This will make such documentation easily usable at the point of application

5.3.5. Project review, dissemination and integration into strategy plan

The process of project review, dissemination and integration into the strategy plan will occur towards the end of the project. As part of the documentation of the evaluation and review, this BIM adoption and implementation project will be measured and assessed by using a capability maturity model at stage 5 of the project.

In regard to sustaining new products and processing offerings, one new product that has been identified is the production of BIM information to better meet the post completion facility management of the projects. The required research and infrastructure development is ongoing to enable JMA to provide with Facility Management services to its clients. In respect to evaluation and dissemination of the project, a tangible benefits log has been maintained throughout the BIM implementation project. This will form the basis of an evaluation report that is to be written at the conclusion of the project. As part of the dissemination of the project, presentations in different conferences, events and workshops for industrialists and academics, and involving in exhibitions have already been undertaken.

6. Conclusion

The progress on the BIM implementation in JMA is ongoing and this chapter highlighted the strategies and outcomes from the stage 1 to stage 5.

Visit to Finland and obtain lessons learnt from BIM implementation that is represented in the concept map has provided a good basis for setting the strategies for this project will be used in this KTP project. It is understood that the BIM implementation strategy should be comprehensive and employ human centred, data and process driven methodologies because BIM implementation is as much about people and process as it is about technology.

It is envisaged that when the project is completed, it will provide a clearer vision and roadmap with detailed strategies, methods and techniques for successful BIM implementation. Furthermore, based on the current findings and optimistic behaviour and culture evolved during the project, it will re-engineer the operational and IT processes and broaden the knowledge of existing staff and stakeholders up and down the supply chain. The impact of the KTP has already been realised during the project that it has improved JMA's practice: eliminating the risk of calculation, misinterpretation of design, improve communication, provide interoperability between stakeholders and, ensuring control and sharing of documentation. This is because BIM is the foundation for implementing an efficient process and invariably leads to lean-orientated, team based approach to design and construction.

Finally, the KTP enabled JMA to establish itself as one of the vanguard of BIM application giving them a competitive edge because BIM enables the intelligent interrogation of designs; provide a quicker and cheaper design production; better co-ordination of documentation; more effective change control; less repetition of processes; a better quality constructed product; and improved communication both for JMA and across the supply chain.

Author details

Yusuf Arayici and Paul Coates
The University of Salford, UK Paul Coates The University of Salford, UK

7. References

Arayici, Y., Coates, P., Koskela, L., Kagioglou, M., Usher, C., O'Reilly, K., (2011) "BIM adoption and implementation for architectural practices", Structural Survey, Vol. 29 Iss: 1, pp.7 – 25

Aouad, G., & Arayici, Y 2010, Requirements Engineering for Computer Integrated Environments in Construction, Wiley-Blackwell, Oxford, UK

Arayici, Y., Coates, P., Koskela, L., Kagioglou, M., Usher, C., O'Reilly, K., (2009), "BIM Implementation for an Architectural Practice", Managing Construction for Tomorrow International Conference, October 2009, Istanbul Turkey

Bernstein, P.G., Pittman, J.H. (2004). "Barriers to the adoption of building information modelling in the building industry", Autodesk Building Solutions, White paper

Betts M., (1999), "Strategic Management of IT", ISBN 0 632 04026 2, Blackwell Science

Beyer H, Holtzblatt K, (1998), "Contextual Design, Defining Customer-Centred Systems", Morgan Kaufmann Publishers, San Francisco.

Checkland, P., Poulter, J., (2010), "Systems Approaches to Managing Change: A Practical Guide", Springer London, ISBN 978-1-84882-808-7, 2010-05-11

Cheng Tai Fatt (2005), An IT Roadmap for Singapore's Construction Industry, IAI Industry Day, Oslo, May 2005

Coates, P., Arayici, Y., Koskela L., Kagioglou, M., Usher C., O'Reilly, K., (2010), "The key performance indicators of the BIM implementation process", ICCBE 2010, Jun 30 2010, Nottingham

Durward K., Sobek, II, (2008), "Understanding A3 Thinking: A Critical Component of Toyota's PDCA Management System", Taylor & Francis Group, New York.

Finkelstein, C., (1992), "Information Engineering, Strategic System Development", Addison Wesley Longman Publishing, Boston, USA, ISBN: 0201509881

Gerber & Rice, (2009), "The Value of Building Information Modelling: Can We Measure the ROI of BIM?" AECbytes Viewpoint (Analysis, Research and Reviews of AEC Technology, Issue 47, (August 2009), http://www.aecbytes.com/viewpoint/2009/issue_47.html

Grint, K., Willcocks, L., (2007), "Business Process Reengineering in theory and practice: business paradise regained?" New Technology, Work and Employment, Vol. 10, Issue 2, pp. 99-109.

Jordani, D (2008), "BIM: A Healthy Disruption to a Fragmented and Broken Process", FAIA, Jordani Consulting Group, Journal of Building Information Modeling: Spring 2008, Matrix Group Publishing, Houston

Kam C, Fischer M, Hänninen R, Karjalainen A and Laitinen J (2003), The Product Model and Fourth Dimension project, ITcon Vol. 8, Special Issue IFC - Product models for the AEC arena, pg. 137-166, http://www.itcon.org/2003/12

Koskela, L. J. (2003), 'Theory and Practice of Lean Construction: Achievements and Challenges', in: Proceedings of the 3rd Nordic Conference on Construction Economics & Organisation. Hansson, Bengt & Landin, Anne (eds). Lund University (2003)

Koskela, L J & Ballard, G 2006, 'What is Lean Construction - 2006.', -Construction in the XXI Century: local and global challenges - ARTEC - Rome, Italy

Malmi, (2001), "Balance scorecards in Finnish Companies: A Research note", Management Accounting Research, Vol.12, Issue 2, pp.207-220.

Mihindu, S., and Arayici, Y. (2008). "Digital construction through BIM systems will drive the re-engineering of construction business practices", 2008 International Conference Visualisation, IEEE Computer Society, CA, ISBN 978-0-7695-3271-4, P29-34.

Novak, J. D. & A. J. Cañas, The Theory Underlying Concept Maps and How to Construct Them, Technical Report IHMC CmapTools 2006-01 Rev 01-2008, Florida Institute for Human and Machine Cognition, 2008", available at: http://cmap.ihmc.us/Publications/ResearchPapers/TheoryUnderlyingConceptMaps.pdf

Oakley, P. (2007). "CAD Enough?", CAD User AEC Magazine, Vol 21 No 01, 2008

Schevers, H., Mitchell, J., Akhurst, P., Marchant, D., Bull, S., McDonald, K., Drogemuller, R., Linning , C., "Towards Digital Facility Modelling For Sydney Opera House Using IFC and Semantic Web Technology", July 2007 at http://itcon.org/2007/24/

TEKES, (2008), "Sara – Value Networks in Construction 2003–2007", Technology Programme Report 2/2008, Helsinki, ISBN 978-952-457-392-4.

TOCOMAN, (2008), "Benefits", http://www.tocoman.com/default.asp?docId=13339, [Accessed 20/04/08].

US-GSA. (2008). "3D-4D Building Information Modelling", http://www.gsa.gov, [Accessed 25/04/08].

Voss, C., (2006), "Successful Innovation and implementation of new processes", Business Strategy Review, Vol.23, Issue 1, pp.29-44.

Section 4

Culture and Life of Human

Chapter 10

Virtual Reality in Village Folk Custom Tourism

Zhuowei Hu and Lai Wei

Additional information is available at the end of the chapter

http://dx.doi.org/10.5772/48666

1. Introduction

With the prosperous development of socialist construction in China, the tourism is increasingly becoming new growth point of economy and one of the main pillars of the tertiary industry. It becomes hotpot in current international tourism industry because of rich national cultural connotation and strange exotic ambiance.

Some famous tourist cities of China, such as Xi'an, establish the tourism resources information system in natural landscape, human landscape, heritage, and achieve a modern tourist information services and management through the advanced network geographic information technology. Although there are a lot of development examples of tourism information system, they have various deficiencies. Using of information technology has penetrated into modern tourism industry. It brings new business revolution for rapid development of tourism. However, present tourism system is out of keeping with development requirement of village folk custom tourism industry. Application of virtual reality technology in tourism not only can play a part in drumbeating, influence and attractiveness, but can also meet the tours and aesthetic demands of those people who haven't or not be capable of getting there in a certain level. We can combine with virtual reality and real reality to make system more unfeigned. At the same time, 3D visualization and virtual reality makes up for insufficient of space scenes expression in WebGIS. It can make geospatial data realistically exhibit in real space, dynamically and figuratively depict objective phenomenon of landscape, and provide new technology for decision maker in reasonable planning of scenic spot. Therefore we integrated WebGIS, Network, spatial information, 3D modeling, 3D roaming and multimedia technology to establish the "Village Folk Custom Tourism Service System". It can use virtual reality technology to make virtual reconstruction and 3D simulation for typical folk custom information.

This system is based on spatial information technology and multimedia virtual reality technology. It can display famous scenic site, local customs and practices, entertainment and tourist transportation, deeply mine local characteristics of village, build external propaganda window, establish visualization and publishing platform, achieve systemic organization and efficient management, promote culture exchange and protect excellent traditional folk custom tourism resource.

This system can use virtual reality technology to simulate and display typical folk custom information. We put some data, such as geographical data and tourism thematic, into a computation module, and make intuitive information. Through the comprehensive analysis and evaluation, we can provide statistical analysis information for user and decision maker by internet.

This system mainly includes 4 function modules. They are management and analysis of village resoureces, e-commerce of town and village folk tourism, town and village folk tourism landscape display and self-service of village folk tourist information.

2. System functional design

2.1. Management and analysis of village resoureces sub-system

We design the management and analysis of toen and village resource sub-system according to characteristic of folk custom tourism resource, business process or requirement of mamagement, system flexibility or security and efficient or convenience of development. Then we divide the system in function.

2.1.1. Management module

The goals of this sub-system are specification of folk custom tourism resource, effective management and accurate analysis. It integrated tourism landscape virtual display and provide folk custom tourism resource data and analysis result for other sub-system. Data information has been classified and evaluated in collection of folk custom tourism resource.

The management system has 5 parts according to different stages of data flow. There are information collection and classification, folk custom tourism resource evaluation, subsidiary information management, attribute of layer management and system information management.

The information collection and classification module can put the single information to the database according to specification data. If there are not tourism resource single data, we can use GPS to measure the coordinate and manually put them into the database. After that, we classify the data according to some classification methods.

The folk custom tourism resource evaluation module is used to evaluate the single resource information according to evaluation model. Then we evaluate the tourism resource within study area through single evaluation information and attribute from database, such as folk custom tourism resource density, population density, economic capacity density and so on. It can propose a reasonable management for tourism enterprise and village management.

The subsidiary information management module manages the scenic spot information, tourist information, socio-econom, and naturalenvironment information.

The attribute of layer management module can manage the basic information of folk custom tourism resource, monomer tourism level, different kinds of image and description information of reflecting the appearance.

The system information management moduel can add, delete and modify the system user.

2.1.2. Analysis module

Analysis module is based on collection, classification, evaluation and specification data of management module. It contains 4 parts, such as information inquiry and statistics module, spatial query module, spatial analysis module and folk custom tourism resource planning.

The information inquiry and statistics module can do condition query by attribute of folk custom resource. The system can provide search according to study area, number, level and type. Then it can display and print the search result by image, report and statistic chart.

The spatial query module can use to do research between the attribute and image. On the one hand, we can do research for folk tourism resource by roi which selected by people, on the other hand, we also can do research according to single attribute and highlight it.

The spatial analysis module can achieve density analysis, buffer analysis, network analysis and so on of folk custom resource. It can support the folk custom tourism resource planning module.

The folk custom tourism resource planning module can design and plan the tourism with GIS spatial analysis. Then it can analyze priority development area

2.2. E-Commerce of town and village folk tourism

This module can combine with folk tourism industry and e-commerce technology and achieve management of business information, local information display, public information display and information search for tourist, tourism enterprise and village administrator department. It can use information technology to improve competitiveness of tourism industry and quality of market service.

2.2.1. Business-oriented folk tourism e-commerce

Some business can use single self-service to establish small web site themself. This system can provide 2 functions.

1. Add Information

This function provide some operating of text edit, picture display, panorama show and audio/video display. The business can add some information about folk scenic spot into system and display them.

2. Message Reply

The system can provide message board function. Tourist uses this function to evaluate the service quality.

2.2.2. Travel-oriented folk tourism e-commerce

This module can provide some functions through centralized service platform, such as standard template and advanced customization electronic map making, blog prepared, 3D simulation making, audio/video management, message reply and so on. If user wants to display scenic spot by general function, they can chooes standard template. If user wants to make a panorama, they can choose advanced customization.

2.2.3. Trourist-oriented folk tourism e-commerce

1. Release of Demand Information

It can provide 2 ways, such as standard template and advanced customization.

2. Business Space Management

This system provides some functions, such as electronic map making, blog prepared and so on.

2.3. Town and village folk tourism landscape display

This sub-system contains 2 modules. There are 3D GIS and augmented virtual reality.

2.3.1. 3D GIS module

1. Geographical Environment Multi-Scale Display

The multi-scale detail of landscape can simulate some information in different status, angles and ranges.

Scale Visualization: It can simulate change of size and clarity in different distances and movements.

Adaptive display: It is a simple form for landscape information display. It can add some detail information into the simple model according to some demands.

Omnibearing display: We can use mouse to choose different viewpoint for omnibearing display.

2. Interactive of 2D Map and 3D Scene

2D map can provide tourist information on plane, such as distribution of tourism resource, service facilitity and travel traffic.

Distribution of tourism resource: It contains distribution of attraction, tourism project and ecological landscape, such as farm courtyard, folk games and river.

Distribution of service facilitity: It contains restaurant, hotel and internet café.

Travel traffic: It contains travel route in scenic spot, such as bus line and tourist route.

Eagle eye function: We choose some destination point to see the 3D scene.

3. Scenic Tour

We can use mouse to select interest area and roam in 3D scene. We also can set start and stop, then roaming by tour line. It can help tourist to achieve self-navigation.

2.3.2. Augmented virtual reality

1. 3D Model Display
    1. Single Object Stereo Display

It can support e-commerce for volk custom tourism. Then it also can model and display folk characteristic landscape and feature product by stereo.

2. Freedom Browse by Mouse Control

We can choose different modes of mouse to display single object in omnibearing.

1. Small Regional Virtual Display
    1. Small Regional Virtual Display in Scenic Spot.

It can make model of scenic spot. Then it cans virtual display the model.

    2. Panorama Display in Scenic Spot

It cans virtual display the scenic spot by panorama.

2.4. Self-Service of village folk tourist information

2.4.1. Overall function of sub-system

This sub-system is a guide information service program, which is based on mobile terminal, such as PDA and mobile phone. User cans download the program and install it in their mobile terminal. The program can determine tourist position by GPS signal recived. Then it can obviously display information about nearby scenic spot and give some routes for navigation. Then it also can provide voice service, such as location, special resource and so on.

This sub-system also can manage guide resource and provide download site. User can download the map and navigation data to mobile terminal by wired and wireless.

2.4.2. Intelligent guide

The system can determine the position of tourist by GPS. Tourist can set the auto-play voice guide information and image. In different terminal platform, it provides different guide services. It combines with GPS module and provides self-navigation and voice guide service.

2.4.3 Guide service information

It can provide attraction introduction, characteristic picture, recommended tourist route and distance of current location.

2.4.4. Mobile tour guide information service system

It can provide data information of guide information by different ways. User can add, modify and manage information, which related with attraction. Then user also can obtain other information in wide range of ways.

The map and navigation data can be downloaded to mobile terminal by many ways, such as local cable, mobile communication network, wireless, Bluetooth and internet.

2.4.5. Mobile guide terminal

The software adapt to different mobile terminals.In smart phone or PDA with GPS, it can achieve the multimedia guide service through GIS and GPS. In smart phone or PDA without GPS, it can achieve simple voice guide service.

3. Design proposal

3.1. Management and analysis of village resources

The overall design thinking of this sub-system is achieving data base management of tourism resource basic information, scoring information, classification information and multimedia information; establishment model base of folk tourism resource classification, evaluation, development and planning; achieving conditional query, interaction query, visualization query of tourism single source basic information. It can provide release and management service of tourism attraction, tourism facilities and traffic information for village management department.

In order to simplify deployment and management of system, the logical structure of system uses multilayer structure based on BS. It is good for management of data and service. The system can be divied into presentation layer, web layer, application layer and data layer. It is shown in Figure 1

The presentation layer is public interface for user accessing system. It is mainly forward user request to web service through internet and intranet by browser. Then the server returns the logical organization information to user. In this layer, it do not achieve the real business logic, it is only for forwarding the user request.

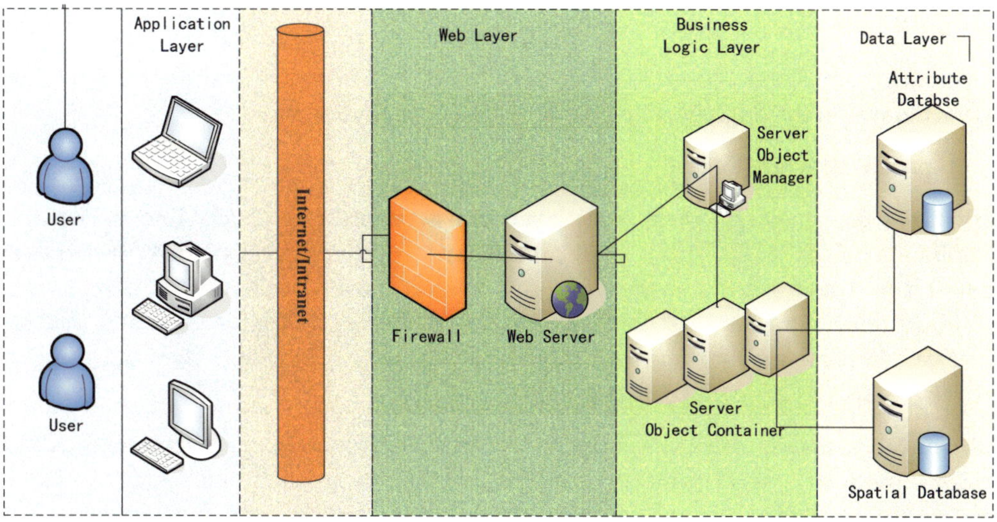

Figure 1. Design Proposal of Management and Analysis of Village Resoureces

The web layer is under the presentation layer. It can receive the request of user from presentation layer and reject the illegal request through firewall. So it can ensure the security of system operation. In web layer, we dispose the netword application system, which is developed by ArcGIS Server and ADF foR JAVA. It can process non-spatial data without GIS analysis function.

The business logic layer is GIS server center which is based on ArcGIS Server platform. Whole GIS analysis inner system is achieved in server. Server object manager can equal divide the complex and expensive GIS operation into server object container through load balancing and cluster technology. The server object container can call the spatial data to complete the operation and return the result to web layer.

Data layer mainly intergrates the basic data, which are from folk custom tourism resource management and analysis system. There are 2 databases for storing data. One is attribute database, other is spatial database. Data layer can make a relationship between 2 databases.

The system architecture of enterprise GIS has a clear level and division. Different level can achieve different function. It is good for full use of resource and maintenance of system. This structure can improve system stability, decrease system bottle-neck effect with complex operation for GIS data, increase processing power with high concurrency.

1. System User Role

The system user role has 2 parts. One is user, another is administrator. It can restrict modify permission of system data and ensure system data security.

   1. System Administrator

System administrator is administrator of government and management department of tourism resource. They can login management system and modify the data and user permission.

2. System User

System user is business operation personnel of relative department and tourist. Then only access the system for obtaining information without modifying database.

1. Database Structure Design

Spatial database mainly contain basic layer and thematic layer of folk tourism resource distribution, which is shown in Figure 2. Basic layer contains administrative, river system, traffic road, remote sensing image and so on. Thematic layer contains distribution map of folk tourism resource and best travel route map. Intergration of basic layer and thematic layer can simulate reality thing and display on the system interface. User can make an interactive analysis by spatial data layer.

Attribute data mainly contain information of basic layer, landscape information of folk tourism resource, socio-economic information, environmental information, tourist information, classification, evaluation indicator and system user information. Each information stores into a table. It is managed by SQL Server.

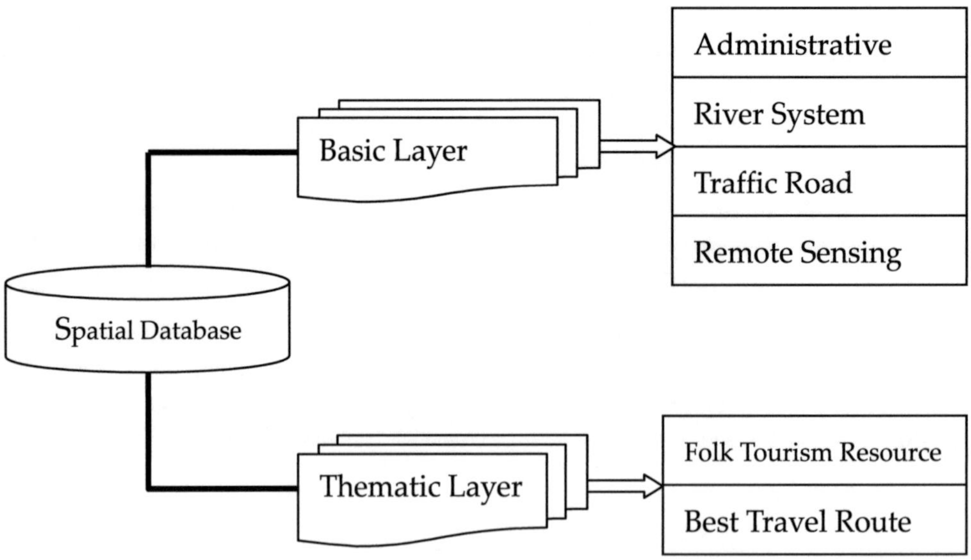

Figure 2. Hierarchy Structure of Spatial Database

3.2. E-Commerce of town and village folk tourism sub-system

Structure of e-commerce of village folk tourism sub-system is shown in Figure 3.

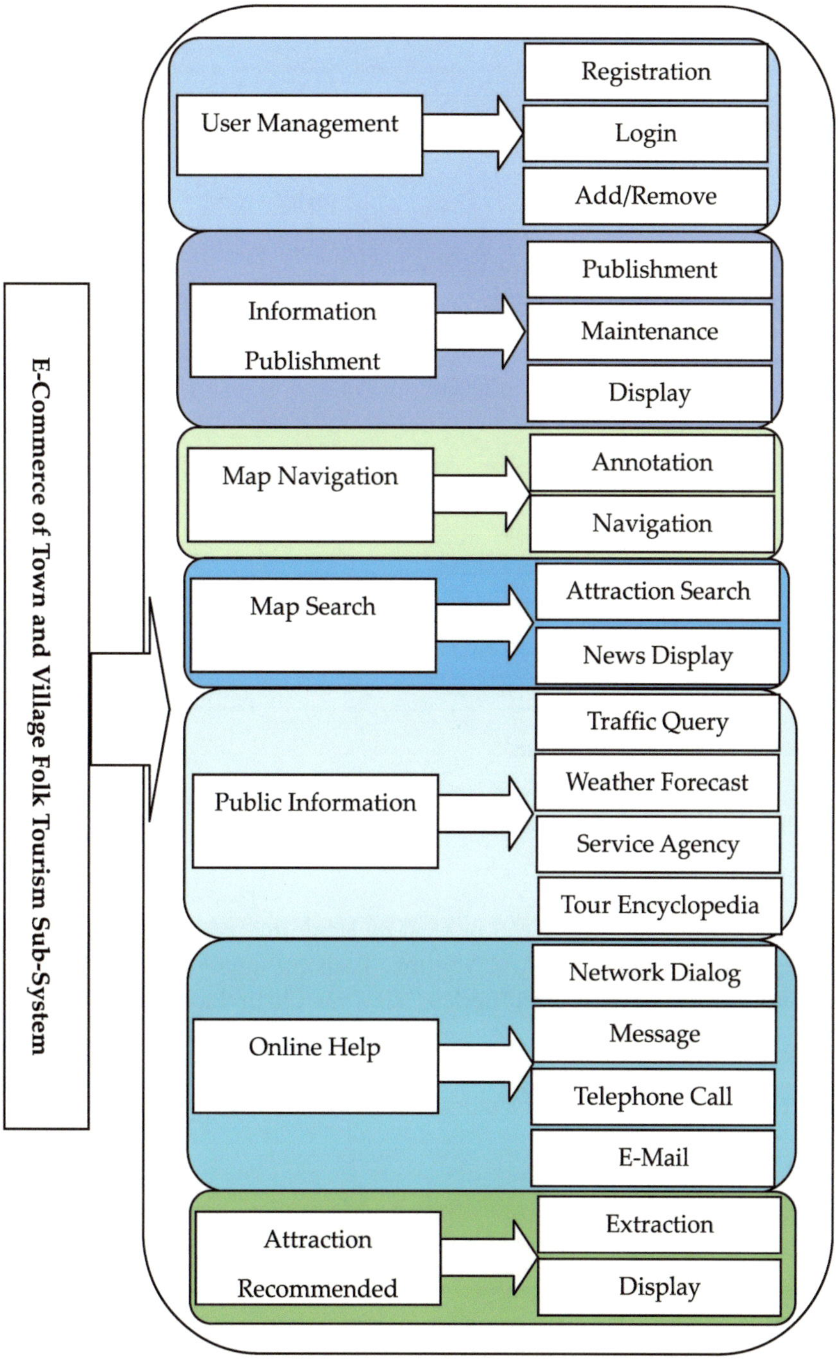

Figure 3. Structure of E-Commerce of Town and Village Folk Tourism Sub-System

3.2.1. User registration module

The Figure 4 shows categories and permissions of users.

Function describe: user account verification, information detail record, user management

Enterance parameter: User ID

Database operation: We can store data and modify data through user registry.

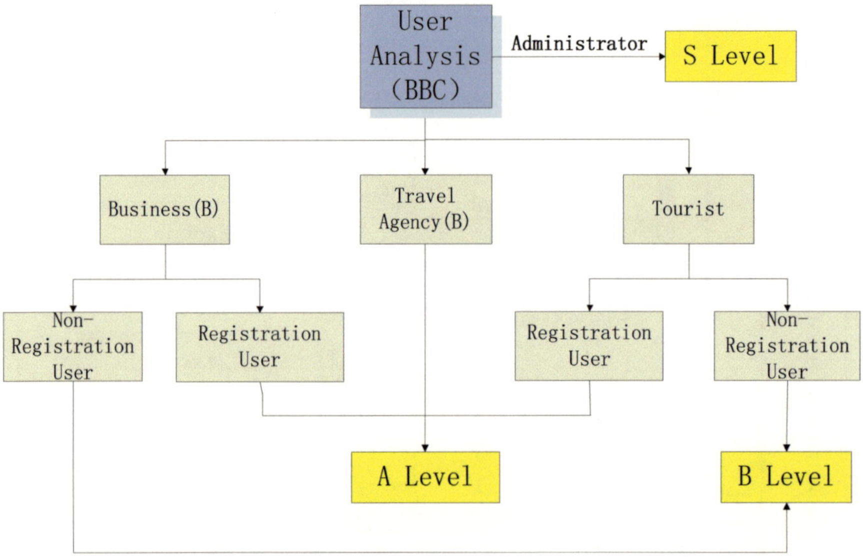

Figure 4. User Categories and Permissions

3.2.2. Information publishment module

1. Information Publishment

Business, tourist and travel agency can publish their information after registration. We can entry information through click "Add" button. Each information is relationship with a record of businessinfo. Database uses "update" statement to update.

2. Information Maintenance

The information maintenance contains manual and automatic ways.

1. Manual

It is managed by web administrator. When information contains false, reactionary, superstitious and violation information, we can use "delete" statement to manual delete.

2. Automatic

It is depand on database. It use automatically retrieve to analyze information. If there is time-out, then delete it. It can reduce the record redundant of database.

3. Category Display

It can provide a variety of classification system for use. It contains source category, region category, folk characteristic category, basic tourism project category and so on.

3.2.3. *Map navigation module*

1. Attraction Navigation

When mouse move to a certain province, the system can automatically displays totals and news of folk tourism in this province. If I click a province, the system automatically displays the map of this province.

User can choose interest attraction to obtain detail of attraction, scuh as text, picture, video, panorama and so on.

2. Map Annotation

It is achieved by system administrator. When user adds some information, he can put forward request through message and call. System administrator receives request and make an annotation in the map. Then he makes a relationship with attribute of shape file.

3.2.4. *Map search module*

1. Attraction Search

User can entry the name of attraction into the system. System can match data from business database and display the result to user. The result is made relationship with attribute of shape file and show in map.

2. News Show

When user click the attraction in result, the system can show some information and news of this attraction, such as organize activity, favorable price policy and so on.

3.2.5. *Attraction recommended module*

1. Information Extraction

To do attractions recommended must first be extracted from the business information form and tourists on their evaluation. Through attractions search system selects the top of the evaluation of data and displays on the homepage.

2. Information Display

When attraction information has been extracted, we need dislay these informations. It contains text, picture, audio, video, panorama and so on.

3.2.6. Public information module

Public information module can provide daily information service for tourism, such as traffic routing, weather forecast, local service agency and so on. This information can provide tourism through superlink.

3.2.7. Online help module

1. Network Dialog

It can display in floating windows by QQ dialog. If user wants to consult, he can click on the dialog.

2. Electronic Message

It is message board. User can leave a message to administrator. System administrator can solve the question by message.

3. Telephone Call

In homepage, there is telephone number of administration. User can call the number for help.

4. Email

User can send a email to administrator. Administrator can reply email in 1-2 work days.

3.3. Town and village folk tourism landscape display

Town and Village folk tourism landscape adaptive display component divided to two functional modules horizontal. One is the 3DGIS module, and it strengthen the virtual reality module.3DGIS module in charge of display the geographical elements of the village folk landscape. This module displays the real landscape in multi-scaled 3D and roam. It also has the assist function of spatial query and analyze. Strengthen the virtual reality module is to show independent 3D model and small region virtual reality landscape more meticulous and vividly based on the 3DGIS landscape display. In the same time, multimedia technique display village tourism humanity landscape which could not be displayed by 3DGIS.

Adaptive display component could be divided to three levels from bottom to top, which is database and model, interface and function. The database and model level bring various kinds of base data to database and then abstract to model base. Adaptive display component achieve model management interface of model base inside, and service interface to other subsystems outside. These interfaces recombine and realize the main function of adaptive display component.

The realization flow of town and village folk tourism adaptive display component mainly composes of four level contents, data, model, interface and display. Every level is supported by a higher level. Finally, the whole component supply concise calling method and other subsystems acquire adaptive display related service through external interface.

The base data is multi-source data. Part of the data need to acquire by field measurement and graph-taking. Database management most of the data, and some special data is managed by file style.

Model is the general name of abstract data structure and data management method. It includes 3D model and other virtual reality model. The gathering of various kinds of model and mutual association compose the model base.

Interface is divided into internal model interface and external service interface. The former realize model objectification function, and form adaptive displayed concrete object. The later supplies methods for other system to call this component.

After model instantiation, the component displays the village tourism omnidirectional stereo by virtual reality method at last. And it displays the user concerned tourism information by spatial analysis and inquire supplied by 3DGIS at the same time.

3.4. Self-Service of village folk tourist information

3.4.1. System structure and function module

Mobile intelligent tourist guide termination and information system general structure shows as Figure 5 follow. The system is divided into tour guide information service system and mobile tour guide termination.

3.4.2. Mobile intelligent tour guide termination system and function

As shown as Figure 6 following. Mobile intelligent tour guide termination platform divide into termination with operating system above Windows mobile6.0 kernel and ordinary mobile phone. The termination provides different kinds of tour guide information service base on developable interface offered by the system and hardware platform system function.

On PDA and intelligent mobile phone with Window mobile6.0 kernel, the termination supply GPS orientation and map service mainly formed voice tour guide and data system service.

On the develop interface limited ordinary mobile phone, it allows user to press button operation to supply voice tour guide and data system service.

3.4.3. Tour guide information data service system

Shown as Figure 7, the main function of tour guide information data service system is to receive and accept tour guide service information data. And it realizes data management, provides multiple data interface, and allows mobile tour guide termination or remote computer users to visit local data. Based on applying for data, it provides tour guide map data, voice data and information service data for download.

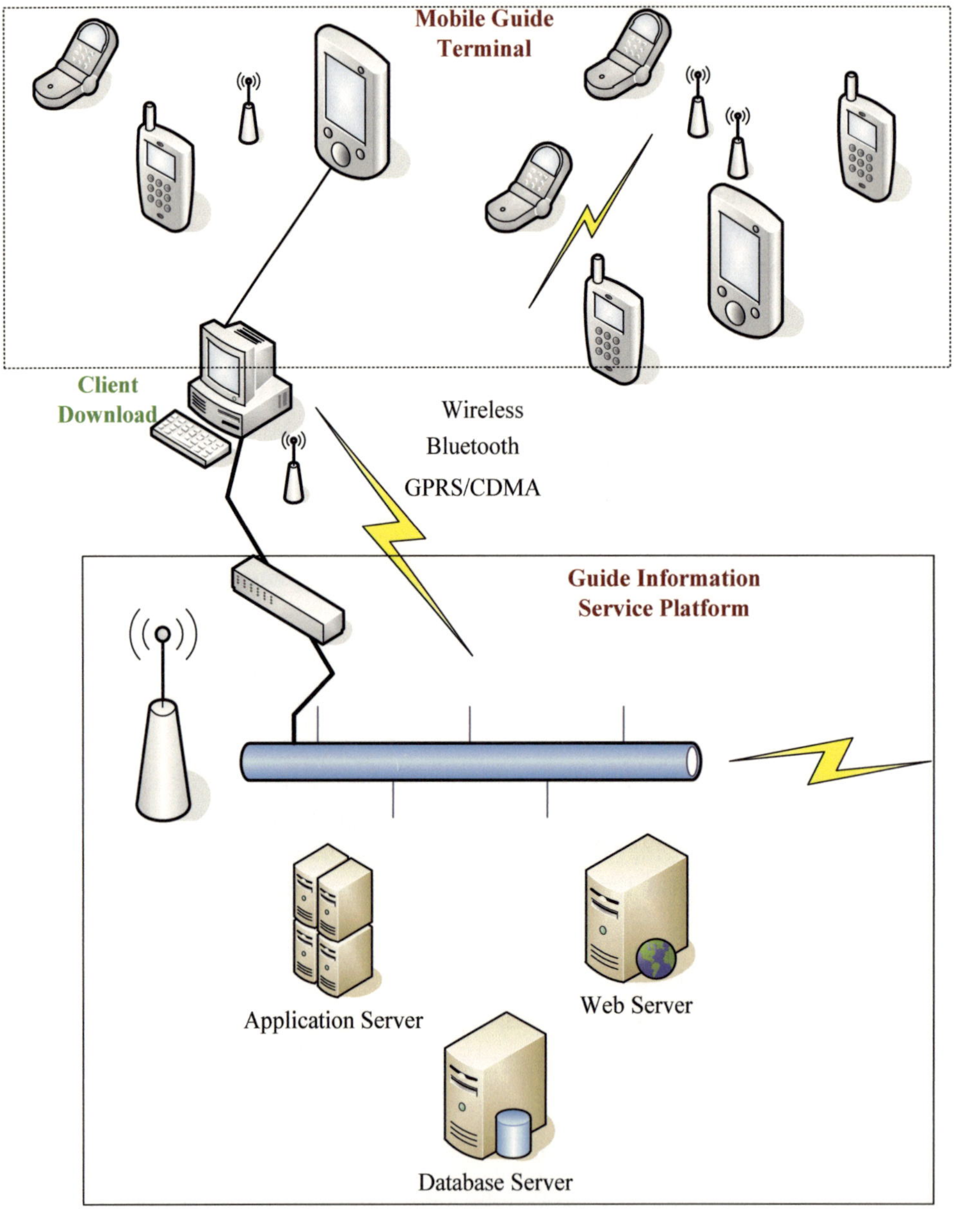

Figure 5. System Structure of Mobile Intelligent Guide Terminal and Information Service

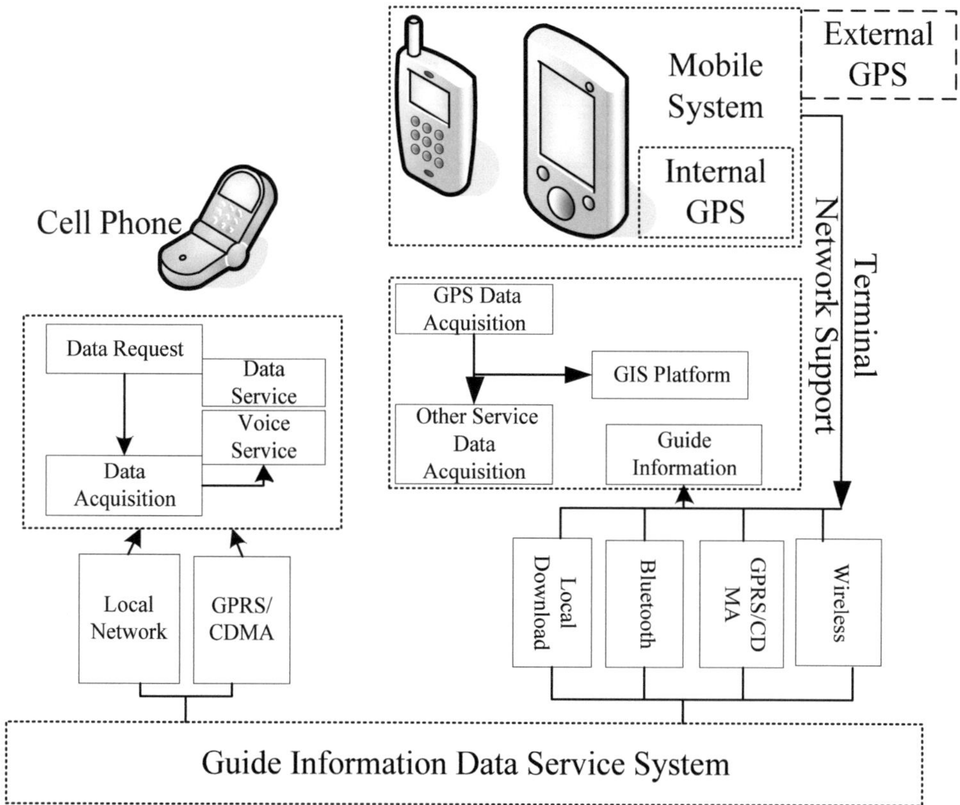

Figure 6. Function Structure Diagram of Mobile Intelligent Tour Guide Terminal

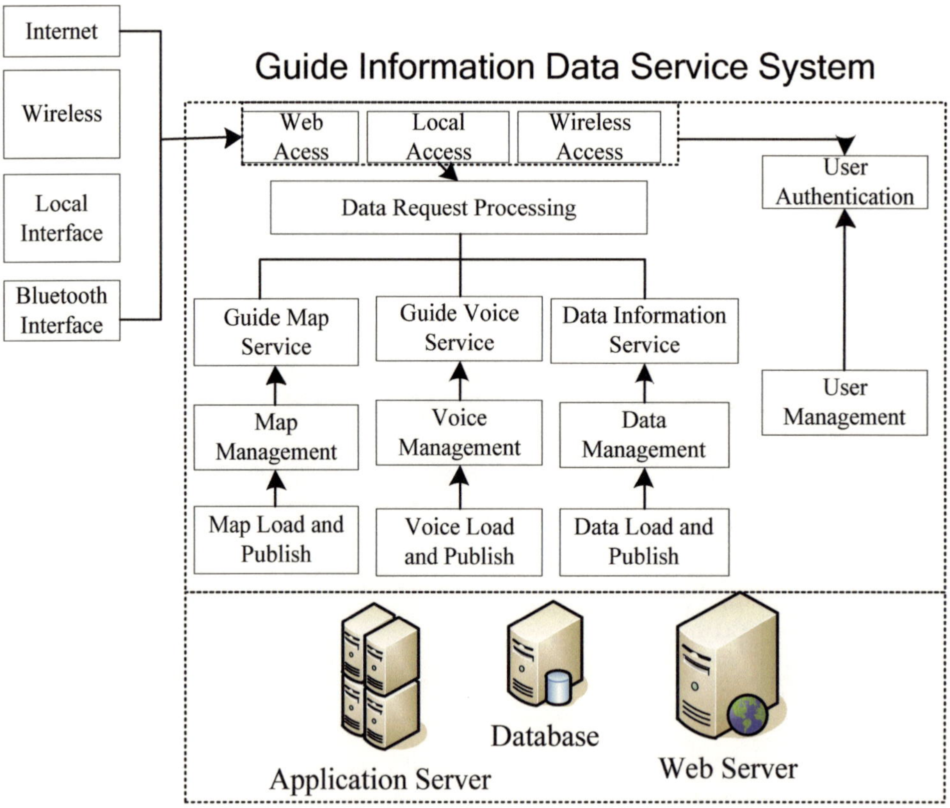

Figure 7. Function Structure Diagram of Tour Guide Information Data Service System

3.4.4. System interface design

The system interface design is shown in Figure 8.

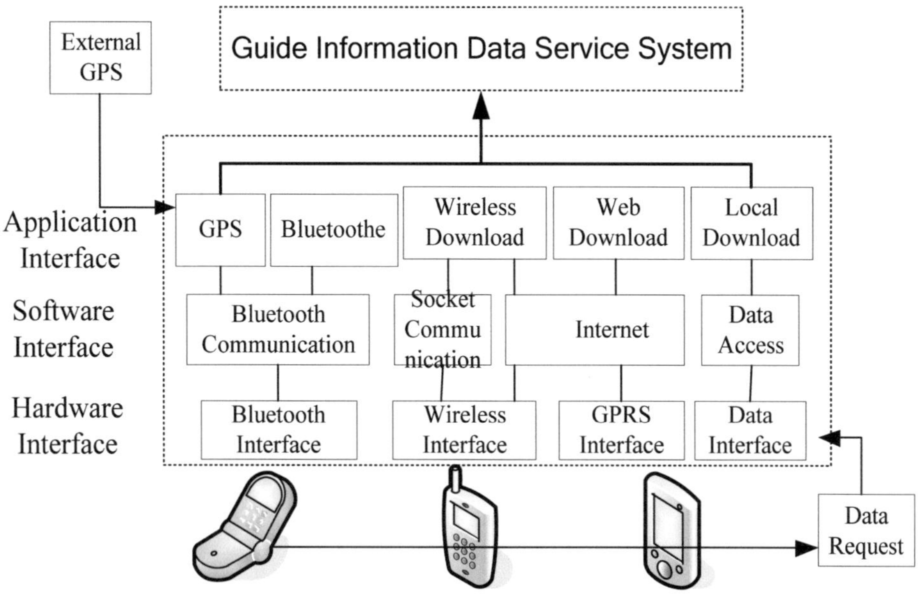

Figure 8. Mobile Intelligent Tour Guide Termination System Interface Design

4. Conclusion

Nowadays, the development of rural folk tourism industry is going on a high-speed way as a typical information-depended industry.It is urgent to solve the problem with the information management of rural folk tourism .So the chapter carrys out the study about it. It is to achieve a scientific and effective management about the information of rural folk tourism resources.

At present there are still the some shortcomings: 1. The way of rural folk tourism resources management is less efficient,updated data is not convenient.Tradition methods of rural folk tourism resources management are based on the type of rural folk tourism resources to set up various databases to manage all kinds of folk resources data.The method is of great inconvenience to add or amend data in future.Additonally,it is likely to result in defferent types of rural folk tourism resources in defferent information storage standard and causes much in convenience for the informtion retreval of rural folk tourism resources.the realization of tradition information management system about rural folk tourism resources is based the client-server software architecture model. A direct result is poor sharing of rural folk tourism resources information in the way. It is difficult to achieve the interactive effects between the tourists and rural folk tourism industy. 2. The developed information system of rural folk tourism resources integrates resources management and analysis-evaluation of rural folk tourism resources. To manage the information of rural folk tourism resources is for the purpose of better managing and making use of the rural folk resources and furtherly offer a scientific basis of usage ,protecion and exploitation.the traditional management method is separated from management and evaluation,when need to evalute,we must be though statistical analysis software to compute.In additon,the types of rural folk tourism resources is diverse and distribution of scattered, This will not only increase the difficulty of evaluation but also less efficient.

To deal with problems above, the main contents of this chapter are as followed: 1.because the type of rural folk tourism resources is complex, in a great amount, and it need to be updated frquently, a database of rural folk tourism resources based on centralized database model is constructed, in which all kinds of the rural folk tourism resources data is stored in standard catalogs. Spatial data and attribute data are stored in the same database by ArcSDE and achieve the effective correlation between them.2.To develop the information system of rural folk tourism resources based on the Browser-Server software architecture model, management and analysis-evaluation of rural folk tourism resources are closely integrated.It manages vectora and information data altogether. Types, scale, hierarchy, function, value of rural folk tourism resources are evaluted by the AHP-based method of evalution and the results of evalution are get. The experience for the rational use of rural folk tourisms resources, protection of the environment, the overall effect of playing is offered. Scientific data which determines the construction order of tourism is provided and improve the efficiency of evaluation.

This chapter fully studys the ideas of design, implementation and key technologies.the methodology of development integrated the access interface of database based ArcSDE which make use of Java and ArcGIS Server develops the information management system of rural folk tourism resources.The resources of rural folk tourism are Scientifically managed, analyzed and evaluted.

Author details

Zhuowei Hu and Lai Wei
College of Resources Environment and Tourism, Capital Normal University, China
Key Lab of Resources Environment and GIS, Beijing, China
Key Lab of 3D Information Acquisition and Application, Ministry of Education, China

5. References

Tang Yong, Zhou Ming-Tian, Zhang Xin. Overview of Routing Protocols in Wireless Sensor Networks[J]. Journal of Software, 2006, 17(3): 410-421.

Yan Quan-Feng, Zou Bei-Ji, Huang Zhao. Wireless Real Time Multimedia Communication System[J]. Microelectronics & Computer, 2003, 8: 22-26.

Liu Jun-Yong, Tao Yang. Transmission of QoS-Adaptive multimedia over 3G network[J]. Journal of Chongqing University of Posts and Telecommunications, 2004, 16(1): 60-62.

Xu Ming, Wang Nan, Hou Zi-Feng, Song Jian-Ping. Implementation and Design of a Bluetooth Simulation Software[J]. Mini-micro Systems, 2004, 25(8): 1565-1568.

Ma Jin-Xing, Chen Qi-Jun. Analysis and Implementation of RFCOMM Layer in Bluetooth Protocol Stack[J]. Computer Engineering, 2004, 30(8): 112-113, 125.

Ding Zhen, Ou Hong Wu, Wang Yun-Qin. The Software Design and Realization of Integration Mobile Information System[J]. Journal of the Academy of Equipment Command & Technology, 2006, 17(1): 90-93.

Zhang Lei. Design of Multi-model Mobile Guide System Based on Context Awareness[J]. Computer Engineering, 2007, 33(6): 272-272, 282.

Luo Yue-Tong, Liu Xiao-Ping. Prospect and Key Technologies of Applying Virtual Reality in Tourism Publications[J]. Science & Technology Review, 2007, 25(19): 75-80.

Jiang Wen-Yan, Zhu Xiao-Hua, Chen Chen. Research Progress of Virtual Tourism[J]. Science & Technology Review, 2007, 25(14): 53-57.

Wang Ai-Guo, Liu Chun-Lei, Xu Cun-Hua. The Application of 3D GIS technology in Land Resources Management[J]. Modern Surveying and Mapping, 2007, 30(2): 44-46.

Chen Qian-Lin, Chen Ding-Fang. Application of VRML in the Internet Electronic Commerce[J]. Journal of Hubei Polytechnic University, 2003, 18(2): 53-54, 59.

Yang Ji, Chen Xiao-Wei. Research and Implementation of VR Model Based on Panorama[J]. Application Research of Computers, 2004, 1:249-254.

Ge Yan-Hong, Li Wen-Feng, Liu Xu-Guang. Realization of Streaming-media Real-time Transmission with Java Based on RTP[J]. Computer and Modernization, 2007, 2: 63-65.

Wei Qun, Zhang Yong-Ming, Gao Li, Gong Xue-Jing, Xiong Zhang. Virtual Space Building and Roaming System[J]. Computer Engineering and Applications, 2004, 40(4): 114-117.

Wang Xiao-Yan, Dai Qing, Hao Li. Summarize of Navigation System based on Panoramic View[J]. 2006, 22(6): 227-230.

Mao Yan-Ping. Study on Problmes and Counter-measures in the Development of China's Tourism Electronic Business[J]. Commercial Research, 2003, 11: 129-131.

Luo Gui-Xia. A Trial Discussion of the Development or E-business of Tourism in China[J]. Tourism Science, 2001, 2: 33-35.

Liu Da-You, Yang Kun, Chen Jian-Zhong. Agents: Present Status and Trends[J]. Journal of Software, 2000, 11(3): 315-321.

Zeng Ya-Ling. Thinking about developing folk customs tour of Jilin province[J]. Journal of Changchun University, 2007, 17(3): 22-26.

Cui Guang-Bin, Zheng Yan. Several Thinking on the Development of Folk Custom Resources in National Regions[J]. Heilongjiang National Series, 2007, 1: 66-70.

Ku Rui. Shaanxi folklore tourist resources to be developed[J]. Journal of Xi'an University of Post and Telecommunications, 2007, 12(2): 39-42.

Turnock D. Sustainable rural tourism in the romanian carpathians[J] . Geographical Journal ,1999 ,18 (3) :192 - 199.

Zha Fang. Studying on the Origin and Definition of Rural Tourism[J]. Journal of Ankang Teachers College, 2004, 16(12): 29-32.

Wang Rui-Hua, Zhang Bing, Yin Hong. The Prelimitary Discussion of The Developing Modes of Rural Tourism in Overseas[J]. Yunnan Geographic Environment Research, 2005, 17(2): 73-76.

Xiong Jian-Ping, Liu Cheng-Liang, Yuan Jun. On E-Commerce Development and Its Network System Construction of Rural Tourism[J]. Economic Geography, 2006, 26(2): 340-345.

Cali F, Conti M, Gregori E. IEEE 802.11 protocol: Design and performance evaluation of an adaptive backoff mechanism[C]. IEEE Journal on Selected Areas in Communications, 2000,18(9):1774-1786.

Bianchi G. Performance analysis of the IEEE 802.11 distributed coordination function.[C] IEEE Journal on Selected Areas in Communications, 2000,18(3):535-547.

Chapter 11

The Use of Virtual Reality in Studying Complex Interventions in Our Every-Day Food Environment

Wilma Waterlander, Cliona Ni Mhurchu and Ingrid Steenhuis

Additional information is available at the end of the chapter

http://dx.doi.org/10.5772/46410

1. Introduction

'An apple a day keeps the doctor away'. This saying illustrates how a healthy diet can contribute to the prevention of some major diseases. Despite the fact that most people are more or less aware of the importance of healthy eating and the fact that most governments and public health organisations make large effort in educating the public about healthy eating, unhealthy population diets are still a major concern. Industrialized countries suffer from the consequences of overconsumption and excessive intakes of sugar, salt, and saturated fatty acids on the one hand and insufficient intakes of fibre, fruits and vegetables on the other. These unhealthy dietary patterns contribute largely to the growing prevalence of non-communicable diseases such as cardiovascular disease, diabetes type 2, obesity and cancer. For example, the prevalence of overweight and obesity in the United States has risen to the massive number of 68% in 2007-2008 [1]. Unhealthy population diets and its consequences put a growing burden on public health, and both the World Health Organization (WHO) and the Federal Agricultural Organization (FAO) have called for action [2, 3]. Moreover, the first-ever High-Level Meeting of the UN General Assembly on non-communicable diseases held in September 2011 demonstrated that one of the major challenges in today's society is creating healthier population diets [4]. The impact of reaching healthier population diets is well illustrated by a recent UK modelling study which found that 33,000 deaths per year would be prevented as a result of improvements in the population diet to a level that is in line with government recommendations [5].

In the challenge of improving population diets, structural interventions such as lowering fruit and vegetable prices, increasing prices of unhealthy foods, front-of-pack (FOP) nutrient labelling or food reformulation are becoming more frequently mentioned as being promising interventions as opposed to nutrition education (alone). The sustainability and affordability of educational programmes are key continuing challenges, especially when it is aimed to reach whole populations. Besides, educational programmes do not address the strong societal forces (e.g., food availability, costs, merchandising, etc.) that work against individual behaviour change [6]. These societal forces may be of key relevance since there is a large body of evidence from the field of consumer psychology showing that consumer choices are mostly not rational, but merely unconscious and heavily influenced by environmental factors [7]. This means that, even if people are well educated about what a healthy diets looks like, they still have a great chance of making unhealthy food choices because at the point of purchase they do not consider all options rationally and are instead driven by factors such as price, convenience, branding, etc.

Swinburn and colleagues developed a framework for understanding the role of our food environment in food choice behavior and for prioritizing environmental components for intervention: the ANGELO-Framework (Analysis Grid for Environments Linked to Obesity). The model makes a distinction in the size (e.g., micro level or macro level) and the type of the environment (e.g., physical, economic, political and socio cultural) [8]. The physical environment refers to the presence of food in all settings including supermarkets, vending machines, restaurants and worksites. The political environment refers to laws and regulations that apply for food, for example Value Added Tax (VAT) regimes or food safety standards. The socio-cultural environment includes components such as traditions and religion which have a powerful influence on peoples' dietary rituals and habits. Finally, the economic environment refers to both food costs and income [8].

In large parts of the world, supermarkets are the dominant food environment [9, 10]; this is the place where people buy most of their food [11, 12]. For example, the market share of Dutch supermarkets for food purchases is around 86%. It is therefore interesting to study how changes in the retail environment (such as different prices, products or placing) could be used to stimulate healthier food choices. However, such evidence is currently very small [13]. The main reason for this lack of evidence is that supermarket studies are complex and costly to conduct. This is especially true for randomized controlled trials (imagine that you would have to modify all supermarket food prices). Besides, opposition from the food industry on several intervention strategies is an important reason for the lack of experimental studies. In order to find a solution to this problem, we developed a research tool which can be used to study the effects of interventions in a virtual-reality setting: the Virtual Supermarket. This software tool can be used to study various interventions in a supermarket setting without having to rely on a complex implementation process.

1.1. Chapter outline

In this chapter we will go more deeply into: 1) the design of the Virtual Supermarket software; 2) potentials of the Virtual Supermarket in food behaviour research and the importance of this new research; 3) how the Virtual Supermarket has been used in experimental studies and an overview of participant feedback on the software; 4) an overview the newest updates and information about future research; 5) new ideas for the Virtual Supermarket such as modifying the software to a serious game.

2. Design of the Virtual Supermarket software

The Virtual Supermarket is a three-dimensional software application in which study participants can shop in a manner comparable to a real supermarket. The application was developed in the Netherlands at the Department of Health Sciences of the VU University Amsterdam in collaboration with SARA Computing and Networking Services Amsterdam. Recently, we published a paper in BMC Public Health about the working, design and development of the software [14]. In this section, we will provide some of the most important features of the application and will give an overview about the working of the program.

The Virtual Supermarket is a computerized web-based supermarket which is very suitable for experimental research on food choice behaviour in a supermarket environment. The program contains a front-end which can be seen by study participants and a back-end that enables researchers to easily manipulate research conditions. The front-end was designed in the image of a real supermarket using an Amsterdam branch of the Dutch market leader supermarket as a model (see Figure 1). When study participants open the Virtual Supermarket on their computer, they see a three-dimensional supermarket model with isles, shelves and a range of food products to choose from. Photographs of real products were used to compose the product models. The current supermarket model contains 512 different food products which form a representation of a normal Dutch supermarket assortment. The program does not include all food products normally present in a supermarket because it was unfeasible to model all these products. In order to make a representative product selection, we used numbers provided by one of the major Dutch supermarket specialist journals and information from the market leader's website [15]. An average Dutch supermarket offers about 7,000 different food products; this number includes, for example, approximately 200 different types of cheese and 250 varieties of wine. The market leader's website categorizes these products in 38 different food categories. These categories comprise, for example, potatoes, vegetables, poultry, fish, soft drinks, confectionary, and bread [15]. Within each product category, a sample representing approximately 10% of the usual stock was selected by choosing popular and frequently consumed products. Since there were no Dutch sales data available showing market shares of individual products and brands, the product selection was conducted by two individual researchers. However, when developing new versions of the Virtual Supermarket, we recommend researchers to use sales data in order to ensure that the program contains the most popular food products. In order to widen the product availability, we created a function by which products in the Virtual Supermarket could represent a number of product varieties. For example, grapes represented red and white grapes and fruit yoghurt represented peach/strawberry/and forest fruit flavours. An overview of the entire product categories as well as the number of products per category in the Virtual Supermarket is given in Table 1.

The 512 food products were placed in three-dimensional supermarket shelves, making a supermarket model which closely resembles a real supermarket. Study participants can download the software on their home computer and start grocery shopping right away. Navigating the virtual supermarket goes easily by using the cursor keys. Participants can select groceries by clicking on them and the product then appears in their shopping cart. After they have finished shopping, participants can move to the cash desks which are located in a similar position as in a regular supermarket. The shopping procedure is however virtual and not real, meaning that participants do not receive the products they have purchased and do not have to pay with real money. If researchers however have the capability to link the virtual supermarket with a real product delivery system (comparable to online shopping) this would be of great interest. Also, there lies potential in collaborating with supermarkets in order to make the virtual shopping procedure real.

Figure 1. Screenshots of the Virtual Supermarket

	Food Category	Total products (n)	Healthy products (n)[a]
1	Potatoes and potato products	10	7
2	Fruits	10	10
3	Vegetables	41	41
4	Ready to eat meals	19	4
5	Meat/ Fish/ Poultry	29	13
6	Meat products	18	4
7	Salads (e.g., crab salad, egg salad, etc.)	8	3
8	Appetizers/ snacks	6	1
9	Cheese	19	3
10	Dairy drinks (e.g., milk, yoghurt drink, etc.)	15	8
11	Desserts	21	4
12	(Whipped) cream	5	-
13	Butter	6	2
14	Eggs	2	-
15	Bread	15	6
16	Pastry	14	4
17	Snacks/ refreshments	12	3
18	Frozen snacks	10	-
19	Ice (cream)	8	1
20	Frozen pastry	2	-
21	Coffee	7	-
22	Evaporated milk/ sugar/ sweeteners	9	2
23	Baking products	13	4
24	Sweet sandwich fillings	10	3
25	Breakfast products	13	6
26	Pasta/ Rice/ Noodles	12	4
27	Mixes for sauces	12	1
28	Seasonings	9	1
29	Herbs and spices	10	-
30	Oils/ Sauces and pickles	26	9
31	Soups	12	2
32	Canned foods (excluding fruits and vegetables)	10	3
33	Beverages (excluding soda)	6	3
34	Soda	24	14
35	Alcoholic beverages	19	-
36	Candy	14	3
37	Chocolate	20	-
38	Crisps/ nuts/ toast	16	3
	Total	512	172 (33.6%)

[a] Healthy products are defined following the Choices front-of-pack nutrition label criteria which are based on the international WHO recommendations regarding saturated fat, trans fat, sodium, and added sugar [16]

Table 1. Outline of product categories and number of products in the web-based supermarket

The back-end of the Virtual Supermarket is designed in such a way that it can be used by researchers to change research conditions in the application without the assistance of an expert programmer. Researchers can use the back-end to change for example food prices, food labels, the placement of signs, and to configure questionnaires. The back-end can also be used to create different research conditions. For example, research condition A can be linked to regular food prices and research condition B to a situation where a fat tax is introduced. Participants who log in to the application with login code A (1-1000) will see regular prices and participants who log on with login code B (1-1000) will receive the changed (taxed) prices. Changing the above mentioned aspects works via Excel sheets, using comma-separated values. The application keeps track of all products purchased by a participant, the time at which the products were selected, the allocated budget, total expenditures and answers to configurable questionnaires. When a respondent completes the virtual shopping task, data is automatically sent to a server and stored in a unique comma-separated value file under the respondent's personal code. The individual data can subsequently be transferred to an Excel or SPSS data file using a link which compresses the data of all participants that are available on the server.

2.1. Have a closer look at the software

The Virtual Supermarket is free to watch and to test for scientific purposes (e.g., non-commercial). The application is available for both MS Windows (Windows 2000 and all newer versions e.g. Windows XP and Windows 7) and Mac (OS10 and all newer versions) and is built to accommodate a wide range of computer arrangements, by allowing the user to choose different screen sizes and graphical quality. Researchers can download the application for free and in a way that preserves their anonymity.

The Virtual Supermarket can be downloaded for:

- Windows: http://www.falw.vu/boodschappen/Supermarket_0027_windows.zip;
- Mac: http://www.falw.vu/boodschappen/Supermarket_0027_mac_universal.zip.

The installation consists of unpacking a compressed file to the desired location. When opening the program, it first asks you about the graphic quality you want to use; you can just click on 'play' in this window. Following you have to fill in a participant number, this can be anything starting with an alphabetic letter (A-Z) followed by a number from 2000 (e.g., A2000). Subsequently, the current version asks you to fill in your household composition; you can fill in the appropriate numbers here. After that, you'll find yourselves at the entrance of the Virtual Supermarket. Feel free to try the program out!

3. Potentials of the Virtual Supermarket in food behaviour research

Key strong points of the Virtual Supermarket are that it can be used to test several intervention strategies (such as food pricing strategies, food labelling, shelf spacing) in a highly controlled experimentally design without a complex implementation process. In this section, we will describe why this type of research is so important, what it adds to the current scientific literature and what the exact potentials of the Virtual Supermarket are in food behaviour research.

3.1. Research that is not supported by the food industry

First, the Virtual Supermarket is very useful to conduct controversial research. During the formation of new pricing, labelling, or other health-stimulating strategies, there is a massive lobby from the food industry aiming to ban new legislations that aim to limit the purchase of certain foods. For example, a recent WHO nutrition report was heavily criticized on its credibility because the draft strategy was delayed for a month in order to give the United States and several small, sugar-producing countries (the so-called G77) an opening to lobby for a softer strategy [17].

David Ludwig and Marion Nestle have published an insightful commentary paper in the Journal of the American Medical Association (JAMA) about the role of the Food Industry in obesity (research) [18]. This paper highlights the problems that occur when academics and governments work together with the food industry when trying to find successful interventions to stimulate healthy eating. The major problem is that food corporates must make the financial return to stockholders their first priority, in other words, they must sell as much food as possible. This goal contradicts the public health goals which focus on increasing the consumption of healthy foods such as fruits and vegetables, and on *de*creasing the intake of calories from fat and sugar. As highlighted later in this chapter, most of food industries' profit comes from convenience foods such as fast food and snacks which is illustrated by the fact that nearly 70% of the annual $33 billion spending on food advertisements and promotions goes into these convenience foods [19] . Due to this profit making structure, food producers have no real incentive to participate in health stimulating behaviour and may even contradict this aim. For example, pricing strategies are frequently mentioned as a promising strategy to stimulate healthier food choices. In a Delphi Study, we asked representatives from academia, food industry and government organizations what the most feasible and effective pricing strategies would be. An interesting outcome of this study was that taxing unhealthy food was generally indicated to be an effective strategy, but not feasible, especially from the food producers view point [20]. Brownell and colleagues at the Yale Rudd Centre have argued for the introduction of taxes on sugar-sweetened beverages [21], but encountered some thorough opposition from the sugar sweetened beverage industry stating that such taxes would lead to higher alcohol consumption. Numbers show that PepsiCo, Coca-Cola Co and the American Beverage Association have spent the huge amount of US$ 70 million on lobbying against proposed soda taxes [22]. Moreover, Vermeer *et al.* concluded in their study on the feasibility of interventions aimed at portion size that "The respondents indicated that, from a perspective of responsible entrepreneurship, their companies were willing to play an active role in combating this social problem. However, that this willingness was subject to the condition that any such intervention would not harm commercial interests" [23]. Finally, in front-of-pack labelling research (see also later in this chapter) there are issues with labels indicating products as being unhealthy. From the public health viewpoint, there is growing consensus that FOP labels should identify food products both as being healthy or unhealthy where applicable [24]. An example of such a system is the multiple traffic light format [25] using colour schemes to indicate the products healthiness. In general, food producers do not favour this system since it could give their products a clear red mark indicating the product as being unhealthy, which could in turn lower the sales. In general, food producers are willing to think about practices to stimulate healthy eating, as long as their profits are not affected. When truly thinking about successful interventions, we do however might want to achieve lower sales and lower profit making in the food industry sector, especially with regard to unhealthy convenience foods.

Ludwig and Nestle highlight that 'Academia's role is to investigate by rigorous scientific investigation of nutrition and health. To minimize the corrosive effects of financial conflicts of interest, universities should institute systems to ensure independent review of industry-sponsored research, including critical oversight of hypotheses, design, data collection, data analysis, interpretation, and decisions to publish' [18]. However, this level of independence is hard to accomplish when trying to examine the effectiveness of interventions in the real-life food environment. For example, if you want to conduct a trial on shelf spacing in the supermarket, you rely on the willingness of the supermarket to corporate. Also, testing the effectiveness of interventions that are not favoured or rejected by the food industry (such as traffic light labelling or soft drink taxes) is very complicated to conduct. The Virtual Supermarket does not have to deal with such issues and maintains researcher independence and avoids conflicts of interest that may arise from industry collaboration. In the following paragraphs, we will list some different types of interventions that are interesting to study using the Virtual Supermarket.

3.2. Social marketing

Traditional nutrition education interventions are based on social-cognitive models, which assume that behavior change is a rational process. Examples of such models are the 'Theory of Planned Behavior', the 'Health Belief Model' or self-regulation theory [26, 27]. Key elements in these theories are health beliefs, intentions, goal setting et cetera. However, often behavior is unconscious, irrational and driven by other motivators than health. Marketing makes use of this knowledge by nudging people towards a product by using default behaviors (i.e. the tendency to choose the middle size or the one which is labeled as 'normal' or 'medium'), building on human preferences (i.e. to make it easy, convenient and requiring low effort) and by using the 'fun factor'. Social marketing is a process "that applies marketing principles and techniques to create, communicate, and deliver value in order to influence target audience behaviors that benefit society (public health, safety, the environment, and communities) as well as the target audience" [28] Social Marketing is more customer oriented than traditional health education; it uses marketing research to understand market segments; positions the 'product' or behavior in an appealing way to the chosen target market (more appealing than the competing products or behaviors); and uses a marketing mix in which product, place, price and promotion are the key elements. Social marketing differs from commercial marketing in the sense that the main goal of commercial marketing is to make a financial profit, while the main goal of social marketing is to benefit both the individual and the society. An important principle in both commercial and social marketing is the exchange theory. In order for an exchange to take place, people must perceive benefits greater or at least equal to the perceived costs [28].

Both social marketing and the classic marketing mix use the concept of four p's to describe the determinants that can be used to steer consumer behaviour: product, place, price and promotion [29]. This concept implies that if you want to sell something to a consumer (for example healthy eating) you could intervene on the product (develop a new type of healthy bread); on the place (self-spacing in the supermarket); price (subsidy on fruits); and/or promotion (advertising). Especially, it is important to be aware of the fact that all four p's should be 'correct', for example: if you have a very healthy, tasty new type of bread, which is placed in every supermarket and heavily promoted, it will still not sell if it has not the right price. It is interesting to study these four p's in relation to health promotion since they show potential as primers to steer consumers decision processes [7]. In this section, we will provide an overview of the potentials of the virtual supermarket in research on the use of these four p's.

3.3. The first P: Pricing

Price has been listed as *the* factor to steer consumer behaviour [30]. Indeed, economists state that they have no idea how to change people's preferences; the way to change behaviour is to change the cost [31]. It is true that economic strategies have previously been successful in reducing the use of alcohol and tobacco [32]. Moreover, when thinking about our every-day food environment, it is clear that marketers use price a lot to attract consumers towards their product. Another way to use price is via de-marketing obesity [33]. Social marketing not only focuses on attracting people towards a certain product or behaviour, but also on decreasing their attraction towards unwanted behaviours. With regard to food pricing, one could think about making the relative costs of unhealthy foods more expensive in order to make them less attractive.

Different governments around the world are considering (or have already introduced) food pricing strategies to improve the quality of population diets. In October 2011, Denmark introduced a fat tax. Specifically, the measure consisted of a price increase of around €2.15 on every kilo of saturated fat on any food that contains more than 2.3% saturated fat. Also Hungary introduced a tax on unhealthy food items [34] and France recently introduced a tax on sugary soft drinks (the tax of around one Euro cent per can is expected to bring in tax revenues of €120 million). Moreover, in December 2011, the Dutch Council for Public Health and Health Care (RVZ) advised the government to look at food pricing strategies as a measure in the prevention of welfare diseases. Their particular advice was to explore how a fat tax or a higher Value Added Tax rate for all foods could be realised [35]. Furthermore, also the WHO advises member states to consider fiscal policies to stimulate healthy food choices [34]. Interestingly, however, the effects of these fiscal measures on health are unknown and are some gaps that need to be filled before pricing strategies can be designated as a solution in health promotion [36].

3.3.1. Evidence on the effectiveness of food pricing strategies

One way of studying the effects of food pricing strategies, is the use of simulation modelling studies. These studies simulate the effects of tax reforms using real data on food expenditures such as national household consumption surveys. These data are used to determine the price elasticity of demand of the studied food products. Price elasticity of demand is defined as the responsiveness of the quantity demanded of a certain good due to a price change of this good [37]. If, for example, the demand of hamburgers decreases drastically due to a fat tax (price increase) this is considered an elastic good. A recent review on the price elasticity of food (based on a selection of 160 studies) revealed that food is elastic and that the highest price elasticity was found for food away from home, soft drinks, juice, meats, and fruit and the most inelastic demand for eggs [11].

A second way of studying the potential of food pricing strategies is to ask consumers how they would react to changing food prices using qualitative methods or quantitative surveys. This type of research has shown that price is an important factor in food choice and that consumers expect that they will eat more healthy food if this becomes cheaper [38, 39]. Third, experimental studies are highly relevant to gain insight into consumer responses towards price changes. Well known examples of experimental pricing studies in the field of health promotion is the work by French and colleagues. They conducted experiments in vending machines where prices of low-fat snacks were reduced by 10, 25 and 50 per cent and found that sales of these products raised by 9, 39 and 93 per cent respectively [40]. These results were duplicated in later studies of the same group [41]. Also, they found that reducing prices of fruits and vegetables with 50 per cent in school canteens lead to a two-fold increase in vegetable and four-fold increase in fruit purchases [40]. Other experimental studies are the work by Epstein and colleagues who conducted a study on several pricing schemes in a laboratory supermarket [42], the work by Nederkoorn and colleagues on a high caloric tax in a web-based supermarket [43], and the work by Giesen and colleagues on taxing high caloric university lunch menus [44]. All these studies revealed significant effects of the price changes.

While the previous paragraph illustrates that there is some good scientific evidence to support the effects of food pricing strategies, it still does not give insight into the effectiveness of these measures to stimulate population health. The major issue with the effects of food pricing strategies on health outcomes is the potential side effects of these measures. For example, if fruits become cheaper people may use the money to buy more pizza. Or, if fatty foods become more expensive people may compensate their loss by buying less fruits and vegetables [42, 45]. This side effect of food pricing strategies is known as 'cross price elasticity of demand', e.g., the responsiveness of the demand for a good as a result of a price change of another good [37]. Cross-price elasticity is consequently referred to as being highly complex [45]. The majority of simulation modelling studies have not modelled complete demand systems to estimate the effects of price changes on both targeted foods and non-targeted foods. Moreover, most studies have only modelled through to the effect of fiscal regimens on overall purchases of targeted foods and nutrients; there are very few examples where modelling has been extended to determine effects on health and disease [36] or across socio-economic groups. The same issue applies to experimental studies. A review on randomized controlled trials on food pricing found that the published trials studied small sample sizes, were of short duration and also only studied a small number of products [46].

3.3.2. *What type of research is needed?*

In order to gain insight in the multifaceted effects of food pricing strategies, it is of importance to conduct experiments in larger food environments, where people buy most of their foods, that is retail settings [11, 12, 47]. Randomized controlled trials (RCT's) are especially important to conduct because, in the hierarchy of evidence that influences healthcare policy and practice, this type of research is considered to be the most reliable methodology. For example, the National Health and Medical Research Council of Australia designated "Level I" evidence as that "obtained from a systematic review of all relevant randomised controlled trials" and "Level II" evidence as that "obtained from at least one properly designed randomised controlled trial. Moreover, the results of RCT's form an important input for the data used in simulation modelling studies. A recent review on experimental food pricing research has revealed that only four supermarket food pricing experiments have been published up to date [48]. These trials include for example the New Zealand SHOP study [47] and a recently published French study on the effects of fruit and vegetable vouchers [49]. All four studies focused on the effects of providing discounts on healthier foods and did not contain detailed data on substitution effects [48]. The main reason for the absence of large experimental trials on the effects of food pricing strategies is that those are complex, costly and sometimes even impossible to conduct in real-life. It is hard to change prices in real supermarkets and it also difficult to find good a good control group (that receives regular prices) which is crucial for a randomized controlled trial. Moreover, it is hard to extract the effects of the pricing strategy from other factors that may influence consumer choices (e.g., branding, shelf placement, etc.).

The virtual supermarket offers a great solution to the difficulties surrounding the implementation of RCT's on the effects of food pricing strategies. The software is suitable to experimentally study various pricing interventions in a highly controlled supermarket setting without having to rely on a complex implementation process. Besides, the Virtual Supermarket can be used to study the effects of food pricing strategies that are not favoured by the retail or food sector such as different types of taxes (soda tax, fat tax, etc.). The results of such studies can form a good input for policy and practise and can also be used in subsequent simulation modelling studies.

3.4. The second P: Product

A second way of stimulating healthier food choices is by the introduction of new healthy food products or the reformulation of existing food products towards a healthier nutrient composition. One way by which food producers can be encouraged to develop healthier products is by the introduction of a front-of-pack (FOP) nutrition label [50]. FOP labels can roughly be divided into non-directive, semi-directive and directive labels [51] and aim to provide clear and direct information about the healthiness of a food product and thereby support consumers in making healthier food choices. FOP labels show potential to promote healthier product selection by consumers (as will be explained in section 3.5) but show also potential with regard to food reformulation and the development of new food products with a healthier product composition. Food producers are generally keen to heave a healthy food label on their product or just don't want a red traffic light stating that their product is unhealthy. In order to reach this goal, food producers are encouraged by FOP labels towards a healthier product composition.

3.4.1. Evidence on the effect of product interventions

Research on a FOP label (the Choices Healthy Food Label) revealed that this label stimulated food manufacturers to develop new healthier products and to reformulate existing products towards a healthier nutrient composition [52]. Moreover, a New Zealand study observed that the Pick the Tick logo lead to a reduction in sodium content of a small number of products [53]. When food products are reformulated as a consequence of FOP labels, this could have large implications for public health since people will then automatically select healthier products (because the products became healthier). A Dutch simulation modelling study using national food consumption and food composition data revealed that a diet modelled to contain more products that complied with the Choices FOP label could contribute to cardiovascular risk reduction [54]. Second, a study using a randomized parallel design examining the effects on sodium excretion of dietary education to choose foods identified by either Australia's National Heart Foundation Tick symbol or by the Food Standards Australia and New Zealand's low-salt guideline, revealed that sodium excretion decreased significantly in both groups after 8 weeks [55].

3.4.2. What type of evidence is needed?

Comparable with food pricing research, large randomized controlled trials on the effects of food reformulation and new product development form a gap in the literature. There is evidence that FOP labels lead to healthier product development and there is evidence that the consumption of healthier products leads to improved health status, but we don't exactly know how consumers react to the introduction of new or improved products. Will consumers indeed buy these new products, or will they stick with their regular purchases? Or will consumers purchase more products if they perceive them as being healthier? The virtual supermarket can be a very useful tool to conduct such research since it allows the placement of new products in the assortment. Therefore, the effects of new products can be studied in a highly controlled environment without other disturbing factors such as pricing or branding. The software enables to link the virtual purchases with food composition data, meaning that the effects of new products on nutrient purchases can be easily calculated. The Virtual Supermarket could be similarly useful to study the introduction of new sustainable, organic or fair-trade products. Different studies have shown that there is a large gap between environmental awareness and conducting actual environmentally friendly behaviour. The same issues apply to health: most people list their health as being one of the most important factors in their life, but still, they have trouble in taking part in healthy behaviour. While numerous studies have been undertaken to explain this gap, there is no definite answer yet [56]. The Virtual Supermarket has the unique advantage of providing the possibility to study environmental friendly related or health related behaviour experimentally. Will product innovation actually pay of? What is the right price for a new product when it enters the market? How should the new product be positioned and how does it work amongst different types of consumers? There lies great potential in conducting research on these aspects. Later in this chapter, we talk about the possibilities of linking the Virtual Supermarket to eye-tracking research. This technique captures how long consumers look at a certain product and where they look at. The combination of both tools shows great potential in studying the effects of new products in the market place.

3.5. The third P: Promotion

Promotion has great potential in stimulating healthier food choices. Here there are different types of promotion we could consider, for example, promoting the healthiness of a product, promoting the price of a product, promoting a new product, advertisements, etc. The huge amount of money that goes in food promotion each year (in 1999, US food companies spent more than $33 billion annually on advertising and promoting their products and nearly 70% of this money was spent on advertisements for convenience foods such as fast food and snacks) illustrates that at least food producers expect good results from this marketing strategy [19]. It would be very interesting to study how different type of advertisements would affect consumer food choices and how these could be used to stimulate healthier food choices. The virtual supermarket could be used to display different types of signs or people could be exposed to different types of commercials before entering the supermarket.

3.5.1. Evidence on the effects of promotion

There is a large body of evidence, especially within the field of marketing and retail research, about the effects of promotions. For example, research showed that people have the tendency to buy a product simply because it is on sale or cheaper now [57, 58]. Going beyond that, there is evidence that people react to a sale sign without an actual price discount. Anderson and Simester found that using the word 'sale' beside a price (without actually varying the price) can increase demand by more than 50% [59]. Also the way of framing the price seems to be important. Research found that the use of $9/€9 endings increases demand because people link this ending to a promotion price [60]. This extra effort seems important since it was found that people tend to remember prices badly and are dependent on cues to update their expectations about relative prices and future product availability [61].

Besides informing about special offers, it was found that consumers are interested in information telling them about the healthiness of a product [39]. FOP labels form a potential effective strategy to promote healthy products among consumers. As described above, there are generally three different types of FOP labels. First, non-directive labels provide information about the (core) nutrients in a product, but leave the decision about whether this nutrient content is healthy or not to the consumer (for example the Daily Intake Guide, DIG). Second, semi-directive labels provide some guidance, but leave the final healthiness interpretation to the consumer. An example is the colour-coded multiple traffic lights label (MTL) which ranks total fat, saturated fat, sugar and sodium and codes these with a colour [25]. Finally, directive FOP labels include quality marks – a healthy food logo. Mostly, this logo defines a healthier product within a certain product category. A recent review revealed that consumers are interested in nutrition labeling and favor the idea of a simple label on the front of pack of food products [62]. There is a considerable amount of evidence on consumer understanding of different FOP schemes and also their use in the supermarket [62, 63]. For example, A German study tested consumer understanding (n=420) of different FOP label formats. Results revealed that German adults profit most from the traffic light label [64]. Next, A new Zealand study on use, understanding and preferences among ethnically diverse shoppers revealed that traffic light labels demonstrated high levels of understanding while consumers had more difficulties with the mandatory nutrition information panel[65]. Finally, a Dutch observational study examined the evaluation and use of the Choices front-of-pack logo among supermarket shoppers [66]. This study found that 62% of the study sample was familiar with the logo and that it regularly occurs that shoppers purchase products with the logo unintentionally [66].

3.5.2. What type of evidence is needed?

There is need for experimental research on the effects of different types of product promotion on food purchases. With regard to FOP labelling it is a problem that most studies are based on self-report; experimental evidence about the effectiveness of FOP labels is roughly absent [62]. The main reason for the absence of experimental studies about the effects of FOP labels on food choices is that, similar to food pricing, these are complex to conduct. FOP labels are mostly introduced nation-wide without the presence of a good control group (that did not receive the new FOP labels). Moreover, different FOP labels already exist in the market place, which makes it hard to extract the effect of the new label only. Finally, it is complex to measure the pure effects of FOP labels apart from other influencing factors such as food packages, branding and price. It is highly important to get more insight into the effects of FOP labels on actual purchases, both for research and policy purposes. First objective measures are needed because these effects may differ largely from reported behaviour. Moreover, it is important to carefully monitor the effects of FOP labels because they may result in negative side effects. For example, it is expected that consumers eat more of a product when they think the product is healthy and also there are also indications that health messages may be counteractive because people link health with a bad taste [67]. Stakeholder views are polarized with regard to the best FOP label format [24]. For example, most food producers do not favour the traffic light system [25] because it will give their products a clear red mark indicating the product as being unhealthy. Most public health workers, on the other side, do favour such a system [24]. Without the presence of solid experimental evidence it is hard to inform policy makers about the best format. If we aim for stringent food labels (such as the traffic light system) solid evidence is needed to work against the strong lobby of the food industry.

Also for other type of promotion strategies more experimental research is warranted. Most marketing and retail research has not focused on public health outcomes, but instead measured the effects of promotion on a couple of single products. The effects found in such studies cannot be directly related to the effects of promotion on public health nutrition. For example, the effects of increased sales due to a promotion could work via different mechanisms being "product substitution", "forward buying", "purchase acceleration", "brand switching", "product testing", or "repeat purchasing" which all are expected to have different effects on the definite consumption pattern [30]. Similar concerns apply to the effects of the communication of pricing strategies. As mentioned before, it may be more important to tell people that a product is discounted than to actually discount it. The effects of communicating pricing information (promotion) also seems relevant in relation to price increases; it may be more important to tell people that products are taxed than to actually tax it [68, 69]. This discussion is referred to as 'tax salience' in the economic literature; in which salience has indeed been found to have large effects on behavioral responses on tax changes [70]. Nevertheless, the evidence is currently limited to theoretical analysis [70] and experimental studies are needed to gain insight into this topic.

The virtual supermarket could be a useful tool in conducting experiments on different promotion strategies and in finding out how taxing, subsidizing or FOP label schemes should best be addressed to consumers. For example, researchers can design an experiment with different sales labels ('two for the price of one' versus '50% discount') and the effects of communicating new taxing measures (for example placing signs stating 'warning: this product has been taxed').

3.6. The fourth P: Place

There is growing recognition that our food environment is obesogenic, that is defined as "the sum of influences that the surroundings, opportunities, or conditions of life have on promoting obesity in individuals or populations"[6, 8]. Another interesting area for investigation would therefore be product placement and the amount of shelf space that is awarded to a certain product. What happens if healthy foods form 90% of the supermarket assortment and unhealthy food is more difficult to locate?

3.6.1. Evidence on the effects of place

The effects of shelf spacing and product placement have not been heavily studied, but there are some studies that show promising results. For example, a study found that the sales of fruits and vegetables increased by 40% after doubling the shelf space [71]. Moreover it has been observed that all store types (supermarkets, convenience stores, specialty shops, etc.) devote more shelf space to unhealthy items compared to healthy items [72]. Finally, a group at Deakin University (Australia) has done some work on the shelf spacing aspect and found that supermarkets in lower socio-economic areas dedicate significantly more shelf space to unhealthier products (soft drinks, snacks) compared to supermarkets in higher socio-economic areas. Besides shelf spacing, also the location of products in the supermarket is expected to have a large influence on food purchases. This includes for example the location of products near the entrance, or placing products on eye-level [73].

3.6.2. What type of evidence is needed?

Altogether, there are indications that changes in shelf spacing of healthier and unhealthier foods can be an effective intervention to stimulate healthier food choices. However, up to date, there are no published experimental studies that have examined the effects of interventions with regard to product place on food purchases [73]. Moreover, there are roughly no studies on the effects of the placement of products on eye level, the placement of products near the cash desk area, the placement of products in special eye-catching locations (including for children); changing the proportion of healthy versus unhealthy products; or changing the total amount of products available [73]. We expect that one of the main reasons for the absence of such studies is that those are very complicated to conduct. This would require the adjustment of a whole supermarket layout which is very complex and costly. The virtual supermarket has potential in studying such interventions. Besides, we do expect that the retail industry has some useful data on the effects of product placement in the supermarket; however, this information has not been published or provided to public health researchers so far. We are therefore dependent on other types of data collection to get insight into these effects.

3.7. Summary of the main potentials of the virtual supermarket in food behaviour research

This section revealed that the Virtual Supermarket has great potential for experimental research about the effects of interventions in a retail setting on food purchases. The virtual supermarket provides a highly controlled environment and makes it easy for researchers to change research conditions such as price, product place, promotion or other strategies. Besides the four P's from the marketing mix, researchers could use the Virtual Supermarket for various other intervention studies. For example, what is the influence of music? Work by North and colleagues revealed that French music played in a store led to higher sales of French wine whereas German music led to higher German wine sales [74]. Researchers could also think of the influence of colour schemes, lighting, adding extra service, providing consumers with a clear map of the supermarket (or via a smartphone application), the influence of hunger and thirst, impulsivity, stress and many other things. For example, Nederkoorn *et al* have used a virtual supermarket in the form of 640 food products that could be chosen via drop down lists (comparable to the current form of most online stores) to examine the effects of impulsivity and hunger on calorie purchases [75]. Moreover, Giesen et al., have used this similar type of virtual supermarket to examine the role of impulsivity on the effects of calorie taxes and subsidies [76].

4. Results of experimental research with the Virtual Supermarket

The development of the Dutch Virtual Supermarket software has been completed in 2010. Since then, the software has been pilot tested among 66 consumers and it has been successfully used in five scientific experiments among 557 study participants. In the sections below, we will provide an overview of the experiments that have been conducted with the

Virtual Supermarket so far. These experiments were mainly focused around the effects of food pricing strategies and give an indication about how virtual reality can be used in behavioural research. Besides, during the pilot phase and as part of the experiments, we asked consumer feedback about the software and requested them to judge the validity of the tool on several quality indicators. The results of these quality observations will be presented at the end of this chapter.

4.1. The effects of a 25% price discount on fruits and vegetables

The first experiment in the virtual supermarket examined the effects of a 25% price discount on fruits and vegetables. The results have been published in the International Journal of Behavioral Nutrition and Physical Activity [77]. In this experiment, 115 Dutch adults from the general population shopped one time in the virtual supermarket. Half of the sample was randomized to a condition with normal food prices and the other half of the sample was randomized to a condition with a 25% price discount on fruits and vegetables. Most participants completed the experiment at home and they were instructed to undertake a typical shop for their household for one week. The main outcome measure was fruit and vegetable purchases (in grams and items). Next, also purchased calories (kcal) and expenditures in unhealthier food categories were measured (e.g., desserts, soda, crisps, candy, and chocolate). Before entering the Virtual Supermarket, participants were asked some background variables including: sex; age; ethnicity; household composition; degree of being responsible for the groceries; weekly food budget; education level; employment status; and household income. Results of this experiment revealed that the group in the 25% price discount condition purchased nearly 1 kilogram of fruits plus vegetables more for their household for one week compared to the group that received normal food prices ($p<.05$). Differences between both research conditions for fruit (B=481; 95% CI: -69, 1,030; $p=.09$) and vegetable purchases (B=504; 95%CI: -64, 1071; $p=.08$) separately also showed large differences, but these were not statistically significant.

Furthermore, both groups purchased an equal number of food items and an equal amount of calories, indicating that participants in the discount condition did not spend the money they saved from the discounts on other foods than fruits and vegetables. More details of the results can be found in Figure 2.

While it is important that future studies expand and validate these findings to a real supermarket setting, the results were the first to report the effects of discounting fruits and vegetables in a retail setting and found that this measure is effective in stimulating purchases of those products which could have major implications for public health.

4.2. The effects of price discounts combined with price increases

The second experiment in the Virtual Supermarket concerned the effects of combining discounts on healthier food products (no discount; 25% discount or 50% discount) with price increases on unhealthy products (5%; 10%; 25% price increase) on food purchases. The results of this experiment have been recently published in Preventive Medicine [69]. The experiment contained nine study (three x three) conditions and study participants shopped once in the virtual supermarket. Participants were sent an USB-device with the web-based supermarket software, instructions and a personal log-in code by post. Every participant was asked to conduct a typical shop for their household for one week. Data of in total 117 participants were included in the statistical analysis. Results revealed that the discounts were effective in stimulating healthier food purchases; participants that received a 50% discount purchased significantly more healthy foods than participants with no discount (mean difference was 6.62 items) or a 25% discount (mean difference was 4.87 items). However, higher price discounts were also associated with more food purchases overall (including unhealthier products). Participants that received a 50% price discount purchased in total 10.4 more food items compared to the participants that received no discount. Moreover, the 50% discount group purchased 10,505 more calories (kcal) for their household for one week compared to the group with no discount (p=.001). We did not find an effect of the price increases on food purchases. Also we did not find that participants in the study conditions with price increases on unhealthy foods purchased less food products, nor that the effects of the discounts (extra calories) were balanced by the price increases. To our knowledge, this is the first study examining both separate and simultaneous effects of multiple price discounts and price increases in a retail environment. Different authors have emphasized the importance of such studies [11, 12]. This study therefore provides important new evidence into the effectiveness of varying price discount and price increase schemes on food purchases. An important aspect to consider is that our results may be an underestimation of price strategies in practice, because the pricing strategies were silent. As mentioned earlier in this chapter; it may be more important to tell people that a price has changed (either increased or decreased) than actually changing the price [57, 58, 68]. It is therefore important to validate our results in a real supermarket setting and to include the effects of communication strategies. Finally, it would be interesting to study the effects of higher tax levels (25% onwards) since different studies have revealed that such high levels are required to result in behaviour change[42, 76]. The virtual supermarket could also be a useful instrument to study such effects as well.

4.3. The effects of price discounts in combination with sales and promotion signs

The third virtual supermarket experiment studied the effects of different signs ('healthy choice', 'sale' and 'sale & healthy choice') in combination with price discounts (10%; 25% and 50%) on healthy foods on food purchases. The results of this experiment have been submitted for publication [78]. The experiment contained nine study conditions (three x three) and study participants shopped once in the virtual supermarket. The types of signs were chosen to segregate the effects of pointing out that a product was either on sale, healthy, or both. The signs were placed noticeably next to the healthier products in the web-based supermarket (Figure 3). Healthy products were defined following the Choices front-of-pack nutrition label criteria which are based on the international WHO recommendations regarding saturated fat, trans fat, sodium, and added sugar [16]. Main outcome measures were: healthy and unhealthy food items (number and proportion); fruit and vegetables (gram); and calories (kcal). All outcomes were measured per household per week. The final study sample included n=109 participants and differences between conditions were tested using two-way factorial ANCOVA, where factor 1 indicated the level of discount and level 2 the promotion sign. In line with the previous experiments, the results of this experiment showed that discounts are effective in stimulating healthy food purchases. We did however not observe significant differences between the effects of the sales signs. A limitation of this study was that it did not include a condition with no promotion sign, which makes it hard to separate the pricing and the promotion effects. It is interesting to examine this in more detail in future studies.

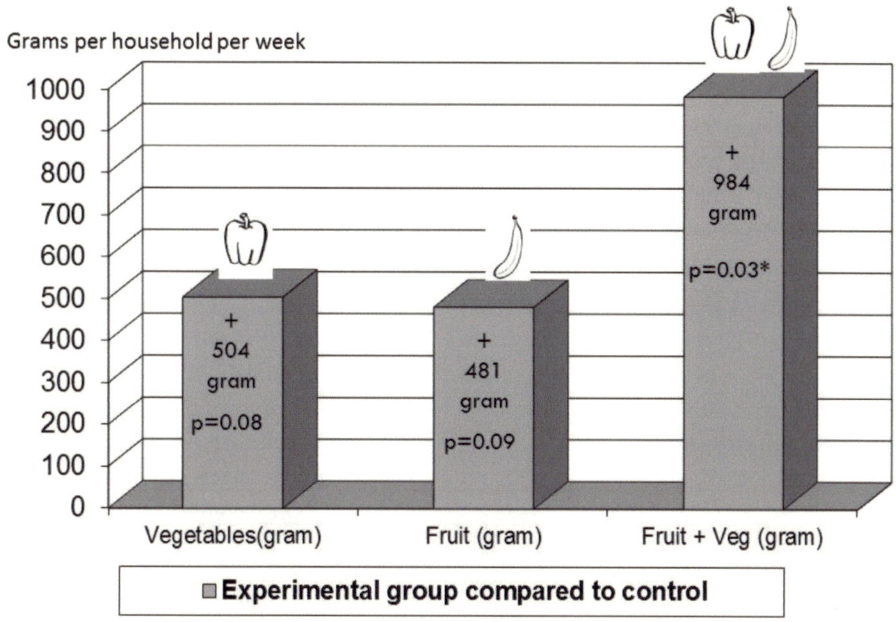

Figure 2. Results of experiment 1 in the virtual supermarket: difference in purchased amounts of fruit and vegetables (in grams per household per week) between the experimental group (25% discount on fruits and vegetables) and the control group (normal food prices)

Figure 3. Sales signs in the Virtual Supermarket

4.4. Unpublished results

The results of the fourth and fifth experiment in the virtual supermarket have not been published and fully analysed yet. The first of these experiments studied the effects of a tax measure on sugar-sweetened beverages. This pricing measure has particular interest in the United States and also France recently implemented a soda tax. The experiment we conducted contained two study conditions: one with normal prices and one with a tax increase on sugar-sweetened beverages from the regular 6% to the high tax level of 19% (which is the same as the Dutch tax level for alcohol). Table 2 gives an overview of the control and experimental prices. 94 Participants were included in statistical analysis. Results of initial analysis showed promising effects of such a tax on the purchase of sugar sweetened beverages and are expected to be published next year. The second of these experiments studied how different discount percentages on healthier foods affected food purchases. In this experiment we asked participants to shop four times in the virtual supermarket. During every shopping event participants were provided with different prices on healthier food products (no discount; 10% discount; 25% discount and 50% discount). Participants received the price discounts in different orders and were not informed about the price changes. The data of this experiment have not been analysed yet, but they promise to provide valuable new information because they can give insight into the effects of price changes both within and between consumers and also show which discount percentage is needed to find significant results.

	Control Group (price in €)	Experimental group (price in €)
Lemonade/ syrup	1.53	1.71
Cola	1.14	1.28
Orange	1.14	1.28
7-up/ soft drink	1.14	1.28
Spa fruit drink	1.09	1.21
Cassis soft drink	1.09	1.21
Ice tea	0.64	0.71
Tonic	1.35	1.51
Energy drinks	1.72	1.98
Red-bull	4.32	4.83
Ice coffee	1.05	1.17
Apple juice	1.06	1.19
Orange juice	1.25	1.40
Grape juice	0.95	1.06
Multi fruit juice	1.21	1.35
Chocolate milk	0.86	0.96

Table 2. Overview of the control and experimental prices in the soda tax experiment

5. Participant feedback on the Virtual Supermarket software

Besides the primary outcome measures on food purchases, the Virtual Supermarket also enables to review how participants experienced the software. In all five experiments, we measured participant feedback with a list of questions. It was observed that this feedback was generally very good. For example, in experiment 1, it was observed that 91% of the participants scored ≥ 4 (scale 1-5) on comprehension of the software. Furthermore, 87% scored ≥4 on the question asking whether they could envision doing their normal groceries using the web-based supermarket. Finally, 80% scored ≥4 on the question asking whether their purchases at the web-based supermarket gave a good indication for their normal groceries [77]. In experiment 3, we found comparable results showing that ninety-one percent of the participants scored ≥5 (1=lowest; 7=highest) on comprehension of the software. Furthermore, 85% scored ≥5 on the question asking whether their experimental groceries corresponded with their regular groceries and 94% scored ≥5 on the question asking whether the products in the web-based supermarket were good recognizable [69].

The virtual supermarket was also pilot-tested among 66 consumers as described in our paper in BMC Public Health [14]. Results (see also Figure 4) of this pilot study revealed that the majority of respondents considered the Virtual Supermarket easy to understand (n = 55 agree, n = 7 neutral, n = 4 disagree) and could easily find their way around the Virtual Supermarket (n = 48 agree, n = 11 neutral, n = 7 disagree). Around half of the respondents agreed that the Virtual Supermarket had a sufficient variety of products in stock (n = 37 agree, n = 14 neutral, n = 15 disagree), and thought that the stock of the Virtual Supermarket resembled the stock of a real supermarket (n = 34 agree, n = 11 neutral, n = 21 disagree). Moreover, most respondents indicated that the products they selected in the Virtual Supermarket corresponded to their normal weekly groceries (n = 52 agree, n = 7 neutral, n =7 disagree).

The experimental results and the results from the pilot study show that the Virtual Supermarket is a good-quality tool to measure shopping behaviour. Study participants state that they can envision doing a typical grocery shop using the software and most participants indicate that their virtual groceries correspond well with their regular groceries. Especially when combined with other methodologies to unravel the effects of interventions in the supermarket environment (simulation studies, questionnaires, experiments in smaller settings), the results can provide imperative insight in the effects of different intervention strategies. Especially since electronic shopping is becoming increasingly common these days. Moreover, there is evidence that peoples' virtual behavior largely corresponds with their actual behavior. Sharpe et al. (2008) validated food and beverage choices made in a virtual road trip survey by comparing those choices with choices made in a real McDonalds a week later. The authors concluded that peoples' simulated purchasing behavior is highly predictive of their real behavior [79].Virtual shopping behaviour may thus also be fairly comparable to real-life shopping behaviour. A point for improvement would be the number of products that is available in the Virtual Supermarket since some participants indicated that the product variety was low. Besides, it could be valuable to provide participants with a map of the supermarket showing them which products are available and where they are located; more than half of the participants in the pilot study indicated that they could not easily find all products [14].

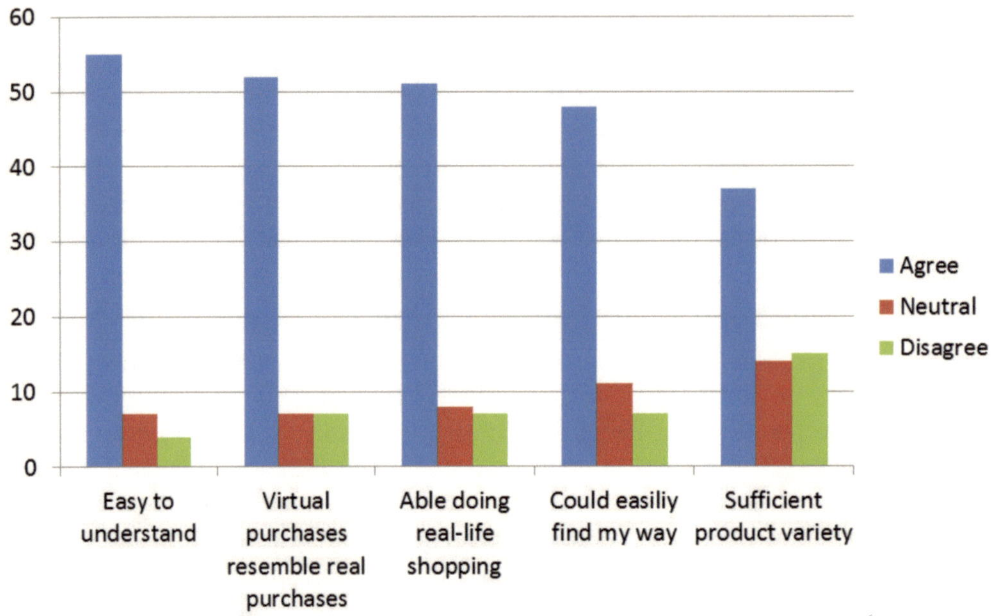

Figure 4. Participant feedbacks from 66 consumers on the Virtual Supermarket software. Each bar represents the number of participants that fitted in that category. For a more detailed overview see [14]

6. What's next: Upcoming research and an English language version of the Virtual Supermarket

The virtual supermarket has successfully been used in several experimental studies and shows great potential for further food choice studies. In order to ensure that the quality of the software is high and to enable the use of the software outside the Netherlands, we are currently working on new research. This research encompasses the validation of the software and the development of a New Zealand version of the virtual supermarket.

6.1. Validation of the virtual supermarket

An important limitation of the virtual supermarket in food choice research is that the found effects may be different compared to a real supermarket. Behaviour in a real setting may differ from a virtual setting because real life concerns real money and real products and this may lead virtual shopping to be taken less seriously. It is therefore of major importance to validate the Virtual Supermarket against real-life food purchases.

In the Netherlands, we are conducting a virtual supermarket validation study at this moment. In this study, we have asked study participants to conduct a typical weekly shop at the Virtual Supermarket and subsequently to collect their (real) grocery receipts from the following week. We aim to collect data for around 100 study participants. The data from this study will be used to analyse to what extend the virtual and the real purchases overlap and how this varies across different food categories. Next, we will measure which products were purchased in real life but for which no good alternative was available in the virtual supermarket. Moreover, participants will be given a set of questions asking about the quality of the software and whether or not they missed any products. We aim to finish data collection in April 2012 and expect the results to be published early 2013. We aim to update the software based on the results of this validation study.

6.2. New Zealand Virtual Supermarket

At the National Institute for Health Innovation (NIHI), the University of Auckland, New Zealand we are working on a New Zealand version of the Virtual Supermarket at this moment. This version will contain more product items compared to the Dutch version and will contain many new features.

The New Zealand version will enclose an assortment that is representative for an average New Zealand supermarket. The product selection will be based on the products that are available in a regular supermarket and we aim to enclose around 1,500 products (this is three times more than the Dutch version). In contrast to the Dutch version, The New Zealand Virtual Supermarket will contain different brands. In order to select the most popular products from each product category we use data from the Australian Grocery Guide. This guide gives an overview of market sizes and market shares of all retail products in Australia. While Australian data may differ somewhat from New Zealand, the guide does provide a good starting point for product selection. Other features of the New Zealand version include that it will have signs at each isle indicating what product categories are located there. Moreover, we will incorporate a function that enables to select fruits and vegetables per gram (instead of per package) and we will enable participants to set their own shopping budget based on their normal expenditures.

After finishing the virtual supermarket software, we will initially test it among the University staff. Based on this internal feedback, we will create an updated version of the software. The next step is to validate the New Zealand virtual supermarket and test it among New Zealand consumers. For this purpose we will conduct a study in which we ask a selection of study participants to conduct a typical shop at the virtual supermarket. After their shop, they will be asked a set of questions about the software, for example, about the product assortment or the easiness of navigation. Besides, we will use insights from previous work on perceptions of virtual environments by measuring level of presence and realism (e.g., the feeling of being there). Also, we will ask participants to collect their grocery receipts from the past week and compare their real groceries with the virtual ones. The software will be updated based on the results of this validation study. We aim to finalize the

New Zealand Virtual Supermarket software by the end of 2012 and we have planned an experiment on the effects of front-of-pack labelling using this new application.

7. The virtual supermarket as a serious game

All the above sections describe the use of the Virtual Supermarket as a research instrument, e.g., an innovative way to measure here food choice behaviour in the retail setting. A final very promising aspect of the software that we would like to mention is modifying the application to an intervention tool. Here one could think of the Virtual Supermarket as a serious game or eHealth instrument.

Serious games form a very promising approach in the stimulation of health behaviours [80], especially among children and young adults. Today's children and young adults spend a great deal of their time on video games and video games can attract and maintain attention, which form key components for effective behaviour change [80]. A review on the use of games for health related behaviour change indicated 25 different serious games available in the literature and revealed that these studies mostly showed significant effects on knowledge, attitude, behaviour, and other health-related changes [80]. The review showed that there are two primary methods by which video games can influence behaviour. The first involves the insertion of behaviour-change procedures (e.g., goal setting) into the process of playing the game. The second involves the use of story (narrative series of events) and inserting behaviour-change concepts in the story [80].A good example of a serious game focused on improving nutrition intakes is Squire'sQuest! The design of this American game was an interactive multimedia game for elementary school children [81]. This game used the concept of a story line. The story was about a kingdom that was invaded by enemies and who were attempting to destroy the kingdom by destroying the fruit and vegetable crops. The children had to defend the kingdom and defeat the invaders. In order to succeed this, the child had to take on some challenges which involved skills and goals related to eating more fruit, 100% fruit juice, and vegetables [81]. This example shows that it is important to include a game element in the intervention tool in order to make it successful. It would be possible to do something similar with the Virtual Supermarket. Possible ideas include to let people make their own supermarket empire and letting them get higher scores if their product selection is healthy; develop some kind of supermarket shopping race; or letting people try to see through marketing tricks. There lies also potential of distributing the virtual supermarket game through social media such as Facebook. Finally, there lies potential in the use of the Virtual Supermarket by dieticians or other public health workers. There is some good evidence showing that guided tours through the supermarket by a dietician are effective in stimulating healthy food purchases. Within this approach, a dietician accompanies a consumer during grocery shopping and shows him/her how he/she could make healthier food choices. A limitation of this approach is that it is very costly and time consuming and it is not feasible to reach a whole population with this method. It is therefore potentially a good idea to use the virtual supermarket for these type of guided tours. For example, researchers could make a video with a dietician in the virtual supermarket or it would be possible to let people shop and show health messages by the choices they make.

The modification of the Virtual Supermarket into a serious game would require some serious software changes, but it is definitely an idea worth considering. We are happy to engage in this type of research in the future.

8. The Virtual Supermarket one step further

Technology is developing rapidly and recently some interesting tools have been introduced in the market which could be linked with the Virtual Supermarket. For example the 'Carl Zeiss Cinemizer OLED' are video glasses which can be placed in front of the eyes. The device contains head tracking and can be used to 'walk' through three-dimensional virtual rooms. The new devise shows great potential for the gaming industry, but could also be used for scientific research and could be linked with the virtual supermarket software. Another example of new technology is the use of a virtual supermarket model by the retail industry. For example, Woolworths (Australia) is currently running a trial on its virtual supermarket concept in the Town Hall railway station in central Sydney. They have created a virtual wall of labels representing available groceries online from the company. Shoppers can use the Woolworth's smartphone application to select products from this wall, which will be subsequently ordered online. The wall features 120 product lines from Woolworths' online catalogue. Also, the Korean branch of Tesco has recently installed billboards in train stations around the country which show all the products one would expect to find in its traditional stores. The model is similar to the Australian one and people can purchase the products by scanning them with their smart phone. The order will then be delivered to the consumers' home address. The Korean billboards have been evaluated and concluded that the project is very popular; more than 10,000 customers have used the virtual stores so far, while the online sales of the store have increased by 130 per cent.

A final possibility for the Virtual Supermarket lies in the combination with eye-tracking research. Eye-tracking technology tracks where a person is looking by using either light or dark spot eye trackers. The eye-tracking devise works via shining low levels of infrared light on to the participants face to identify the pupil location. Eye-tracking devises can be accurate to 5mm and allow great latitude for movement [82]. The underlying hypothesis in eye-tracking research is that 'we look at what we like', and 'we like what we look at' [82]. So far, most eye-tracking research has focused on showing study participants with some samples of pictures and testing where the participants look at. For example, eye-tracking could be used to examine how much time consumers spend reading the different sections of information on a nutrient information panel (which is normally provided at the back of pack of food products) and also in which order they look at the information. A limitation of current eye-tracking research however is that it is mostly laboratory based and has not been implemented in real life situations such as for example making product selections in the supermarket. An important reason for this is that most devises do not work well outside the laboratory. The Virtual Supermarket shows therefore great potential. It could serve as a balanced mix between using eye-tracking in real life and in a (controlled) laboratory environment, especially since eye-tracking works better when working with objects on a computer screen as opposed to real objects [82]. Examples of eye-tracking research in combination with the Virtual Supermarket include experiments on the notice of FOP labels, prices, different types of promotions or shelf spacing.

9. Conclusion

The Virtual Supermarket is an innovative and unique research tool with great potential in the study of food choice behaviour. This type of research is of significant importance since the prevalence of several non-communicable diseases such as diabetes type 2, obesity and cancer is growing rapidly. Creating healthier population diets could bring a major contribution in the prevention of these chronic diseases. However, food choice behaviour is highly complex and traditional approaches to stimulate healthy eating (such as education) have shown little effectiveness so far. Traditional nutrition education interventions are based on social-cognitive models, which assume that behavior change is a rational process. However, often behavior is unconscious, irrational and driven by other motivators than health such as convenience or habit. Marketing makes use of this knowledge by nudging people towards a product by using default behaviors (i.e. the tendency to choose the middle size or the one which is labeled as 'normal' or 'medium'), building on human preferences (i.e. to make it easy, convenient and requiring low effort) and by using the 'fun factor' and the effects of interventions. Most importantly, the four P's from the marketing mix e.g., price, product, place and promotion show potential to stimulate healthier food behaviour.

One of the best ways to study the effects of interventions on product, price, place or promotion is by the use of randomized controlled trials (RCT's) in retail environments. Supermarkets form the dominant food environment and are the place where people buy most of their food. However, the design and implementation of supermarket intervention studies is complicated. First, such studies require the modification of supermarkets which is costly and complex, second it is hard to find a good control group (people that do not receive the intervention) and third it is hard to extract the intervention effects from other disturbing factors (e.g., if a new product is introduced, this comes with a certain price, promotion and place). Finally, conducting experiments in the food environment often requires corporation with the food industry which could threaten researcher independence and could lead to conflicts of interest. Virtual Reality can bring a great solution to this complexity by designing environments comparable to real life and using these for experimental research. The virtual supermarket is a great example of how virtual reality can be used in food choice research.

The Virtual Supermarket is a three-dimensional software application in the image of a real supermarket. The program contains a front-end which can be seen by study participants and a back-end that enables researchers to easily manipulate research conditions. The front-end was designed in the image of a real supermarket using an Amsterdam branch of the Dutch market leader supermarket as a model. Study participants can do grocery shopping using this application comparable to real-life grocery shopping. Researchers can use the tool to easily manipulate research conditions, such as changing food prices or shelf placement. Such interventions show great potential to stimulate healthier food choices, but are very difficult to conduct in real life.

Up to date, the virtual supermarket has been successfully used in multiple experiments and has shown to be a valuable research instrument. The Virtual Supermarket is a valuable tool precisely because it offers high levels of controllability, it allows prices to be easily be manipulated, and because a complex implementation in a real-life setting is avoided. Moreover, participant feedback indicated that consumers view the Virtual Supermarket as a reliable research tool and are able envisioning doing their groceries in it comparable to the real-life situation.

Limitations of the Virtual Supermarket include that it has not been validated against real purchases, that the product selection is not based on sales data, that the product selection is relatively small and that the current version is only available in Dutch. We are however working on improving all these aspects. First, we are currently conducting a validating study in the Netherlands among around 100 participants aiming to test the compatibility of the virtual purchases against real purchases. Second, we are working on the development of a New Zealand version of the Virtual Supermarket. This version will include around 1500 products and the product selection will be based on sales data and market shares. This version will also be validated against real purchases and is expected to be launched by the end of 2012.

The Virtual Supermarket is a good-quality research tool and has great potential to become a multifunctional, well-used and valid instrument. There is interest for the software from around the globe (including the United States and Switzerland) and there are a great number of ways in which the software could be used. Examples include studies on the effects of pricing, food labelling, place, location in the supermarket, and even the modification of the program into a serious game. While the current software requires further validation, the possibilities are endless and it is expected that the software can grow into a high-quality research instrument in a close period of time.

Author details

Wilma E. Waterlander
VU University Amsterdam, The Netherlands

University of Auckland New Zealand

Cliona Ni Mhurchu
University of Auckland New Zealand

Ingrid H.M. Steenhuis,
VU University Amsterdam, The Netherlands

10. References

[1] Flegal KM, Carroll MD, Ogden CL, Curtin LR (2010) Prevalence and Trends in Obesity Among US Adults, 1999-2008. Jama: doi:10.1001/jama.2009.2014

[2] Joint WHO/ FAO Expert Consultation (2003) Diet, nutrition and the prevention of chronic diseases. (WHO ed. Geneva: WHO.

[3] World Health Organization (2009) Global health risks: mortality and burden of disease attributable to selected major risks. Geneva: WHO.

[4] United Nations. General Assembly (2011) Scope, modalities, format and organization of the High-level Meeting of the General Assembly on the Prevention and Control of Non-communicable Diseases. New York.

[5] Scarborough P, Nnoaham KE, Clarke D, Capewell S, Rayner M (2010) Modelling the impact of a healthy diet on cardiovascular disease and cancer mortality. J Epidemiol Community Health. doi:10.1136/jech.2010.114520.

[6] Swinburn BA, Sacks G, Hall KD, McPherson K, Finegood DT, Moodie ML, Gortmaker SL (2011) The global obesity pandemic: shaped by global drivers and local environments. Lancet. 378:804-814.

[7] Dijksterhuis A, Smith PK, van Baaren RB, Wigboldus DHJ (2005) The unconscious consumer: Effects of environment on consumer behavior. Journal of Consumer Psychology. 15:193-202.

[8] Swinburn B, Egger G, Raza F: Dissecting Obesogenic Environments (1999) The Development and Application of a Framework for Identifying and Prioritizing Environmental Interventions for Obesity. Prev Med. 29:563-570.

[9] Hawkes C (2008) Dietary implications of supermarket development: a global perspective. Development Policy Review. 26:657-692.

[10] Vorley B: Food, Inc. (2003) Corporate Concentration from Farm to Consumer. London: International Institute for Environment and Development.

[11] Andreyeva T, Long MW, Brownell KD (2010) The impact of food prices on consumption: a systematic review of research on the price elasticity of demand for food. Am J Public Health. 100:216-222.

[12] Ni Mhurchu C (2010) Food costs and healthful diets: the need for solution-oriented research and policies. Am J Clin Nutr. 92:1007-1008.

[13] Glanz K, Hoelscher D (2004) Increasing fruit and vegetable intake by changing environments, policy and pricing: restaurant-based research, strategies, and recommendations. Prev Med., 39 Suppl 2:S88-93.

[14] Waterlander WE, Scarpa M, Lentz D, Steenhuis IH (2011) The Virtual Supermarket: An Innovative Research Tool to Study Consumer Food Purchasing Behaviour. BMC Public Health. 11:589.

[15] Groceries (boodschappen). URL:http://webwinkel.ah.nl/ [http://webwinkel.ah.nl/]

[16] Roodenburg AJC, Popkin BM, Seidell JC (2011) Development of international criteria for a front of package food labelling system: the international Choices Programme. Eur J Clin Nutr. 65:1190-1200.

[17] Vastag B (2004) Obesity is now on everyone's plate. Jama. 291:1186-1188.

[18] Ludwig DS, Nestle M (2008) Can the food industry play a constructive role in the obesity epidemic? Jama. 300:1808-1811.
[19] Nestle M (2007) Food Politics. How the industry influences nutrition and health. Berkely: University of California Press.
[20] Waterlander WE, Steenhuis IH, de Vet E, Schuit AJ, Seidell JC (2010) Expert views on most suitable monetary incentives on food to stimulate healthy eating. Eur J Public Health. 20:325-331.
[21] Brownell KD, Frieden TR (2009) Ounces of Prevention -- The Public Policy Case for Taxes on Sugared Beverages. N Engl J Med. 360(18):1805-1808.
[22] Stanford DD (2012) Anti-Obesity Soda Tax Fails as Lobbyists Spend Millions: Retail. In Bloomberg Business Week.
[23] Vermeer WM, Steenhuis IHM, Seidell JC (2009) From the point-of-purchase perspective: A qualitative study of the feasibility of interventions aimed at portion-size. Health Policy. 90:73-80.
[24] White J, Thomson G, Signal L (2010) Front-of-pack nutrition labelling: where to now? NZMJ. 123:12-16.
[25] Food Standards Agency (FSA) (2009) Comprehension and use of UK nutrition signpost labelling schemes. London, UK: Food Standards Agency.
[26] Ajzen I (1991) The theory of planned behavior. Organizational Behavior and Human Decision Processes. 50:179–211.
[27] Rosenstock IM (1990) The health belief model: Explaining health behavior through expectancies. In Glanz K, Lewis FM, Rimer BK (Series Editor). Health behavior and health education: Theory, research and practice. San Francisco, CA, US: Jossey-Bass.
[28] Kotler P, Zaltman G (1971) Social Marketing - Approach to Planned Social Change. Journal of Marketing. 35:3-12.
[29] McCarthy J (2001) Basic Marketing: A managerial approach. 13th ed. Homewoon Illinois: Irwin.
[30] Hawkes C (2009) Sales promotions and food consumption. Nutr Rev. 67:333-342.
[31] McCarthy M (2004) The economics of obesity. Lancet. 364:2169-2170.
[32] Chopra M, Darnton-Hill I (2004) Tobacco and obesity epidemics: not so different after all? Bmj. 328:1558-1560.
[33] Wansink B, Huckabee M (2005) De-marketing obesity. California Management Review. 47:4
[34] Holt E (2011) Hungary to introduce broad range of fat taxes. Lancet. 378:755-755.
[35] Dutch Counsil for Public Health and Health Care (RVZ) (2011) Prevention of Welfare Diseases (Preventie van Welvaartsziekten). The Hague, The Netherlands.
[36] Thow AM, Jan S, Leeder S, Swinburn B (2010) The effect of fiscal policy on diet, obesity and chronic disease: a systematic review. Bull World Health Organ. 88:609-614.
[37] Perloff JM (2007) Microeconomics. 4 edn. Boston: Pearson Education.
[38] Steenhuis IH, Waterlander WE, de Mul A (2011) Consumer food choices: the role of price and pricing strategies. Public Health Nutr. 14:2220-2226.
[39] Waterlander WE, de Mul A, Schuit AJ, Seidell JC, Steenhuis IHM (2010) Perceptions on the use of Pricing Strategies to stimulate Healthy Eating among Residents of deprived

Neighbourhoods: a Focus Group Study. Int J Beh Nutr and Phys Act. 7:doi:10.1186/1479-5868-1187-1144.

[40] French SA (2003) Pricing effects on food choices. J Nutr. 133:841S-843S.

[41] French SA, Hannan PJ, Harnack LJ, Mitchell NR, Toomey TL, Gerlach A (2010) Pricing and availability intervention in vending machines at four bus garages. J Occup Environ Med. 52 Suppl 1:S29-33.

[42] Epstein LH, Dearing KK, Roba LG, Finkelstein E (2010) The Influence of Taxes and Subsidies on Energy Purchased in an Experimental Purchasing Study. Psychological Science. 21:406-414.

[43] Nederkoorn C, Havermans RC, Giesen JC, Jansen A (2011) High tax on high energy dense foods and its effects on the purchase of calories in a supermarket: An experiment. Appetite., 56:760-765.

[44] Giesen JC, Payne CR, Havermans RC, Jansen A (2011) Exploring how calorie information and taxes on high-calorie foods influence lunch decisions. Am J Clin Nutr. doi: 10.3945/ajcn.110.008193.

[45] Mytton O, Gray A, Rayner M, Rutter H (2007) Could targeted food taxes improve health? J Epidemiol Community Health. 61:689-694.

[46] Wall J, Mhurchu CN, Blakely T, Rodgers A, Wilton J (2006) Effectiveness of monetary incentives in modifying dietary behavior:a review of randomized, controlled trials. Nutr Rev. 64:518-531.

[47] Ni Mhurchu C, Blakely T, Jiang Y, Eyles HC, Rodgers A (2010) Effects of price discounts and tailored nutrition education on supermarket purchases: a randomized controlled trial. Am J Clin Nutr. 91:736-747.

[48] Epstein LH, Jankowiak N, Nederkoorn C, Raynor HA, French SA, Finkelstein E (2012) Experimental research on the relation between food price changes and food-purchasing patterns: a targeted review. Am J Clin Nutr doi:10.3945/ajcn.111.024380.

[49] Bihan H, Mejean C, Castetbon K, Faure H, Ducros V, Sedeaud A, Galan P, Le Clesiau H, Peneau S, Hercberg S (2011) Impact of fruit and vegetable vouchers and dietary advice on fruit and vegetable intake in a low-income population. Eur J Clin Nutr.

[50] Institute of Medicine (US) (2011) Front-of-package nutrition systems and symbols. Promoting healthier choices. Report Brief 2011, October.

[51] Bonsmann SS, Celemin LF, Grunert KG (2010) Food labelling to advance better education for life. Eur J Clin Nutr. 64:S14-19.

[52] Vyth EL, Steenhuis IHM, Roodenburg AJC, Brug J, Seidell JC (2010) Front-of-pack nutrition label stimulates healthier product development: a quantitative analysis. International Journal of Behavioral Nutrition and Physical Activity. 7: doi 10.1186/1479-5868-7-65

[53] Young L, Swinburn B (2002) Impact of the Pick the Tick food information programme on the salt content of food in New Zealand. Health Promotion International. 17:13-19.

[54] Vyth EL, Hendriksen MA, Roodenburg AJ, Steenhuis IH, van Raaij JM, Verhagen H, Brug J, Seidell JC (2011) Consuming a diet complying with front-of-pack label criteria may reduce cholesterol levels: a modeling study. Eur J Clin Nutr. doi:10.1038/ejcn.2011.193

[55] Ireland DM, Clifton PM, Keogh JB (2010) Achieving the Salt Intake Target of 6 g/Day in the Current Food Supply in Free-Living Adults Using Two Dietary Education Strategies. Journal of the American Dietetic Association. 110:763-767.
[56] Kollmuss A, Agyeman J (2002) Mind the Gap: Why do people act environmentally and what are the barriers to pro-environmental behavior. Environmental Education Research. 8:239-260.
[57] Anderson ET, Simester DI (1998) The role of sale signs. Marketing Science. 17:139-155.
[58] Blattberg RC, Briesch R, Fox EJ (1995) How promotions work. Marketing Science. 14:G122-G132.
[59] Anderson ET, Simester DI (2003) Mind your pricing cues. Harvard Business Review. 81:97-103.
[60] Anderson ET, Simester DI (2003) Effects of $9 price endings on retail sales: evidence from field experiments. Quantitative Marketing and Economics. 1:93-110.
[61] Vanhuelle M, Laurent G, Dreze X (2006) Consumers' immediate memory for prices. Journal of Consumer Research. 33:163-171.
[62] Grunert KG, Wills JM (2007) A review of European research on consumer response to nutrition information food labels. J Public Health. 15:385-399.
[63] Sharf M, Sela R, Zentner G, Shoob H, Shai I, Stein-Zamir C (2011) Figuring out food labels. Young adults' understanding of nutritional information presented on food labels is inadequate. Appetite. 58:531-534.
[64] Borgmeier I, Westenhoefer J (2009) Impact of different food label formats on healthiness evaluation and food choice of consumers: a randomized-controlled study. Bmc Public Health 9: doi 10.1186/1471-2458-9-184
[65] Gorton D, Mhurchu CN, Chen MH, Dixon R (2009) Nutrition labels: a survey of use, understanding and preferences among ethnically diverse shoppers in New Zealand. Public Health Nutr. 12:1359-1365.
[66] Vyth EL, Steenhuis IH, Vlot JA, Wulp A, Hogenes MG, Looije DH, Brug J, Seidell JC (2010) Actual use of a front-of-pack nutrition logo in the supermarket: consumers' motives in food choice. Public Health Nutr. 13:1882-1889.
[67] Horgen KB, Brownell KD (2002) Comparison of price change and health message interventions in promoting healthy food choices. Health Psychol. 21:505-512.
[68] Lacaniloa RD, Cash SB, Adamowisz WL (2011) Heterogneous consumer responses to snack food taxes and warning labels. The Journal of Consumer Affairs. 45:108-122.
[69] Waterlander WE, Steenhuis IH, de Boer MR, Schuit AJ, Seidell JC (2012) Introducing taxes, subsidies or both: The effects of various food pricing strategies in a web-based supermarket randomized trial. Prev Med. doi:10.1016/j.ypmed.2012.02.009
[70] Chetty R, Looney A, Kroft K (2009) Salience and Taxation: Theory and Evidence. American Economic Review. 99:1145-1177.
[71] Curhan RC (1974)The effects of merchandising and temporary promotional activities on the sales of fresh fruits and vegetables in supermarkets. Journal of Marketing Research. 11:286-294.

[72] Farley TA, Rice J, Bodor JN, Cohen DA, Bluthenthal RN, Rose D (2009) Measuring the Food Environment: Shelf Space of Fruits, Vegetables, and Snack Foods in Stores. Journal of Urban Health-Bulletin of the New York Academy of Medicine. 86:672-682.

[73] Campo K, Gijsbrechts E, Goossens T, Verhetsel A (2000) The impact of location factors on the attractiveness and optimal space shares of product categories. International Journal of Research in Marketing. 17:255-279.

[74] North AC, Hargreaves DJ, McKendrick J (1997) In-store music affects product choice. Nature. 390:132-132.

[75] Nederkoorn C, Guerrieri R, Havermans RC, Roefs A, Jansen A (2009) The interactive effect of hunger and impulsivity on food intake and purchase in a virtual supermarket. Int J Obes., 33:905-912.

[76] Giesen JCAH, Havermans RC, Nederkoorn C, Jansen A (2011) Impulsivity in the Supermarket: Responses to Calorie Taxes and Subsidies in Healthy Weight Undergraduates. Appetite. doi:10.1016/j.appet.2011.09.026.

[77] Waterlander WE, Steenhuis IH, de Boer MR, Schuit AJ, Seidell JC (2012) The effects of a 25% discount on fruits and vegetables: results of a randomized trial in a three-dimensional web-based supermarket. Int J Behav Nutr Phys Act. 9:11.

[78] Waterlander WE, Steenhuis IHM, de Boer MR, Schuit AJ, Seidell JC (2012) Sign or discount? The effects of various promotion strategies on food purchases in a randomized controlled trial at a three-dimensional web-based supermarket. Submitted.

[79] Sharpe KM, Staelin R, Huber J (2008) Using extremeness aversion to fight obesity: Policy implications of contaxt dependent demand. Journal of Consumer Research. 35:406-422.

[80] Baranowski T, Buday R, Thompson DI, Baranowski J (2008) Playing for real - Video games and stories for health-related behavior change. American Journal of Preventive Medicine. 34:74-82.

[81] Baranowski T, Baranowski J, Cullen KW, Marsh T, Islam N, Zakeri I, Honess-Morreale L, deMoor C (2003) Squire's Quest! Dietary outcome evaluation of a multimedia game. Am J Prev Med. 24:52-61.

[82] Maughan L, Gutnikov S, Stevens R (2007) Like more, look more. Look more, like more: The evidence from eye-tracking Brand Management. 14:335-342.

Chapter 12

Post Disaster Virtual Revival: 3D CG Manual Reconstruction of a World Heritage Site in Danger

Elham Andaroodi, Mohammad Reza Matini and Kinji Ono

Additional information is available at the end of the chapter

http://dx.doi.org/10.5772/46406

1. Introduction

Cultural heritage is an irreplaceable witness of the traditions and developments of the past. They are evidence of the history of various civilizations around the world. The ICOMOS Venice Charter stated (International Council on Monuments and Sites, [ICOMOS], 1964):

> "People are becoming more and more conscious of the unity of human values and regard ancient monuments as a common heritage. The common responsibility to safeguard them for future generations is recognized. It is our duty to hand them on in the full richness of their authenticity."

Modern technologies have caused several changes in lifestyles. Traditional functions have been replaced by new ones and monuments such as caravanserais, houses, and ancient castles have lost their original use. New infrastructures that are the fundamental basis for recent developments have posed numerous risks to heritage monuments and sites. Several natural or human disasters such as earthquakes, tsunamis, wars, and urban or industrial development have damaged physical bodies or the authenticity of heritage buildings. As Ben Kacyra (who established the CyArk to cyber archive heritage buildings through a 3D laser scanning system) stated (Kacyra, 2011):

> "We are losing the sites and the sorties faster than we can physically restore them. It is apparent that we are fighting a losing battle. Basically we are losing our sites and the stories as a significant piece of our collective memories. Imagine us as a human race not knowing where we came from."

There are at the moment 35 properties in the list of the world heritage sites that that have been identified as sites in danger that need specific attention and protection. For example changes in climate, erosion, and abandonment damaged the Rice Terraces of the Philippines Cordilleras. The development of agriculture around the archaeological site of Abu Mena in Egypt increased the level of the water table, softened the clay soil, and risked the collapse of buildings. The Bamiyan Valley and its heritage have suffered abandonment, military action, and dynamite explosions. Bam and its cultural landscape were destroyed by a strong earthquake in 2003 in our case study (United Nations Educational Scientific and Cultural Organization [UNESCO], World Heritage Centre [WHC], 2004).

However, new opportunities to preserve heritage buildings have been created in recent decades. Digital technologies such as 3 Dimensional Computer Graphics and Virtual Reality, Close Range Photogrammetry, and 3D Laser Scanning Systems have made it possible to make highly accurate digital replicas of heritage buildings. The Internet has provided an environment to disseminate data on digitally resituated heritage to end users. Digital tools are a key to saving heritage buildings and preserve them virtually. They can enrich our knowledge about the past and transfer this to future generations.

We introduce our research on 3 Dimensional Computer Graphics manual reconstruction of a world heritage site in danger, i.e., the citadel of Bam, as an example of post-disaster virtual revival in this chapter. A devastating earthquake destroyed the city of Bam and its rich heritage in 2003. Ten thousand lives were lost and an ancient mud-brick citadel with a unique combination of different types of Persian architecture was converted into debris. The citadel and other significant heritage of the city consisting of its urban landscape and specifically the Qanat water management system was inscribed on the list of world heritage sites in danger as 'Bam and its Cultural Landscape" in 2004 (UNESCO, WHC, 2004).

3D CG reconstitution of the citadel of Bam began right after the earthquake in December 2003. We joined post-disaster endeavours for virtual revival of the destroyed city's heritage using digital technologies as part of the Digital Silk Roads Project of the National Institute of Informatics, in collaboration with organizations and universities including the Iranian Cultural Heritage, Handicraft, and Tourism Organization (ICHHTO), Waseda University (Japan), the University of Tehran, the Razahang Architectural Firm (Iran), and the Espace Virtuel de Conception en Architecture et Urbaine (France).

The high-precision process of 3D CG reconstitution of the site faced several challenges. The citadel was vast and comprised various types of buildings and nine residential districts with a castle on top of a hill. Since most of the buildings were destroyed, precise surveying techniques such as close range photogrammetry and laser scanning could not be applied. The architectural 2D or 3D drawings and images were incomplete and several locations within the citadel had not been documented before the quake. The complicated traditional Persian adobe architecture of the buildings was difficult to comprehend, especially with the lack of reliable documentation before its destruction. Normal 3D CG surface modeling techniques could not replicate the citadel's complicated shapes of mud-brick vaulted facades and domed roofs. Our project was part of academic collaboration between universities and it involved students of architecture or CG experts from different cultures. Thus, facilitating coordination between the team members and producing a coherent 3D CG model were major challenges to be faced (Ono et al., 2008a).

Figure 1. Citadel of Bam after earthquake in 2003

We will discuss our research methods of 3D CG reconstitution of the citadel of Bam and solutions that we followed to cope with these challenges. We will introduce the key results from our research projects as a demonstration of the virtual reality of the citadel in the situation it was in before the earthquake struck and the distribution of output data accompanied by their semantics on a knowledge-based website.

2. Historical background

The citadel of Bam is part of an ancient city that is located along the Silk and Spice Road in the south east of Iran in Kerman province. The city flourished because of its textile products that were carried along the ancient routes to cities far away. The route started from the sea corridors of the Indian ocean, extended to Hurmoz port in Persia, and passed through the roads of the city of Bam to reach the east-west Silk Road.

The city was also developed for its ecological location as a basin in the middle of the desert. It gathered water through the advanced Qanat water management system that originated from distant mountains. One of the most ancient Qanats dating back to the Achaemnian period (500 B.C.) was discovered north east of the city (Adle, 2004). Several agricultural products supported the economy of the city such as cotton and dates. Travelogues such as those by Ibn Hawqal (who travelled there from 943–969 CE) described the city and its citadel (Hawqal, 1966):

> "Bam city has a pure weather and several quarters. A grand and well known citadel is located inside this city and it has three Jame mosques including a mosque inside the citadel. In Bam a beautiful, elegant and durable cotton textile is woven and is exported to lands and cities far away. The scapulars that are made in this city are very fine and made from delicate silk. Several other fine clothes are made that are sold in Khaorasan, Iraq and Egypt. Bam textile are very good quality and can be found in treasures of kings."

Such strategic locations made the city flourish during the centuries. However, the citadel inside the city has a longer history. Its original date of construction is mysterious but can be guessed from archaeological findings, resemblance of architectural styles, and even myths and stories. Discoveries after debris was removed from the citadel, such as pieces of pottery, some of which date back to the 3rd millennium B.C. (Ahmadi, 2008), and coins that belonged to the Parthian period (150 BC- 224 AD), (Armanshahr, 1993) support its origins. Archaeological findings prove the area of Bam and Baravat (south of Bam) was inhabited during the Achaemenid (550–330 BC) and Parthian (150 BC– 224 AD) periods (Ataai, et al., 2006).

The citadel is referred to in ancient myths and poems like those by Ferdowsi (Persian poet 940–1020 CE). There are stories about some parts of the citadel such as an old gate (Kod-e-Kerm) where a magical worm was kept. The worm could secrete a delicate thread (probably a silk worm) and it brought wealth and fortune to the inhabitants (Ferdowsi, 1974). There was also a deep water well that was dug by Rostam (national hero of Greater Iran) and Egyptian craftsmen in the middle of the castle of the citadel in the rocky mountains (Vaziri Kermani, 1967).

Some critical resemblance in architecture indicates the citadel might have had a more important function in ancient times. Some buildings in the governor's district, on top of the cliff of the citadel, most probably resemble an important temple in FirouzAbad (built by the Sassanid dynasty (226–651 AD)). Similar elements are the fire tower, (watch tower for the citadel), the four vaults (Chartaghi) that held fire (Four Seasons or the ChaharFasl monument of the citadel), and water resources, like springs or water wells, that were dug inside rock because ancient Persians believed that Nahid or the Water Goddess was born from stone, (deep water well in the governor's district of the citadel near the governor's bath), (Nourbakhsh, 1974).

Newer layers were destroyed after the earthquake and older mud-brick structures became evident with large mud bricks similar to those used in ancient constructions from the Elamit period (3200 BC–539 BC) (Mehryar, 2004).

The citadel has witnessed several historical events, flourishing civilizations, or destructive inventions during the last 20 centuries. When the city of Bam was an important industrial, agricultural, and trade centre in the middle of Persia in the 10th century, it accommodated vast houses with huge mud brick walls (Tayari, 2005). However, its defensive function threatened its existence during insecurity in the region. In a fight with Arsalan Seljuk and his army in 1183 AD, the citadel was mostly destroyed; they diverted water from a river and filled the moat and destroyed the city's walls. After this event, and during the invasion by Ghoz into Kerman, the region was mostly destroyed, especially the Qanat systems (Aasefi Heravi, 1964), which weakened the economy of the city. The inhabitants who remained after the vast destruction in the bigger city entered the walls of the present day citadel and the large citadel shrank to its contemporary size. They replaced the large buildings and rich districts with smaller everyday houses. This event appears to have happened in 1409 AD on the order of the Teimorid governor of the city (Tayari, 2005).

However, major reconstruction of the citadel occurred during the Qajar period (1785 to 1925 CE), while the area flourished again for its date gardens. The citadel's life as a city ended in the middle of this period, when its inhabitants deserted it and created the new city of Bam south of the citadel. At the beginning of the current century, it accommodated minor military forces and finally it was registered on the National Heritage of Iran list in 1966. Although the citadel was destroyed and rebuilt several times during the last 20 centuries of habitation, no power was greater than nature, which changed the great heritage site into debris in 12 seconds.

3. Features of 3D CG reconstitution

We investigated the architectural characteristics of the buildings inside the citadel to reconstitute the citadel of Bam in 3D CG. Later, we studied the level of destruction of each case of the buildings after the earthquake. We studied different tools that were available, methods, and experience in parallel, specifically those introduced by the International Scientific Committee for Documentation of Cultural Heritage (CIPA) to choose an appropriate digital technique for reconstitution. We introduce the process that resulted in 3D CG manual modeling of major architecture of the citadel in this section.

3.1. Multi-technique approach to 3D CG development

Knowledge-based records of heritage buildings need to virtually replicate every point of their surfaces through digital techniques. Existing systems for buildings such as close range photogrammetry or laser scanning can produce points of clouds and create precise surfaces of buildings. Examples of best practices are heritage sites such as ancient Merv (Turkmenistan), Angkor (Cambodia), and Rapa Nui (Easter Island), which have been digitized by the CyArk non-profit organization. The points of cloud data and surface models of these sites, together with 28 other sites have been disseminated over the Internet.

However, these processes pose greater challenges for heritage in danger that has partially or completely been destroyed. The original shapes of buildings cannot be laser scanned as they do not exist anymore. If sites have been photographed with calibrated cameras before destruction, then CRP can help to extract points of surfaces. The three metric images acquired in Bamiyan in 1970 by Professor Kostka could be used to reconstruct the Bamian Great Buddha with VirtuoZo digital photogrammetric systems (Grün et al., 2004).

Unfortunately, such metric on-site images were not available for the citadel of Bam. Yet an aerial photograph of the citadel in 1994 was available, which could be used for cartography to generate a 3D drawing with remote sensing techniques. Although such systems can be used to extract the major dimensions and geometry needed for the heights and plans of buildings, they have shortcomings in elevation and interior spaces.

Manual 3D CG modeling was a traditional but effective method in our case study by enabling the geometry of surfaces from 2D architectural drawings to be created. Tools such as Auto CAD ® provide a metric environment for precise modeling specially with lines, such as the borders of arches and the edges of walls. 3DS MAX ® has a powerful interface for generating curves and free-form surfaces such as the mud-brick constructions of the citadel.

The site was surveyed before the earthquake and 2D architectural drawings as plans, section facades, and perspectives were available (Iranian Cultural Heritage, Handicraft and Tourism Organization materials). Several onsite photos were also available to help disambiguate interior spaces.

Therefore, we chose a multi-technique approach for 3D CG reconstitution. We exploited a 3-D photogrammetric map (which was made available to us under the Irano-French 3-D Cartographic Agreement on Bam (IFCA) and the Iranian National Cartographic Centre (NCC)) that had been reconstituted by Prof. Adle and his team from aerial photos of the citadel of Bam from 1994, as a basic resource to provide planar dimensions. We later used 2D drawings and photographs to complete a 3D model of the buildings both from the interior and exterior (Ono et al., 2008 b).

Our main decision was to find suitable case studies and to choose manual or automatic techniques of 3D CG modeling. Manual 3D CG modeling of destroyed buildings with the high degree of precision and the multi-technique approach we previously discussed is a time consuming and difficult task and needs accurate basic documents. Consequently, we needed to select the buildings carefully according to their architectural features.

3.2. Architecture of the citadel

We had to study the citadel's architectural style carefully to create a 3D CG reconstitution of it. The citadel was divided into three important sections of a district for the public and general inhabitants, an area for military buildings and residences, and the governor's district. These districts had different levels with different heights (of around 50 meters). There were various types of buildings in each district that were partly damaged or totally ruined after the earthquake.

The major architectural features of the citadel can be divided into six parts:

1. Surrounding Walls

There are five defensive walls that surround different sections of the citadel. The first and longest wall with an approximate length of 2000 meters embeds the whole citadel. The second wall separates the military and governor's district from the areas for the public. More than 40 watch towers divide the surrounding walls into shorter sections. There are embankments at both sides of the wall to strengthen its defensive functions. A moat was dug at the outer side of the wall to fortify the city.

The third, fourth, and fifth wall successively surround the governor's castle and were built in different centuries.

Figure 2. Architecture of citadel of Bam and its different types of buildings. Photographic credits: ICHHTO (top left, center, bottom center, and right) and NCC (top right and bottom left)

2. Gates (Entrances)

The citadel has only one main entrance gate that is located at the south side of the first defensive wall. This entrance has an octagonal small yard that is strongly fortified by watch towers. The second gate is located on the south side of the second defensive wall. A winding narrow path starts from the second gate, goes through the military buildings, and ends at the governor's castle. There are two old gates belonging to earlier centuries of the citadel that were closed by later defensive walls. The gates of the citadel are made of a vestibule that is protected by two adjacent defensive towers and guard rooms watching over the entrances.

3. General Populace Districts

There are nine districts in the citadel that were inhabited by ordinary people. These districts consist of one or more large complexes of houses and several other small ones that are separated by narrow streets. The houses are closed to the outside so mud-brick walls with entrances to houses can only be seen in the streets. Most of the large houses were restored before the quake and have an important architectural style for courtyard houses in the desert. However, the small houses are partly ruined and eroded and do not have distinguishable architectural forms. The borders of small houses are hardly visible and their shapes are vague. Before the earthquake they were not restored and left in ruins.

4. General Buildings

General buildings of the citadel that are used by the public are common to other types of Persian architecture. A bazaar starts from the main gate and divides the general populace district of the citadel into two sections. A mosque is located near the most important quarter of the citadel. A Madrasa or school and residences for pupils are located in front of the mosque. A ceremonial building with a large plaza called Tekiyeh is located beside the bazaar. Some caravanserais are located adjacent to the public buildings to accommodate outside travellers. These buildings were restored before the earthquake and have characteristic architectural features.

5. Military Buildings

The military facilities are located right after the second gate and defensive wall of the citadel. There is a stable that once had the capacity to house 200 horses with dwellings for superior officers. The military facilities also have barracks and a water well, a house for the commander, and a wind mill. They are a well-designed combination on the lower slope of the hill of the citadel.

6. Governor's District

This section has the most important monumental buildings of the citadel. There is a house for the governor with a spacious courtyard and vast Iwans overlook the whole city from the top of the hill. There is also a high square watch tower, the governor's bath, and a deep water well. The most important symbolic building is located on top of the citadel. It is a monument called the Four Seasons and it has a room with four archaic doorways facing north, south, east, and west. The governor could welcome his guests in this building and could show them the whole city in the south, the mountains in the north, and the palm gardens in the east and west. It might have had a regional purpose with such a unique architecture and spectacular views (as was mentioned in Section 1) in earlier periods.

3.3. Types of 3D CG modeling

According to our survey on the architectural characteristics of the citadel, the situation with the buildings after the quake struck, and the available material, we divided the citadel into three parts.

1. Less Important Areas

The general populace districts, which were the largest of the three areas, did not have a specific architectural form (as explained in Section 3.2 (3)) and the main documentation for them was in the form of aerial photographs. No precise 2D drawings were available and the 3D photogrammetric map could not be directly used to distinguish the architecture of the buildings. Therefore, manual 3D CG modeling of the site was not an appropriate method. A semi-automatic process with the help of a 3D photogrammetric map was tested simply an elevated plan and create areas filled with images of the district before the earthquake struck.

2. Moderately Important Areas

The surrounding walls of the citadel (as explained in Section 3.2 (1)) were the longest of the three areas; their documentation was similar to that of the less important areas but their architectural form could be better recognized. Manual 3D CG reconstruction of the wall was time consuming and unnecessary. Therefore, automatic 3D modeling was tested by giving volume to different sections of the wall along specific paths.

3. Very Important Areas

The general buildings, military buildings, and the governor's district (as explained in section 3.2 (2), (4), (5), (6)) were combined together in a complicated way over the slope and the hill of the citadel. Documentation for these buildings was available. Removing debris made it possible to measure their remaining walls, foundations, and vaults and assist the documents.

3D CG manual modeling of the buildings in this category was started in two major phases of research, from 2005 to 2007 and 2007 to the present, which will be discussed in the next section (Matini et al., 2008).

4. Manual 3D CG modeling of very important areas of the citadel

Manual 3D CG modeling of the citadel was primarily based on the documents surveyed before the earthquake. Several sources of architectural information were investigated as a first step and different types of data were collected. We prepared a manual 3D CG model of the most important buildings from 2005 to 2007 by directly applying heterogeneous data. We improved our method based on this experience and completed the 3D CG model of all very important areas of the citadel by using a CAD-based 3D drawing as a basic resource for 3D CG modeling. We will explain the processes and discuss their shortcomings in this section.

4.1. Heterogeneous data collection

We provided a database of heterogeneous information as a basic document for 3D CG restitution of the citadel. Although 2D architectural drawings of some of the buildings' plans, sections, and facades were available, they were not precise. Due to the irregular shapes of the mud-brick structures and application of traditional methods of construction such as arch-and-vaults or domes, the surveyed drawings had errors or contained insufficient information. Therefore, we investigated other resources, specifically images. Immediately after the earthquake struck, we made a call for participation over the Internet and collected several photographs of the citadel taken by tourists from around the world on our website (http://dsr.nii.ac.jp/bam/index.html.en). The photo-database was completed with resources provided by organizations such as ICHHTO, NCC, and NHK. These resources included onsite, satellite, and aerial photographs. However, the photos were mostly low resolution, too many of them were of popular views, and very few images were of private buildings or residential districts. There was also a lack of images of interior spaces, no data were related to settings on cameras, and no photos were available from metric cameras.

Aerial photos were complementary data for creating the 3-D models, which were taken over seven different years (the first dating from 50 years ago), and those with a scale of more than 1: 2000 were provided by the National Cartography Centre and Digital Globe. These photos revealed the changing situation with the citadel during the last 50 years. In fact, we recognized three different periods before 1971 in which the citadel had been abandoned and suffered damage from nearby human habitation; the citadel was partially restored from 1971 to 1993. The citadel underwent massive reconstruction as one of five large ICHTO projects from 1993 to 2003.

We decided to reconstitute the citadel virtually to the physical form it had right before the earthquake struck in 2003.

Figure 3. Heterogeneous data are needed for 3D CG reconstruction of citadel of Bam.

On-site images (top: 1st and 2nd from left), aerial photo (top: 3rd from left), 3D photogrammetric map (top: 1st from right), sketch (middle: 1st from left), on-site image after quake (bottom: 1st from left), 3D CG rendered image (bottom: 1st from right).

We made several sketches of different spaces within the citadel to find the original shapes of missing spaces such as interiors or details after questioning experts who had worked there before the earthquake struck, especially about the shapes of vaulted ceilings and roofs. This method was practical specifically for interior spaces with no records of documentation (as shown for 3D of ceiling of the north middle room of Sistani House, big yard in figure 3).

One major document was 3D photogrammetric restitution of the citadel (IFCA project) using aerial photos of the citadel dating back to 1994. The 3D photogrammetric map helped us to correct errors in 2D architectural drawings, to ascertain building heights and dome shapes, and specifically to locate every building at the site by using a *Universal Transverse Mercator* (UTM) system (Ono et al., 2008b).

Figure 4. Application of 3D photogrammetric map (IFCA project of prof. Adle and NCC) for adjustment of 3D model (top: 1st from left), adjustment of height of tower of stable, white lines are 3D photogrammetric map. (top: 2rd from left), extraction of counter lines of the domes of roof of Four season monument, (top: 1st from right), adjustment of shape of slopes of the hill from topographic lines (bottom: 1st and 2nd), adjustment and extrude of counter lines of ordinary houses.

We watched every available video of the citadel in parallel with the map and took snapshots from the videos and processed the extracted images specifically to reduce contrast and darkness, and we used the images to disambiguate details of interiors or decorations as no photos were available. We studied different textual resources about the history and architecture of the citadel of Bam to support semantic annotations of the buildings, and to support conceptual representations of 3D CG modeling.

4.2. 3D CG modeling by direct application of heterogeneous data

3D CG modeling was started by using two buildings featured at the citadel: the main gate and the Four Seasons monument (by the Waseda University team). Five major public buildings, each of a different type were added to the work (by the University of Tehran and Razahang teams). Teams of 3D CG modelers simultaneously used different types of data for the first phase of manual 3D modeling. However, the lack of precise 2D drawings for many of the citadel's buildings made it necessary to use heterogeneous data directly in 3D CG modeling. Such data can help the team to find more information about the spaces to be modeled, but it is not always easy to use.

The CG modelers used the heterogeneous data by themselves to model the seven buildings in 3D. They followed a two-step process:

4. They superimposed the 2D drawings onto the 3D photogrammetric map, corrected the dimensions of the plans, adjusted the heights, and completed details such as the shapes of domes on the roof (which were precise in the 3D photogrammetric map)
5. They extracted several missing details on the facades and interior spaces by acquiring the geometry and proportions from on-site or aerial photos and corrected the 3D models.

This process required high levels of expertise in both architecture and 3D modeling. Applying the two types of data simultaneously led to confusion regarding domain knowledge on the part of the CG modelers, because they were not familiar with traditional Persian architecture.

To ensure the resulting 3D models were precise, we checked carefully the models provided in this stage.

4.2.1. Systematic 3D CG modeling in different layers

A layer management strategy was proposed to name each component of a 3D model on the basis of the component's type, its location, and the resources used for 3D modeling. We devised a simple methodology similar to morphology by defining affixes to name different layers as a single string. A prefix was designed to indicate the type of building. An infix specified the data type that was used for 3D modeling such as architectural maps (plans, façades, and sections), 3D photogrammetric maps, photos, movies, and sketches. A suffix was defined to show a building component or an architectural element and its location as an interior or exterior part.

The layer manager in MAX® is a function for organizing and managing objects in complex scenes. Each layer has some attributes such as colour. Semantic layer management of the 3D models of the citadel of Bam provided a systematic model with several advantages. The supervising team could turn the layers on or off and analyze the components of the 3-D model, or it could make one or more layers transparent (by changing the 'opacity' of the component in the 'material editor' function of MAX®) and check the correctness of the rear of the target component. As each layer could have a different colour, it was easy to recognize when the components of the 3-D model interfered with one another. The user could also search inside the 3-D models to retrieve specific components according to the layer management metadata.

The most important advantage of layer management is during the process of merging individual 3D models into a unified one. Our final output to reconstruct very important areas with 3D CG consisted of at least 25 models that were prepared by different teams. The 3D CG modeling tool had default-layer naming and if a layer-naming system had not been implemented, the components of the models would have had similar layer names and errors would have occurred. We merged the 3D models with correct coordinates of the UTM system for each building without error on a ground surface model extracted from a 3D photogrammetric map with this method (Ono et al., 2008b).

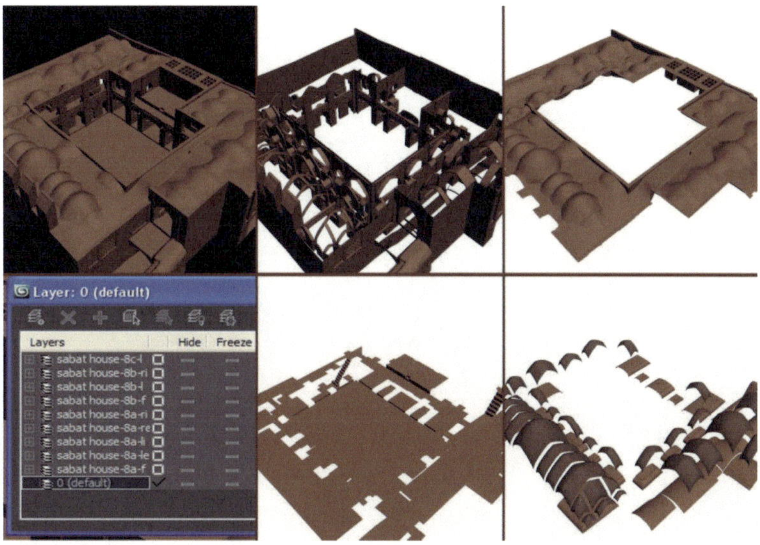

Figure 5. Implementation of layer management system for 3D model of Four Seasons monument

4.2.2. Quality control of 3D CG models

Quality control on the 3D models was carried out to ensure the 3D reconstruction process was correct. The scale of 3Ds was unified and the geometric coordinates of the elements and their correct positions within the citadel as a whole were specified. The initial 3D models that were developed by the team of CG experts were evaluated to identify incomplete parts or components with errors. The interior spaces, vaulted ceilings, or ornaments had problems due to a lack of accurate 2D drawings. Therefore, the architecture for the 3D models was controlled by analytically interpreting relics using the heterogeneous resources in the following categories:

6. Architectural
a. Superimposition of different architectural drawings

We superimposed plans of different levels of selected buildings, facades, and sections, and compared them with 3D models. Displacements were found that confused the modelers about the dimensions of walls on the ground and first floor, the alignment of load-bearing walls over each other at different levels, and the heights of towers. We merged 3D models with a 3D photogrammetric map based on some reference points. The correct measurements of heights and exterior borders of buildings were marked and reported.

b. Comparison with photos, sketches based on oral explanations by experts, and videos

The complicated architecture of the citadel had missing details in the 2D drawings. The exact shapes of arches, details on decorations, and correct forms for the domed surfaces of roofs were major errors in the 3D models. Photos had to be used to disambiguate the details. We tried to extract as much information as possible from the photos using scalable components such as human scale. We made a library of traditional Persian arches common to the architecture of the citadel and gave the 3D modelers drawing instructions.

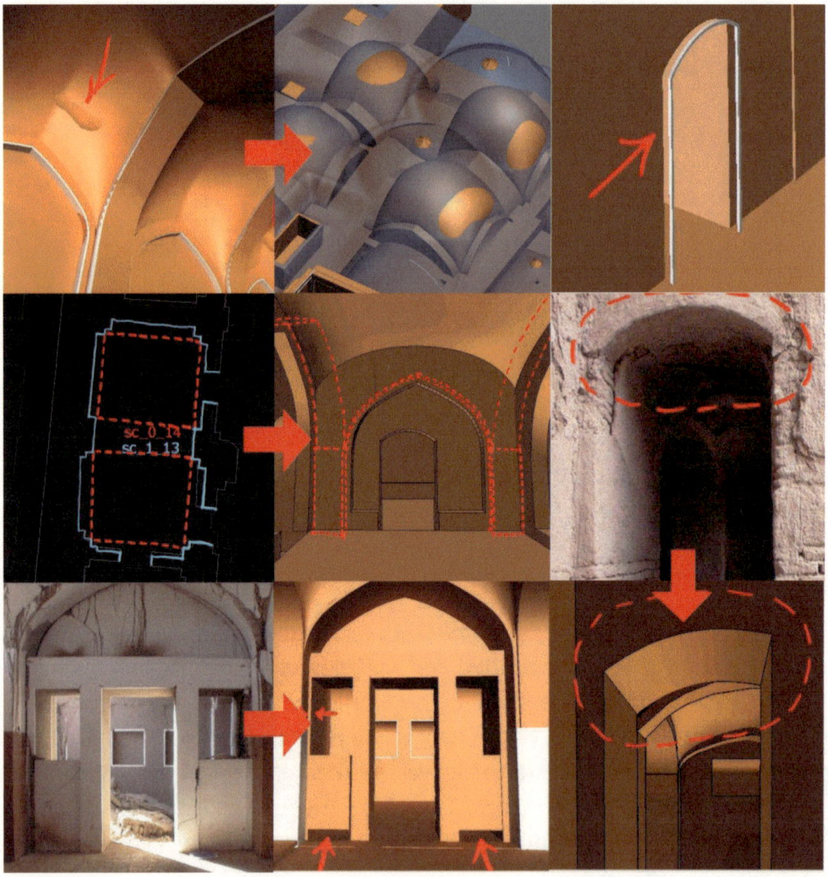

Figure 6. Errors in technical 3D CG models during first phase of project

c. Comparison with similar styles of construction

Of the different components of 3D models, the interior spaces of less well known buildings had the least basic information and contained errors. We tried to compare the geometry of the spaces with other similar spaces inside the citadel or inside the city of Bam and found similar styles. This method was specifically useful for interior vaults. The aerial photos were helpful to deduce the locations of walls and styles of coverings. Specific instructions were provided for modeling and reporting the most well-known vaults in the citadel. The instructions included simple models of the details of ornaments such as chalk bands around vaults and columns or brick-work decorations.

7. Technical 3D CG modeling

a. Selection of suitable surface modeling technique

We selected Auto CAD ® and 3ds Max ® from the different tools available for 3D CG modeling for our work. These tools have different functions and can cover different applications. AutoCAD provided a coordinated environment to draw precise lines and dimensions. Therefore, 2D drawings were first matched together to form initial 3D drawings of extruding solid surfaces of walls with this tool. However, problems started with 3D modeling of the free-form surfaces of the adobe of the citadel.

There were insufficient 3D meshes that were formed between four-sided volumes in the tool. Although newer versions (AutoCAD 2012 ®) are empowered with more sophisticated surface modeling such as *non-uniform rational basis* (NURB) splines, the 3D modeling that was started with the tools in 2005 had shortcomings for our purposes. Therefore, several initial drawings were imported from AutoCAD ® to 3ds Max ® for modeling.

As the process had errors with some surfaces, specifically the meshes of vaults, the modeling of ceilings, vaults, roofs, and details were started from scratch with the 3ds Max ® tool. The tool provided different methods of surface modeling where each was suitable for particular forms. We proposed mesh surfaces for barrel or cloister vaults that had four specific sides that were symmetric. Roofs or non-geometric surfaces of the ground were modeled by using polygons or NURBs. These two allowed a case-by-case approach to modeling to fill in all the surveyed geometries and the surfaces of arched vaults or roofs as each room of the buildings was different in its own way.

b. Selection of proper level of details

3D CG modeling of the buildings inside the citadel of Bam with a one-to-one scale of details needed every detail of one centimetre or less to be precisely reconstituted. Modeling adobe architecture with tools such as 3ds MAX ® was like digitally rebuilding a site from mud; soft and curved surfaces of mud brick needed high levels of detail of their surfaces. This made the models heavy, which will be a problem when all models are merged and rendering is carried out. We checked the size of meshes or polygon details and the geometry of intersecting solids or surfaces to optimize the level of details and avoid unnecessary large size files.

c. Control of adjacency of 3D components

Seams between components, e.g., at the joints between facades and interior spaces, interference by 3D solid parts, such as ceilings with exterior walls, chalk decorations with mud brick walls, and similar errors, were evident and checked in the 3D models. Layer management helped us to separate different components such as walls, roofs, and ceilings and check their adjacencies and report the errors (Matini, Ono, 2010).

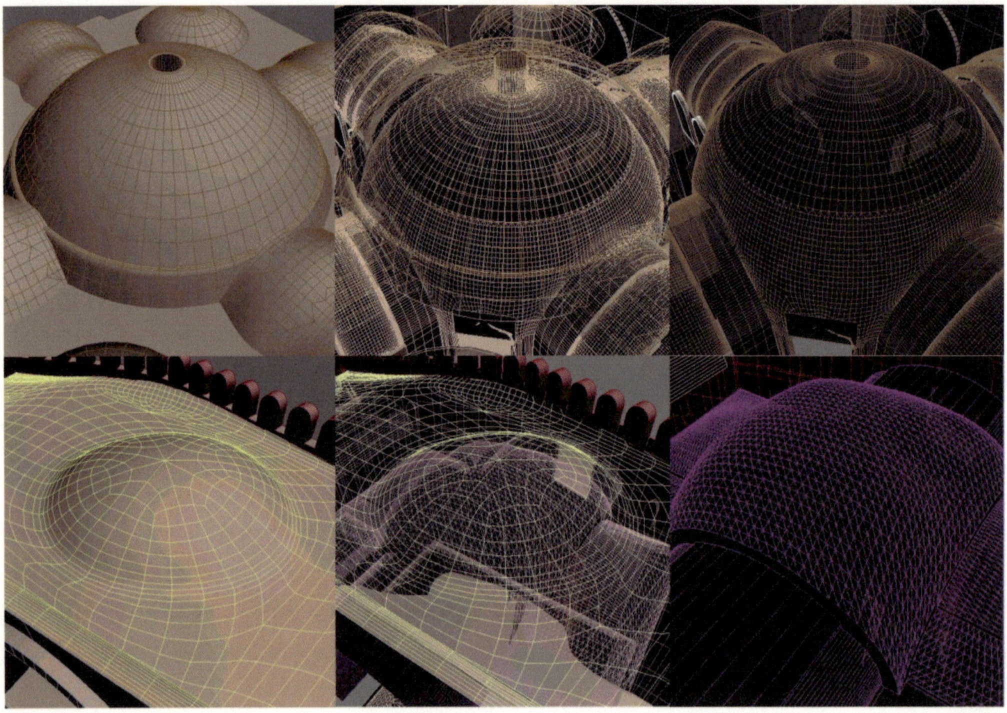

Figure 7. Different methods of surface modeling for ceiling and roofs in citadel of Bam (outer surface of roof and inner surface of ceiling below it are showed)

4.2.3. Evaluation reports

According to the quality control specified above, we took snapshots of the errors and compared them with our data by using knowledge on the geometry, proportions, structure, and scale of the adobe buildings. From 2005 to 2007, during which the first phase of 3D modeling of the seven buildings was almost completed, we evaluated the 3D models of all buildings during the development phase at least three times and identified between 100 and 200 errors (architectural and technical) each time that needed to be modified. We also provided evaluation reports to ask for corrections and also organized meetings and discussions with the modelers. Hundreds of pages of questions for evaluation were prepared and sent to different teams of CG modelers (Waseda University, Prof. Kawai's laboratory in Tokyo, the University of Tehran, Prof. Einifar's laboratory in Tehran, ENSAPVS, Prof. Bouet and Prof. Dell's laboratory of EVCAU in Paris).

The errors were carefully observed by the CG modelers and corrected. They provided answers to the corrected errors and created the final results for the first phase for the seven buildings with the best possible precision.

4.3. 3D modeling by CAD-based 3D drawings as basic resources

The correction process for the first phase of 3D modeling was complicated. Several problems resulted from the modelers' application of heterogeneous data and their corrections took a great deal of effort. Sometimes remodeling was easier than making modifications to some errors.

To solve this problem in the second phase of the project (beginning October 2007), we developed CAD-based 3D technical drawing as a unified method of basically drawing the citadel. The drawing was developed in a sequential modification process using the domain knowledge and contribution of architectural experts. They could comprehend the chronology and the original shapes of the mud-brick buildings.

First, an initial drawing for the interior spaces was developed from 2D drawings. In some cases, we surveyed the remains after the earthquake struck, but in many cases no measurable remains were available and only 2D drawings surveyed before the earthquake were used. Later, the 3D photogrammetric map was directly used as an initial drawing for exterior borders of the buildings, roofs, and heights. Initial 3D drawings were adjusted and completed through a number of different modification steps. One architectural aspect of the model was evaluated in each step and modified by applying one or more heterogeneous data items. The modifications were made sequentially rather than simultaneously to avoid confusion and the possibility of missing important features. The modifications comprised geometrical, structural, and proportional changes and the adding of details, which are discussed below.

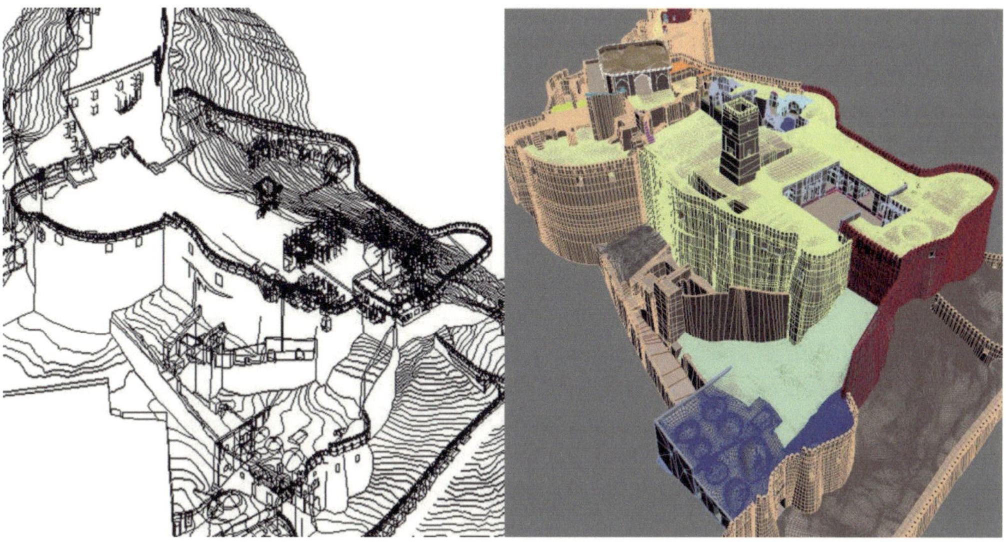

Figure 8. CAD-based 3D drawing as basic resource for 3D CG modeling of governor's section and 3D model

8. Geometrical Modifications

The incomplete parts of the 3D models that were identified during the first phase of the project were mostly from spaces without information, specifically interiors. Geometrical features of an architectural element helped us to sketch and modify these spaces.

For example, the shape of the roof visible in aerial photos can specify the geometry of an interior ceiling or location of a wall. Shadow and light visible on the floor or wall in a photo can reveal architectural elements such as windows. A symmetric space can help to mirror an available section. Similarities between components such as niches can also help to identify the shapes of missing parts of the 3D models.

9. Structural Modifications

Traditional adobe buildings have limited features of construction. Load-bearing walls are covered by specific types of roof systems such as barrel-vault, cloister-vault, or arch-vault types of covering. However, adobe has less resistance as a material than brick, and the domes or vaults might not be completely symmetric; minor changes can also be found in different centuries of construction such as the shapes of arches and the heights of domes.

The height of interior ceilings was one of the most serious problems in the drawings. Measurements based on the 2D drawings were insufficient and some ribs of ceilings reached outside the surface of the roof in the 3D models.

The outer surface of the roof was modeled in this stage by using the 3D photogrammetric map. As the domes were not symmetric, two orthogonal splines were drawn for the curvature of the domes. Therefore, the style for the roofing structure was extracted, and the thickness of the ribs or vaults was determined (around 12 cm for vaults and 32 cm for arches). Finally, the surface of the ceiling was modeled.

This process needed an on-site survey. Some vaults were not completely destroyed and could be measured after the quake. Some portions of the vaults or arches were surveyed after debris was removed from the citadel and the 3D drawings were correctly completed based on structural features.

10. Proportional Features and Details

Traditional Persian buildings have specific module of dimension that specifies their proportions. For example the span of a doorway, 103 cm, is a module that controls the proportions of rooms. Therefore heights, angles, spans, thicknesses, and other parameters were drawn in a wireframe model according to extracted proportions. Photos were primary resources to make proportional modifications. Unfortunately, we could not find a metric photo to provide a rectified image and directly take measurements from photos. However, we could use some functions of the MAX ® tool such as camera matching, and could find approximate perspectives for scenes. Then, scalable parts in scenes, such as floor tiles and the human scale could be identified and the approximate proportion of whole scenes could be extracted; as a result, the geometry of 3D drawings could be completed. This method was helpful specifically for details such as niches, columns and chalk band decorations.

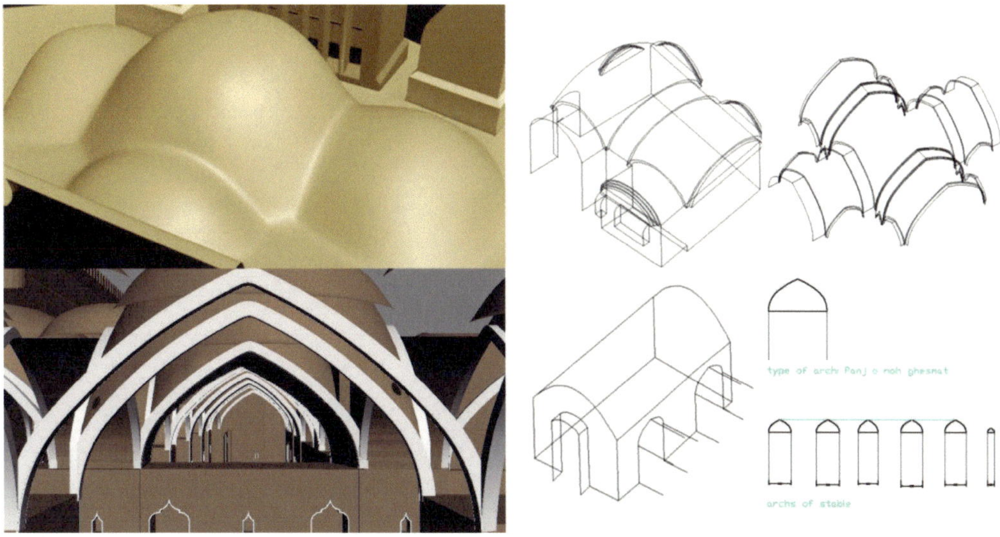

Figure 9. Geometric and structural modifications to make the wire frame of the ceiling and the roof and complete the 3D CG modeling

CAD-Based 3D drawing, which was prepared by complementary application of heterogeneous data, had detailed specifications on the architecture of the citadel. The whole governor's section, surrounding walls, second and old gates, and other complicated spaces of the citadel located on Bam's hills were completed with this method. 3D drawings were easily imported into the 3ds Max® environment and completed by 3D modelers who had little domain knowledge. They imported DWG files into 3ds Max®. Their task was only to define suitable faces between the borders of 3D drawing lines. This reduced the amount of synthesis they needed to do for the original shapes, especially for arches, vaults, domes, and the proportions of niches. In most cases, the lines were given for all details and the only challenge was to choose proper surface modeling or a proper modifier from a large number of tool options, such as polygons or NURBS for cloister vaults and meshes for barrel vaults. We used this method to finish the modeling of 20 buildings and several defensive walls of the citadel between 2007 and 2010 (Matini, et al., 2008).

5. Key results

The results for the 3D CG manual reconstruction of the citadel of Bam demonstrated that we finished 3D modeling of every building in areas of great importance that had been restored and made safe before the earthquake. For moderate or less accurate areas, we tested methods of automating the modeling process to reduce the time and cost required for reconstruction. One method that was proposed for semi-automatic modeling was to refine the photogrammetric map toward the 3D models of unimportant buildings and paste texture from tourist photographs onto the models (Kitamoto et al., 2011).

Figure 10. Results for 3D CG reconstitution of very important buildings of citadel of Bam

5.1. Bam 3D CG ontology driven website

We presented our visual output data as rendered images, Quick Time Virtual Reality (QTVR) videos, or walkthrough videos as part of the conceptual process of our project on the Bam3DCG Website (http://dsr.nii.ac.jp/Bam3DCG/). In comparison to the architectural process, conceptual modeling is about representing our knowledge of cultural heritage by defining the semantic relationship between knowledge of the domain and output data. Since we were dealing with heterogeneous data, the data needed to be explained with semantic annotations linked to various concepts associated with the data. We developed the Bam 3DCG ontology-based Website for this purpose.

To acquire the semantics of the citadel of Bam, we designed an ontology knowledge model called Bam 3D CG ontology using three major schemas: a metadata-based schema, which was conceptualized using different metadata standards, a referencing-based schema, which provided the location or bibliographic attributes such as a historical summary of each building from different travelogues or historic references), and a lexical-based schema, which provided terminological specifications for every building in the citadel.

Every piece of information, or visual output data, is an entity connected to other entities by semantic links in this ontology designed using the Protégé knowledge acquisition tool as a Resource Description Framework (RDF) file. These links are descriptive attributes of entities. Each homogeneous group of information is hierarchically categorized in classes with subclasses.

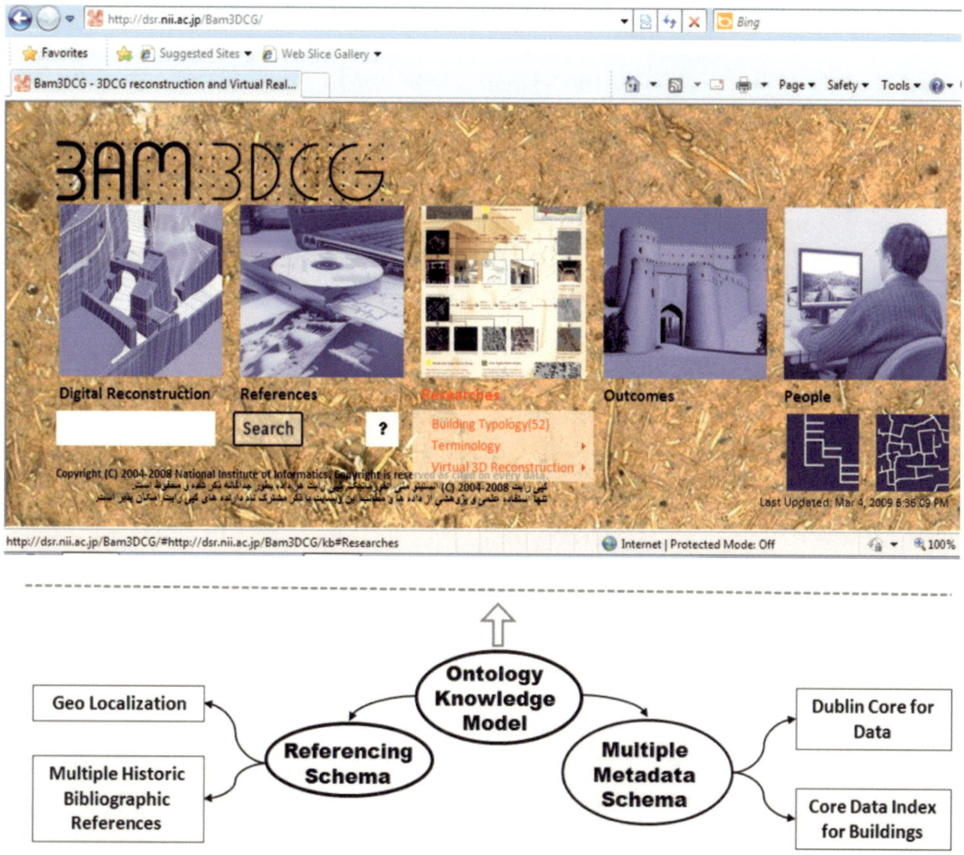

Figure 11. Architecture of Bam 3D CG ontology driven Website

We selected the Core Data Index to Historic Buildings and Monuments of the Architectural Heritage (Thornes, Bold, 1998), which was part of the Object ID standard to describe the attributes of the buildings (such as name, location, date, material, etc.). We used the Dublin Core Metadata Element Set, which is a standard vocabulary of fifteen properties for use in resource descriptions to describe and catalogue visual data that consisted of photos, videos, architectural drawings, and sketches. The multilingual lexical schema of the ontology provides the semantics of all buildings in different languages. We designed a Website generation and maintenance system to browse the RDF graph created on Protégé so that people could browse knowledge bases using a standard Web browser.

Bam 3D CG displays rendered snapshots, QTVR, or walkthrough videos of the 3D models of different buildings, photos of them before the earthquake, and their geo-referencing by using the UTM system on satellite photos. Their names are provided in five languages with the date, physical condition, and material of each building, the history of the buildings from multiple references, people that contributed to the 3D CG process, and several other data. The Website also renders maps of buildings on the satellite photos of sites that enable users to gain access to building information (Andaroodi, Kitamoto, 2010).

5.2. Virtual reality demonstration

We represented QTVR videos of the virtual citadel on the Bam 3D CG Website, which allowed users to look at different directions with variable resolution. However, the interactivity offered by Quicktime VR was limited, because users could not move from the camera location to another point. A more advanced mechanism is to use a virtual reality system for real-time rendering. We presented the Bam 3D CG reconstruction as part of a virtual reality (VR) demonstration. The VR space of the completed 3D CG models is intended to be the basis for future restoration work.

The space was built using the OmegaSpace VR presentation software developed by Solidray Co., Ltd. OmegaSpace is also space construction software that enables real-time rendering in a PC environment and can be used in various fields. It can also be extended to a cyberspace type of system on a network, allowing two or more users to simultaneously use a single VR file. This enables the VR space to be shared and cooperative work to be done in it.

The model was output in VRML form with coordinate information to create a VR file and was read into OmegaSpace. The model was lit arbitrarily and two or more cameras were set up in each building. The walk-through was done by switching cameras with a joystick. We also added a collision-detection mechanism to prevent the operator from walking into walls and other objects in the model.

The VR demonstration enabled users to interact with computer-simulated spaces and walk virtually inside the buildings displayed on the screen. This might be the only chance for them to discover the heritage of Bam. We used a Z-800 3D Visor head-mounted display to test the effectiveness of the VR technology for our model.

The preliminary VR demonstration was presented in a workshop that was held at the citadel of Bam in September 2006. The open house at NII in June 2007 also held a virtual tour inside the digitally restored citadel. A virtual demonstration was broadcast by NHK in its 'SOS from World Heritage' program in May 2006. The VR demonstration revived buildings of the citadel of Bam, which are now impossible to visit in the real world (Ono et al., 2008b).

Figure 12. Test of virtual reality demonstration in Bam 3D CG Reconstruction

The main limitation of the VR system is that users need to go to places where special devices are available. It may be useful for specific exhibitions, but this is not a good solution for the general public. The best solution is to build a system on the Internet where users can interactively navigate through the 3D model at any time from any place with a browser.

The simplest solution available is to use a virtual reality modeling language (VRML) version of the 3D models online so anyone with a VRML browser can download the data and interactively render the 3D model. We could not use this method as free distribution of data was not considered. The ideal solution is to protect the original model on the server side, and only transfer the rendered output to the client side in an interactive manner in real-time. We are now seeking a solution to fulfil this idea (Kitamoto et al, 2011).

6. Conclusion

The 3D CG reconstruction of the citadel of Bam was a post-disaster effort to virtually revive large adobe structures after its destruction in the earthquake. We investigated several techniques to create a 3D CG reconstitution of the site. 3D CG manual modeling was our best solution as the site had been destroyed and direct techniques of measurement could not be applied. We used a photogrammetric 3D map that was reconstituted from aerial photographs as a basic resource (IFCA project). We added several other heterogeneous data such as on-site photos, videos, and sketches to complete knowledge of the original shapes of the buildings.

We collaborated with various 3D modeling teams as part of an academic-research effort. There were two phases of 3D modeling to reconstitute all extremely important buildings in the citadel. First, the CG modelers directly used heterogeneous data for 3D modeling. Unfortunately, the initial data were more incomplete than we expected, and several spaces were ambiguous in form. The work of 3D modelers was controlled several times to create a precise 3D model and 10 buildings were completed from 2005 to 2007.

Later, we developed CAD-based 3D drawings as basic resources in the second phase by gradually implementing the heterogeneous data. The modelers used 3D drawings as basic resources and just defined faces between lines to complete the 3D model. This second phase lasted till 2009 and more than 20 buildings were reconstructed in the citadel. We represented our results at a conceptual level on an ontology-based Website. The output was several rendered images, QTVR, and walkthrough videos. Data were linked with knowledge of the buildings and represented their history, material, and locations.

The virtual reality (VR) demonstrations of the reconstructed buildings were presented inside the OmegaSpace tool, and were viewed with an HMD in 3D by several visitors of buildings that had been destroyed and did not exist in the real world.

Our future work is to complete 3D CG reconstruction by automatically or semi-automatically generating less important areas of the citadel such as its surrounding walls or residential districts.

We investigated ways of building a system on the Internet where users could interactively navigate through a 3D model of the citadel with a browser at any time through an online Virtual Reality system.

The Citadel of Bam is under physical reconstruction now but several locations such as the Governor Section have suffered serious damages and it seems to be very difficult to physically restore them. Our Virtual Reconstruction is the only chance for the visitors to view the site. Therefore a VR theatre that is constructed in the site beside the Citadel can provide the chance for the visitors to see the heritage in its original shape before the earthquake. The 3D stereoscopic image that is provided by a 3D projector and viewed on a wide screen in a VR theatre can present a better 3D stereoscopic presentation effect and help the visitors to experience a high quality three dimensional walkthrough inside the heritage.

Another application is to provide an Augmented Reality (AR) presentation of the site with different tools. The visitors can experience the destroyed heritage and the 3D CG reconstructed images provided by AR system at the same time and compare them together.

Different VR or AR presentation systems of the destroyed heritage that is reconstructed by 3D CG techniques are the key applications to revive the site virtually and to preserve it for future generation.

Author details

Elham Andaroodi and Mohammad Reza Matini
University of Tehran, Iran

Kinji Ono
National Institute of Informatics,Japan

Acknowledgement

The 3DCG reconstruction and virtual reality of the citadel of Bam was a collaborative research project between the Iranian Cultural Heritage and Tourism Organization (ICHTO), the DSR project of the National Institute of Informatics (NII) and the University of Tehran's Faculty of Architecture. The 3D photogrammetric map was provided by the Irano-French Cartographic Agreement (IFCA) of CNRS of France and NCC of Iran led by Prof. Chahryar Adle.

The authors would like to express their sincere gratitude to Prof. Alireza Einifar from the University of Tehran's Faculty of Architecture, and Mr. Alireza Einifar from the Razahang Architectural Firm for supervising and 3D CG modeling the six case studies in the first phase and the other 3D models in the second phase of the project. We would like to extend our thanks to Prof. Asanobu Kitamoto of NII, Prof. Takashi Kawai of GITI, Prof. Olivier Bouet of EVCAU, and Prof. Eskandar Mokhtari of the Bam Recovery Office.

We are also grateful to the other contributors who provided us with photos, movies, and documents related to Bam especially Mr. Ryoichi Ogane (NHK) and Ms. Chihiro Ohkubo. Special thanks go to the CG modelers, Messrs. Human Kian-Ersi, Pouya Khosro Jerdi, Morteza Hengofti, Nobuaki Abe, Ha Young Yoon, and Ms. Vida Gholipour. Special thanks also go to Mr. Benoit Guillou, Ms. Sahar Ghaderi, and Messrs. Majid Bequali, Tiago Da Silva, Natchapon Futragoon, and Ms. Xining Chen. We would also like to thank Mr. Tomohiro Ikezaki for implementing the Bam3DCG Website generation system. The ontology was developed using the Protégé open-source Knowledge Acquisition Tool.

7. References

Aarmaanshahr, Architecture and Urbanism Consulting Engineers. (1993). *Studies of the master plan of Bam region and Bam city, volume 1*. Ministry of Housing and Urban Planning, General Office of Kerman Province. Kerman

Andaroodi, E. & Kitamoto, A. (2010). Architectural Heritage Online: Ontology-Driven Website Generation for World Heritage Sites in Danger. *Proceeding of the Digital Heritage, Third International Conference, EuroMed 2010. Lecture Notes in Computer Science*, 6436, ISSN: 0302-9743, Cyprus, November 2010

Aasefi Heravi, A.H. M. (1964). *Seljuqs and Ghaz in Kerman*. Tahouri. Tehran

Adle, C. (2004). Oldest Qanat System in Iran Was Discovered. Cultural Heritage News Agency. Date of access 2012/03/10. Available from: http://www.chn.ir/News/?section=2&id=9252

Ahmadi, N. (2008). Pottery dated back 5,000 years were discovered in the Citadel of Bam after removal of debris. Cultural Heritage News Agency. Date of access 2012/03/10. Available from:http://www.chn.ir/news/?Section=2&id=47372

Ataai, M.T. & Ahmadi, N. & Zare, Sh. (2006). the area of Bam and Baravat was inhabited during the Achaemenid and Parthian periods Cultural Heritage News Agency. Date of access 2012/03/10. Available from: http://www.chn.ir/News/?section=2&id=35866

Cyark. (March 2012). Available from:http://archive.cyark.org/

Dublin Core Metadata Element Set. (March 2012) Available from: http://dublincore.org/documents/dces/

Ferdowsi, A. (1974). *Shahnameh, volumn 5*. Pocket Book Co. Tehran.

Grün, A.& Remondino, F. & Zhang, Li (2004). Photogrammetric reconstruction of the Great Buddha of Bamiyan, Afghanistan. *The Photogrammetric Record*, Volume 19, Issue 107, (September 2004), pp. 177-199. Online ISSN: 1477-9730.

Ibn HAWQAL, M.A.K. (1966). *Surat-al-Ardh*. Cultural Foundation of Iran. Tehran.

International Council on Monuments and Sites. (March 2012). Available from: www.international.icomos.org/charters/charters.pdf

International Scientific Committee for Documentation of Cultural Heritage. (March 2012). Available from:http://cipa.icomos.org/

Kacyra,B. (2011). Ancient Wonders Captured in 3D. *TEDGlobal*. (March 2012). Available from: http://www.ted.com/talks/ben_kacyra_ancient_wonders_captured_in_3d.html

Kitamoto, A. & Andaroodi, E. & Matini, M. & Ono, K. (2011). Post-Disaster Reconstruction of Cultural Heritage: Citadel of Bam, Iran. *Proceeding of IPSJ SIG Computers and the Humanities Symposium*, Kyoto, December 2011.

Mehryar, M. (2004). *The History of the Citadel of Bam*. Iranian Cultural Heritage and Tourism Organization, Tehran.

Matini, M. R. & Andaroodi, E. & Kitamoto, A. & Ono, K. (2008). Development of CAD-based 3D Drawing as a Basic Resource for Digital Reconstruction of Bam's Citadel (UNESCO World Heritage), *Proceeding of Conference on Virtual Systems and Multimedia Dedicated to Digital Heritage (VSMM-Full papers)*. ISBN: 978-963-8046-99-4, Cyprus, October 2008

Matini, M. R. & Ono, K. (2010). Accuracy Verification of Manual 3D CG Reconstruction: Case Study of Destroyed Architectural Heritage, Bam Citadel. *Proceeding of the Digital Heritage, Third International Conference, EuroMed 2010, Lecture Notes in Computer Science*, 6436, ISSN: 0302-9743, Cyprus, November 2010

Nourbakhsh, H. (1974). *Arg-e-Bam and a Summary of the History of Urbanism in Iran* , Cultural Heritage Documentation Center, Tehran

Omega Space ®. (March 2012). Available from: http://www.solidray.co.jp/product/omega/index.html

Ono, K. & Kitamoto, A. & Andaroodi, E. & Onishi, M. & Nishimura, Y. & Matini, M.R. (2008). Memory of the Silk Road -The Digital Silk Road Project. *Proceeding of the Conference on Virtual Systems and Multimedia Dedicated to Digital Heritage (VSMM-Project papers)*, Cyprus, October 2008

Ono, K. & Andaroodi, E.& Matini, M.R.& Einifar, A.& Abe, N.& Kawai, T. & Kitamoto, A & Bouet, O & Chopin, F. & Mokhtari, E. & Einifar, S. (2008). 3DCG Reconstitution and Virtual Reality of UNESCO World Heritage in Danger: the Citadel of Bam. *Journal of Progress in Informatics*. 5th issue. (March 2008). pp. 99-135. Print ISSN: 1349-8614 , Online ISSN : 1349-8606

Tayari, H. (2005). *The Citadel of Bam.* Bam Recovery Office, Iranian Cultural Heritage, Handicraft and Tourism Organization, Tehran

Thornes, R. & Bold, J. Documenting the Cultural Heritage (1998). The J. Paul Getty Trust. 1998. (March 2012). Available from: http://archives.icom.museum/object-id/heritage/index.html

United Nations Educational Scientific and Cultural Organization [UNESCO], World Heritage Centre [WHC]. List of World Heritage in Danger. (March 2012). Available from: http://whc.unesco.org/en/danger

Vaziri Kermani, A. (1967), *Geography of Kerman*. Scientific Publisher. Tehran

Chapter 13

Fun Computing

Kazunori Miyata

Additional information is available at the end of the chapter

http://dx.doi.org/10.5772/51043

1. Introduction

Initially, the main applications of virtual reality (VR) included various walkthroughs with real-time graphics. At present, VR applications have been extended to various fields including telecommunications, training, scientific exploration, collaborative work activities, and entertainment. In particular, in the entertainment field, not only VR but also mixed reality (MR) and augmented reality (AR) technologies are actively used for human–machine interfaces in application building. For example, a number of major amusement parks operate amazing VR rides, and numerous museum exhibits have interactive installations using VR/MR/AR technologies.

In addition, the factor of entertainment is currently adopted in education and skill development applications. LEGO® mindstorms® provides an excellent learning environment for engineering and programming subjects. It promotes self-learning of basic computing logic and machinery mechanisms while having fun. The term "edutainment" is used to indicate video games that teach players by a game-based learning approach. For example, players can learn about a historical background by playing simulation games such as *Civilization* and *Nobunaga's Ambition*. Serious games are developed as educational tools and mainly focus on teaching rather than entertaining. Gamification is a framework used to apply game design methods to nongame matters. Foursquare, which is a location-based SNS, is an example of gamification. Concerning rehabilitation, there are many computer-based programs that encourage rehabilitation while playing games or singing songs along with hand gestures.

The common theme among such programs is "motivation." Motivation is the reason why people act or behave in a particular manner[1]. It is important to determine the method to motivate people faced with a tedious task or those unwilling to work. "The Fun Theory[2]"

[1] from Oxford English Dictionary
[2] http://www.thefuntheory.com/

holds that something as simple as "fun" is the easiest way to change people's behavior for the better. For example, the "Piano Staircase" project installed a giant piano keyboard covering the stairs leading out of a subway station in Stockholm. This keyboard plays a note when people step on it. As a result, people soon preferred going up and down the stairs while making music rather than using the escalator. An objective test revealed that 66% more people than normal chose the stairs over the escalator. Consequently, the element of fun rather than words changed people behavior for the better.

For its part, "Fun Computing" is a coined term that means the use of media technology to entertain people. Fun computing may motivate people to engage in more physical activity or perform burdensome work in a fun manner.

2. Media interaction

Unlike physical simulations and mathematical computations, the design of an interactive system is indirect, sensuous, and fuzzy because human behavior is involved.

2.1. Interaction

Computer-based media, also known as digital media, are characterized as interactive media. People can freely access, edit, and share digital media content through computers. According to the AIP cube model proposed by Zelter [1], interaction is an essential factor of VR. Interaction is a process-related communication feature. In computer science, "interaction" is interpreted as two-way communication in which a system reacts to the user's action and the user reacts to system response, as illustrated in Figure 1.

In computer science, interactivity can be quantitatively measured as follows:

1. How quickly does the system respond to user input (speed)?
2. How accurate is the system output (accuracy)?
3. How many reaction variations does the system provide (richness)?

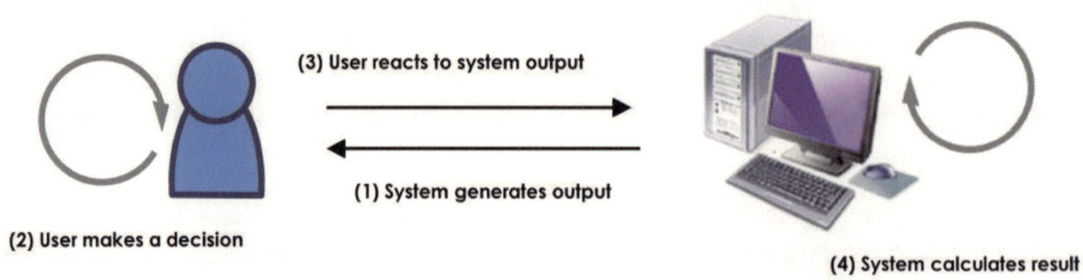

Figure 1. Interaction Model

The speed of a system depends on its computational power, sensing frequency, and machinery response time and directly affects the user's satisfaction with the system. The accuracy of system output primarily depends on the computational model and affects system reliability. In the design of an interactive system, there is often a tradeoff between speed and accuracy. Richness is the variety of system reactions and influences a user's sense of boredom. If a system only provides simple and predictable reactions, the user would easily get bored with the system.

2.2. User experience

It is important to design an interactive entertainment system from the viewpoint of the players by focusing on the quality of the user experience. That is, we design what the player should experience, how the player might feel using a system, what kind of enjoyment and surprise a system provides, among other features. In fun computing, we focus on designing a system that is not technology oriented, although the idea of an entertainment application using emerging technology such as VR and AR tends to emphasize technical fascination. However, the user experience of a game is more important for a player. An application is often designed by scripting a short story to illustrate a concept, and then, sketching the user experience to embody the concept. Figure 2 shows the storyboard of the VR application "Landscape Bartender," which is described in Section 3.5.

Figure 2. Example of a storyboard

2.3. Media integration

The following should be considered while implementing an attractive entertainment application using media technologies:

1. Robustness

Robustness has two aspects. One is the ability of the software system to deal with errors and handle unusual or atypical inputs. The other is durability with repetitive use. A user, especially a child, often operates a system in a random and rough manner. Therefore, robustness is the most important feature of an interactive system.

2. Safety

Safety is an important issue for an interactive system if it has a mechanical force feedback because it may harm the player. The visual feedback of the system should also be considered. Visual interface artifacts may contribute to player sickness such as headaches, asthenopia, and nausea. The image resolution, field of view, refresh rate, and time delay to update a scene of the display are the main causes of sickness.

3. Intuitiveness

In human–computer interaction, an intuitive interface is regarded as one that is easy to use. People can intuitively use an application with little knowledge or directions on its usage. That is, the users apply prior knowledge to the new system. Therefore, to design an intuitive interface, it is essential to fill the gap between users' current knowledge and target knowledge needed to use the new system.

4. Immersion

Immersion is the state of being mentally involved in a game; that is, the players do not feel any physical borders around them. The sensation of immersion in a VR application can be described as presence within the virtual space surrounding a player. The naturalness of the virtual space, that is, the reality of the environment and prompt responses from the system, are the key factors for promoting the sense of immersion.

3. VR applications

In this chapter, we consider VR applications that use an intuitive interaction model to entertain people.

3.1. Ton^2

3.1.1. Overview

Ton^2 is a new body-sensory style VR application that is implemented using an intuitive and robust interaction model, as shown in Figure 3 [2]. This application captures the player's motion data as displacement values by means of distance sensors and uses the data for its interaction model.

We have revived an old Japanese traditional game, *Paper-Sumo*. This game is normally played on a board using paper and cardboard; however, we have designed it as a game that can be played under water. We used water as the media and not just as an element of enjoyment, but the players could experience the comfort of pressing down the water surface. Moreover, when players respond to their opponents' moves, the game provides feedback similar to the original game. In the 3D imagery projected on a screen floating on the water surface, both players push down the water surface in order to control the movements of the sumo wrestlers. This gives a sense of a sumo wrestling performance.

3.1.2. System configuration

This system consists of four modules, as depicted in Figure 3 (a): (1) A projector that projects the image on the screen, which floats on water, as shown in Figure 3 (b). (2) Wave Generator Cubes (WGCs) that produce waves from the pressing action of the players. There are three WGCs on each side of the tank. (3) Distance sensors record displacement data. Four sensors are placed at the corners of the screen and six (one for each WGC) are set under the tank. (4) The computer controlling the entire system calculates the input data from an A/D conversion board.

The process flow of the system is as follows:

(P1) The distance sensors obtain displacement data from the six WGCs and four corners of the screen.
(P2) The computer calculates the velocity of the hold-down action of the WGCs and the change in the slope of the floating screen on the basis of displacement data.
(P3) By using the results of P2, the computer determines the influence on the movement of the Paper-Sumo wrestler.
(P4) The system calculates the interference and reaction of both wrestlers. At the same time, it determines whether either of the wrestlers has won or lost.
(P5) The projector displays the 3D imagery generated for both wrestlers on the screen.

3.1.3. Result

The players experienced "Paper-Craft Sumo" underwater and enjoyed the game in a typical manner. The 3D imagery projected when the Sumo wrestling is held underwater provides visual enjoyment and the generated waves, which move back and forth in the tank, also give the participant rhythmical comfort while having fun playing the wrestling match. In Ton^2, because the input is not a direct handling of the wrestler and instead the wrestler is influenced by the waves, a participant must rely on his/her intuition and no technique is required to play the game. Therefore, participants of any age can play Ton^2 equally well. This was one of the fascinations of the traditional Paper-Sumo. Moreover, the physical act of influencing the wrestlers and the visual sensation of the wave movement stimulate the participants. As a result, there is both physical and visual feedback to the players.

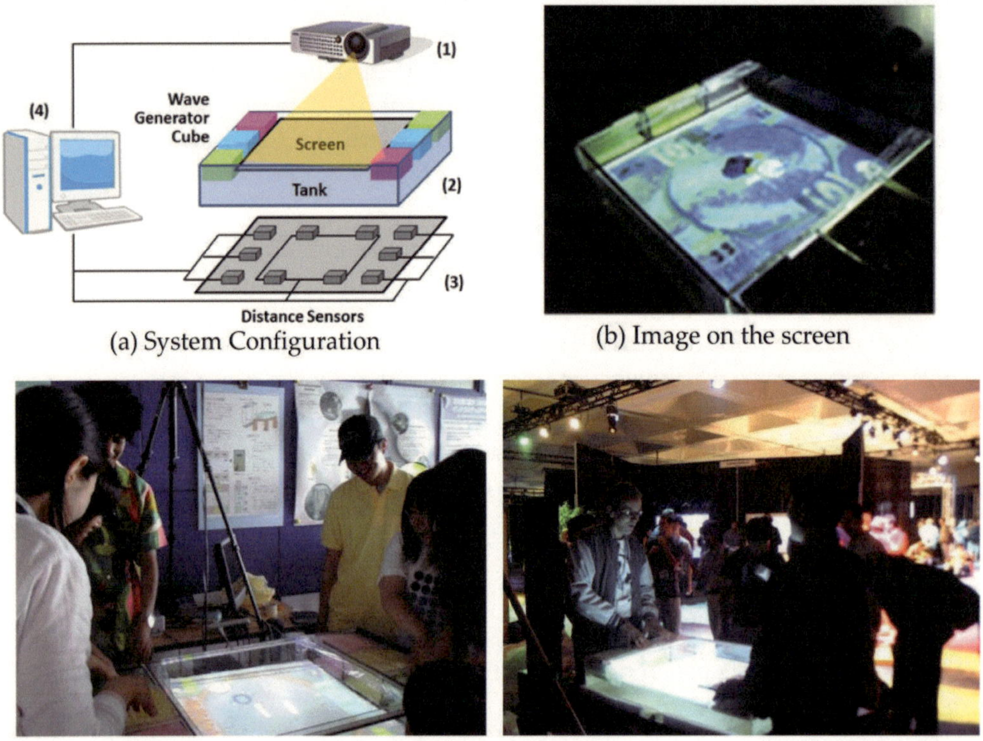

(a) System Configuration

(b) Image on the screen

(c) User Experiences

Figure 3. Ton^2

3.2. Kyukon

3.2.1. Overview

Traditional sports video games use buttons or sticks as user interfaces. These are unnatural interfaces for playing sports. *Kyukon* creates a virtual pitching experience through a nonwearable interface. Our system allows the control of a ball similar to a real pitcher. The nonwearable interface employs wireless sensing technology and a strip screen. There are no physical restrictions; hence, a user can freely pitch a ball.

The strip screen smoothly connects a player to the virtual stadium projected on the screen. The objective is to strike out the batter. As the player throws the ball toward the screen, the ball smoothly passes through the screen. At the same time, the virtual ball will be projected at the exact position the player threw the ball, which also reflects the speed and rotation of the thrown ball. The player can also pitch a miracle ball with a particular rotation and speed.

A player can attempt controlling his/her arm and wrist to pitch a miracle ball. For example, a faster ball will become a *Flaming Miracle Ball* that flies with the flame effect, as shown in

Figure 4 (c), whereas a rapidly revolving ball will become a *Tornado Miracle Ball* with the spiral effect.

3.2.2. System configuration

The strip screen is a novel display system that seamlessly connects the real and virtual worlds, as shown in Figure 4 (a). It is composed of white vinyl and is divided into many strips. A thrown ball will pass through the strip screen with a minimal distortion of the screen. The screen immediately reforms and displays the virtual ball. We developed a combination of a wireless accelerometer and optical sensors to create a nonwearable interface system for pitching. The wireless accelerometer is placed inside the ball, as depicted in Figure 4 (b2). It detects the time at which the ball is released from the hand and the rotation of the ball. Optical sensors are installed behind the strip screen, as shown in Figure 4 (b1). They detect the time when the ball reaches the screen and the position where it passes through the screen.

3.2.3. Result

Kyukon, which is an intuitive interface for pitching a ball, enables various controls without any physical restrictions owing to the nonwearable sensors. Moreover, we developed a method for connecting the virtual and real worlds by enabling a continuation of objects using the physical data of the player's natural motion. This innovation enhanced the experience of the sport.

In addition, we installed *Virtual Petanque*, as shown in Figure 4 (d2). The player can throw a ball similar to a pitcher into a virtual field projected on the screen. The players could find a new sense of fun while playing *Virtual Petanque.*

3.3. Interactive fountain

3.3.1. Overview

There are various computer-controlled fountains in the world. However, these computerized fountains spray water in only some preset patterns. Dietz et al. demonstrated three interactive water displays [3], but the water performance was not very dynamic, and the displays were not too different from conventional fountains. In addition, Mann developed a fluid-based tactile user interface with an array of fluid streams that work like the keys on a keyboard [4].

This project suggests the possibility of a fountain with a novel display system that reacts to a player's motions. Our version of the interactive fountain is so compact that it can even be installed in a living room. The system provides an ambient display with changing water jets and color illumination. The goal of this project is to change the fountain into a design element, such as the interior decoration of a room, and to demonstrate the possibilities of the fountain's interface by providing an exciting experience of fountains that react to a player's actions.

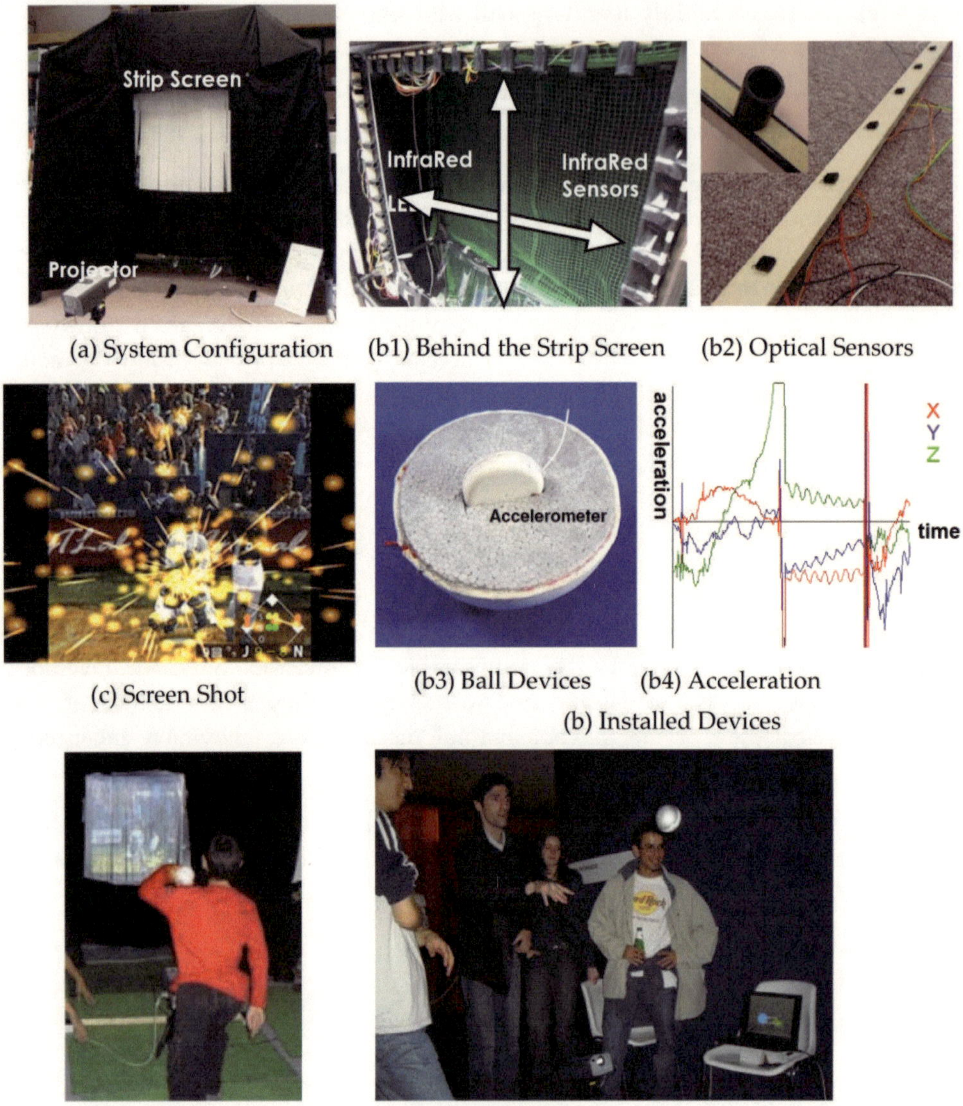

(a) System Configuration (b1) Behind the Strip Screen (b2) Optical Sensors

(c) Screen Shot (b3) Ball Devices (b4) Acceleration

(b) Installed Devices

(d1) Original (d2) Virtual Petanque

(d) User Experiences

Figure 4. Kyukon

3.3.2. System configuration

This system consists of a PC, a fan-type controller, a CCD camera, seven speakers, two MIDI-controlled 4ch dimmer switches, and seven fountain units. Each metallic nozzle head is surrounded by nine full-color LEDs, as shown in Figure 5 (b). The MIDI-controlled dimmer switches supply electricity to the underwater pump. Electric current varies with the MIDI signal and changes the height of the water jet. A self-illuminated fan is used as the body of the controller. A wireless three-axis accelerometer is mounted on the controller handle. Figure 5 (c) shows the difference between the acceleration measurements of "waving" and "cutting" motions. The system can distinguish between "waving" and "cutting" motions by considering the changing ratio along the y- and z-axes. The system changes the strength of the water jets and the illumination color on the basis of the measured acceleration. Moreover, it detects the position of the controller by a background image subtraction method. The detected position of light is used to select the fountain to be activated.

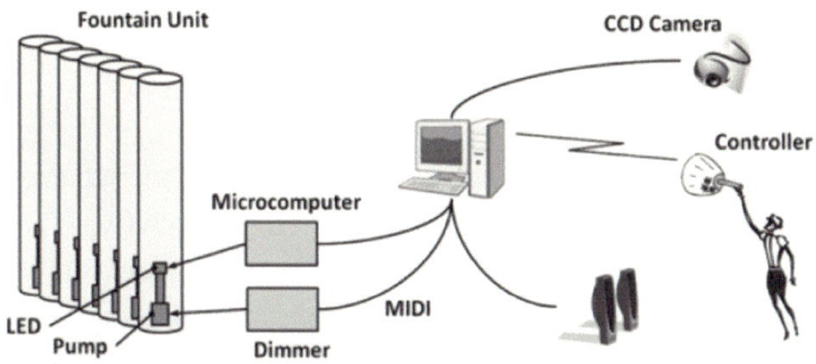

(a) System Configuration

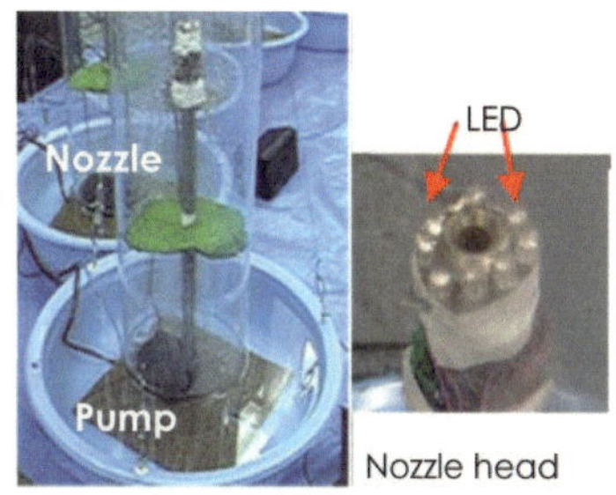

(b) Fountain Unit

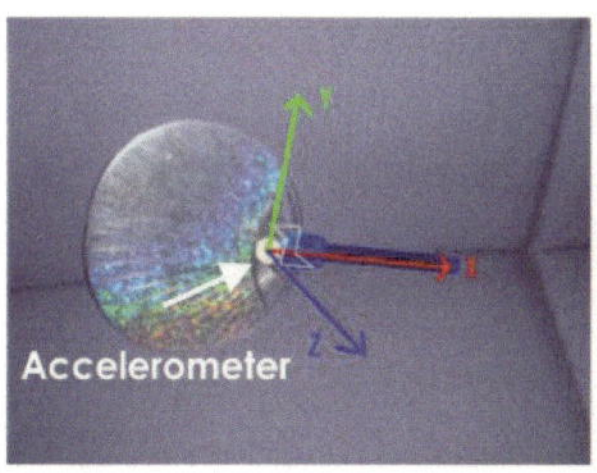

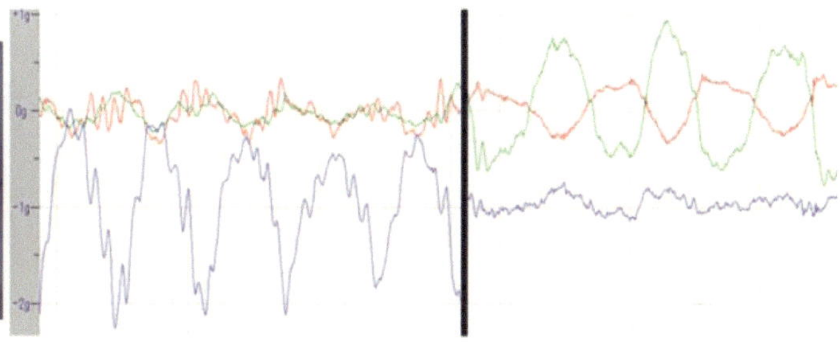

(i) waving (ii) cutting

(c1) Controller (c2) Acceleration Measurement Data (x: red, y: green, z: blue)

(c) Fan-type Controller

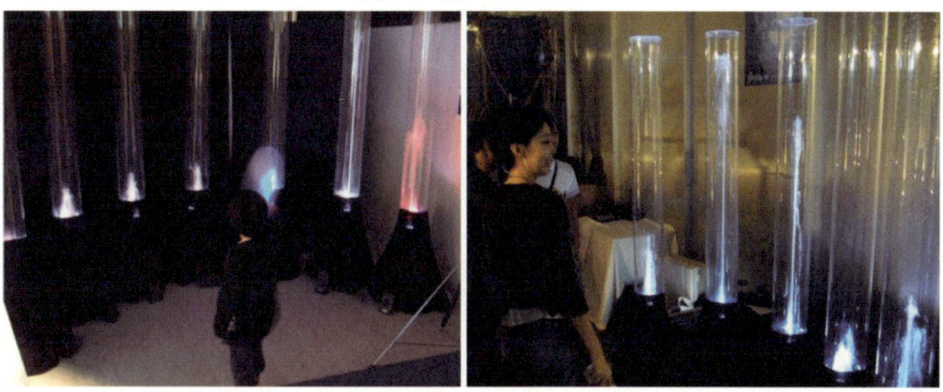

(d) User Experiences

Figure 5. Interactive Fountain

3.3.3. Result

In our system, the strength of the water jets as well as the illumination of water and sound effects are dynamically changed according to player's motions. Therefore, our interactive fountain performs as a novel interactive water display.

The fountains instantly react to user motion, thus changing the water jet strength, illumination colors, and sound effects. As shown in Figure 5 (d), a player can intentionally control interactions using real water that cause the effect of water being scattered by the wind.

3.4. Witch's cauldron

3.4.1. Overview

This project presents a novel interactive application that causes virtual objects to fracture by stirring them with a wand. This application calculates the collision force for each object, and an object breaks apart when it collides forcefully with others. The player interactively crashes the objects with haptic sensation and simultaneously watches computer-generated imagery of the fracture.

3.4.2. System configuration

Figure 6 (a) shows the system configuration. This system consists of (1) a screen that shows the virtual world, (2) a rear-screen projector, (3) an interface to sense the movement of a player and to display haptic sensations, (4) an electric circuit to control the stirring interface, and 5) a PC to control the application.

Figure 6 (b) shows the stirring interface and Figure 6 (c) shows the data flow of the system. When the player turns a wand, the universal joint turns the axis of a motor as shown in Figure 6 (c) (1). The system measures the rotation signal as shown in Figure 6 (c) (2) of the rotary encoder, which is transferred from the motor control board. Finally, the system calculates the status of the virtual wand using the measured rotation signal as shown in Figure 6 (c) (3).

The system provides haptic sensation via the wand as follows. The force information to be applied to the stirring interface is transferred to the microcomputer as shown in Figure 6 (c) (4). The microcomputer outputs a pulse wave modulation signal to the short brake circuit as shown in Figure 6 (c) (5). The rotation speed is controlled with the short brake circuit as shown in Figure 6 (c) (6), and the player experiences haptic sensation as shown in Figure 6 (c) (7).

Virtual objects are physically simulated in real time using a physical engine. When the virtual objects are stirred with a wand, they receive an impulsive force from the wand. The status of the wand is determined on the basis of the information transferred from the microcomputer. The breakable object is composed of fragments that are connected to each other with a joint force, as shown in Figure 6 (d). When a strong impulsive force is applied, the joint is separated and the object is broken into fragments. A 3D CGI is generated in real time and the image is projected on the screen.

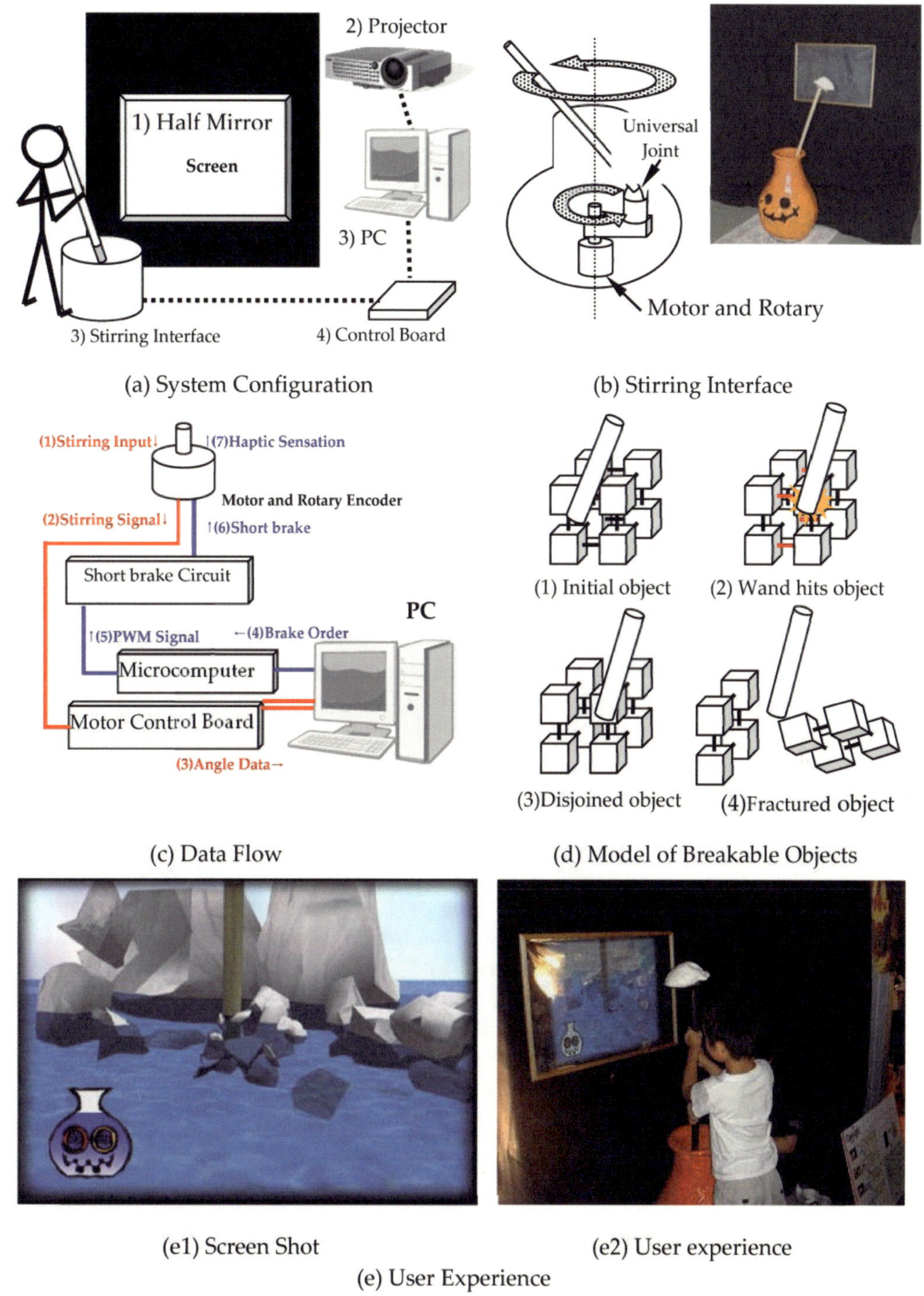

Figure 6. Witch's Cauldron

3.4.3. Result

Today, the opportunity for physical exercise has decreased. As a result, the population is becoming overweight. It is difficult for an overweight child or a person past middle age, whose muscles are weak, to vigorously exercise without any training. There are many training and fitness programs. However, people do not like to use conventional training equipment such as dumbbells and jumping ropes because of their monotonousness. We believe that they need exercise that uses their entire body and is fun.

The player of *Witch's Cauldron* has to use his/her entire body to break the objects with the wand. As a result, a fun activity is performed while exercising the entire body. Unlike conventional VR applications, it can be effective in promoting physical health.

We believe that our technology can be applied not only to the destruction of virtual objects but also to other kinds of operations. For example, we can equip a cooking trainer or a simulator for heavy equipment with haptic sensation.

3.5. Landscape bartender

3.5.1. Overview

Some cocktails names compare cocktails to landscapes. For example, tequila sunrise compares orange juice and grenadine to the morning sky with the glow of the sun. These two elements generate a sunrise landscape. This project presents a system that generates landscapes using a cocktail analogy [5]. With this system, users can generate landscapes in the same manner that they make a cocktail, that is, by combining "ingredients." Each ingredient of the landscape cocktail, i.e., each landscape element, is actually water in a different bottle. The player selects a bottle containing the intended landscape element and pours a suitable amount of water into a shaker.

The system has eight elements: sand, rock, water, plants, sun, moon, stars, and clouds. The elements of landscape are categorized into two groups—a) soil: sand, rock, water, and plants; b) sky: sun, moon, stars, and clouds. The mixture ratio of these two element groups determines the ratio of the ground and sky in the image. The amount of water used from each bottle determines the ratio of the landscape elements. The ratio of sun and moon changes over time with the altitude of sun/moon. If the ratio of the sun element is high, a daytime scene is generated, as shown in Figure 8 (d1); otherwise, a nighttime scene is generated, as shown in Figure 8 (d3). If the ratio of sun and moon is equal, an evening scene is generated, as shown in Figure 8 (d2). Moreover, plants are grown only if water and sand/rock are present.

The contour of the ground and the position of each element are changed by shaking the shaker. The contour of the ground becomes rough if the controller is shaken vertically and becomes smooth if it is shaken horizontally. Moreover, the sun shifts horizontally if the controller is shaken horizontally. To give the player the feeling of generating his/her own landscape, the system displays a vague in-progress image while he/she is shaking the shaker. The in-progress image is unclear, and the contents of the shaker cannot be seen.

After shaking the shaker, the player pours water into the cocktail glass. The resultant landscape can be seen clearly only when the cocktail glass is placed on the coaster.

3.5.2. System configuration

The system consists of four modules, as shown in Figure 8 (a): (1) a shaker-type controller with a three-axis wireless accelerometer hidden inside the cap of the shaker; (2) a measuring module comprising eight digital scales for sensing the volume of water: a scale is used for sensing the amount of each landscape element, and the data is used for the combining process; (3) a counter-type image display unit; and 4) a PC. Acceleration data is used to change the contour of the ground and the position of each element.

The sensing module for detecting the placement of the glass on the coaster is installed in the counter-type image display unit. A magnetic chip is placed on the base of the glass. Furthermore, a digital compass is used as the sensing module, which detects the approach of the glass. The data from each module is transmitted to the PC via a serial connection and a wireless signal.

The ground of a landscape is generated using a height map of resolution 256 × 256. Uniform balls are set out on a grid at the initial condition, as illustrated in Figure 8 (c1). The size of each ball is varied according to the strength of a shake in the vertical direction or averaged according to the strength of a shake in the horizontal direction. The final surface model of the ground is obtained from the deformed balls, as shown in Figure 8 (c2).

3.5.3. Result

This system provides the enjoyment of creating one's favorite scenery. The technique of designing a landscape follows the actual procedure of making a cocktail; therefore, a player can easily understand the instructions.

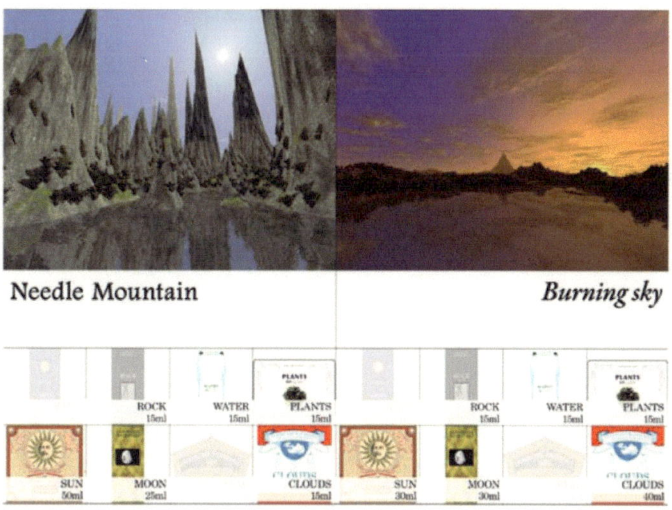

Figure 7. Recipe Book

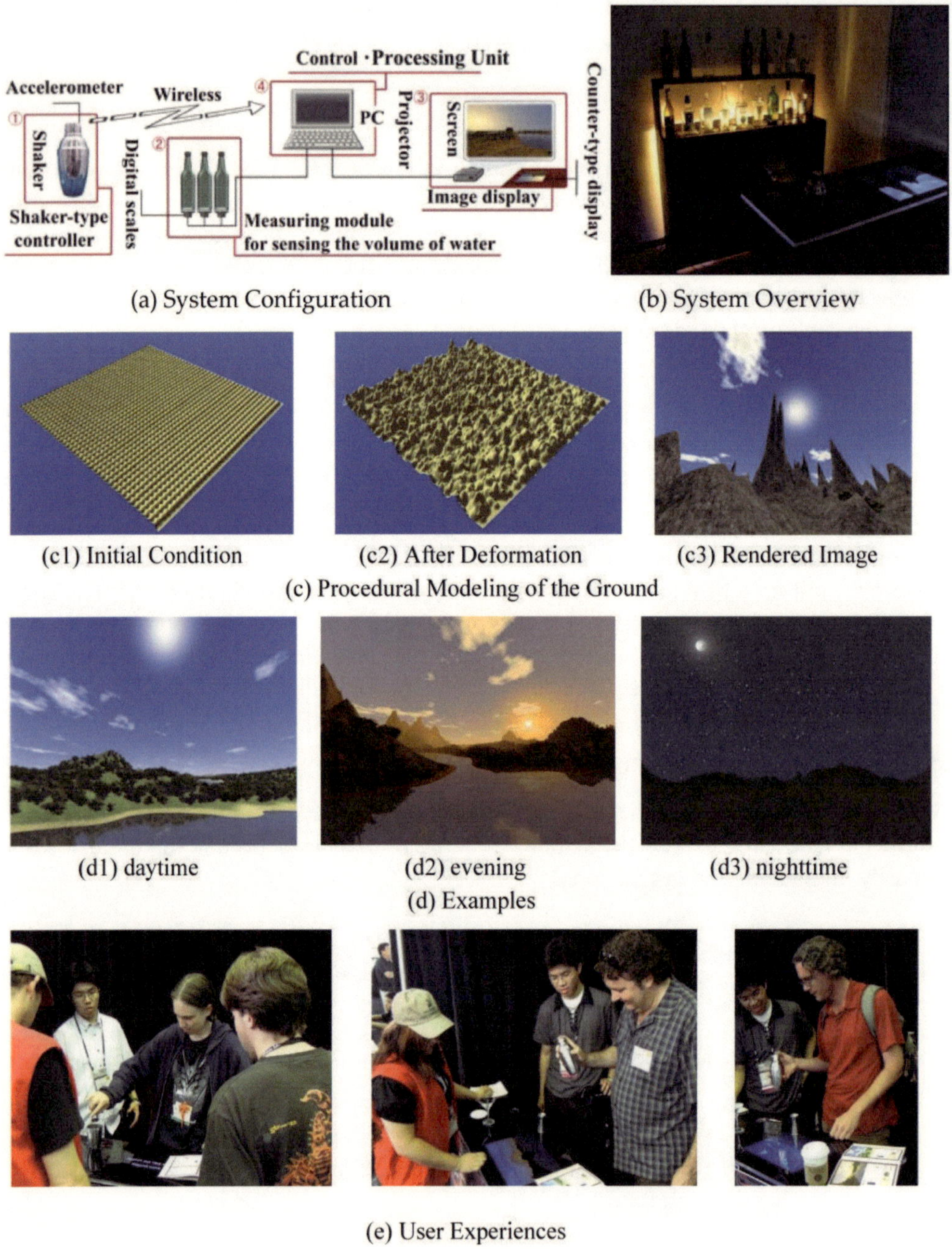

Figure 8. Landscape Bartender

The digital scale measures weight in units of cubic centimeters. Hence, the combination of ingredients becomes almost infinite. The contour of the ground and the position of each element are changed by shaking the shaker. Therefore, the system can generate a once-in-a-lifetime scene. In addition, we provided a "recipe" book, shown in Figure 7, as a reference to design scenery. However, most people enjoyed designing their own scenery like a chemistry experiment.

3.6. Spider Hero

3.6.1. Overview

A superhero has overwhelming speed and power. The special ability of a superhero is his most important characteristic. In this VR application, the user can jump from one building to another by using a web, which is stuck to the user, similar to the famous superhero Spiderman™. In fact, the aim of this application is to provide the user the enjoyment of using Spiderman's superpower [6].

The user wears the web shooter illustrated in Figure 9 (b), which is a device used to shoot a web. The user aims at a target building with this device. Then, when the user swings his/her arm forward, the web is launched, thus sticking to the target building on the screen. Next, the user's arm is pulled in the direction of the target building by the pulling force feedback system, which can provide the feeling of being pulled directly and smoothly as if attached to an elastic string. Finally, the user moves toward the target building.

3.6.2. System configuration

This system consists of three components: a feedback system, input devices, and effects. The feedback system includes an air module that gives the user the feeling of wind and a pulling force feedback system that gives the user the feeling of being pulled. In this system, the user's arm is connected to an elastic line, and this line gives the user the sense of being pulled. This line is attached to a rubber plug. This rubber plug is activated by a vacuum device. However, without a limit on the system, the user will be indefinitely pulled by this system. Hence, we introduce an openable cap using a servomotor. Using this openable cap, we can control the strength of the pulling force. When the cap is closed, the pulling force is the strongest. On the other hand, when the cap is open, the pulling force is zero. These feedback systems provide the user with a force feedback of flying from one building to another by means of the spider web.

As input devices, the user can use a pressure sensor and two web shooters. The sensor allows the user to change his view by shifting his/her weight, and the web shooters are interfaces to aim at a target building and launch the spider web.

To make this application as immersive as possible, we need to work on visual and sound effects. This is particularly important to enhance the user experience of speed and exhilaration. For visual effects, we use motion blur and focusing effects, as shown in Figure 9 (d1). Furthermore, we use sound effects of wind and a virtual city environment. The wind sound effect uses a sound loop of wind and the pitch of this sound is modified depending on motion speed. In the environment sound effect, we use nine sound sources in the virtual city, as shown in Figure 9 (d2). When the user moves from the one place to another, he/she notices a change in the environment's sound because each sound source includes different sounds.

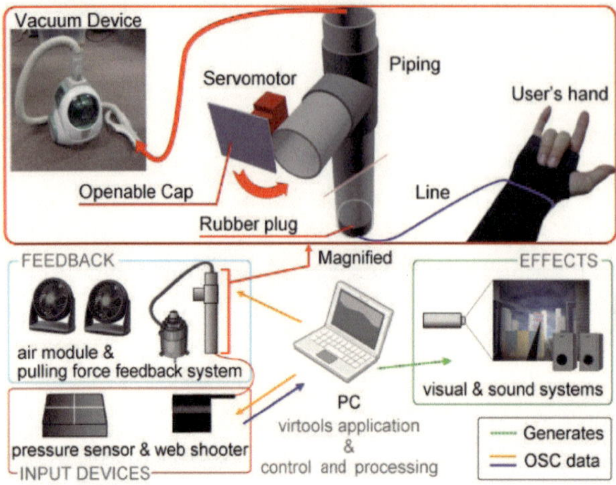

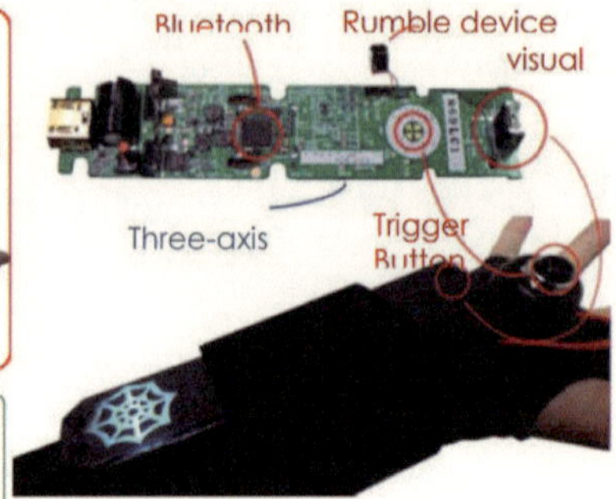

(a) System Configuration

(b) Web Shooter

(d1) Motion Blur and Focus Effect

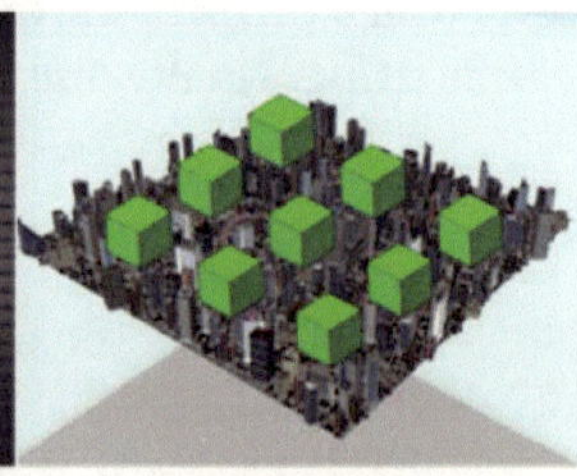

(d2) Sound Sources (green boxes)

(c) Screen Shot

(d) Effects

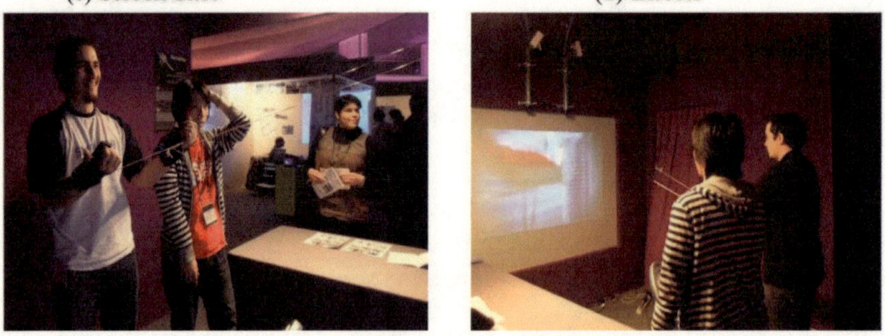

(e) User Experiences

Figure 9. Spider Hero

3.6.3. *Result*

This application has a dreamlike feel. The objective is to provide everyone with the enjoyment of using super powers. In the application, the user can feel being pulled and can feel the wind through a force feedback system. Visual and sound effects immerse the user in this VR experience. Moreover, the intuitive interface increases the operability of this VR application. However, through experimental evaluation, we confirmed that the operability is inadequate, and hence, we plan to improve the devices. On the software side, to provide a better experience, we need to speed up the motion and wind. Our current pulling force feedback system handles the pulling force only in one direction. We plan to overcome this limitation by including a few pipes with openable caps and improving the content to increase the sense of immersion.

This VR application requires the user to have a sense of balance in order to change the user's viewpoint and to swing both arms at a sufficient rate of speed. Therefore, this application would be effective for whole-body exercise.

3.7. Extreme can crusher

3.7.1. Overview

Recently, environmental awareness has increased worldwide. One of the simplest actions that can contribute to environmental conservation is crushing a can. It reduces the bulk of cans, thus reducing recycling costs and environmental pollution. However, crushing cans is a tedious and boring task. This project proposes a sustainable method for crushing cans by applying the gamification approach.

The player places a can in the can crusher and his/her foot in the slipper. After engaging in a walking-like motion wearing the slipper, a rocket is fueled up and launched. Here, the amount of fuel is proportional to the speed of the player's walking motion. The launching direction is displayed cyclically within a half-round direction on the screen, and it is determined by the timing of the foot motion. While the rocket is flying, it sows the soil with seeds, and flowers bloom. The color of the flowers is related to the dominant color of the crushed can.

3.7.2. System configuration

The system consists of three components: (1) a PC, (2) web camera, and (3) can crusher, as shown in Figure 10 (a). Two vibrators are installed on either side of the slipper in which the user places his/her foot. These vibrators imitate the rumbling of the ground when the rocket is launched. An eccentric motor is used as a vibrator to display noticeable strong and long-period vibrations. An infrared distance sensor is installed in the lower part of the can crusher to detect the speed of the player's foot motion. The height of rocket launch is determined by the speed of the foot motion; the faster the motion, the higher the rocket flies. A web camera is used to capture the surface of a can. After an image is captured, the system extracts the image region that contains the can by using image background subtraction. Then, it analyzes the dominant color of the can by an image histogram method. The extracted dominant color is used as the color of flowers that will bloom.

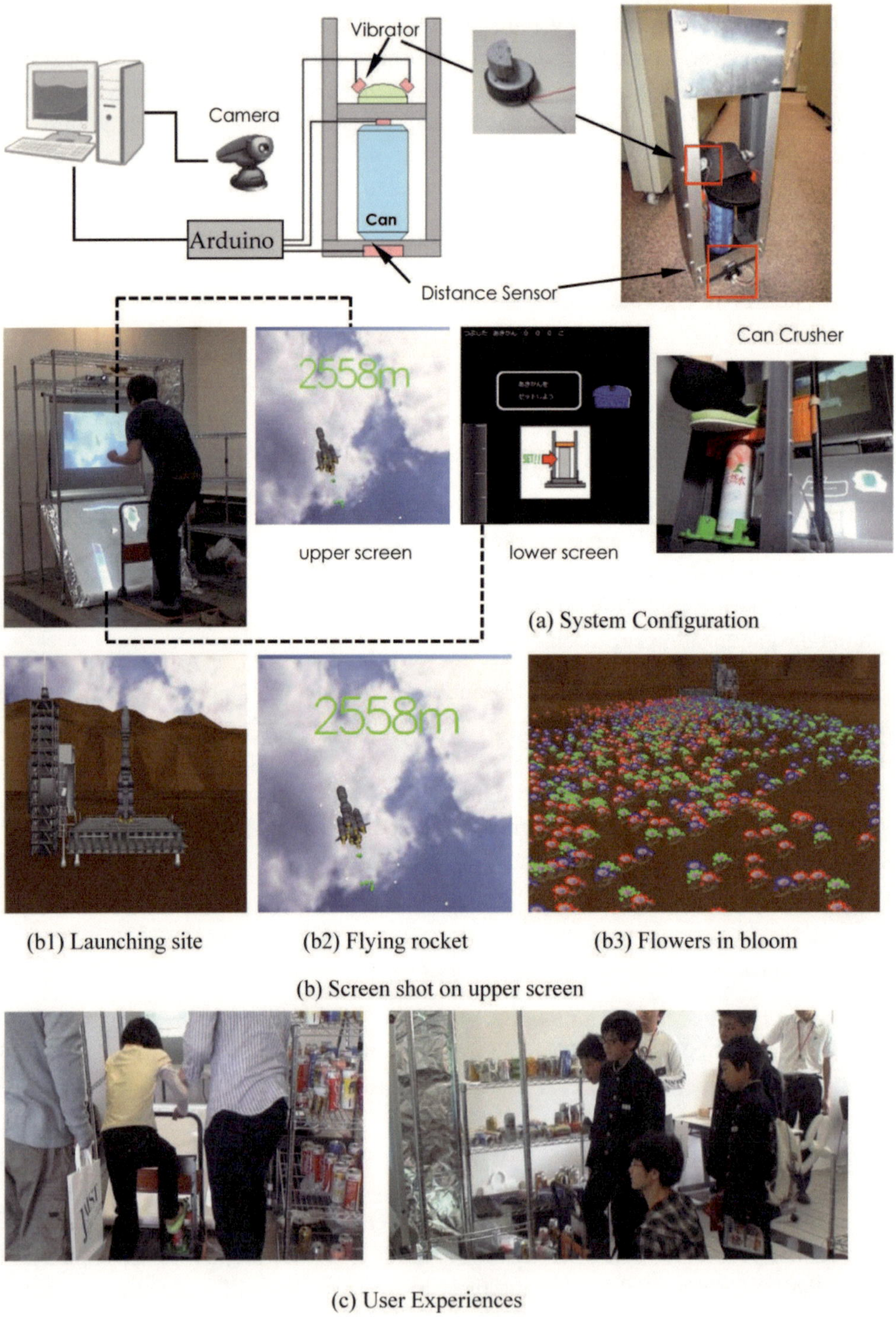

Figure 10. Extreme Can Crusher

The system uses dual screens; the upper screen displays a scene of the flying rockets with real-time graphics, as shown in Figure 10 (b), and the lower screen shows system instructions, cheering characters, and a launching guide.

3.7.3. Result

It is observed that players enjoyed the ordinarily monotonous work of crushing a can because the system makes it fun. The system displays the flight distance of the rocket and the players tend to compete against one another. Some players gathered empty cans to use with this system. We noticed that this application may contribute to the cleanliness of public spaces and eco-conscious actions.

4. Conclusion

This chapter provided an overview of the basic concept of fun computing—a form of entertainment that uses media technology. We reviewed the interaction between humans and a VR environment and analyzed an interaction model. In addition, we outlined some VR applications that entertain people by using an intuitive interaction model and showed how "fun computing" helps motivate people's actions and change human behavior. Fun computing is widely applicable not only for entertainment but also for physical training, rehabilitation, and moral consciousness improvement. Development of fun computing applications is a comprehensive process and requires various skills— not only hardware and software knowledge but also aesthetic design and storytelling abilities. Among them, designing user experience is the most important and difficult skill needed to develop an attractive application.

Author details

Kazunori Miyata
Japan Advanced Institute of Science and Technology, Japan

5. References

[1] Zelzter D (1994) Autonomy, Interaction and Presence. Presence. 1: 127-132.
[2] Yabu H, Kamada Y, Takahashi M, Kawarazuka Y, Miyata K (2005) Ton2: A VR Application With Novel Interaction Method Using Displacement Data. ACM SIGGRAPH 2005, E-Tech.
[3] Dietz P.H, Han J.Y, Westhues J, Barnwell J, Yerazunis W (2006) Submerging Technologies. ACM SIGGRAPH 2006 Emerging technologies, Article #30 ·
[4] Mann S (2005) Interactive arts 1: interfaces for audio and music creation: “"fl Huge UId streams": fountains that are keyboards with nozzle spray as keys that give rich tactile feedback and are more expressive and more fun than plastic keys. Proceedings of the 13th annual ACM international conference on Multimedia '05. 181–190.

[5] Noda T, Nomura K, Komuro N, Tao Z, Yang C, Miyata K (2008) Landscape Bartender: Landscape Generation Using a Cocktail Analogy. ACM SIGGRAPH 2008, New Tech Demo SIGGRAPH Core.

[6] Ishibashi K, Luz T.D, Eynard R, Kita N, Jiang N, Segi H, Terada K, Fujita K, Miyata K (2009) Spider Hero: A VR application using pulling force feedback system. Proceedings of VRCAI2009. 197-202.